The Fathers on the Bible

This book offers an overview of how the Church Fathers used and interpreted biblical texts. It brings together a range of different Christian confessional and social perspectives to explore the biblical basis and impact of their thinking. The contributors cover different ages and traditions, with each chapter focusing on a specific individual and theme. The book takes an ecumenical approach to the relationship between the Church Fathers and Holy Scripture and fosters a better understanding of the relationship between Christian tradition and the Bible. It will be of interest to scholars of Christian theology, the history of Christianity, biblical studies and patristics.

Nicu Dumitraşcu is Professor of Patristics, Mission and Ecumenism in the Faculty of Orthodox Theology "Episcop Dr. Vasile Coman" at the University of Oradea, Romania. His previous book with Routledge is *Basil the Great: Faith, Mission and Diplomacy in the Shaping of Christian Doctrine* (2018).

Routledge New Critical Thinking in Religion, Theology and Biblical Studies

The *Routledge New Critical Thinking in Religion, Theology and Biblical Studies* series brings high quality research monograph publishing back into focus for authors, international libraries, and student, academic and research readers. This open-ended monograph series presents cutting-edge research from both established and new authors in the field. With specialist focus yet clear contextual presentation of contemporary research, books in the series take research into important new directions and open the field to new critical debate within the discipline, in areas of related study, and in key areas for contemporary society.

God After the Church Lost Control
Sociological Analysis and Critical-Constructive Theology
Jan-Olav Henriksen and Pål Repstad

Religion and Intersex
Perspectives from Science, Law, Culture, and Theology
Stephanie A. Budwey

Exploring Theological Paradoxes
Cyril Orji

African Churches Ministering 'to and with' Persons with Disabilities
Perspectives from Zimbabwe
Nomatter Sande

The Fathers on the Bible
Edited by Nicu Dumitrașcu

The Theological Imperative to Authenticity
Christy M. Capper

For more information about this series, please visit: https://www.routledge.com/religion/series/RCRITREL

The Fathers on the Bible

Edited by
Nicu Dumitraşcu

Routledge
Taylor & Francis Group
LONDON AND NEW YORK

First published 2023
by Routledge
4 Park Square, Milton Park, Abingdon, Oxon OX14 4RN

and by Routledge
605 Third Avenue, New York, NY 10158

Routledge is an imprint of the Taylor & Francis Group, an informa business

British Library Cataloguing-in-Publication Data
A catalogue record for this book is available from the British Library

ISBN: 9781032209562 (hbk)
ISBN: 9781032226613 (pbk)
ISBN: 9781003273592 (ebk)

DOI: 10.4324/9781003273592

Typeset in Sabon
by codeMantra

Contents

Contributors

Pablo Argárate is Professor and Head of Department at the Institute for Ecumenical Theology, Eastern Orthodoxy and Patristics at the Faculty of Catholic Theology at the University of Graz (Austria).

Nicu Dumitraşcu is Professor in Patristics, Mission and Ecumenism of the Faculty of Orthodox Theology "Episcop Dr. Vasile Coman", University of Oradea (Romania). He currently directs the *Ecumenical Patristic Society*, a formal Research Association for Patristics, History and Christian Spirituality.

Ștefan Florea is Professor of Systematic Theology at the Faculty of Orthodox Theology and Educational Science, "Valahia" University of Târgoviste (Romania).

Gunnar af Hällström is a retired Professor of Systematic Theology and Patristics at the Åbo Akademi University in Turku (Finland).

Piotr Kopiec is Professor of Ecumenical Theology in the Ecumenical Institute and Lecturer of Sociology in the Institute of Family Studies at the John Paul II Catholic University in Lublin (Poland). He also is President of the Theological Commission of the International Ecumenical Fellowship and Secretary of the Editorial Board of "Roczniki Teologiczne" (Annals of Theology).

Anni Maria Laato is Adjunct Professor in Dogmatics at the Åbo Akademi University, and in Patristic Studies at the University of Helsinki. She is also the chair of the Finnish Patristic Society.

Krzysztof Leśniewski is Professor of Orthodox Theology at the John Paul II Catholic University of Lublin (Poland).

John Anthony McGuckin is the Nielsen Chair of Ancient Church History Emeritus at Union Theological Seminary, and Emeritus Professor of Byzantine Christian Studies at Columbia University in New York. He is currently a member of Oxford University's Theological Faculty, and directs the *Sophia Institute*, an International Research Centre for Eastern Orthodox culture.

Carl Séan O'Brien is Lecturer in the Department of Philosophy, Ruprecht-Karls-Universität Heidelberg (Germany).

Adina Voichița Roșu is Assistant Lecturer of Classical Language, and Patristics at the Faculty of Orthodox Theology "Episcop Dr. Vasile Coman", University of Oradea (Romania).

Hector Scerri is Professor in Systematic Theology (Christology, sacraments and eschatology) and Ecumenism at the University of Malta (Malta).

Gheorghe Ovidiu Sferlea is a Lecturer in Mission and Ecumenism at the Faculty of Orthodox Theology "Episcop Dr. Vasile Coman", University of Oradea (Romania).

Anca Tomoioagă is a Lecturer of Romanian Literature and Romanian Language for Foreigners at the Faculty of Letters, University of Oradea (Romania).

Florin Toader Tomoioagă is a Lecturer in Systematic Theology at the Faculty of Orthodox Theology "Episcop Dr. Vasile Coman", University of Oradea (Romania).

Victor Yudin is a Lecturer in Patristics and Dogmatic Theology at H. Johannes de Theoloog College (Brussels/Ghent, Belgium) and Deacon at St. Matthew's Orthodox Parish (Leuven, Belgium).

Preface

The history of European culture and civilization cannot be conceived without the contribution and influence of Christianity, whether we are talking about literature, poetry, education, art or even technology. Even though, in recent decades, the process of secularization has shifted the center of gravity of life and culture in general, from God to man, leading the latter to believe that he could become the master of the universe, he rather turns himself into its prisoner, because the progress of science, in all its forms, unfortunately comes with spiritual regression. Convinced that reason will allow him to rule nature and the outside world, modern man is no longer interested in heavenly paradise, but in the construction of an earthly paradise, which ultimately turns out to be a chimera and a source of unhappiness. Therefore, the return to traditional Christian values and their preeminence in the hope of regaining the spiritual balance in contemporary society seems a recurring theme, which never loses its importance. In other words, although for many young people today, theology is an exotic field, fixed somewhere in time, as a relic of the past, it can always be a factor of the permanent renewal of life and relationships between people, because it came always with an answer to most of the problems that humanity has faced throughout its history. And its most important representatives were, without a doubt, the Church Fathers.

They are the champions of the interpretation of the Holy Scripture and the transmission of its message over the ages to the present day because they can answer, through their own experiences, the essential questions people ask, regardless of faith, race or ethnicity, old or young, men or women. They do not address, as was sometimes mistakenly believed, only monks, ascetics or practicing Christians, pietists or even fundamentalists, but all people who want to discover (or rediscover) their vocation as "imitators" of Christ. They contributed, through their faith, eloquence and sacrifice, to the correct understanding of the Old Testament's relation with the New Testament and the fulfillment and continuity of the former into the latter, to the establishment of Christian spirituality in a world permanently marked by crises and confrontations which turned it away from God, the

Creator of the Universe, and turned it from an eternal ally of man into a permanent source of danger and failure.

In addition to their exclusively theological role, the Church Fathers must be seen as promoters of a fair, honest ecumenism, because they – by interpreting the Holy Scriptures as faithfully as possible – provide the basis for the Christian conception common to the three great traditions: Orthodox, Catholic and Protestant, with the condition that none of them manifests an exclusivism that would rather drive them apart, rather than bring them closer. Moreover, in order to remain in this optimistic (positive) horizon, we should also note the growing interest of Protestants in the life and work of the Church Fathers, especially in their biblical commentary and historical interpretation of the Holy Scripture, which leads us to believe that the patristic culture can prove to be a bridge between Christians everywhere.

In this spirit must also be understood the initiative of a small group of theologians and scholars, belonging to the three major Christian historical denominations, to transform friendship into a concrete collaboration through regular meetings, every two years, each time in a different country, in another Christian culture, under the umbrella of an informal association, symbolically called the Ecumenical Patristic Society, during which to discuss the special relationship between the Church Fathers and the books of the Bible.

The Holy Fathers, through the enlightenment of the Holy Spirit, have acquired the ability to penetrate beyond what is revealed to us in the letter of Scripture. They do not add, improve, or supplement the gospel of Christ, but contribute to the knowledge of the truth by continuing and amplifying its meanings. And this is because they view Scripture as an expression and formulation of the truth and not the Truth himself, who, of course, cannot be contained in any book. They knew better than anyone that the interpretation of the Holy Scriptures is an integral part of the act of preaching and transmitting the Word of Christ to the world, which must be constantly explained for each age, taking into account its historical, social and cultural context, in the language understood by believers.

In other words, their theological contribution must always be seen in collaboration with the truth of the Holy Scripture and never in opposition to it. The novelty they bring to the whole world is how they have understood how to interpret the messages of Christ contained in the Holy Scripture and make them accessible to people of all times and places because they are "vehicles" of the Holy Spirit, who probes the deepest meanings of the divine wisdom. Therefore, the Church Fathers should not be ignored by any Christian who wants to understand better what is hidden in every parable, in every exhortation, in every word that Christ addresses to his disciples and which they record in their Gospels. Ignoring the Fathers and their teachings can lead to a separation of the Bible from the experience of the prophets and Apostles, although the Bible itself presents the process of their deification and creates the premise of its understanding by those who consider this reality. It would be quite difficult, if not impossible, for anyone to explain the evolution of the history of dogmas and their content without knowing the foundations of the prophetic, apostolic and patristic experiences, because the Church Fathers dogmatized on the basis of their lived experience of deification, and not on philosophical reflection on those contained in Holy Scripture.[1]

The Fathers remain the most credible "instruments" through which the teaching of the Church is transmitted and the message of Jesus Christ is better (more correctly) understood by all Christians, regardless of confession, because they support their doctrinal position through a double, biblical and practice, argumentation. More specifically, they always construct their argumentation by direct reference to the word of Holy Scripture, which they then validate (and give authenticity to it) by their own experience, which they relate to that of the prophets and apostles. In other words, the personal experience of the Church Fathers and of the living saints in every age is the guarantor of the understanding of the truths of Holy Scripture.

Unfortunately, either because of the busy schedule of the participants or because of the COVID pandemic, which has shaken the whole world for the last three years, there were only two conferences, both held in Romania, a predominantly Orthodox country with a very active Christian life and with a flourishing monasticism. In fact, the first, entitled The Fathers of the Church and Monastic Spirituality, took place in 2014 at the Voroneț Monastery, also known as the "Sistine Chapel of the East", due to its special blue in the exterior iconography, and the second only in 2018, also in Bucovina, at the Râșca Monastery, with the title The Fathers on the Bible. This volume contains the lectures given at this latter conference, to which were added a few others sent later by some colleagues who were unable to attend in person.

Following the editor's Preface, professors from different countries and denominations give contributions, as follows: *McGuckin* offers a consideration of the historical background to Athanasius' Letter to Marcellinus on the Interpretation of the Psalms, and of its message, in the light of its sources both in terms of antecedents in Hellenistic philosophical literature and the prior Christian exegetical schools of Alexandria. *Lesniewski* shows the Hesychast tradition is characterized by the relationship of practicing psalmody and the spiritual condition of man. *Laato* speaks about the centrality of the Book of Isaiah for the early Latin-speaking Christians. *Scerri* focuses upon the way a number of patristic texts have read into the third temptation of Jesus according to the Gospel of Matthew, and *Sferlea* provides an informative study of defending the Scriptural legitimacy of ousia language in the vision of St Athanasius and Basil of Ancyra. *F. Tomoioagă* analyzes the origin of human sexuality in Genesis 1, 26–27 in the view of Gregory of Nyssa, while *Yudin* offers a fresh understanding of revising the Stoic interpretation of the concept of enslavement (Genesis 25) in the thinking of Philo of Alexandria and Ambrose of Milan. *Dumitrașcu* gives an overview on how the Church Fathers interpreted the dialogue between Christ and a high-ranking official, showing how wealth and power enslave the human being. *Argarate's* study focuses upon memra 19 of enigmatic Liber Graduum, which turns around the non-biblical distinction between road and paths. *Hällström* offers an analysis of the Theological Principles in the Formation of the Biblical Canon according to Athanasius, bishop of Alexandria, while *O'Brien* examines the coherence of Augustine's methodology of scriptural exegesis. *Roșu* explores the way in which Gregory the Great shows that the Song of Songs is to be considered as one of the oldest biblical revelations of divine love; *A. Tomoioagă* provides the reader with an understanding of Ethos in Gregory Nazianzus's First Theological Orations, *Florea* discusses the concept of Pauline hamartiology in the thinking of John Chrysostom, and *Kopiec* reviews Augustine's impact on Luther's teaching on Marriage.

In short, this volume takes a multifaceted approach to exploring the significant contribution that the Church Fathers made – by interpreting biblical texts to later Christian thought up until the present day.

They are and will remain the barometer of Christian normality in a world marked by so many social, moral, ideological or economic inequities. Therefore, I believe that any scientific contribution to the way in which the Church Fathers understood how to interpret and live the gospel of Christ transforms them into our own contemporaries. Because they themselves confessed their fears, weaknesses and falls, but overcame them all, as we are also invited to do today, through sincerity, spiritual flexibility, humor, humility and simplicity, constantly relating to the principles and the truths of Holy Scripture. Their life began and ended with the Holy Scripture, never at odds with it, but in a continual search for its deepest meanings.

Nicu Dumitrașcu
University of Oradea
January 30, 2022
The Feast of the Three Holy Hierarchs

Note

1 Ioannis Romanides, *Teologia Patristică [Patristic Theology]* trasl. into Romanian by G. Mândrilă (București: Metafraze Press, 2011): 237–238.

1 St. Athanasius of Alexandria on the Interpretation of the Psalms

John Anthony McGuckin

St. Athanasius of Alexandria (295 or 230–373) was one of the most influential bishops of one of the most important of all Christian intellectual centers in the ancient world. His predecessor in the city, the theologian Origen (c. 184-253), even though forced by episcopal pressure to leave his ancestral city in mid-career, had placed the Alexandrian Christian school internationally on a high-level footing and had been followed, relatively early on, after the time of the Alexandrian Archbishop Dionysius (190–265), by a series of highly sympathetic theologians who valued and used his work. Athanasius' mentor and predecessor in the See of St. Mark, Alexander (250–327), who was to take Athanasius while still a deacon to be a protagonist with him at the Council of Nicaea (325), had indeed partly initiated the Arian crisis by debating with his own presbyter Arius the terms of the Son's generation from the Father, on the lines of that unfinished *aporia* laid down by Origen that the Son was eternally born of the Father, yet as derived he was not unoriginated. Hammered at once more, between Alexander and Arius, the fault lines of that continued discussion ran off into controversies about the Son's co-equal, or subordinate, ontological status, which impacted the entire Christian world, and would take more than a generation to resolve. When it did, in the Neo Nicene movement, one of the ways forward taken by Gregory the Theologian, was to hold up the life and work of Athanasius as a paradigm of pastoral and theological rectitude. Gregory's *Oration* 21 is, in fact, the ancient 'canonization sermon' which seven years after his death calls Athanasius both the 'pillar of the faith' and gives him the enduring title of 'the Great'.

The shock waves caused by the great crisis before and after the Council of Nicaea made Athanasius' canonical episcopal succession of Alexander a more complicated matter than it might otherwise have been. He was elected to the see on June 8th 329, after a highly traumatic and conflicted process, and more than a year's hiatus after the death of his predecessor. His and Alexander's theological arch-enemy, Eusebius of Nicomedia had just been released from his temporary exile and was bent on causing as much trouble for Athanasius as he could. Allied to this, the reconciliation Alexander had only recently made with the Melitian schismatics in Egypt had broken

DOI: 10.4324/9781003273592-1

down in disarray after Athanasius' election. Of the list of bishops Melitius had submitted to Alexander who would now acknowledge his episcopal authority, almost half had reneged on their agreement. The terms of the reconciliation dictated by the council of Nicaea (that the rival Melitian bishop in any given diocese should be subordinated to the local bishop who had already been appointed or recognized by Alexander) meant in effect that most Meletian hierarchs were entirely excluded from the process of the election of Athanasius.

Athanasius, to continue his effectiveness for the Nicene cause on the international scene, desperately needed stability and wide support on the local Egyptian front. To achieve this the new and very young hierarch started to travel throughout the Egyptian countryside. Certainly, since the early third century, if not before, the Alexandrian church had been unusual in its format and institutional structures. Almost everywhere else in the Church, by this stage, regarded episcopal governance within a diocese as monarchical within collegial supervision. Each individual diocesan bishop was subject to the mind and governance of the synod of his local episcopal colleagues, headed by a senior bishop (or Archbishop). But it was the synod, not the Archbishop, which proceeded to moderate the individual local 'monarchies' by process of synodical control. Not so in Egypt, where the bishops of Alexandria (the country's only major metropolis in the early Christian period) had accumulated such power and resources (principally of law and wealth and school) that every other country bishop throughout Egypt more or less played the role of the suffragan of the Alexandrian hierarchs, and were made to take personal oaths of loyalty to him at their consecrations.

Knowing the sensitivities of his position, soon after his election, Athanasius decided he needed to secure the loyalty not only of the hierarchs whom he could count on, but also the favour of the common Christian people: chief among whom were the monks of Inner Egypt. Their spiritual reputations counted for much and could secure for Athanasius the stable base he needed. His first trip, of several, was in 330 to the Thebaid to call back to his allegiance the smaller number of monasteries who had seceded; and it was followed by a visit to Pentapolis in 332. From 330 onwards, Constantine's court was applying pressure on him and in 331 he was summoned to answer charges before the emperor at Psamathia near Nicomedia. Meletian clergy had protested that in demanding they supply linen tunics for ecclesiastical use Athanasius had broken imperial law which made clothing imposts only permissible to the army commanders. The Melitian party present at Psamathia also sponsored the accusation raised against him by the dissident country priest Ischiras, that he had sent his cleric Macarius from Alexandria to break up his local community worship and, in the process, smashing his chalice. Athanasius was able to answer all the charges successfully, even managing to turn Ischiras back to his own side and encouraging him to write a letter asking to be readmitted to the mainline Alexandrian clergy.[1]

In the latter part of 332, however, the new leader of the Melitian schism, John Arkaph capitalized on the strange disappearance of bishop Arsenius of Hypselis (he had escaped from house arrest by one of Athanasius' more zealous episcopal friends). Someone or other produced a dead man's hand (they were often used in antique magic rituals) and putting two and two together, to make five, the rumour mill declared that Athanasius had taken Arsenius away into the desert to murder him. When John Arkaph formally raised this as a charge against Athanasius, the latter put together a search party of his deacons and was able to flush Arsenius out of hiding, and bring him before the magistrates, demonstrating that he still had two hands and had been hidden away by Melitian sympathizers from the outset. This was in some sense a point of respite for Athanasius, however temporary, for it brought about a formal letter of support for Athanasius from Constantine, as well as forcing an apology out of the embarrassed John Arkaph. But in 334 Athanasius received a summons from the Emperor to attend a new synod at Caesarea in Palestine, to prepare the ground for a major council planned to be held at Tyre in 335. This, the Tricennalia of Constantine, and thus ten years after Nicaea, was meant to be a 'grand finale' to the Nicene settlement and was to show how the imperial policy had brought a lasting peace to the international church.

Athanasius, knowing that the preliminary processes were being orchestrated by Eusebius of Nicomedia, realized that it was in fact going to be a question of the rehabilitation of Arian theologies, and so he refused the imperial command to attend. When the council of Tyre finally opened it proved disastrous for Athanasius who came with 48 bishops, all of whom were forbidden to attend, while their Archbishop was deposed. This began the second series of struggles for his very existence as bishop theologian, one that would result in no less than five exiles from his see, several intruders positioned there in his place, and no lasting peace for Athanasius until he resumed his Alexandrian throne, for the last time, in 366, less than seven years before he was to die.

Even from this very cursory review of his life and crises, it follows, then, that all of Athanasius' writings, even those written before the Arian crisis broke, were produced in a context of no small ecclesiastical turbulence. In all the tensions arising from his conflicted election, from the ongoing resistance of the Melitian clergy, and from his imperial persecutions, the one safe audience he felt he could rely on was the monks of Inner Egypt. The majority of their monasteries had always been faithful to Alexander and himself. His composition of the *Life of Antony*, not merely an encomium of the ascetical lifestyle which his church had championed, and even exported widely, but also the formal text canonizing Antony as a saint worthy of veneration, would soon gain him overwhelming prestige in monastic circles.

It is in this overarching context, writing with one eye on the favour of the monastics, that his composition of the text *To Marcellinus on the Interpretation of the Psalms,* ought to be located. This short treatise, focused on the use of the psalms and sent to a friend who was recuperating from illness, is in many ways a synopsis of the larger treatment of the psalms to which he gave considerable attention in the course of his theological writing, most notable his *Expositions on the Psalms*, whose fragments are now contained in *Patrologia Graeca* volume 27.[2] The present essay will focus chiefly on the *Ad Marcellinum*, but some notice of the *Expositiones* is in order to contextualize his general approach. Gilles Dorival (1980) had set aside the numerous proofs from antiquity assembled by Montfaucon (1857) asserting the Athanasian authorship of the *Expositiones*. He found that the author had used not only Origen, but also Eusebius of Caesarea's psalm commentary, a text issued in 330 (as Rondeau had earlier argued). Dorival went on to discover literary dependences even on Apollinaris, Didymus the Blind and Cyril of Alexandria, making him conclude, from his survey of the *Catena* evidence (where this 'treatise' largely resided in fragments) that the authors of the text in Migne were Evagrius and an unknown 'Pseudo-Athanasius' of the fifth century. Dorival's very precise allocation of citations that he finds from later authors is, however, suspect in that almost all of them were close disciples of Origen, whose voluminous Psalm commentaries have themselves been scattered across the *catenae*.[3] Citations of authors into the fifth century may thus largely be explained on the basis of the common reference to the great Alexandrian of the third century. Given that both Athanasius and Eusebius of Caesarea (the greatest Origenian disciple of the fourth century) were both quite explicitly referencing Origen in their respective works, we might apply the principle of Occam's razor to much of Dorival's authorial speculation.

Madame Rondeau's study of the issue (1968) first raised the claim that the Athanasian text had used Eusebius of Caesarea, and if this is accepted then we have a fairly precise window for the work which is surely between 330 and the council of Tyre in 335, when there was a definitive break between Athanasius and Eusebius, whom he thenceforward classified as an enemy on the Arian side of the struggle. The *Expositiones* has tended to be placed, by recent historical scholars to around 370, but few seem to have taken in the literary arguments. After Rondeau, and noting the arguments of Dorival and Stead, Bouter's more recent and full-scale analysis of the *Expositiones* has strongly argued a case for restoring the ascription of authorship to the real Athanasius. We should, however, take cognisance of Stead's (1985) pertinent observation of the impact of the evidence of the Manuscript Vaticanus Graecus 754, which clearly shows two sources being combined to create a larger treatise in the *Expositiones*. The comments are listed in two different systems, one with minuscule setting out each psalm separately; and the other with uncial numeration, dealing with psalms in groups of 100 comments at a time. Vian (1982), followed by Stead (1985, p. 70) has argued, convincingly, that the minuscule series belongs to Evagrius of Pontus (another who himself used Origen's psalm commentaries) while the Uncial series is indeed authentically Athanasian. As Stead remarked, the formal critical edition still needs to be issued, but anyone with Vian's article and a blue pencil can mark off the genuine Athanasiana for themselves.

Stead's own article (1985) gives a good synopsis of the key components of the Athanasian treatise, as does that of Sieben (1973), while Bouter (2001) has certainly provided the first in-depth systematic analysis of the theological content. With the *Expositiones* now reassigned, together with the *Epistle to Marcellinus*, one can gain a strong impression of how Athanasius approached the psalm exegesis. It is also probable that we should relocate the psalm works more to the 330s (few have been able securely to locate the *Ad Marcellinum* to date[4]). At this period in his life, he was just setting out to visit the monasteries of the Thebaid, in the cause of strengthening their allegiance to him, in the face of the Melitian challenges to his episcopal election.

In the *Expositiones* (and here I am indebted to Bouter) Athanasius continues that approach to exegesis (with which we can note he famously ends his *De Incarnatione*[5]) one that sees the scripture as one single voice of God revealing his salvific plan to humanity, but in a revelation that requires ascetical conversion on the part of the hearer, so that he might receive the message clearly. This, of course, is entirely in accord with Origen's principles of exegesis. Similarly as Origen set out, Athanasius insists that the careful exegete must identify the speaker in any given oracle or text.[6] This clarification of prosopography was an element of the Hellenistic literary process already established at the Great Library of Alexandria,[7] and Origen and Athanasius both show themselves to be literary commentators in a careful 'scientific' style. Athanasius advanced on Origen's style here (and it becomes a chief characteristic of his overarching approach in the *Expositiones*) to make the speaker predominantly Christ, but Christ speaking in the name of all Mankind. Athanasius makes the Christocentric focus, where Christ tells Mankind of his salvific process, and calls them into it, much more stressed in 'incarnational' terms (where Origen had envisaged more a focus on the advent of the transcendent Logos to the world). He does this, in a sense, as part of the repairing he consistently makes to Origen's Christology: making it more in line with Nicene standards.[8] Athanasius also makes more use of the Psalm headers (*tituloi*, taken from the LXX). He sets them as 'markers' of the story of salvation. He argues that the Psalms of Degrees (Pss.119–133) are a generic account of the phases of salvation history in its historical (Pss.119–126) and religious (Pss.127–133) aspects.

Lastly, Athanasius consistently moves from symbol to symbol by means of word association linking various biblical texts together in an oracular set of connected illuminations. This too is a deeply Origenian style of exegesis. As Bouter notes, these various technical presuppositions of his approach correspond with the handbook of literary criticism (*Progymnasmata*) of Aelius Theonos and would have identified his work on the psalms to his contemporaries as that of a learned Alexandrian scholar. The overarching message of his *Expositiones* is that the Psalms call out as Christ's own voice addressed to the world. The Saviour here speaks as the archetypal Man calling humanity back to himself in a covenant of salvation.[9] Athanasius sees this appeal to the world to return to the union as further divided into two appeals: first that Mankind would rise to his stature in the Church, a New Israel gathering the worldwide faithful back to God; and thereafter the hope for regathering the Israelite people.[10] The Church is the New Israel, the Jews, the Old. Athanasius has hopes that the final fulfilment of all salvation at the Eschaton would be preceded by the conversion of the Jews so that the Church would be the united fulfilment of humanity in Christ.

Throughout the work there is an appeal to personal asceticism, the struggle of repentance that will make this great scheme of salvation in Christ effective on the personal level of the individual. This recurring theme makes it clear that for Athanasius the dogmatic works of his career are not a separate genre from the so-called ascetical works: but both are one and the same exercise in two closely related modalities: the metaphysical structures and the personal appropriations.

Within the turbulent context of Athanasius' life which we have already noted, and his envisaged theological audience (Alexandrian), the appeal of any advocacy of the Psalter as a paradigmatic prayer book to clergy and laity, but especially to the monastic movement, is self-evident. Throughout the entirety of the *Apophthegmata Patrum*, taking such a text to stand for the core monastic mentality, it is the Psalms which are far and beyond the single most cited scriptural source.[11] Such a work shows at one and the same time Athanasius' status as *Magister* in both the dogmatic and ascetical domains and is a loudly implicit claim to authenticity as the rightful occupier of the *thronos* of Christian Alexandria in spite of the chief canonical claim raised by the Melitians against this; namely, that he was too young to accede. The monks had already taken the Psalter as the backbone of the system of daily offices of prayer that the majority of common life monasteries had adopted. Theodoret tells us[12] that from early morning through to the late afternoon, in Syria, the monks vocalized the Psalm texts while working and walking for exercise. Cyril of Scythopolis[13] adds that it was St. Sabba's practice never to allow a young monastic to move from the coenobium to the Lavriotic lifestyle until he could command the entire psalter. This too was taken in several parts of the ancient church as a necessary qualification for ordination. As Brakke has observed, the recitation of the psalms was integral to the ascetic exercises of the early monks. As the recitation of the Psalms brings harmony to the mind and stability to the soul this in itself: 'Is a verbal appropriation of the physical victory over the movements of the flesh that Christ won in his Incarnation'.[14] This sense of coming to the ordering of the thoughts is a key aspect of much monastic teaching and corresponds exactly with Athanasius' intent in his writing to Marcellinus, just as it did in the *Expositiones*. Regrettably, some of the English translations of the *Ad Marcellinum* widely available on the Internet have bowdlerized exactly this part of Athanasius' argument where he speaks of how the psalms bring order and harmony into a disturbed soul.[15] In the *Ad Marcellinum*, Athanasius returns to this point several times:

> Reason desires that the soul which possesses the mind of Christ (as the Apostle says) ought not to be subject to disordered anxiety, but should have this as our Guide which will bring order both to the affects of the soul, and control to the members of the body, like a lyre that has been well tuned. This is exactly what the Psalter does to a man.[16]

We do not know who Marcellinus was, but it was his illness that was the immediate occasion of Athanasius sending to him a treatise which became the closest thing he ever wrote to an actual commentary on scripture. This work[17] is a very dense coverage of all the psalms, showing a close personal knowledge of their contents. It fits exactly within the theological prescripts shown in the *Expositiones*, thus further attesting to the authenticity of the Athanasian *catena* line demonstrated therein. This parallelism can be seen, theologically speaking, especially in the way Athanasius' argument runs from the generic statement of salvation offered in Christ, who personally summates, and stands for, Mankind, to the particular sense of how this Christ-life is individually appropriated through the soul-ordering (τάξις) of personal ascesis.

The structure of the *Ad Marcellinum* is relatively simple even though its coverage (for such an occasional letter) is immense. After a brief prolegomena in epistolary form (though the 'letter' soon emerges as a short treatise of practical ecclesiastical nature), there are two primary arguments, each one followed after its initial statement by a developed exposition of details supporting that statement. The third argument is added in the form of a set of practical reflections on the necessity for chanting the psalms in a style that does not alter the original text[18]; and a final short postlude. A synoptic view of it can stand as follows:

> *Prolegomena*: Commendation of Marcellinus in his trials and in his resolve to adopt a rule of scriptural study. [ch. 1].
>
> *Argument 1. General Overview of the Progress of Salvific Revelation.* [ch.2].
>
> All scripture is useful but the Psalms are a special treasure:

a The Pentateuch deals with Creation.
b The Historical books deal with the offer of salvation to Israel.
c The Prophets speak of the coming of Christ: His Passion and Glory.

> *Development of Argument 1.* [chs. 3–9].
>
> All the various scriptural books are like gardens, each with their own respective fruit. But the Psalter is a garden that has its own special treasures and also all the fruits of the others in it.

Argument 2. Specifics of Salvific Revelation in the Individual Soul. [chs. 10–13].

a The special grace of Spirit is given to the reader of the Psalms. The Psalter portrays all the lineaments of the Soul for us to see and learn [ch. 10].
b The words of the saints are here set out, but more so the Words of Christ himself which paradoxically become our own words as we pray them: we thus enter into Christ mystically [ch. 11].
c Reprise of (a) above: the psalms become a mirror of the soul: our pattern of repentance [ch. 12].
d Reprise of (b) above: by a special philanthropy Christ lays down his own words and life pattern for us to follow. The Psalms give a sketch of it for us.

Development of Argument 2. [chs. 14–26].

Athanasius offers a veritable *Typikon* of which psalms are appropriate to use for which liturgical moment, or which condition in which the soul finds itself.

This *vade mecum* of which Psalm to employ prepares the reader like a course in appropriate oratory before approaching a King.

Argument 3. Practical afterthoughts on the use of Psalms in the Church. [chs. 27–28].

The Psalms ought to be sung not said, and this because:

a This is how they were first conceived by the saints who wrote them.
b Singing makes us commit our full powers and focus.
c Singing has a unifying and harmonizing effect on our spirit.
d Whoever sings well tunes up their soul in the process.

Conclusion [chs. 30–33]

a The Psalms are a garden for all to find there what they need spiritually.
b But they must not be altered as compositions: but kept as the saints originally composed them [ch. 31].
c God will give grace and assistance to all who pray the Psalms.

Their chanting puts demons to flight. [chs. 32–33].

We learn from the prologue that Marcellinus is recovering from an unspecified debility, and Athanasius has sent this letter to him as a work of consolation and encouragement. Kannengiesser[19] describes it as the composition that 'more than any other of his writings...illustrates his attitude to the Bible'. From the outset, we learn that the letter is meant to encourage Marcellinus in his ascetical struggle: a notable theme of antique philosophy and Christianity alike[20]: the rendering into harmony of one's belief and moral practice. This concern to render harmonious may also be contextualized in Athanasius' concern to forge a stronger bond between Alexandria, the great city, and the desert inhabited by monks. Anxious in case any schism happens between the two (something the Melitians threatened as far as he was concerned) Athanasius wishes to point out that this life of ascesis is central both to urban Christians and desert monks alike. In this strategy, he called the urban ascetics of Alexandria to his side (especially the numbers of female ascetics already present there since before the time of Antony) making the basis of a strong alliance between the chief episcopal see and the network of urban ascetics who – apart from any spiritual allegiance they might have felt towards the desert monks – were also important to the inner desert ascetics who needed the favour of the urban Christians to market their wares and financially support themselves.

Athanasius uses clearly recognizable sophistic terms telling Marcellinus that fashioning his life according to the psalms will be an essential part of his 'care for the self' (προςέχω σεαυτοῦ) and that his immersion in the psalms will be a tool to re-model himself (τυπω ἑαυτὸν). Whether Marcellinus is an actual monastic or an Alexandrian lay zealot is not clear; but it is clear that the treatise, once composed, would not only appeal to the monastics (proving Athanasius' credentials as a true ascetic himself) but would have a lively uptake in the urban Christian circles of Alexandria, demonstrating his capacity as a spiritual guide to the Church members, and as a worthy sophist to the Alexandrian scholars.

The treatise, in short, serves as a practical handbook. Before he assigns particular psalms to various theological demonstrations, personal occasions and festal (liturgical) celebrations, Athanasius has made the key point that the overarching purpose of the Psalter's use in the Church is that the soul will repent, and find an order (τάξις) for the soul, by following the footsteps of the saints who mirrored there all human life. But the saints are not, in this case, mere moral examples for Christians. Athanasius follows Origen's insistence that it is Christ Himself who speaks as the main voice through the Psalter; giving the clearest indication of the final plan of salvation (outside of the Gospels). In assigning such detail as to appropriate usage of the Psalter, it is clear that the treatise turns from a generic reflection into an early form of *Typikon* for the Alexandrian church. The *Typikon* remains to this day in the eastern Churches, a genre of liturgical literature that is required in every sacristy of every church; and this aspect surely accounts for the great popularity of this Athanasian text in antiquity: something which Athanasius may have already had in mind as a strategy to ensure the work's command of a wide and authoritative circulation. Unfortunately, some of the English translations of the *Ad Marcellinum*, especially those widely available on the Internet, have deliberately abbreviated the extent of the psalms that Athanasius lists, offering only a (very) select abbreviation.[21]

Evidently, the concept of the liturgical *Typikon* has here fallen victim to the haste of the paraphraser.

The Christocentric mysticism and ascetic power of the *Ad Marcellinum* demonstrate it as clearly an Athanasian treatise that bridges the all-too-common, but inappropriate, classification of his writings into dogmatic or ascetical treatises: a false division that has also, too often, been used to make dubious assumptions about historical datings. Here, in the *Ad Marcellinum,* just as in the *Expositiones,* in the hands of a masterly patristic theologian we are shown how scriptural theology, Christological dogma, soteriological hope, and ascetical endeavour, are all one and the same Spirit-driven impulse that forms the Church into the image and likeness of the Saviour, and thus remakes a pattern for a New Humanity.

Notes

1 He would soon fall away, and this time, because he had broken a civil oath, Athanasius had him temporarily committed to prison.

2 See Montfaucon (1857); Vian (1982); Stead (1985).

3 They are still being discovered in recent times. Not only have 14 previously considered lost Homilies of Origen on the Psalms recently been found in the (re) discovery of Bayerische StaatsBibliothek Codex Graecus 314; but also V. Peri ('Omelie origeniane sui Psalmi', Studi e Testi 289. Vatican City, 1980 – and see also *Tractatus sive homiliae in Psalmos*, ed. G. Morin, CCL 78, Turnhout 1958) has restored to Origen a total of 74 homilies on the Psalms once attributed to Jerome, who was, it now appears, merely their translator. Further see *Origene – Gerolamo. 74 omelie sul libro dei salmi*, intr., trad. e note di G. Coppa, Milano 1993, pp. 13–32. Their overall dependence on Origen was especially asserted by V. Peri, *Omelie origeniane sui Salmi. Contributo all'identificazione del testo latino*, Città del Vaticano 1980.

4 Ferguson (2017) put it in Constantius' or Julian's reign (early 360's) because of the reference in the text to tumultuous rulers. But even in 330 Athanasius knew that Constantine (advised by the arch-Arian Eusebius of Nicomedia) was preparing a summons against him. There was no ruler, in Athanasius' experience to whom the psalmist's words: 'Put not your trust in princes' (Ps. 146.3), could not fruitfully be applied.

5 Athanasius, *De Incarnatione*. 54. 1–2:

> But for the searching or the Scriptures and true knowledge of them, an honourable life is needed, and a pure soul, and that virtue which is according to Christ; so that the intellect guiding its path by it, may be able to attain what it desires, and to comprehend it, in so far as it is accessible to human nature to learn concerning the Word of God. 2. For without a pure mind and a modelling of the life after the saints, no man could possibly comprehend the words of the saints.

6 Bouter (2011), ch. 3.

7 Stoic writers had already applied it to the exegesis of the Homeric canon, and the Neo-Platonic commentators used the method in exegeting the Platonic *Dialogues*.

8 Origen, in his early work *On First Principles*, had famously made a strict distinction between the Logos who comes to earth within the Soul of Jesus,

and the Soul Jesus himself who assumes human flesh in order to facilitate the Logos' entry to the earth. Athanasius follows Dionysius of Alexandria in abolishing this two-step Christology and making the Logos the direct personal (*hypostatic*) assumer of the flesh.

9 Bouter (2011), ch. 4.
10 Bouter (2011), ch. 5.
11 See D. Burton Christie, *The Word in the Desert: Scripture and the Quest for Holiness in Early Christian Monasticism*. Oxford, OUP, 1993, 97.
12 Theodoret of Cyr, *Historia Religiosa*, 2.5.
13 Cyril of Scythopolis. *Lives of the Monks of Palestine*, 113, 1–20.
14 Brakke (1995), 196.
15 See Athanasius. *Ad Marcellinum*. 28, Migne, P.G. 27.40.
16 Athanasius. *Ad Marcellinum*. 28, Migne, P.G. 40.B; see also *Ad Marcellinum* 12–13, where he treats the Psalms' capacity to conform the soul to Christlike status.
17 There are three recent English translations currently available: Ferguson (1978); Gregg (1980) and Bright (1986).
18 This is, I think, not so much a criticism of the works of the two Apollinarii (in the time of Julian), but more of a caution against the heterodox practice of making cento pastiches of sacred texts for dinner party recitation to flute accompaniment.
19 Kannengiesser (2006, 709).
20 Further see: Hadot (1995). See *Ad Marcellinum*, ch. 28. PG 27.40.
21 See *Ad Marcellinum*, 14. Migne, P.G. 27.25.

Books References

P. F. Bouter, *Athanasius von Alexandrie en zijn uitleg van de Psalmen* (Een onderzoek naar der hermeneutiek en theologie van een psalmverklaring uit de vroege kerk). Zoetermeer: Uitgeverij Boekencentrum, Rijksuniversiteit Utrecht, 2001.

D. Brakke, *Athanasius and Asceticism*. John Hopkins University Press, Baltimore, 1995.

P. Bright, 'On the Interpretation of the Psalms', in C. Kannnengiesser (ed), *Early Christian Spirituality*, Fortress Press, Philadelphia, 1986, pp. 56–77.

G. Dorival, 'Athanase ou Pseudo-Athanase?' *Rivista di storia e letteratura religiosa*, 16, 1980, 80–89.

E. Ferguson, 'Athanasius' Epistle to Marcellinus', *Ekklesiastikos Pharos* (Alexandria), 60, 1978, 378–403.

R.C. Gregg, *Athanasius: The Life of Antony and The Letter To Marcellinus* (Classics of Western Spirituality Series). Paulist Press, New York, 1980.

P. Hadot, 'Forms of Life and Forms of Discourse', in A. Davidson (ed), *Philosophy as a Way of Life: Spiritual Exercises from Socrates to Foucault*, Blackwell, Cambridge, 1995, 49–70.

P.R. Kolbet, 'Athanasius, the Psalms, and the Reformation of the Self', *The Harvard Theological Review*, 99(1), 2006, 85–101. (Also idem. ch.4, of B. Daley & P.R. Kolbet (ed), *The Harp of Prophecy: Early Christian Interpretation of the Psalms*, University of Notre Dame Press, Indiana, 2015).

B. de Montfaucon, 'Admonitio in Sancti Athanasii Expositiones in Psalmos', in J.P. Migne (ed), *Cursus Completus Patrologiae Graecae*, vol. 27, cols. 45–54. Paris: Parisiis, Garnier, 1857.

M.J. Rondeau, 'L'epitre a Marcellinus sur les psaumes', *Vigiliae Christianae*, 22 (1968), 176–197.

H.J. Sieben, 'Athanasius uber den Psalter', *Theologie und Philosophie*, 48, 1973, 157–173.

G.C. Stead, 'St. Athanasius on the Psalms', *Vigiliae Christianae*, 39(1), 1985, 65–78.

G.M. Vian, 'Il Testo delle Expositiones in Psalmos di Atanasio', *Studia Patristica*, XVII, 3, 1982, 1041–1045.

2 Psalmody in the Hesychastic Tradition

Krzysztof Leśniewski

The psalms are very important in both the community and personal prayer of Christians.[1] This results from the fact that,

> The book of Psalms provides the most reliable theological, pastoral, and liturgical resource given us in the biblical tradition. In season and out of season, generation after generation, faithful women and men turn to the psalms as a most helpful resource for conversation with God about things that matter most.[2]

The psalms, as inspired songs, were taken from the Semitic tradition as prophecies[3] that can only be fully understood in the light of the paschal mystery of Christ.[4] This hermeneutic principle was given by the Saviour Himself:

> These are my words which I spoke to you while I was still with you, that everything written about me in the law of Moses and the prophets and the psalms must be fulfilled. Then he opened their minds to understand the scriptures.
>
> (Luke 24: 44–45)

It is evident that,

> In making the psalms his own Christ gave them their definitive meaning. They are the prayers of the man-God who is also the Son of God. He became incarnated, so to speak, in them. For this reason a Christian understanding of the psalms cannot neglect any dimension of these prayers that contributed to their original meaning, since that is the meaning taken up into the prayer of Christ.[5]

Already in apostolic times, the faithful sensed in the psalms the announcement of the salvation which was to be fulfilled in the New Covenant, and because of this the psalms were interpreted more deeply than just in a strictly literal sense. In Christianity, the psalms have been considered as a

DOI: 10.4324/9781003273592-2

record of existential experiences arising as a result of man's encounter with God as expressed through prayer, supplication, thanksgiving, and worship. This is because the hopes sung by the psalmists were realized.

From the very beginning of Christian monastic life, the psalms were an important part of both common and personal prayers. This fact is confirmed by the oldest documents regarding monasticism in Egypt, Palestine, Anatolia, Mesopotamia, and Syria. The existence of monastic typicons, containing detailed information about the content and method of prayer in the first centuries of Christianity, allows us to have an insight into the complex reality of the process of shaping liturgical prayer, which in a more developed form existed in Byzantine Christian worship as a combination of secular and monastic elements.[6] Usually, Hesychast spirituality is understood as a way of life of Eastern Christians, both monks and laymen, which is based mostly on the practice of the Jesus prayer. But it must be stressed that the natural milieu of the development of Hesychast spirituality should be placed in Eastern Orthodox monasteries, where psalmody plays the important role in the whole structure of common prayers. In this chapter, the significance, value, and teaching of the psalms in Hesychast spirituality will be examined. The method and way of practicing psalmody according to the Philokalic Fathers will be presented as well.

The Significance and Value of the Psalms in Hesychast Spirituality

What significance do the psalms have in Hesychast spirituality? Why has the chanting and quiet recitation of the psalms for centuries been one of the most basic structures of a monastic prayer life? What value do the psalms have in the therapeutic experience of God? The answers to these questions can be found in Philokalic works.

The great authority of psalmody, especially in monastic life, can be testified for by the deep conviction of St. John of Karpathos that God calls us to pray and recite the psalms.[7] If someone asks persistently for the gift of prayer with the psalms,[8] then God will answer their prayer.[9] Deeply experiencing and praying the psalms is based on the love of God. Psalmody is one of three practices blessed by God, through which the Hesychast can obtain God's blessing. This is completed through prayer and the reading of God's Word.[10] The practice of psalmody is possible through the fear of God,[11] and its purpose is to sing the glory of God. In the admiration of God and in praising His immeasurable goodness, as is shown in the psalms (especially in Psalm 104), the whole of creation joins with man, namely, the angels and all invisible powers, as well as wild animals, cattle, birds and reptiles.[12] The psalms are very helpful for those Christians who fight passions, especially those who attack these desires as soon as they begin to manifest. St. Nilus of Ancyra came to this interpretation when considering the last verse of Psalm 137: "Happy shall be who takes your little ones and dashes them against the rock!" (Psalm 137: 9). When one of the brothers asked Abba Philimon why he got more joy in the psalms than in any other part of the divine Scripture, he answered:

> My son, God has impressed the power of the psalms on my poor soul as He did on the soul of the prophet David. I cannot be separated from the sweetness of the visions about which they speak: they embrace all Scripture.[13]

Blessed is the man who constantly suffers a hunger for learning the Word of God and makes prayer and the psalms his food and drink. He strengthens himself thanks to the reading of God's glory in the Scriptures.[14] The Christian constantly praises his Lord Jesus Christ by learning and practicing the psalms.[15] St. Peter of Damaskos considered psalmody as a bodily activity aimed at the purification of the intellect.[16] He described psalmody as the fourth form of body discipline (Gr. *somatikon prakseon*).[17]

The psalms, hymns, and spiritual songs were treated by Hesychasts as a weapon that was necessary to overcome passions and evils in themselves.[18] Psalmody played the role of a rod that struck the demons who caused distraction of the intellect during prayer, as well as prompted a change of this negative behavior.[19] It must be stated that every kind of demon hates the chanting of the psalms, especially when it is practiced by someone who leads his life according to God.[20] Psalmody, by its very nature, is good. For the Hesychast, it is important to practice psalmody without vanity. When somebody chants psalmody with understanding and rhythm he can then be released from passions and curb the uncontrolled impulses of the body.[21] Just as the stars do not outweigh the sun, so do psalmody and prayer not surpass the worship, propitiation, and invocation of God that a priest does on behalf of sinners during the Divine Liturgy.[22] Prayer is better than psalmody, just as silence is more valuable than speech.[23]

The Teaching of the Psalms in Hesychast Spirituality

What do the psalms teach? How can they be helpful for a deeper understanding of Scripture? The Philokalic Fathers joyfully relied on the verses of the psalms, treating them as an authority that confirmed the truths the Fathers proclaimed. In their opinion, the psalms teach, among others, obedience to God (cf. Psalm 62,5 LXX),[24] the value of poverty (cf. Psalm 68,10–11 LXX),[25] and the perfect hatred toward demons.[26] Careful examination of the sung content of the psalms helps to overcome an ignorance of God's matters.[27] The psalms are also the source of warnings addressed to those tempted by pleasures, anger, or vanity, so that they could escape the scorching heat of their enemy.[28] The psalms can help in awakening a desire for contemplation and a deeper knowledge of God. Thanks to the psalms it is easier to understand that there is no contradiction in the Holy Scriptures, with these contradictions seen by an unenlightened intellect (Gr. *nous*).[29]

What do the psalms encourage? First of all, the psalms hearten to unceasing and uninterrupted prayer so that one will be heard by the Lord (cf. Psalm 34: 15).[30] The psalms are also helpful in fighting with ungodly thoughts that attack the soul and passions of the body.[31] The psalms urge us to live a virtuous life and to explore spiritual knowledge in anticipation of God's advent (cf. Psalm 101:1–2).[32] What is the role of the psalms in the process of the spiritual progress of Hesychasts? Do the psalms have the same meaning regardless of one's stage on the path leading to union with God? The psalms are a special kind of prayer aimed at the entering of the Christian into a personal relationship with God. Somebody's contact with God as a Person presupposes a concentration and directing of someone's awareness of Him. Prayer combined with the psalms makes it easier to focus on God, but also requires effort in praying for a long time without distraction and with attention. In this context, the remark of Ilias the Presbyter is very interesting. He claimed that if someone remains distracted in prayer and does not try to achieve concentration and attention, he finds the psalms uncouth.[33] Authentic piety is born of faith, hope, and love. True faith awakens within the Christian a desire to understand more deeply the Word of God and to praise God with the psalms.[34] The literal repetition of the psalms is especially recommended for beginners on their spiritual journey.[35] A beginner's intellect cannot bear to be forced to pray for a long time. They are similar to the colt that, when spring comes, wants to leave the stable, where it takes food from a manger and eagerly gallops, "into the fields of natural contemplation" (Greek: *epi to platos tes fisikis theorias*) to devote itself to psalmody and spiritual reading.[36] The Psalter is a very effective medicine for beginners, especially if they fall into vanity.[37] Reciting the psalms in solitude is helpful in a prayerful dialogue with God. In this way, one can build oneself. Nikitas Stithatos distinguishes between two levels of prayer with the psalms: the first when we pray and psalmodize inwardly in tongue, and the second when prayer is combined with responsibility for the Church. For Stithatos, his foundation for such a distinction was the 14th chapter of the First Letter to the Corinthians. The teaching of St. Paul presented there Nikitas Stithatos refers to as prayer with the psalms. Admittedly, this is quite an unusual exegesis of the teaching of the Apostle to the Nations, but this kind of approach to the Word of God was popular in Greek patristics. For someone who cares about spiritual gifts, and especially for someone who wants to love, it is not enough to talk to God through prayer with the psalms in private. Someone who is touched by God's love prophesizes with the language of sacred teaching in order to edify God's Church (cf. 1 Corinthians 14:2–4), i.e. to teach a neighbor how to fulfill God's commandments and how to live according to God's will. If someone does not speak to those brethren for whom he is responsible, whether by inspiration of the Holy Spirit, through his knowledge of God's mysteries, with a received prophetic gift of foresight, or by making manifest a call to teach the wisdom of God (cf. 1 Corinthians 14:6), what could be the benefit? The shepherd taking responsibility for his disciples should prepare them for battle against the passions and demons (cf. 1 Corinthians 14:8). This can be done through clear instructions addressed to one's flock in writing or by word of mouth. Someone can build oneself with psalmody alone because this kind of prayer falls deeply into the soul. It is not enough, however, for the intellect to benefit (cf. 1 Corinthians 14:4) and to contribute to the edifying of the Church. For this reason, St. Nikitas Stithatos encouraged only the following of the example of St. Paul who taught: "[...] nevertheless, in church I would rather speak five words with my mind, in order to instruct others, than ten thousand words in a tongue" (1 Corinthians 14:19), except that in his interpretation instead of "ten thousand words in a tongue," one must make "ten thousand words of psalmody in private."[38] The instructions of the Church are much more fruitful than praying with the psalms in private.

To all those who do not yet see it as worthy to enter into contemplation and spiritual knowledge, words of encouragement are directed to their intellects to practice prayer with the psalms and troparia. In this way, those with some inhibitions will start some kind of meditation that can be possible at different times of the day. It is well known that monks memorized the psalms. They chanted or recited them both during work and travel.[39] According to St. Symeon the New Theologian, the diligent practice of psalmody is at the second rung or stage of spiritual growth, i.e. reflects the development of adolescence to youth. When somebody will manage to limit the scope of the influence of passions, psalmody brings delight to the tongue, which is welcomed by God. The necessary condition for this task is to guard the heart so that it does not become a source of passion. The Hesychast should remember that it is not possible to sing to the Lord in a foreign land (cf. Psalm 137:4) from an impassioned heart.[40] At a more advanced stage of the spiritual path, St. Gregory of Sinai recommended moderate psalmody complemented by silent prayer. If the exhaustion caused by the continuous noetic invocation of God and intense concentration overwhelms the intellect, it is good to allow it to relax in the amplitude of psalmody. Chanting of the psalms is therefore the perfect medicine for the overworked intellect.[41]

Many Hesychasts, like the desert fathers before them, wondered about the intensity of psalmody.[42] Some taught that it is necessary to devote a lot of time to chanting and reciting the psalms, others suggested that it is enough to spend a moderate amount of time reciting the psalms, and others considered that psalmody is not needed at all because it will suffice to focus only on the prayer of the intellect and physical activities (such as handicrafts or prostrations). The answer given by St. Gregory of Sinai was at the heart of the problem. His answer was based on his personal experience gained on the road to God. In his opinion, the multitude of stances and standpoints regarding the intensity of psalmody results from excessive attachment to one's own spiritual experiences. It usually happens that after passing a certain part of the spiritual path, personal and ascetic experiences take on a normative meaning, which is certainly good, because it leads to an ever closer relationship with God. But, one should remember that it is dangerous to discredit the way of attaining the achievements of other people. In its extreme form, the power of one's experiences becomes so compelling that the spiritual experiences of other people are denied and there is no recognition of truthfulness and action of God's grace in their hearts.[43] These explanations lead the thought of St Gregory of Sinai to a detailed conclusion, namely, that psalmody prepares man for contemplation. Those who are advanced on the spiritual path can stop reciting the psalms because they have already reached a state of enlightenment. At this stage, it is more appropriate to cultivate silence, unceasing prayer, and immersion in God.[44]

The Method and Way of Practicing Psalmody According to the Philokalic Fathers

How to pray with the psalms? What method and way of practicing psalmody was taught by the Philokalic Fathers? When, with what frequency, and in what position of the body should the dialogue of the Hesychast with God take place through the psalms? Answering these questions will allow us to have a closer look at psalmody in relation to the tradition of constant concentration on God, which is the essence of Hesychast spirituality. The introduction to continuous prayer (cf. 1 Thessalonians 5:17) in the monastic environment presupposed that everything should be done in accordance with regulations and at specific times and hours.[45] This general recommendation also applied to prayer and psalmody.[46] St. Theoliptos precisely explained a way of praying the psalms:

> When chanting psalms, do this in a low voice, with your intellect fully attentive: do not allow any phrase to go uncomprehended. Should anything escape your understanding, begin the verse again, and repeat this as many times as necessary, until your intellect grasps what is being said. For the intellect can attend to the chanting and simultaneously can recollect God. You may learn this from everyday experience: you can meet and speak with someone and also focus your eyes on him. Similarly, you can chant the psalms and focus on God through recollectedness.[47]

The Hesychast should devote himself to the remembrance of God and stillness of heart. From early morning, he is obliged to participate in daily services, which in large part consisted of the psalms and hymns. The third, sixth, and ninth canonical hour was to be chanted, while the other canonical hours were to be recited.[48] Only when the Hesychast began to pray continuously was he no longer obliged to give glory to the Lord seven times a day, at certain times of day and night (cf. Psalm 55:17), as the Psalmist testified (cf. Psalm 119:164).[49] Nikitas Stithatos taught that the prayerful recitation of the psalms should be pronounced with perseverance and attentiveness because it is of great importance for spiritual life. Thanks to the quality of the recitation of the psalms the soul becomes fertile. The recitation of the psalms consists in becoming aware of the meaning hidden in Holy Scripture, so that the heart is filled with wonderful thoughts of God and the light-creating energy of the Holy Spirit.[50] The presence of the Holy Spirit in man, in turn, influences the quantity and quality of the prayerful recitation of the psalms[51] because God stimulates man to glorify Him more and more perfectly. According to St. John Climacus, it is good to spend most of the night for prayer of the intellect, and what is left is found only in psalmody.[52] From the earliest times, in the monastic tradition of the Christian East, the psalms were chanted in a standing position. This is confirmed by numerous testimonies in the apophthegmata of the Desert Fathers as well as in broadly understood philokalic literature. St. Gregory of Sinai advised that the whole of night vigils (Gr. *agrypnia*), of which an important part was the chanting of the psalms, should be adjusted to the degree of one's advancement on the spiritual path. He also recommended that beginners should sleep during the first part of the night and spend the second half of the night in prayer keeping vigil. Those midways on the path and the perfect were instructed that they should remain awake and keep vigil after nightfall for one or two hours, then sleep for four hours, then rise for matins and chant the psalms and pray for six hours until daybreak, then chant the first hour, and after that sit down and practice stillness. Perfect Hesychasts, who are already far down the spiritual path, can stand in prayer with the psalms, keeping vigil uninterruptedly all night.[53] According to St. Peter of Damaskos, it is good to keep moderate vigils (Gr. *agrypnia symetros*). This form of ascetic discipline consists of sleeping for half the night and devoting oneself to the recital of the psalms, to prayer, compunctive sorrow, and tears for the other half.[54] In his work *On Prayer*, St. Gregory of Sinai once again returns to the problems related with psalmodizing and gives a concrete justification for its use. Psalmody has been given to us because of our grossness and indolence, so that we may be led back to our true state. Frequent chanting of various psalms is recommended for beginner Hesychasts as it helps them gain spiritual knowledge.[55] Hesychasts, who are entirely focused on God and do not succumb to images suggested by their senses as cast by evil spirits, no longer need to psalmodize. St. Gregory of Sinai recommended moderation in this work to all those on their way to achieving interior tranquility. The intensity of psalmody should be adapted to the quality of somebody's spiritual life. If someone has already tasted God's grace, then, according to the Fathers, he needs more time for the prayer of the intellect and less time for praying the psalms. The role of the psalms can be compared to the oars that move a sailing ship when it is stopped in silence. When a fair wind swells the sails of the ship, it is then driven lightly across the salt sea of the passions. But when the ship loses speed it has to be propelled by oars or towed by another boat. So, the psalms are not needed when the wind of constant prayer of the intellect inflates the sails of the ship and thus it goes to the port of internal stillness.[56]

"Shall I read and sing psalms with my mouth only?"[57] – St. Peter of Damaskos asked, pointing out that the purpose of psalmody is more than just singing the glory of God. Metropolitan Theoliptos taught that the richness of content taken from the psalms is to descend into the depths of man's heart. To make this possible, someone must have the intellect fully attentive and he should try to understand the meaning of each of the sung verses as deeply as possible. If the meaning of the verse is districted and lost, it is good to return to it and repeat it as many times as the intellect needs to grasp its contents. When chanting (in a low voice) the psalms, one should simultaneously focus on God through recollectedness.[58] It often happens to novices that during chanting of the psalms, their tongues utter the words of the verses while their intellects are overwhelmed by the distraction caused by passion-charged thoughts and fantasies. The result of such a dispersion of thoughts is a misunderstanding of the sung psalm content and a lack of concentration on God.[59] As soon as the Hesychast discovers that his intellect is distracted during the recitation or chanting of the psalms, he must stop this recitation or chanting, regardless of whether this discovery was made at the beginning, in the middle, or at the end of the psalm, and start it again, but now without distraction. It is recommended that this process should always be repeated as many times as needed so that a psalm is chanted or recited with full attentiveness and understanding.[60] Demons are interested in getting the intellect distracted. Through various tricks of deception, they try to influence the soul's attention in such a way as to change the verses of the psalms into blasphemies. As a result of this loss of attention to the soul, words that should not be said can be spoken, verses can be dropped, or there is a momentary obscuration of consciousness which occurs while reading the psalm so that one cannot remember the last verse just read. By succumbing to Satan's traps, someone becomes neglectful and listless. Protecting yourself from all these dangers requires perseverance and concentration on the words of the psalm chanted or spoken slowly. In this way, one can profit from psalmody and his soul can be filled with the light of the Holy Spirit.[61] It is possible to learn how to pray with the psalms by meditating carefully on their contents so that they become understood by the intellect. Quoting two verses from the Bible, namely: "Sing the psalms with understanding" (Psalm 47:7) and "Search the Scriptures" (John 5:39), St. Peter of Damaskos explains that:

> He who pays attention to them is illumined, while he who pays no attention is filled with darkness. For unless a person attends to what is

said in divine Scripture, he will gather but little fruit, even though he sings or reads them frequently.[62]

Psalmody has a beneficial effect on night rest. When one of the brothers told Abba Philimon that he had many vain fantasies during his sleep, the experienced old man pointed out that he should go to sleep after reciting the psalms and after inward meditation.[63] The psalms, often repeated, like the Jesus prayer, descend to the heart. However, the Hesychast needs to focus on them, both in his dreams and during the day, regardless of what he does. When someone wants to introduce the psalms to his heart then it is required to chant them as well as reflect intensely on their words.[64] St. Peter of Damaskos set out many practical recommendations on how to pray with the psalms. The entire Psalter is divided into 20 sections in the liturgical tradition of the Eastern Church. Each of these sections is called *kathisma* and every *kathisma* is divided into three subsections, each called *stasis* or *antiphon*. Psalmody meditated by Hesychasts was expanded with additional elements, i.e. prayers and prostrations aimed at keeping the intellect focused on the chanted or recited content. According to the rule of praying the psalms described by St. Peter of Damaskos, after directing oneself to God in the Trinity with the words: "God our Master, Father Almighty, Lord Jesus Christ, the Only-begotten Son, and the Holy Spirit, One Godhead, One Power, have mercy on me a sinner," one should immediately address his own thoughts and say three times: "O come, let us worship and fall down before God our King." Then the psalms should be chanted, with there being recitation of the Trisagion after each subsection of the Psalter. After the Trisagion, someone was obliged to say, "Lord, have mercy" 40 times and then to make a prostration and confess within himself, "I have sinned, Lord, forgive me." On standing, the Hesychast should stretch out his arms upward (in a gesture of the *oranta*) and say again: "God, be merciful to me a sinner" and start another subsection of the Psalter in the same way. He should pray until God's grace inflames a feeling of compunction in his heart, which will enable the intellect to bath in tears. Then the Hesychast must stop reciting the psalms, because every bodily activity, and thus also psalmody, is aimed at the purifying of the intellect and uniting it to God in prayer free from any rational imaginations, i.e. free from all form and figure.[65] St. Gregory of Sinai also taught about the incorporation of the Trisagion hymn into psalmodizing. In his opinion, it is good to include the recitation of several penitential *troparia* and the Alleluia in the chanting of the psalms because this is helpful for the intellect in keeping one's thoughts from wandering. Referring to his own experience, St. Gregory of Sinai pointed to psalmody as a remedy for an exhausted intellect by the practice of stillness. For if the Hesychast stays in a sitting position for a long time in a state of long-lasting silence and does not succumb to accidental thoughts and images, whether sensory or conceptual, that rise up from the heart, but prays to God in humility, then his intellect falls into fatigue and his body begins to feel pain. Intense concentration on the constant calling of the Name of Jesus leads to such suffering. In such a state it is good to stand up and chant the psalms standing alone or with brothers.[66] The Metropolitan of Philadelphia, Theoliptos, testified to the benefits of this form of prayer: "When in God's name you gather together with the brethren, present yourself bodily to God and offer Him psalms chanted orally; and likewise keep your intellect attentive to the words and to God Himself, aware of who it is that your intellect addresses and entreats. For when the mind devotes itself to prayer actively and with purity, the heart is granted inexpressible peace and a joy which cannot be taken away."[67] Chanting the psalms and reading Holy Scripture can protect the intellect from various distractions. In this way the Hesychast, "shall prevent the intellect from confusing its own utterances with the utterances of grace, and stop it from being led astray by self-esteem and dispersed through over-elation and loquacity."[68] The Hesychast will be able to concentrate wholly on psalmody if he practices prayers in true purity and conducts spiritual readings in due sequence, completing each phase at the right time. During chanting or reading of the psalms, it can be helpful to raise up physical and spiritual eyes from time to time because there are enemies that lie in ambush in the air.[69]

The Philokalic Fathers made the way of praying with the psalms depend on what was happening inside the intellect of the human being.[70] Basically, the psalms are intended for chanting, both in full voice and quietly. Singing recitations, usually in a low voice, is still popular in monastic environments in the Orthodox Church. Chanting of the psalms together with fasting and keeping vigils characterize someone who loves God.[71] The Hesychast method aims to bring the psalms into the heart in order to chant them there in joy and peace, thus praising God. According to St. Diadochos of Photiki, the singing of the psalms with a full voice is typical for someone who is happy with his life for the sake of success and prosperity. Such a person can easily fall into a deceptive and delusory joy because he focuses more on himself and his feelings than on God. However, if someone is energized by the Holy Spirit, then he sings the psalms with spiritual joy and peace and prays in his heart alone. In this condition, he experiences initially spiritual tears and then an inner stillness. This happens when the memory of God is kindled for the sake of abstaining from speech. By chanting the psalms loudly, one can be freed from a deep despondency. All that is needed is to raise a voice with joyful expectation to God and the dense mist of discouragement will be dispersed by the warmth of the psalms.[72] Some elder monks, like Abba Philimon, chanted the entire Psalter[73] quietly during the night, saying the words as if they were talking to someone else.[74] Therefore, they did not treat chanting the psalms as a method of inner healing and purification of the heart, but as a form of dialogue with God. Chanting the psalms with understanding (cf. Psalm 47:7 LXX) is important because it is a condition for gathering an abundant spiritual harvest. The one who draws attention to the meaning of the words of the psalms is enlightened, and the one who speaks them thoughtlessly plunges into darkness.[75] Staying awake while chanting the psalms is helpful in recognizing and not succumbing to the impure and blasphemous thoughts of the enemy.[76]

What does the chanting of the psalms protect and cure? First of all, this chanting defends one from the vain talk that makes it impossible to concentrate on God.[77] Furthermore, psalmody combined with spiritual reading and vigils prevent the intellect from being deceived and deluded by the passions (Gr. *pahti*).[78] Chanting and reciting the psalms is a very effective remedy for the straying intellect in order to lead it to stability.[79] The Psalter used daily by monks was the most known book of the Bible. Psalmody can have a healing effect on the soul. It is a very effective remedy for acedia, anger, and aggressiveness of various origins. Proper prayer with the psalms, consisting in attentive (without distraction) uttering or singing of verses, calms passions and helps to curb the uncontrolled impulses of the body,[80] and facilitates the flow of spiritual energy to the tired intellect.[81] It is beneficial for a man to chant or recite the psalms according to the rule of prayer, as evidenced by a converted robber named David, who became a monk. An angel prevented him from saying anything except the psalms. There are also known biblical examples of what happened to Jonah (cf. Jonah 1:3) and Zacharias (cf. Luke 1:18), who were not eager to listen to God and yet they were prompted to listen to God.[82]

How can the role of the psalms be summarized in Hesychast spirituality? What can be achieved by this method of prayer? The Philokalic Fathers taught that psalmody is particularly helpful in the initial phase of spiritual growth. It facilitates the detachment of the intellect from material things[83] as well as helps to free oneself from impassioned and wicked thoughts.[84] If someone truly loves God, then he can be freed from passions by devoting himself constantly to Him through self-control, love, prayer, and psalmody.[85] Thanks to prayer with the psalms it is easier to achieve a balance of the temperaments of the flesh.[86] If psalmody is completed by spiritual reading, then achieving purity of heart is faster.[87] Through continuous prayer the words of the psalms are lead down into the heart and various spiritual flowers begin to grow therein. Ilias the Presbyter, among the variety of spiritual flowers, particularly indicates three species, namely: "roses, the vision of incorporeal realities; lilies, the luminosity of corporal realities; and violets, the many judgments of God, hard to understand."[88] The regular and intensive practice of psalmody awakens in the intellect a desire for an intimate relationship with God, which makes it easier for one to reject all distracting thoughts surrounding the heart.[89] The analysis of the role, significance, and practice of psalmody in the Hesychast tradition, based on the philokalic writings, fully confirms that it is an important part not only of the monastic formation in the Eastern Orthodox Church, but also is an integral part of the prayerful relationship of each Hesychast with God in the Trinity of the Most Holy Persons.

Acknowledgment

"The project is funded by the Minister of Science and Higher Education within the program under the name "Regional Initiative of Excellence" in 2019–2022, project number: 028/RID/2018/19, the amount of funding: 11 742 500 PLN".

Notes

1 Cf. Richardson, "The Psalms as Christian Prayers and Praises", 326–346; Scott, *The Psalms as Christian Praise*, passim; Gillingham, *Psalms through the Centuries*, 40–42, 47–62; de Candole, *The Christian Use of the Psalms*, passim.
2 Brueggemann, *The Message of the Psalms*, 15.
3 Kraus, *Theology of the Psalms*, 177–194.
4 Braulik, *Psalter and Messiah*, 15–40; Grelot, *Le mystère du Christ dans les psaumes*, passim.
5 Kriegshauser, *Praying the Psalms in Christ, Notre Dame*, 5.
6 Cf. Custer, "The Psaltery, the Harp and the Fathers", 19–31; Dysinger, *Psalmody and Prayer in the Writings of Evagrius Ponticus*, passim; Dysinger, "The Significance of Psalmody in the 'Mystical Theology of Evagrius of Pontus", 176–182; Gelineau, "Les psaumes l'epoque patristique", 99–116; Grisbrooke, *The Formative Period in Cathedral and Monastic Offices*, 358–369; Knowles, "Monastic Prayer: Text and Context", 143–155; Leloir, "Repartition des psaumes et tradition monastique", 254–264; Mateos, "L'office monastique a la fin du IV siecle: Antioche, Palestine, Cappadoce", 53–88; Mateos, "The Morning and Evening Office", 31–47; Stead, "St. Athanasius on the Psalms", 65–78; Taft, *The Liturgy of Hours in East and West*, 57–91.
7 St John of Karpathos, "Ascetic Discourse Sent at the Request of the Same Monks in India", 323 (Ioannou Karpathiou, "Logos asketikos kai panu paregoretikos pros tous apo tes Indias protrepsantas monachous, ton P' kefalaion ton arithmon synapopleron", 299).
8 Cf. Aejmelaeus, *The Traditional Prayer in the Psalms*, 15–42.
9 Evagrios the Solitary, "On Prayer: One Hundred and Fifty-Three Texts" 87, 65 (Neilou Asketou, "Prologos ton peri preseuches ekaton pentekonta trion kefalion" 87, 184).
10 St Gregory of Sinai, "On Commandments and Doctrines, Warnings and Promises; on Thoughts, Passions and Virtues, and also on Stillness and Prayer: One Hundred and Thirty-Seven Texts" 99, 233 (Gregoriou tou Sinaitou, "Kefalia ΔΙ' akrostichidos panu ofelima. Logoi diaforoi peri entolon, dogmaton, apeilon kai epaggelion, eti de kai peri logismon kai pathon kai areton, eti de kai peri hesychias kai proseuches" 99, 47–48). Cf. Hisamatsu, *Gregorios Sinaites als Lehrem des Gebetes*, 382–387.
11 Cf. St Peter of Damaskos, "Book II. Twenty-Four Discourses" 2, 213–214 (Cf. Petrou Damaskenou, "Bilion B', Logoi synoptikoi ΚΔ'. Plereis notes pneumatikes gnoseos" 2, 114–115).
12 Cf. St John of Karpathos, "For the Encouragement of the Monks in India who had Written to Him: One Hundred Texts" 2, 298 (Ioannou Karpathiou, "Pros tois en te India monachous, grapsantas auto, paramuthetika kefalaia P'", 2, 276).
13 "A Discourse on Abba Philimon", 347 ("Peri tou Abba Filemonos Logos panu hofelimos", 244).

14 St John of Karpathos, "For the Encouragement of the Monks in India who had Written to Him: One Hundred Texts" 83, 317–318 (Ioannou Karpathiou, "Pros tois en te India monachous, grapsantas auto, paramuthetika kefalaia P'" 83, 293).

15 St Mark the Ascetic, "On Those who Think that They are Made Righteous by Works: 226 Texts" 226, 146 (Markou tou Asketou, "Peri ton oiomenon eks ergon dikaiousthai, Kefalia ΣΚζ' 226", 126).

16 St Peter of Damaskos, "Book I. A Treasury of Divine Knowledge", 119 (Petrou Damaskenou, "Biblion A', Tes hypotheseos tou bibliou tou osiou kai theoforou patros hymon Petrou Damaskinou", 41).

17 St Peter of Damaskos, "Book I. A Treasury of Divine Knowledge", 91 (Petrou Damaskenou, "Biblion A', Tes hypotheseos tou bibliou tou osiou kai theoforou patros hymon Petrou Damaskinou", 18).

18 Cf. St John of Karpathos, "For the Encouragement of the Monks in India who had Written to Him: One Hundred Texts" 87, 318–319 (Cf. Ioannou Karpathiou, "Pros tois en te India monachous, grapsantas auto, paramuthetika kefalaia P"'87, 294).

19 Cf. St Gregory of Sinai, "On Commandments and Doctrines, Warnings and Promises; on Thoughts, Passions and Virtues, and also on Stillness and Prayer: One Hundred and Thirty-Seven Texts" 16, 215 (Cf. Gregoriou tou Sinaitou, "Kefalia ΔΙ' akrostichidos panu ofelima. Logoi diaforoi peri entolon, dogmaton, apeilon kai epaggelion, eti de kai peri logismon kai pathon kai areton, eti de kai peri hesychias kai proseuches" 16, 33).

20 St Maximus the Confessor, "Various Texts on Theology, the Divine Economy, and Virtue and Vice. Third Century" 70, 227–228 (Maksimou tou Homologetou, "Kefalaia diafora theologika te kai oikonomika kai peri aretes kai kakias. Ekatontas Trite" 70, 103).

21 St Maximus the Confessor, "Four Hundred Texts on Love. Second Century" 35, 71 (Maksimou tou Homologetou, "Ekatontas deutera. Ton peri agape kefalaion" 35, 19). Cf. Evagrios the Solitary, "On Prayer: One Hundred and Fifty-Three Texts" 85, 65 (Neilou Asketou, "Prologos ton peri preseuches ekaton pentekonta trion kefalion" 85, 184).

22 Cf. Theognostos, "On the Practice of the Virtues, Contemplation and the Priesthood" 72, 376 (Cf. Theognostu, "Peri prakseos kai theorias kai peri hierosynes" 72, 270).

23 Ilias the Presbyter, "A Gnomic Anthology. Part I" 4, 34 (Elia Elachisto Presbitero kai Ekdiko, "Anthologion gnomikon filosofon spoudaion. Spoudasthen kai ponethen" 4, 289).

24 St Diadochos of Photiki, "On Spiritual Knowledge and Discrimination: One Hundred Texts" 35, 263 (Diadochou, "Logos asketikos dieremenos eis P' kefalaia praktyka – gnoseos kai diakriseos pneumatikes" 35, 244).

25 St Diadochos of Photiki, "On Spiritual Knowledge and Discrimination: One Hundred Texts" 66, 275 (Diadochou, "Logos asketikos dieremenos eis P' kefalaia praktyka – gnoseos kai diakriseos pneumatikes" 66, 254).

26 St Theodoros the Great Ascetic, "A Century of Spiritual Texts" 63, 26 (Theodorom, "Tou megalou asketou kai episkopu Edesses, Kefalaia panu psychofele P'" 63, 314).

27 Cf. St Peter of Damaskos, "Book I. A Treasury of Divine Knowledge", 194 (Cf. Petrou Damaskenou, "Biblion A', Tes hypotheseos tou bibliou tou osiou kai theoforou patros hymon Petrou Damaskinou", 99).

28 Cf. St John of Karpathos, "For the Encouragement of the Monks in India who had Written to Him: One Hundred Texts" 60, 312 (Ioannou Karpathiou, "Pros

tois en te India monachous, grapsantas auto, paramuthetika kefalaia P'" 60, 288).

29 Cf. St Peter of Damaskos, "Book I. A Treasury of Divine Knowledge", 144 (Cf. Petrou Damaskenou, "Biblion A', Tes hypotheseos tou bibliou tou osiou kai theoforou patros hymon Petrou Damaskinou", 61).

30 Cf. St Theodoros the Great Ascetic, "A Century of Spiritual Texts" 60, 25–26 (Cf. Theodorom, "Kefalaia panu psychofele P"' 60, 314).

31 Cf. St Maximus the Confessor, "Two Hundred Texts on Theology and the Incarnate Dispensation of the Son of God. Written for Thalassios. Second Century" 97, 163 (Cf. Maksimou tou Homologetou, "Peri theologias kai tes ensarkou oikonomias tou hiou tou Theou, pros Thalassion. Kefalia Σ'. Ekatontas deutera" 97, 89).

32 St Maximus the Confessor, "Two Hundred Texts on Theology and the Incarnate Dispensation of the Son of God. Written for Thalassios. Second Century" 98, 163 (Maksimou tou Homologetou, "Peri theologias kai tes ensarkou oikonomias tou hiou tou Theou, pros Thalassion. Kefalia Σ'. Ekatontas deutera" 98, 89).

33 Ilias the Presbyter, "A Gnomic Anthology. Part IV" 114, 62 (Elia Elachisto Presbitero kai Ekdiko, "Praktyka kai theoretika" 114, 310).

34 Cf. St Peter of Damaskos, "Book I. A Treasury of Divine Knowledge", 167–168 (Cf. Petrou Damaskenou, "Biblion A', Tes hypotheseos tou bibliou tou osiou kai theoforou patros hymon Petrou Damaskinou", 79).

35 Ilias the Presbyter, "A Gnomic Anthology. Part IV" 63, 56 (Elia Elachisto Presbitero kai Ekdiko, "Praktyka kai theoretika" 63, 305).

36 Ilias the Presbyter, "A Gnomic Anthology. Part IV" 61, 55 (Elia Elachisto Presbitero kai Ekdiko, "Praktyka kai theoretika" 61, 305).

37 Cf. Symeon the New Theologian, "One Hundred and Fifty-Three Practical and Theological Texts" 123, 52 (Cf. Symeon tou Neou Theologou, "Kefalia praktyka kai theologika PME'" 123, 261).

38 Nikitas Stithatos, "On Spiritual Knowledge, Love and the Perfection of Living: One Hundred Texts" 89, 169 (Nikita Monachou kai Presbiterou, "Deutera fisykon kefalaion ekatontas peri tes noos katharseos" 89, 321).

39 Cf. St Peter of Damaskos, "Book I. A Treasury of Divine Knowledge", 106–107 (Cf. Petrou Damaskenou, "Biblion A', Tes hypotheseos tou bibliou tou osiou kai theoforou patros hymon Petrou Damaskinou", 31).

40 Cf. Attributed to St Symeon the New Theologian, "The Three Methods of Prayer", 73–74 (Cf. Symeon tou Neou Theologou, "Peri ton trion tropon tes proseuches", 88).

41 Cf. St Gregory of Sinai, "On Stillness: Fifteen Texts" 7, 268 (Cf. Gregoriou tou Sinaitou, "Peri hesychias kai peri ton duo tropon tes preseuches en kefalaiois IE'" 7, 74–75).

42 Cf. van der Mensbrugghe, "Prayer-time in Egyptian Monasticism (320–450)", 435–452.

43 Cf. St Gregory of Sinai, "On Stillness: Fifteen Texts" 6, 266–267 (Cf. Gregoriou tou Sinaitou, "Peri hesychias kai peri ton duo tropon tes preseuches en kefalaiois IE'" 6, 73–74).

44 Cf. St Gregory of Sinai, "On Stillness: Fifteen Texts" 8, 268–269 (Cf. Gregoriou tou Sinaitou, "Peri hesychias kai peri ton duo tropon tes preseuches en kefalaiois IE'" 8, 75).

45 Cf. St Symeon the New Theologian, "One Hundred and Fifty-Three Practical and Theological Texts" 118, 50 (Cf. Symeon tou Neou Theologou, "Kefalia praktyka kai theologika PME'" 118, 259–260).

46 P.P. Bradshaw, *Daily Prayer in the Early Church: A Study in the Origin and Early Development of the Divine Office*, 93:

> In the early Christian tradition there were always those who regarded the observance of fixed times of prayer in the course of the day as no more than a second-best way of fulfilling the apostolic injunction to 'pray without ceasing': the ideal was truly continuous prayer day and night.

47 Cf. Theoliptos, "On Inner Work in Christ and the Monastic Profession", 185 (Cf. Theoliptou Metropolitou Filadelfeias, "Logos ten en Christo krupten ergasian diasafon kai deiknyonen brachei tou monadikou epaggelmatos ton kopon", 11).
48 St Gregory of Sinai, "On Commandments and Doctrines, Warnings and Promises; on Thoughts, Passions and Virtues, and also on Stillness and Prayer: One Hundred and Thirty-Seven Texts" 99, 233 (Gregoriou tou Sinaitou, "Kefalia ΔΙ' akrostichidos panu ofelima. Logoi diaforoi peri entolon, dogmaton, apeilon kai epaggelion, eti de kai peri logismon kai pathon kai areton, eti de kai peri hesychias kai proseuches" 99, 48).
49 St Symeon the New Theologian, "One Hundred and Fifty-Three Practical and Theological Texts" 118, 50 (Symeon tou Neou Theologou, "Kefalia praktyka kai theologika PME'" 118, 259–260).
50 Cf. Nikitas Stithatos, "On the Inner Nature of Things and on the Purification of the Intellect: One Hundred Texts" 70, 127 (Cf. Nikita Monachou kai Presbiterou, "Deutera fisykon kefalaion ekatontas peri tes noos katharseos" 70, 316).
51 Nikitas Stithatos, "On the Inner Nature of Things and on the Purification of the Intellect: One Hundred Texts" 71, 127 (Nikita Monachou kai Presbiterou, "Deutera fisykon kefalaion ekatontas peri tes noos katharseos" 71, 316).
52 St John Climacus, *The Ladder of Divine Ascent* 27, 272 (PG 88, 1116C).
53 St Gregory of Sinai, "On Commandments and Doctrines, Warnings and Promises; on Thoughts, Passions and Virtues, and also on Stillness and Prayer: One Hundred and Thirty-Seven Texts" 101, 233–234 (Gregoriou tou Sinaitou, "Kefalia ΔΙ' akrostichidos panu ofelima. Logoi diaforoi peri entolon, dogmaton, apeilon kai epaggelion, eti de kai peri logismon kai pathon kai areton, eti de kai peri hesychias kai proseuche" 101, 48).
54 Cf. St Peter of Damaskos, "Book I. A Treasury of Divine Knowledge", 90–91 (Cf. Petrou Damaskenou, "Biblion A', Tes hypotheseos tou bibliou tou osiou kai theoforou patros hymon Petrou Damaskinou", 18).
55 Cf. C. Harrison, "Enchanting the Soul: The Music of the Psalms", 205–223.
56 Cf. Gregory of Sinai, "On Prayer: Seven Texts" 5, 277–278 (Cf. Gregoriou tou Sinaitou, "Peri tou pos dei kathezesthai ton hesychazonta eis ten euchen kai me tacheos anistasthai" 5, 82).
57 Cf. St Peter of Damaskos, "Book I. A Treasury of Divine Knowledge", 116 (Cf. Petrou Damaskenou, "Biblion A', Tes hypotheseos tou bibliou tou osiou kai theoforou patros hymon Petrou Damaskinou", 39).
58 Theoliptos, "On Inner Work in Christ and the Monastic Profession", 185 (Theoliptou Metropolitou Filadelfeias, "Logos ten en Christo krupten ergasian diasafon kai deiknyonen brachei tou monadikou epaggelmatos ton kopon", 11).
59 Cf. Theoliptos, "On Inner Work in Christ and the Monastic Profession", 182 (Cf. Theoliptou Metropolitou Filadelfeias, "Logos ten en Christo krupten ergasian diasafon kai deiknyonen brachei tou monadikou epaggelmatos ton kopon", 8).
60 Cf. Nikitas Stithatos, "On the Inner Nature of Things and on the Purification of the Intellect: One Hundred Texts" 73, 128 (Cf. Nikita Monachou kai

Presbiterou, "Deutera fisykon kefalaion ekatontas peri tes noos katharseos" 73, 317).

61 Nikitas Stithatos, "On the Inner Nature of Things and on the Purification of the Intellect: One Hundred Texts" 72, 127–128 (Nikita Monachou kai Presbiterou, "Deutera fisykon kefalaion ekatontas peri tes noos katharseos" 72, 316).

62 St Peter of Damaskos, "Book II. Twenty-Four Discourses" 22, 263–264 (Petrou Damaskenou, "Biblion B', Logoi synoptikoi KΔ'. Plereis notes pneumatikes gnoseos" 22, 156).

63 "A Discourse on Abba Philimon", 348 ("Peri tou Abba Filemonos Logos panu hofelimos", 245).

64 "A Discourse on Abba Philimon", 348 ("Peri tou Abba Filemonos Logos panu hofelimos", 244).

65 Cf. St Peter of Damaskos, "Book I. A Treasury of Divine Knowledge", 118–119 (Cf. Petrou Damaskenou, "Biblion A', Tes hypotheseos tou bibliou tou osiou kai theoforou patros hymon Petrou Damaskinou", 41).

66 Cf. St Gregory of Sinai, "On Stillness: Fifteen Texts" 9, 269–270 (Cf. Gregoriou tou Sinaitou, "Peri hesychias kai peri ton duo tropon tes preseuches en kefalaiois IE'" 9, 75–76.)

67 Theoliptos, "On Inner Work in Christ and the Monastic Profession", 183 (Theoliptou Metropolitou Filadelfeias, "Logos ten en Christo krupten ergasian diasafon kai deiknyonen brachei tou monadikou epaggelmatos ton kopon", 9).

68 Cf. St Diadochos of Photiki, "On Spiritual Knowledge and Discrimination: One Hundred Texts" 68, 275–276. (Cf. Diadochou, "Logos asketikos dieremenos eis P' kefalaia praktyka – gnoseos kai diakriseos pneumatikes" 68, 255).

69 Attributed to St Symeon the New Theologian, "The Three Methods of Prayer", 75 (Symeon tou Neou Theologou, "Peri ton trion tropon tes proseuches", 88–89.)

70 Cf. Lingas, "Hesychasm and Psalmody", 155–168.

71 St Maximus the Confessor, "Four Hundred Texts on Love. First Century" 42, 57 (Maksimou tou Homologetou, "Ekatontas prote. Ton peri agape kefalaion" 42, 7).

72 Cf. Diadochos of Photiki, "On Spiritual Knowledge and Discrimination: One Hundred Texts" 73, 277–278 (Cf. Diadochou, "Logos asketikos dieremenos eis P' kefalaia praktyka – gnoseos kai diakriseos pneumatikes" 73, 257).

73 Cf. "A Discourse on Abba Philimon", 346 (Cf. "Peri tou Abba Filemonos Logos panu hofelimos", 243).

74 Cf. "A Discourse on Abba Philimon", 347 (Cf. "Peri tou Abba Filemonos Logos panu hofelimos", 244).

75 St Peter of Damaskos, "Book II. Twenty-Four Discourses" 23, 263–264 (Petrou Damaskenou, "Biblion B', Logoi synoptikoi KΔ'. Plereis notes pneumatikes gnoseos" 23, 156).

76 St John of Karpathos, "For the Encouragement of the Monks in India who had Written to Him: One Hundred Texts" 51, 310 (Cf. Ioannou Karpathiou, "Pros tois en te India monachous, grapsantas auto, paramuthetika kefalaia P'" 51, 287).

77 Theoliptos, "On Inner Work in Christ and the Monastic Profession", 185 (Theoliptou Metropolitou Filadelfeias, "Logos ten en Christo krupten ergasian diasafon kai deiknyonen brachei tou monadikou epaggelmatos ton kopon", 11).

78 St Thalassios, "On Love, Self-control and Life in accordance with the Intellect. Fourth Century" 19, 326 (Thalassiou tou Libuos kai Afrikanou, "Peri agape kai egkrateias kai tes kata non politeias. Pros Paulon Presbiteron. Ekatontas Tetarte" 19, 224).

79 Evagrios the Solitary, "Extracts from the Texts on Watchfulness" 5, 53–54 (Evagriou Monachou, "Ek ton neptikon kefalaion" 5, 58). Cf. Dysinger, "Evagrius Ponticus: The Psalter as a Handbook for the Christian Contemplative", 97–125.
80 Evagrios the Solitary, "On Prayer: One Hundred and Fifty-Three Texts" 83, 65 (Neilou Asketou, "Prologos ton peri preseuches ekaton pentekonta trion kefalion" 83, 184). Cf. Driscoll, "The Psalms and Psychic Conversion", 91–110.
81 Cf. St Gregory of Sinai, "On Stillness: Fifteen Texts" 9, 269–270 (Cf. Gregoriou tou Sinaitou, "Peri hesychias kai peri ton duo tropon tes preseuches en kefalaiois IE'" 9, 75–76).
82 Cf. St Peter of Damaskos, "Book II. Twenty-Four Discourses" 11, 243–244 (Cf. Petrou Damaskenou, "Biblion B', Logoi synoptikoi KΔ'. Plereis notes pneumatikes gnoseos" 11, 138).
83 St Maximus the Confessor, "Four Hundred Texts on Love. Second Century" 54, 74 (Maksimou tou Homologetou, "Ekatontas deutera. Ton peri agape kefalaion" 54, 21).
84 St Maximus the Confessor, "Four Hundred Texts on Love. Fourth Century" 48, 105 (Maksimou tou Homologetou, "Ekatontas tetarte. Ton peri agape kefalaion" 48, 45). Cf. St John Cassian, "On the Holy Fathers of Sketis and on Discrimination", 97 (Cf. Kassianou tou Romaiou, "Pros Leontion Hegoumenon, Peri ton kata ten sketen Agion Pateron kai peri diakriseos logos ofeleias polles anamestos", 84).
85 St Maximus the Confessor, "Four Hundred Texts on Love. Third Century" 50, 91 (Maksimou tou Homologetou, "Ekatontas trite. Ton peri agape kefalaion" 50, 34).
86 St Thalassios, "On Love, Self-control and Life in accordance with the Intellect. Third Century" 35, 321 (Thalassiou tou Libuos kai Afrikanou, "Peri agape kai egkrateias kai tes kata non politeias. Pros Paulon Presbiteron. Ekatontas Trite" 35, 219).
87 St John Cassian, "On the Holy Fathers of Sketis and on Discrimination", 97–98 (Kassianou tou Romaiou, "Pros Leontion Hegoumenon, Peri ton kata ten sketen Agion Pateron kai peri diakriseos logos ofeleias polles anamestos", 83). Cf. Rousseau, "La priere des moines au temps de Jean Cassian", 117–138.
88 Ilias the Presbyter, "A Gnomic Anthology IV" 78, 57 (Elia Elachisto Presbitero kai Ekdiko, "Praktyka kai theoretika" 78, 307).
89 Attributed to St Symeon the New Theologian, "The Three Methods of Prayer", 73–74 (Symeon tou Neou Theologou, "Peri ton trion tropon tes proseuches", 88).

Bibliography

Abbreviations

FtHN A' – *Filokalia ton hieron neptikon*, t. A'. Athenai: Aster, 1982.
FtHN B' – *Filokalia ton hieron neptikon*, t. B'. Athenai: Aster, 1984.
FtHN G' – *Filokalia ton hieron neptikon*, t. G'. Athenai: Aster, 1991.
FtHN D' – *Filokalia ton hieron neptikon*, t. D'. Athenai: Aster, 1991.
FtHN E' – *Filokalia ton hieron neptikon*, t. E'. Athenai: Aster, 1992.
The Philokalia 1 – *The Philokalia. The Complete Text compiled by St Nikodimos of the Holy Mountain and St Makarios of Corinth.* Translated by Gerald E.H. Palmer, Philip Sherrard, Kallistos Ware. Volume I. London -- Boston: Faber and Faber, 1979.

The Philokalia 2 – *The Philokalia. The Complete Text compiled by St Nikodimos of the Holy Mountain and St Makarios of Corinth.* Translated by Gerald E.H. Palmer, Philip Sherrard, Kallistos Ware. Volume II. London – Boston: Faber and Faber, 1981.

The Philokalia 3 – *The Philokalia. The Complete Text compiled by St Nikodimos of the Holy Mountain and St Makarios of Corinth.* Translated by Gerald E.H. Palmer, Philip Sherrard, Kallistos Ware. Volume III. London – Boston: Faber and Faber, 1984.

The Philokalia 4 – *The Philokalia. The Complete Text compiled by St Nikodimos of the Holy Mountain and St Makarios of Corinth.* Translated by Gerald E.H. Palmer, Philip Sherrard, Kallistos Ware. Volume IV. London – Boston: Faber and Faber, 1995.

Sources

"A Discourse on Abba Philimon." In *The Philokalia* 2, 344–357 ("Peri tou Abba Filemonos Logos panu hofelimos," FtHN B', 241–252).

Diadochos of Photiki. "On Spiritual Knowledge and Discrimination: On Hundred Texts." In The Philokalia 1, 254–296 (Diadochou, Episkopou Fotike. "Logos asketikos dieremenos eis P' kefalaia praktyka – gnoseos kai diakriseos pneumatikes," FtHN A', 236–273).

Evagrios the Solitary. "Extracts from the Texts on Watchfulness." In *The Philokalia* 1, 53–54 (Evagriou Monachou. "Ek ton neptikon kefalaion." FtHN A', 58).

Evagrios the Solitary. "On Prayer: One Hundred and Fifty-Three Texts." In *The Philokalia* 1, 55–71 (Neilou Asketou. "Prologos ton peri preseuches ekaton pentekonta trion kefalion." FtHN A', 176–189).

Gregory of Sinai, "On Commandments and Doctrines, Warnings and Promises; on Thoughts, Passions and Virtues, and also on Stillness and Prayer: One Hundred and Thirty-Seven Texts." In *The Philokalia* 4, 212–252 (Gregoriou tou Sinaitou. "Kefalia ΔΙ' akrostichidos panu ofelima. Logoi diaforoi peri entolon, dogmaton, apeilon kai epaggelion, eti de kai peri logismon kai pathon kai areton, eti de kai peri hesychias kai proseuches." FtHN D', 31–62).

Gregory of Sinai. "On Prayer: Seven Texts." In *The Philokalia* 4, 275–286 (Gregoriou tou Sinaitou. "Peri tou pos dei kathezesthai ton hesychazonta eis ten euchen kai me tacheos anistasthai." FtHN D', 80–88).

Gregory of Sinai. "On Stillness: Fifteen Texts." In *The Philokalia* 4, 263–274 (Gregoriou tou Sinaitou. "Peri hesychias kai peri ton duo tropon tes preseuches en kefalaiois IE'." FtHN D', 71–79).

Ilias the Presbyter. "A Gnomic Anthology. Part I." In *The Philokalia* 3, 34–42 (Elia Elachisto Presbitero kai Ekdiko. "Anthologion gnomikon filosofon spoudaion. Spoudasthen kai ponethen." FtHN B', 289–296).

Ilias the Presbyter. "A Gnomic Anthology. Part IV." In *The Philokalia* 3, 52–65 (Elia Elachisto Presbitero kai Ekdiko. "Praktyka kai theoretika." FtHN B', 302–314).

John Cassian. "On the Holy Fathers of Sketis and on Discrimination". In *The Philokalia* 1, 94–108 (Kassianou tou Romaiou. "Pros Leontion Hegoumenon, Peri ton kata ten sketen Agion Pateron kai peri diakriseos logos ofeleias polles anamestos." FtHN A', 81–93).

John Climacus. *The Ladder of Divine Ascent*. Translated by Colm Luibheid, Norman Russell. New York – Ramsey – Toronto: Paulist Press, 1982.

John of Karpathos. "Ascetic Discourse Sent at the Request of the Same Monks in India." In *The Philokalia* 1, 322–326 (Ioannou Karpathiou. "Logos asketikos kai panu paregoretikos pros tous apo tes Indias protrepsantas monachous, ton P' kefalaion ton arithmon synapopleron." FtHN A', 297–301).

John of Karpathos. "For the Encouragement of the Monks in India who had Written to Him: One Hundred Texts." In *The Philokalia* 1, 298–321 (Ioannou Karpathiou. "Pros tois en te India monachous, grapsantas auto, paramuthetika kefalaia P'." FtHN A', 276–296).

Mark the Ascetic. "On Those who Think that They are Made Righteous by Works: 226 Texts." In *The Philokalia* 1, 125–146 (Markou tou Asketou. "Peri ton oiomenon eks ergon dikaiousthai, Kefalia ΣΚϛ'." FtHN A', 109–126).

Maximus the Confessor. "Four Hundred Texts on Love. First Century." In *The Philokalia* 2, 53–64 (Maksimou tou Homologetou. "Ekatontas prote. Ton peri agape kefalaion." FtHN B', 4–13).

Maximus the Confessor. "Four Hundred Texts on Love. Second Century." In *The Philokalia* 2, 65–82 (Maksimou tou Homologetou. "Ekatontas deutera. Ton peri agape kefalaion." FtHN B', 14–27).

Maximus the Confessor. "Four Hundred Texts on Love. Third Century." In *The Philokalia* 2, 83–99 (Maksimou tou Homologetou. "Ekatontas trite. Ton peri agape kefalaion." FtHN B', 28–40).

Maximus the Confessor. "Two Hundred Texts on Theology and the Incarnate Dispensation of the Son of God. Written for Thalassios. Second Century." In *The Philokalia* 2, 137–163 (Maksimou tou Homologetou. "Peri theologias kai tes ensarkou oikonomias tou hiou tou Theou, pros Thalassion. Kefalia Σ'. Ekatontas deutera." FtHN B', 69–90).

Maximus the Confessor. "Various Texts on Theology, the Divine Economy, and Virtue and Vice. Third Century." In *The Philokalia* 2, 210–234 (Maksimou tou Homologetou. "Kefalaia diafora theologika te kai oikonomika kai peri aretes kai kakias. Ekatontas Trite." FtHN B', 91–109).

Nikitas Stithatos. "On Spiritual Knowledge, Love and the Perfection of Living: One Hundred Texts." In *The Philokalia* 4, 139–174 (Nikita Monachou kai Presbiterou. "Deutera fisykon kefalaion ekatontas peri tes noos katharseos." FtHN G', 298–325).

Nikitas Stithatos. "On the Inner Nature of Things and on the Purification of the Intellect: One Hundred Texts." In *The Philokalia* 4, 107–138 (Nikita Monachou kai Presbiterou. "Deutera fisykon kefalaion ekatontas peri tes noos katharseos." FtHN G', 298–325).

Peter of Damaskos. "Book I. A Treasury of Divine Knowledge." In *The Philokalia* 3, 74–210 (Petrou Damaskenou. "Biblion A', Tes hypotheseos tou bibliou tou osiou kai theoforou patros hymon Petrou Damaskinou." FtHN G', 5–111).

Peter of Damaskos. Book II. "Twenty-Four Discourses." In *The Philokalia* 3, 211–281 (Petrou Damaskenou. "Biblion B', Logoi synoptikoi ΚΔ'. Plereis notes pneumatikes gnoseos." FtHN G', 112–168).

Symeon the New Theologian. "One Hundred and Fifty-Three Practical and Theological Texts." In *The Philokalia* 4, 25–63 (Symeon tou Neou Theologou. "Kefalia praktyka kai theologika ΡΜΕ'." FtHN G', 237–270).

Symeon the New Theologian (Attributed to). "The Three Methods of Prayer." In *The Philokalia* 4, 73–74 (Symeon tou Neou Theologou. "Peri ton trion tropon tes proseuches." FtHN E', 67–75).

Thalassios. "On Love, Self-control and Life in accordance with the Intellect. Third Century." In *The Philokalia* 2, 319–324 (Thalassiou tou Libuos kai Afrikanou. "Peri agape kai egkrateias kai tes kata non politeias. Pros Paulon Presbiteron. Ekatontas Trite." FtHN B', 217–222).

Thalassios. "On Love, Self-control and Life in accordance with the Intellect. Fourth Century." In *The Philokalia* 2, 325–332 (Thalassiou tou Libuos kai Afrikanou. "Peri agape kai egkrateias kai tes kata non politeias. Pros Paulon Presbiteron. Ekatontas Tetarte." FtHN B', 223–229).

Theodoros the Great Ascetic. "A Century of Spiritual Texts." In *The Philokalia* 2, 14–37 (Theodorom, Tou megalou asketou kai episkopu Edesses. "Kefalaia panu psychofele P'." FtHN A', 304–324).

Theoliptos, Metropolitan of Philadelphia. "On Inner Work in Christ and the Monastic Profession." In: *The Philokalia* 4, 177–187 (Theoliptou Metropolitou Filadelfeias. "Logos ten en Christo krupten ergasian diasafon kai deiknyonen brachei tou monadikou epaggelmatos ton kopon." FtHN D', 4–12).

Secondary Literature

Aejmelaeus, Anneli. *The Traditional Prayer in the Psalms*. Berlin – New York, NY: Walter de Gruyer, 1986.

Bradshaw, Paul F. *Daily Prayer in the Early Church: A Study in the Origin and Early Development of the Divine Office*. London: SPCK, 1981.

Braulik, Georg P. "Psalter and Messiah. Towards a Christological Understanding of the Psalms in the Old Testament and the Church Fathers." In *Psalms and Liturgy*, edited by Dirk J. Human, Cas J.A. Vos, 15–40. London: T&T Clark International, 2004.

Brueggemann, Walter. *The Message of the Psalms. A Theological Commentary*. Augsburg – Minneapolis, MN: Augsburg Publishing House, 1984.

Candole, Henry de. *The Christian Use of the Psalms*. London: A.R. Mowbray, 1958.

Custer, John S. "The Psaltery, the Harp and the Fathers." *The Downside Review* 114(1996): 19–31.

Driscoll, Jeremy. "The Psalms and Psychic Conversion." *Cistercian Studies* 22(1987): 91–110.

Dysinger, Luke. "Evagrius Ponticus: The Psalter as a Handbook for the Christian Contemplative." In *The Harp of Prophecy. Early Christian Interpretation of the Psalms*, edited by Brian E. Daley, Paul R. Kolbet, 97–125. Notre Dame, IN: University of Notre Dame, 2015.

Dysinger, Luke. *Psalmody and Prayer in the Writings of Evagrius Ponticus*. Oxford: Oxford University Press, 2004.

Dysinger, Luke. "The Significance of Psalmody in the 'Mystical Theology of Evagrius of Pontus." *Studia Patristica* 30(1997): 176–182.

Gelineau, Joseph. "Les psaumes l'epoque patristique." *La Maison-Dieu* 135(1978): 99–116.

Gillingham, Susan E. *Psalms through the Centuries*. Malden, MA: Blackwell Publishing, 2008.

Grelot, Pierre. *Le mystère du Christ dans les psaumes*. Paris: Desclée, 1998.

Grisbrooke, W. Jardine. "The Formative Period in Cathedral and Monastic Offices." In *The Study of Liturgy*, edited by Cheslyn Jones, 358–369. London: SPCK, 1978.

Harrison, Carol. "Enchanting the Soul: The Music of the Psalms." In *Meditations of the Heart: The Psalms in Early Christian Thought and Practice. Essays in Honour of Andrew Louth*, edited by Andreas Andreopolulos, Augustine Casiday, Carol Harrison, 205–223.Turnhout: Brepols, 2011.

Hisamatsu, Eiji. *Gregorios Sinaites als Lehrem des Gebetes*. Altenberge: Oros Verlag, 1994.

Knowles, Peter T. "Monastic Prayer: Text and Context." *St Vladimir's Theological Quarterly* 39, no. 2(1995): 143–155.

Kraus, Hans-Joachim. *Theology of the Psalms*. Minneapolis, MN: Fortress Press, 1992.

Kriegshauser, Laurence. *Praying the Psalms in Christ*. Notre Dame, IN: University of Notre Dame Press, 2009.

Leloir, Louis. "Repartition des psaumes et tradition monastique." *Collectanea cisterciensia* 41(1979): 254–264.

Lingas, Alexander. "Hesychasm and Psalmody." In *Mount Athos and Byzantine Monasticism: Papers from the Twenty-Eighth Spring Symposium of Byzantine Studies, University of Birmingham, March 1994*, edited by Anthony Bryer, Mary Cunningham, 155–168. Aldershot: Routledge, 1996.

Mateos, Juan. "L'office monastique a la fin du IV siecle: Antioche, Palestine, Cappadoce." *Oriens christianus* 47(1963): 53–88.

Mateos, Juan. "The Morning and Evening Office." *Worship* 42(1968): 31–47.

Mensbrugghe, Alexis van der. "Prayer-time in Egyptian Monasticism (320-450)." *Studia Patristica* 2(1957): 435–452.

Richardson, Ronald D. "The Psalms as Christian Prayers and Praises." *The Anglican Theological Review* 42(1960): 326–346.

Rousseau, Olivier. "La priere des moines au temps de Jean Cassian," In *La Priere des Heures* (Lex orandi 35), edited by Bernard Botte, Monseigneur Cassien, 117–138. Paris: Cerf, 1963.

Scott, Robert Balgarnie Young. *The Psalms as Christian Praise*. New York, NY: Lutterworth Press, 1958.

Stead, George C. "St. Athanasius on the Psalms." *Vigiliae Christianae* 39(1985): 65–78.

Taft, Robert. *The Liturgy of Hours in East and West*. Collegeville: Liturgical Press, 1986.

3 How the Latin Christians Started to Read the Book of Isaiah

Anni Maria Laato

Introduction

In the New Testament, the Book of Isaiah is abundantly quoted and alluded to. A quick look at the biblical index in the latest edition of *Novum Testamentum Graece* shows that there are far more references to Isaiah than to any other prophet, and moreover they come from almost all of its chapters.[1] Since the time of the Early Church, the Book of Isaiah has remained central for Christian authors. It has been interpreted Christologically as containing prophecies and prefigurations for the most central beliefs of the Christian faith.[2]

In the Latin West, an excellent example of the centrality of the Book of Isaiah is given by Augustine, who in *Conf.* 9.5.13 thinks back to his youth and recollects how in the autumn of 386, before his baptism, he asked bishop Ambrose's advice as to which book of the Scripture he should read to prepare himself to "understand and receive God's grace". Ambrose told the catechumen to read Isaiah. Augustine writes that at that time he found this book difficult and he soon put it down. Later, however, when considering why Ambrose had recommended the Book of Isaiah, he concluded that it must have been because Isaiah "predicts the truth of the Gospel and liberation of the nations" more clearly than other Old Testament writers (Conf. 9.5).

In this chapter, I intend to look at how Latin Christians started to read the Book of Isaiah from three points of view. First, I shall study how the prophet as a person and his task were presented: this opens a horizon of understanding the reading of the Book of Isaiah. In the early church, the prophet Isaiah was regarded as the author of the Book of Isaiah, and therefore what was said about the person is closely connected to the book. Because Jerome nicely summarizes traditions about the prophet Isaiah, I shall focus on how he characterizes him and singles him out among the other prophets. Second, I shall look at the history of Latin translations of the Book of Isaiah, and study how the Latin authors dealt with the fact that they were operating with Latin translations of Greek translations of an original Hebrew text. Finally, I shall look more closely at three central themes,

DOI: 10.4324/9781003273592-3

Messianic promises, pilgrimage to Jerusalem, and hymns and liturgy, and offer some examples of what kinds of questions the early Latin-speaking Christians met in reading Isaiah. In all these tasks my main focus is on the works of Jerome, the author of the first surviving Latin commentary on Isaiah and the first by-name-known translator of the Book of Isaiah into Latin. Jerome both commented on earlier Greek and Latin translations and discussed theological topics with other theologians. Jerome's work helped change the way the Latin-speaking Christians read the Book of Isaiah.[3]

The Prophet Isaiah Preaching the Gospel

In the early church, the prophet Isaiah, who lived in the eighth century BC, was regarded as the author of the whole text, and therefore, even his character and his mission were important, not only the text he was believed to have produced. According to early traditions, the prophet Isaiah suffered death by being sawn in half.[4] In *Vitae prophetarum,* a Jewish text with later Christian changes, Isaiah is named among the six so-called Martyr-Prophets, most of them presented together with references to their way of death, those responsible for their death, and their burial place.[5] The martyrdom of Isaiah became a popular theme even in western Christian texts and art. Latin authors also presented the prophet Isaiah as an example of patience (Tert. Pat. 14.1) and of courage (Hilary of Poitiers, Contra Constantium imperatorem 4; Ambrose, Exp. Luc. 9.25).

According to several Latin authors, the prophet Isaiah's mission was unique among the prophets. The Old Testament was read first and foremost Christologically i.e. as containing promises, prophecies, and types of Christ and the church. Moreover, because the Book of Isaiah, in particular, was very much used for this purpose, Jerome summarized the character of the prophet as "an evangelist":

> ... he should be called an evangelist rather than a prophet because he describes all the mysteries of Christ and the Church so clearly that you would think he is composing a history of what has already happened rather than prophesying about what is to come. (*Prologue to translation of Isaiah in Vulgate*).[6]

At the beginning of his *Commentary on Isaiah* (written 408–410), Jerome described what he was going to do in his Commentary, and called Isaiah not only an evangelist but even an apostle:

> I shall expound Isaiah in such a way that I will show him not only as a prophet, but as an evangelist and apostle. For he himself says of himself and of other evangelists, 'How beautiful are the feet of those who evangelize, announcing good things, who preach peace' (Isa 52:7; Rom 10:15), and God speaks to him as if to an apostle: 'Whom shall I

> send and who will go to this people', and he replied, 'Here I am, send me' (Isa 6:8).

After the quoted passage, he added:

> The Scripture at hand (=The Book of Isaiah) contains all the Lord's mysteries and proclaims Emmanuel, the one who was both born of a virgin and performed illustrious works and signs, was dead and buried, and by rising from the lower world is the Saviour of the nations. (...) within this volume is contained all the Holy Scriptures.

Jerome thus started his *Commentary on Isaiah* by defining his method and his task: he gave a Christian reading to the Book of Isaiah. He intended to show Isaiah not only as a prophet, but also as an evangelist and apostle. These words, as Christian or New Testament language they may sound today, in fact, come from the Book of Isaiah itself, namely, Isa 6:8 and Isa 52:7. Jerome understood that Isaiah was sent (Gr. *apostello*) to proclaim Christ, that is, to preach the word of God just as the apostles did, and to evangelize (Gr. *euangelizo*), that is, to announce good things and to preach peace. Additionally, according to Jerome, the Book of Isaiah contains all the central points of the life of Christ: the promise of Immanuel, the virgin birth, the miracles, the passion, the death, and the resurrection of Christ. This kind of characterization of the person and the Book of Isaiah emphasizes the unity of Old and New Testaments and their common content and goal.

Jerome interpreted the sending of Isaiah in Isa 6:8 in three homilies and offered some additional thoughts on this. In Homily 22 on Psalm 93 (94), e.g., he gave Isaiah's readiness as an example for everyone:

> When He asks, 'Who,' He is inviting everyone to rise with Him, for just as we read in Isaiah: 'Whom shall I send? Who will go for us?' and Isaiah offers himself, so, too, the Lord invites us with the words: 'Who will rise up for me against the wicked?'

Jerome used the expression "for us" which is based on the Hebrew text, not on the Septuagint. In his explanation, Jerome commented on the difference between the Hebrew text and the Septuagint in this passage and stated that he could not understand why the Septuagint says "to this people" when the Hebrew text uses the word *lanu*, "for us" (*nobis*).[7] He interpreted the words "for us" as referring to the Trinity, just as, according to him, the "us" in Genesis 1:26, "let us make man in our image and likeness", referred to the Trinity. Jerome explained that the persons of God are one in nature, but nonetheless three persons, and therefore he can say that "when the Lord commands, the Trinity commands". Thus, he concluded, the one who called Isaiah to be his messenger was the Triune God.

In Homily 41 on Psalm 119 (120), Jerome gave Isaiah as an example of people whom the Lord first cleanses and subsequently calls to be his messengers. Unclean lips, according to him, cannot prophesy. Jerome eventually wished for "us" (himself or his audience) that "all wickedness from our tongue" would be cleansed.

In Homily 87 on the Gospel of John 1.1–14, Jerome explained who John the Baptist was. In order to expound on what it meant that John was *sent* from God, Jerome compared him with Isaiah, who was also sent. He stated that the one who is sent represented his sender, and "the honor of the sender is recognized and acknowledged in him who is sent". The linguist Jerome then explained to his Latin-speaking readers that "*missus*" in Greek is "*apostolos*", and as an example of the use of this word, he stated that Isaiah was sent and was therefore an apostle. He added that according to John those who are not sent by God are thieves and robbers (cf. John 10:8). John the Baptist received his mission as messenger from the Lord.

In all these homilies, Isaiah is seen as a positive figure; his readiness to be a messenger is presented as something for the audience to imitate.

Jerome, who had read Origen a lot and even translated nine of his sermons on Isaiah into Latin, was, at this point, critical towards his teacher. In his *Commentary on Isaiah,* he reacted to Origen's interpretation of Isa 6:8. He said that "others" (referring to Origen) thought that Isaiah said "send me" so rapidly because he thought he would get something nice to say to the people. Additionally, Jerome claimed that Isaiah's rapid answer was not given in arrogance (as Origen claims) but rather spoke of his confidence which was based on his lips already having been purged and his sins forgiven. Third, like Origen, Jerome compared Isaiah to Moses, but said that both – in their own way – responded out of humility. To sum up, Jerome stated that Isaiah offered himself to be sent not because of rashness, but out of obedience to the Lord.

Jerome emphasized the same idea when, in letters 18A and 18B, he explains – both historically and spiritually – the call of Isaiah in Isa 6:1–9. He claimed that this passage denoted Christ because it was said so in John 12:41. In his letter to Pope Damasus, he wrote similarly,

> Whatever we read in the Old Testament we find also in the Gospel; and what we read in the Gospel is deduced from the Old Testament. There is no discord between them, no disagreement. In both Testaments the Trinity is preached.[8]

Jerome's emphasis that the Triune God sent the prophet Isaiah to proclaim the Gospel demonstrates in a nutshell how he and many other early Christians saw the Book of Isaiah should be read. His way of calling Isaiah an apostle and an evangelist spread in the West. Augustine mentioned that "some authorities" called Isaiah evangelist rather than prophet (*evangelista quam propheta potius diceretur*), and for example, Isidore of Seville and Hugo St Victor repeated the same thought.[9]

Vetus Latina – Translations and Early Latin Commentaries on Isaiah

It was not only the person of Isaiah or the contents of the Book of Isaiah which had their impact on how the early Latin Christians read this prophet, but also the form in which they received the text in their own language. Generally, it can be stated that factors influencing a translation of a Biblical text from Greek to Latin include: first, the text on which the translation is based; second, how the translator reads and understands this text; third, the translators' knowledge in both Greek and Latin; fourth, the qualities (syntax, vocabulary) of both languages; fifth, earlier translations; and finally, the special vocabulary used in the communities for which the translation is made. It is not often easy to prove whether theology or more practical reasons prompted a certain choice of words.[10]

The Latin West received the Old Testament in its Greek form, the Septuagint. For centuries onward, this text was regarded as authoritative. Before Jerome's Vulgate, it served as the basis for all Latin translations.[11] These early translations are preserved in the writings of the Church Fathers: treatises, sermons, letters, and commentaries. Today, together they are called *Vetus Latina*, or sometimes, pre-Vulgate. The translators of the *Vetus Latina* versions remain anonymous. It is clear that not all were highly educated and trained in translation, but were most probably preachers and theologians who had mastered Greek as well as Latin, and who needed Latin translations for practical purposes. Augustine, perhaps exaggerating a little, described the situation like this:

> For the translations of the Scriptures from Hebrew into Greek can be counted, but the Latin translators are out of all number. For in the early days of the faith every man who happened to get his hands upon a Greek manuscript, and who thought he had any knowledge, were it ever so little, of the two languages, ventured upon the work of translation.
> (Doct. chr. 2.11)

The first Latin translations were probably made *ad hoc* by people who knew both Greek and Latin, for the purposes of preaching and liturgy. Soon after, even written translations emerged.

These early translations contain vernacular words and stylistic features. Contrary to the *ad sensum* – principle – common in antiquity – one of the principles of the *Vetus Latina* -translators was to give, when possible, a word-for-word translation which means the Greek word order is sometimes discernible. In the process of translating the Christian message and texts into Latin, new words were sometimes created based on Greek ones, and old ones were given new meanings (the Latin-speaking people had always done so). Sometimes these translations displayed certain freedom regarding the original text, and at times errors were even made.

Thus, during the first centuries, no single, authorized version of the Latin Scripture existed: instead there were several different translations. According to the current view, most probably these had emerged from one single version of each book, in this case, Isaiah, but were later developed into different versions. Because of their faults and shortfalls, these early translations were revised and updated from time to time, which led to the emergence of several different text types, and, eventually, to the need for a high-quality translation.

The first evidence of translations of Isaiah in Latin are found in the works of Tertullian (written 196 CE onwards).[12] In *Adversus Marcionem* alone, there are more than 300 quotations from the Book of Isaiah. Tertullian was bilingual and did occasionally translate *ad hoc* from Greek. His writings, however, also witness earlier, archaic forms of Latin translations, and therefore his quotations form the earliest main textual type of *Vetus Latina* versions. These quotations are not identical to the later so-called African text found in, for example, Cyprian's texts. *The Passion of Perpetua and Felicitas*, which contains one important passage that may refer to the Book of Isaiah and which shall be discussed later, also comes from approximately the same period.

From the third century, the most important witness of the Latin text of Isaiah is Cyprian of Carthage (d. 258). His *Testimoniorum libri III ad Quirinum* (249/250) contains many lengthy quotations of an existing translation of Isaiah. From the fourth century, the most important evidence comes from Hilary of Poitiers and Ambrose. Their version, the so-called European text, differs from the African when it comes to the vocabulary used and with regard to the Greek original upon which it is based. Ambrose knew Greek well and used several Latin and Greek versions. He sometimes commented on and corrected the translations, but he never argued that a new Latin translation would be necessary.

The importance of the Hebrew text was not really understood in the Latin West prior to Jerome, and his translation was not easily accepted even when his arguments for its use became known.[13] A well-known example of this attitude is Augustine, who in *De doctrina Christiana*, written in 396–397, lengthily discusses the Latin translations of the Old Testament, their sources, advantages and problems. For him, the Septuagint was authoritative and inspired by the Holy Spirit, and the existence of several Latin translations was not problematic for him (*Doct. chr.* 2.11–16). He was, however, aware of the necessity of knowing Greek and Hebrew for a correct understanding of the Scripture, even if he himself mainly operated on the basis of the Latin translations (*Doct. chr.* 2.11). He saw no need for one standardized translation; he was especially doubtful about Jerome's project of translating from the Hebrew. This hesitation becomes evident in his correspondence with Jerome, dated 395–405 (Aug. letters 28, 40, 67, 68, 71–75, 81, 82), concerning, among other topics, biblical text forms and translations.

Jerome's Vulgate and Commentary on Isaiah

A new translation of the Bible was needed not only for Christian use, but also in discussions with others. Inaccurate translations posed problems in discussions with the Jews, and the poor quality when it came to language and syntax irritated the well-educated people of pagan birth in particular. These factors led to the need for a reliable, high-quality translation, a task that Jerome undertook at the end of the fourth century.

Jerome started his work, in his own words, on the initiative of Pope Damasus in 383, by revising existing translations of the Gospels against the best Greek manuscripts.[14] His versions became widely accepted, but also received criticism (as he states in letter 27.1 to Marcella). He started his revision of the Old Testament around the year 387 with the help of Origen's Hexapla and the works of Aquila, Symmachus, and Theodotion. The work with Origen's Hexapla, however, caused Jerome to become critical not only towards earlier Latin translations but also towards the Greek texts behind them. He realized the importance of the *Hebraica veritas*, i.e. the Hebrew original. Beginning in about 390, he translated the whole of the Old Testament from the Hebrew, including the Book of Isaiah during the years 393–394, together with the other prophets.

Jerome did not intend for his translation from the Hebrew to become a text for liturgical use, but rather one for scholarly work. He used his new translations mainly in his scientific works; in other texts he used the Septuagint, too.[15] With the Vulgate, Jerome intended to offer a high-quality translation of the Old Testament in order to reach a better theological understanding of the Holy Scripture. Instead of a word-for-word translation, he sought to translate "sense-for-sense" (letter 57.5). His knowledge of Hebrew was, for his time, extraordinary, and sufficient to produce good quality translations and he often refers to *veritas*, (truth; even *terminus technicus* for original text); however, he also used older Greek and sometimes even Latin translations when preparing his translation. Jerome calls himself *vir trilinguis*, i.e. fluent in Latin, Greek, and Hebrew (*Ruf.* 3.6), and certainly, his capacity to work in these languages was far better than any of his Christian contemporaries.

Jerome reports of the existence of Latin commentaries of Isaiah before his own (*Comm. Isa* 1), but these have not survived to our day except for some fragments.[16] Prior to writing his commentary, he had translated Origen's nine homilies on Isaiah, and in 397, he wrote a commentary on the ten visions in Isa 13–23. This work was later included in the *Commentary on Isaiah*,[17] which Jerome wrote in 404–410 and dedicated to Eustochium, a noble lady who, with her mother Paula, had followed Jerome from Rome to Bethlehem and established a convent there.[18] Paula had died somewhat earlier in 404.

Jerome's commentary is sizable. All of its 18 books begin with an introduction. He presented and explicated his new translation and commented on the text not only from a historical viewpoint, but often from a theological point of view, too.[19] In many cases, he discussed the texts of Aquila, Symmachus, and Theodotion, and used interpretations from Origen, Eusebius, Apollinaris, and Didymus, and thus transferred their thoughts to the Latin-speaking readers.

Jerome seldom really claimed that the earlier Latin translations of Isaiah were wrong, but rather stated that they could have been clearer. An example of this is found in his commenting on differences between *Vetus Latina* and his own translation, regarding Isa 21:1–3, where he states,

> The common translation (=*Vetus Latina*) and the Hebrew have many discrepancies between them on this passage. That is why we have briefly touched upon both translations, lest we leave behind an occasion for carping at us (to those who are fond of fault-finding).

He applied the same way of speaking concerning the differences between the Septuagint and the Hebrew text. He clarified the differences between them, as well as between different versions of the Septuagint, but most often he did not want to make that a problem (see his explanation to Isa 58:11–12). He could say, for example, "In this passage we have translated according to the Septuagint in order not to appear to be innovating, since the testimony is widespread" (Isa 58:12, "repairer of the fences"). Another time, however, he stated, "In the Septuagint the meaning is confused, and everything is so disorderly that whatever is said can hardly be understood" (Isa 54:9–10).

There is an interesting report of a discussion between Eustochium and Jerome at the beginning of books 15 and 16. In Book 15, Jerome taught Eustochium a general rule about the use of the Septuagint in the New Testament. He claimed that the apostles and evangelists referred to the Septuagint text only when it agreed with the Hebrew Bible. He returned to this claim at the beginning of Book 16. He explained that having heard this, Eustochium had immediately pointed out that in Romans 3 St Paul quotes texts that are not found in the Hebrew Bible (Ps 5:9; Ps 140:3; Ps 10:7; Isa 50:7–8; Ps 36:1). Jerome eloquently describes how this question was like a punch from a powerful boxer. He subsequently started to investigate the matter and noticed that very much of the letter to Romans was based on the Old Testament, mainly on the Psalms and Isaiah. He concluded that the texts Eustochium asked about were in fact found in the Hebrew Bible and stated that several of the texts were interwoven with each other.

Messianic Promises and Christology

As mentioned above, one of the main reasons a reliable Latin translation of the Old Testament was needed was its use in discussions with the Jews; Jerome stated this clearly in his *Preface to Isaiah in Vulgate* and in *Apology against Rufinus* 3.25. Problems in early translations had become apparent particularly when prophecies of the Messiah were discussed. The main topics concerning the Messianic promises and Christology in the Book of Isaiah were the virgin birth (Isa 7:14) and the idea of Christ as the suffering servant (Isa 42:1–7; 49:1–9; 50:4–9; 52:13–53:12). The Latin authors inherited their Christological reading of these passages from the New Testament and from Christian Greek theologians. A rich collection of Christological proof-texts from the Book of Isaiah is found already in Cyprian's *Testimonia*, book 2.

Because Isa 7:14 was understood as a prophecy of the virgin birth very early on, it is no wonder that several translations of this verse were produced already before the Vulgate. In the modern *Vetus Latina* edition, the presentation of these texts and their use takes several pages. In these translations, the Latin word for "a virgin" is not problematic; all the Latin translations follow the Septuagint and use the word *virgo*. Rather, the problem lay in the interpretation of this word. Jewish discussion partners could and did claim that this passage did not prove virgin birth at all. Unlike Irenaeus (*Adversus haereses* 3.21.1.5), Jerome did not claim that the Jews had falsified the text, but rather admitted that earlier Christian commentators had not been able to defend the Christian interpretation against the Jews. Therefore, he took the task on and explained this translation lengthily in his *Commentary on Isaiah*.[20] He started by stating that the normal Hebrew word for virgin was *betulah*. He then presented all Old Testament passages with the word *almah* and noted that Jewish translators regularly translated that word as "young woman" – except in the Septuagint. He concluded that in Hebrew *almah* does not merely mean young woman or virgin, but has a double meaning, both "hidden" (*apokryphos*) and "marriageable", thus the meaning was a "hidden-away-virgin" of marriageable age; one has never been exposed to the sight of men. Jerome added an argument based on another Semitic language, Punic, where *almah* means "a virgin". Finally, he said that in Deut 22:25–27 and 1 Kings 1, 1–4 *almah* denotes a virgin.

Pilgrimage and the Holy Land

In one passage, the contemporary discussion on the reasons for a pilgrimage to Jerusalem affected Jerome's Latin translation. His interest in Biblical topography is visible in his translation and commentary on Isaiah, and even in a book published in 388, *De situ et nominibus locorum Hebraicorum*, "Book on the Sites and Names of Hebrew Places", a revised translation of

Eusebius' Onomasticon. In this work, he offered Latin translations of many Hebrew names, both of individuals and places.

By the second half of the fourth century, pilgrimages to the Holy Land had increased. Jerome himself had moved to Bethlehem and invited other people to come to the Holy Land, too. Apart from the above-mentioned book, Jerome presented holy places in several letters and together with his disciples promoted the idea of the holiness of the Land. Paula and Eustochium, two Roman noble women and friends of Jerome, settled in Bethlehem in 386 CE. Soon after their arrival, they wrote to their friend Marcella in Rome and urged their friend to travel there. This letter, preserved as among the letters of Jerome (letter 46), is one of the most important documents of the early Christian theology of pilgrimage.[21]

In their argumentation for the holiness of Jerusalem, Isa 11:10, which in *Vetus Latina* versions was translated following the Septuagint, *et erit requies eius honor*, "and his rest will be honor" was important. In the above-mentioned letter and in the Vulgate, however, Jerome and Paula used Jerome's new translation, *et erit sepulchrum eius gloriosum*, "and his tomb shall be glorious". Jerome explained in Comm. Isa. 4.11.10, that the Hebrew word can denote any resting-place, not necessarily a tomb, and claimed that *requies* and *dormitio* could be used as synonyms for *sepulchrum*. He interpreted this passage in the light of John 17:15 and stated that this verse was a prophecy of the Lord's Sepulcher in Jerusalem. In this way, he could support the veneration of the burial place of the Lord and the Church of Holy Sepulchre and exhort Christians to visit there.

Liturgy and Homilies

The earliest witnesses of the use of Isaiah in Christian liturgy relate to the *Trishagion* or *Sanctus*, based on Isa 6:3 and Rev 4:8.[22] Both in the *Vetus Latina* and in the *Vulgate*, the Greek *hagios* and/or the Hebrew *qadosh* in this passage is translated *sanctus*. It is interesting to note that in the North African *Passio Perpetuae et Felicitatis* 12 (about 203 AD), however, *sanctus* is not sung in Latin. Rather, in the middle of the Latin text describing a vision of a heavenly court, the words are in Greek. In my view, the most probable explanation for this is that the Carthaginian Church used these words in their liturgy in Greek. This Isaian text was used in Jewish liturgy too and appears in Greek in Ignatius (Ign. Eph. 4.2) and Clement of Alexandria (Strom. 7.12), and in Latin in Tertullian (Or. 3).

The Book of Isaiah is richly present in early Latin lectionaries. For example, the sermons of Augustine give evidence for certain texts of Isaiah (such as Isa 1:10–17; 2:2; 7:14 and 57:13) as belonging to regularly recurring passages.[23] Isa 7:14, for example, was read at Christmas services, as Augustine witnesses in homily 370, when he says to his congregation, "You just heard the reading from the Book of Isaiah.".

As already mentioned, the Book of Isaiah was used prolifically in Christian homilies. While it is not possible to expand that theme here, I offer an example from an author contemporary to Jerome, Augustine. In his Christmas homilies, one of Augustine's favourite passages is Isa 53:8, which he quotes several times in the form, *Generationem eius quis enarrabit?* "Who shall declare his generation?"[24] The Latin translation *generatio*, birth, is based on the Septuagint and differs from the Hebrew text. Augustine uses this text to highlight the uniqueness of the birth of Christ. He asks whether the prophet Isaiah is speaking about Christ's birth from the Father in eternity, or about his birth from his mother Mary in this particular time. He also uses this Isaian question to emphasize the mystery of the virgin birth. Jerome, in his *Commentary* on this passage, does not comment on the difference between the Septuagint and the Hebrew text. He presents the same two ways of understanding this sentence; it can refer to the divine birth and the virgin birth and extends his explanation to a discussion of the differences between knowing with the mind and articulating the same in speech. In fact, Justin is the first Christian author to connect this passage to the mystic birth of Christ (Dial. 76.2).[25]

Another Isaian passage often referred to in Latin Christmas sermons, is Isa 1:3 "The ox knows its master, the donkey its owner's manger" (homily 369). Augustine explains the ox and the donkey as the ox referring to the circumcised, symbolized by the shepherds, and the donkey as reference to the uncircumcised, that is, the magi. Both groups come to the manger of Christ.

Conclusions

The centrality of the Book of Isaiah for the early Latin-speaking Christians is evident through the large number of quotations and allusions to its texts in the texts of the Latin Fathers. Isaiah himself was regarded as the most important of the Hebrew prophets; Jerome even called him "an apostle" and "an evangelist", pointing to the prophecies of Christ found in the Book of Isaiah. The prophet Isaiah was, thus, presented as an example for Christians; he was exemplary in patience and courage as well as a person whom the Lord first cleansed, and then subsequently called to be his messenger.

The first Latin translations of Isaiah – as well as all Biblical books – were not always accurate or in the best possible Latin, which eventually led Jerome to prepare a new translation of this book, based on the Hebrew text. Jerome comments on both older translations and his own choices not only linguistically and historically, but also theologically. Contemporary practices, such as the emerging pilgrimage, at least at one point, affected his translation.

In time Jerome's translation of the Book of Isaiah and his Commentary of Isaiah became prominent in the West and influenced both theology and praxis. The Book of Isaiah has been used and studied in the West mainly in

Latin translations for over a 1,000 years, and by many of the most important theologians. Therefore, the importance of these translations for Christian theology and praxis cannot be overestimated.

Notes

1 Novum Testamentum Graece. 28th Edition. Eds. Aland, Barbara, Aland, Kurt, Karavidopoulos, Johannes, Martini, Carlo M; Metzger, Bruce M. Nestle, Eberhard, Nestle, Erwin, Strutwolf, Holger. Institut für Neutestamentliche Textforschung Deutsche Bibelgesellschaft 2012. This article is partly based on my article "Isaiah in Latin" in Tiemeyer, L. (ed.) The Oxford Handbook of Isaiah.
2 Childs, *The Struggle*, 5.92; Sawyer, *The Fifth Gospel*, 1–2.21.48–50.
3 For Jerome and his methods in translation, see Brown, *Vir Trilinguis*, and Kieffer, *Jerome: His Exegesis*.
4 Heb 11:37; Tertullian, Scorpiace 8; the Latin translation of the Martyrdom and Ascension of Isaiah; Jerome, Comm. Isa. 15.57.1–2.
5 This work was translated into Latin, possibly in the seventh century. See Schwemer 1995.
6 Isidore of Seville (c. 560–636) repeats Jerome's words and calls for Isaiah to be an evangelist rather than a prophet (*evangelista potius quam propheta*), and adds as an interesting detail that Isaiah wrote his book "in good prose" (Isidore, Etym. 6.2).
7 All Vetus Latina translations follow naturally the Septuagint and read "*ad populum istum*".
8 Letter XVIII To Pope Damasus.
9 Aug. Civ. 18.29; Isid. Etym. 6:2; Hugo St Victor Didascalion 4.8.
10 Vetus Latina 12 (edidit Roger Gryson), pars I 1987; pars II 1993–1997.
11 For the history of Vetus Latina -texts, see Schultz-Flügel, The Latin Old Testament Tradition; Stummer, *Einführung*; and Houghton, *The Latin New Testament. For Isaiah in the Septuagint*, see Seeligman, *The Septuagint Version*.
12 See O'Malley, T., *Tertullian and the Bible. Language.Imagery, Exegesis.* passim.
13 Brown, *Vir Trilinguis*, 55.
14 For Jerome and his methods in translation, see Brown, *Vir Trilinguis*, and Kieffer, *Jerome: His Exegesis*.
15 Brown, *Vir Trilinguis*, 61–62.
16 Victorinus of Pettau's commentary is lost, as is most of Ambrose's commentary.
17 Hieronymus Stridonensis, *Commentariorum in Esaiam libri* 18 (CCL 73–73A). English translation: St. Jerome Commentary on Isaiah, Homilies 1–9 on Isaiah Ancient Christian Writers – The Works of the Fathers in Translation) 68. Thomas P. Scheck. Published by Paulist Press (2015).
18 Jay, *L'Exégèse de saint Jérome*; Childs, *The Struggle*, 94–99; Laato, "What Makes," 172.
19 Childs, *The Struggle*, 96–99.
20 *Comm. Isa.* 3.15 (on Isa 7:14). See Childs, *The Struggle*, 95.99; Kamesar, The virgin birth of Isaiah 7:14 JTS 41, 1 1990; Scheck 2015, 980.
21 Laato, "What Makes" 172–173.
22 Werner, The Genesis of the Liturgical Sanctus; Sawyer, *The Fifth Gospel*, 51.60–61.
23 Margoni-Kögler, *Die Perikopen*, 56; 105; 109; 243; 432.
24 Sermones, 184; 195; 196; 372. Here quoted in the King James Version.
25 See Laato, "Who Is the Servant of the Lord," 234.

Bibliography

Sources

Biblia Sacra iuxta Latinam Vulgatam versionem. Editio tertia emendata quam paravit Bonifatius Fischer OSB cum sociis H.I. Frede, Iohanne Gribomont OSB, H.F.D. Sparks, W. Thiele. Stuttgart, 1983.

Esaias, in: Vetus Latina 12 (edidit Roger Gryson), pars I, Freiburg: Herder 1987; pars II, Freiburg: Herder, 1993–1997.

Hieronymus Stridonensis, *Commentariorum in Esaiam libri 18* (CCL 73-73A). English translation: *St. Jerome Commentary on Isaiah, Homilies 1–9 on Isaiah Ancient Christian Writers* - The *Works* of the *Fathers* in *Translation*) 68. Thomas P. Scheck. Published by Paulist Press (2015).

Vetus Latina, die Reste der altlateinischen Bibel, nach Petrus Sabatier neu gesammelt und in Verbindung mit der Heidelberger Akademie der Wissenschaften herausgegeben von der Erzabtei Beuron. Freiburg: Herder, 1949.

Literature

Brown, D., *Vir Trilinguis. A Study in the Biblical Exegesis of Saint Jerome.* Kampen: Kok Pharos, 1992.

Childs, Brevard S., *The Struggle to Understand Isaiah as Christian Scripture.* Grand Rapids Michigan: Eerdmans, 2004.

Houghton, H.A.G., *The Latin New Testament. A Guide to its Early History, Texts, and Manuscripts.* Oxford: Oxford University Press, 2016.

Jay, P., *L'Exégèse de saint Jérome d'après son Commentaire sur Isaie.* Paris: Etudes Augustiniennes, 1985.

Kamesar, A. "The Virgin of Isaiah 7:14: Philological Argument from the Second to the Fifth Century", JTS 41, 1990, 51–75.

Kieffer, R., "Jerome: His Exegesis and Hermeneutics". In Saebø, M. (ed.) *Hebrew Bible/Old Testament. The History of Its Interpretation, Vol 1 From the Beginning to the Middle Ages, Part 1. Antiquity.* Göttingen: Vandenhoeck & Ruprecht (HBOT) I/1, 1996, 663–681.

Laato, Anni Maria, "What Makes the Holy Land Holy? A Debate between Paula, Eustochium, and Marcella (Jerome, Ep. 46)". In Erkki Koskenniemi & Cornelis de Vos (ed.) *Holy Places and Cult.* Studies in Reception History of the Bible 5. Winona Lake, Indiana: Eisenbrauns, 2014.

Laato, Anni Maria, "Isaiah in Latin". In Tiemeyer, L. (ed.) *The Oxford Handbook of Isaiah.* Oxford: Oxford University Press 2020, 489–503.

Laato, Antti, *Who Is the Servant of the Lord?: Jewish and Christian Interpretations on Isaiah 53 from Antiquity to the Middle Ages.* University Park, PA: Eisenbrauns 2012.

Margoni-Kögler, M. *Die Perikopen im Gottesdienst bei Augustinus. Ein Beitrag zur Erforschung der liturgischen Schriftlesung in der frühen Kirche.* Wien: Österreichischen Akademie der Wissenschaften, 2010.

O'Malley, T. *Tertullian and the Bible. Language, Imagery, Exegesis.* Nijmegen/ Utrecht: Dekker & Van de Vegt N.V, 1967.

Sawyer, J.F. *The Fifth Gospel. Isaiah in the History of Christianity.* Cambridge: Cambridge University Press, 1996.

Scheck, T. P. *St. Jerome: Commentary on Isaiah. Including St. Jerome's Translation of Origen's Homilies 1-9 on Isaiah*. Ancient Christian Writers 68. New York: The Newman Press, 2015.

Schulz-Flügel, Eva, "The Latin Old Testament Tradition". In Saebø, M. (ed.) *Hebrew Bible/Old Testament. The History of its Interpretation, Vol 1 From the Beginning to the Middle Ages, Part 1. Antiquity*. Göttingen: Vandenhoeck & Ruprecht (HBOT) I/1 (HBOT I/1), 1996, 642–662.

Seeligman, Isac Leo, *The Septuagint Version of Isaiah and Cognate Studies*. FAT 40. Ed. Robert Hanhart & Herman Spieckermann. Tübingen: Mohr Siebeck.

Stummer, F. *Einführung in die lateinische Bibel. Ein Handbuch für Vorlesungen und Selbstunterricht*. Paderborn: Schöningh, 1928.

Werner, E. "The genesis of the liturgical Sanctus". In Westrup, J. (ed.) *Essays Presented to Egon Wellesz*. Oxford: Clarendon, 1966, 19–32.

4 The Fathers on the Third Temptation of Jesus in Matthew 4:8–11

Hector Scerri

Introduction: The Perennial Relevance of Patristic Texts

The renowned twentieth-century French theologian, Henri de Lubac (1896–1991), once remarked on the "*vitalité explosive*"[1] of the Church Fathers in his seminal work *Paradoxes*. Other expressions which echo forth from the heart and mind of de Lubac include "*l'actualité des Pères*" and "*une actualité de fecundation*."[2] The great patristic scholar, Adalbert Hamman (1910–2000), elaborated upon the "*dynamique explosive des premiers siècles chrétiens*."[3] He is strongly aware that "*chaque fois* [...] *qu'un renouveau chrétien a fleuri* [...] *il a fleuri sous le signe des Pères*."[4] Many scholars, to this very day, are indeed convinced of the truth of these statements.

A bird's eye view of the texts which will be studied in this research reveals an anthropologico-sociologico-existential concern that permeates the thought of the Church Fathers. Most of the Fathers probe the field of convergence between liturgical celebration and social action. Although they often dwell upon the more speculative themes of theology and engage themselves in controversies to oppose heresies, they also opt for more existential real-life situations. Their endeavour was considerably enriched by their familiarity with the social ambience in which they lived. The Fathers' sermons, epistles and commentaries possess a striking applicability to contemporary society. Contemporary readers are gifted with an impressive body of data to ponder upon and an encouraging ideal to follow.

The content of the patristic writings is never dry but ever appealing in its "*quotidienneté*." The Fathers invariably apply the ethical implications of Scripture to daily life. This leads them to exhort Christians to be truly Christ-like – people *for others* and *with others*. The *communio* which springs from worship and the communal listening to the proclaimed word of Scripture flows through the lives of the members of the ecclesial body who reveal that it is called to be a servant Church and a witnessing Church.

The Biblical Text Under Investigation – Mt 4:8–11

The focus of this academic contribution is the third temptation of Jesus in the desert, according to the Gospel of Matthew (4:8–11). What is the

DOI: 10.4324/9781003273592-4

context wherein we encounter the text which will be commented upon, by the Church Fathers? The full text is the following (Mt 4:1–11 NRSV):

> Then Jesus was led up by the Spirit into the wilderness to be tempted by the devil. He fasted for forty days and forty nights, and afterwards he was famished. The tempter came and said to him, 'If you are the Son of God, command these stones to become loaves of bread.' But he answered, 'It is written,
> "One does not live by bread alone,
> but by every word that comes from the mouth of God".'
> Then the devil took him to the holy city and placed him on the pinnacle of the temple, saying to him, 'If you are the Son of God, throw yourself down; for it is written,
> "He will command his angels concerning you",
> and "On their hands they will bear you up,
> so that you will not dash your foot against a stone".'
> Jesus said to him, 'Again it is written, "Do not put the Lord your God to the test".'
> *Again, the devil took him to a very high mountain and showed him all the kingdoms of the world and their splendour; and he said to him, 'All these I will give you, if you will fall down and worship me.' Jesus said to him, 'Away with you, Satan! for it is written,*
> *"Worship the Lord your God,*
> *and serve only him".'*
> *Then the devil left him, and suddenly angels came and waited on him.*

The focus of this work will be on these last four verses in some Church Fathers and early ecclesiastical authors.[5]

An Anonymous Commentary: The *Opus imperfectum in Matthaeum*

This study will commence with an anonymous text, often called the *Opus imperfectum in Matthaeum*, Homily 5, found in the *Patrologia Graeca*. It is available in a Latin translation of a lost Greek original. This work is an early Christian commentary on Matthew's Gospel, dating back, probably to the fourth or fifth century. Its well-known and peculiar name – *Opus imperfectum* – is derived from the fact that it omits a number of texts from Matthew's Gospel and thus possesses lacunae, hence its incompleteness.[6]

> Consider how every promise of the devil is intrinsically irrational and untrue. Certainly, he could not give everything to one person unless he took everything away from everybody. If he took everything away from everybody, he would be adored by no one. Remember that the devil is

> not adored either out of love or out of fear but because he promises and makes deals for riches. So how could the devil take everything away from everyone and give it to one person, in order to be despised by all and worshipped by none?
>
> Nor can we say that anyone could keep his own when the devil has charge of everything. There is no case in which one person is in a situation where he is subject to no one else. This has not happened, nor can it happen. Why? Firstly, because God will not grant the devil such absolute power. Secondly, because of the devil himself, for in what do his joy and glory and power consist except in pride, envy, wrath, vain ambition and the like? When these things come into play, a kingdom cannot stand in unity. It would be necessary to divide up such a kingdom into many kingdoms. But when these things do not come into play, the devil is not reverenced, nor does he reign".
>
> (PG 56:667).[7]

The author of this patristic text, as evident from the above, proceeds gradually, step by step, and in the way in which he writes, he seeks to be logical. In my opinion, he is successful. One is reminded of Aristotelian logic and syllogisms. The method of argumentation sounds philosophical. The reader is invited to observe the style he uses in order to build his argument. He commences with a premise[8]: "Consider how every promise of the devil is intrinsically irrational and untrue." Then he proceeds, seeking to persuade his audience, by moving logically. Note the way he writes:

> He could not ... unless ... If he ... he would not be adored ... So how could the devil ... in order to be despised by all? ... Nor can we say ... nor can it happen ... It would be necessary to ... But when these things do not come into play, the devil is not reverenced, nor does he reign.

What the author successfully brings out is the emphasis he makes on the inconsistency of the devil's promises.

Earlier on in the same anonymous text, the author affirms that "He [Christ] was tempted on your behalf [...] In your stead, he was taken upon a high mountain [...] He was not tempted for the sake of being tempted, but on our behalf" (PG 56:664; 671).

Commenting on the limitations of Satan's power to tempt, the same anonymous text tells us:

> He [Christ] put an end to the Devil's tempting when he said, 'get behind me, Satan!' The Devil could progress no further with his temptation. But we can rightly understand and reasonably ascertain that he withdrew not as though in obedience to the command. Rather it was the divinity of Christ or the Holy Spirit who drove away the devil. This gives us great consolation, for the devil cannot tempt God's people as

> long as he wishes. He can tempt them only so long as Christ or the Holy Spirit who is in them allows him to.
>
> (PG 56:668)[9]

The exegesis is mainly allegorical.[10] The text, as a whole, is strongly existential: man lies in the struggle between good and evil, between the Devil who seduces the flesh and God who assists the free soul in its decisions. The author is showing a markedly pastoral slant. Aware of the fact that the faithful could be discouraged or enter into unwanted tension or incontrollable fear, their hearts are consoled when they are reminded that the Lord is in control, that he has been victorious over Satan, and that he will continue to be so in the life of the faithful.

Another interesting insight in the text we are focusing upon from the *Opus imperfectum* is the "sacramental" aspect. The text states that in contrast to the catechumen, the neophyte, having become a son of God and anointed like an athlete by the Spirit, now belongs to Christ, and like him he is driven into the desert to combat and to win. Because, it is not only Christ who was led into the desert, but all the children of God, because, strengthened by the Spirit they are able to combat (wrestle) against the enemy and to prevail (PG 56:662).

The *Opus imperfectum* is considered to be mildly Arian, and this feature appears in those parts which are doctrinally polemical. In my opinion, the texts presented above do not show this tendency. This is strikingly true when we note what the text affirms, when it clearly affirms the divinity of the Son of God, a truth of faith that the Arians were denying: "Rather *it was the divinity of Christ or the Holy Spirit* who drove away the devil." Simonetti states that the author is probably at the head of a small Arian community that suffered at the hands of dominant Nicene Christians.[11] This is the reason why he insists on the theme of temptation and struggle, which is what we have studied. The author is also being cautious in what he writes, so as not to complicate matters for himself and his community, and so could have affirmed Christ's divinity only grudgingly.

Two Brief Comments by Athanasius

Two very brief texts, from the Christian East, on the topic presented in this study, are those found in the *Vita Antonii* by St Athanasius of Alexandria (296–373): "What the Lord said [with reference to the third temptation in Matthew], he said and carried out *for us*" (*Vita*, 37:1). "The Lord combats *with* Anthony and *within* Anthony" (*Vita*, 5:7; 7:1; 10:2–3; 34:1; 41:5–6; 42:2; 91:3).[12] The theme of temptation and struggle is important in the context of the flight into the desert of certain Christians who desired to live an ascetic life, far from the comforts of the city. So, Athanasius not only wishes to revere the memory of Anthony, but also to encourage Christians who were seeking a more radical way of life.

A Commentary by Hilary – "The Athanasius of the West"

This research now proceeds to the homiletic commentary by Hilary of Poitiers (310–368), often nicknamed "the Athanasius of the West" because of his strong defence against the doctrinal onslaught of Arianism. Hilary has a number of homilies on the Gospel of Matthew. A close and direct encounter with the text is necessary. This is a translation of the critical edition published in *Sources Chrétiennes*:

> But now for the third time, the full ambition of diabolical power is at work. The Lord was taken to a very high mountain. All the kingdoms of the world and the glory of them would be his, he was promised, if only he would fall down and worship. His answer broke through all the devil's suspicions. The devil had enticed Adam with food and led him from the glory of paradise to the place of sin – to the region of the forbidden tree. And he had corrupted him with ambition for a divine name by promising a future similar to that of the gods. In this same way all the power of the world is arrayed against the Lord. The possession of all this is offered to the devil's very Creator, so that in line with the order of the ancient deceit, he whom the devil did not entice with food nor move from place, he would now corrupt by ambition.
>
> But the Lord's response put the matter on a higher plane. He said, 'Be gone, Satan! For it is written, <The Lord your God shall you worship, and him only shall you serve>'. The devil had to live with the outcome of such great recklessness. His crimes were being discovered. He realized that the Lord his God must be adored in the man. By this effective response, the Lord gave us a decisive example. With human power having been disdained and with worldly ambition being held of little account, we should also remember that our Lord and God alone must be adored, especially when the devil's honour has become the common business of every age. After this flight of the devil, therefore, the angels ministered to Christ. With the devil overcome by the man, his head now being crushed, we now can see better the ministering service of the angels and the unfailing courtesies of the heavenly powers toward us.
>
> (*On Matt.*, 3.5)[13]

In this text, one can observe a healthy convergence of several theological themes of prime relevance: Christian anthropology, soteriology and Christology. With regard to the latter, we have to bear in mind the emphasis made by Hilary on the humanity and the divinity of the Son of God, as solemnly enunciated at the First Council of Nicaea (325). With regard to the latter, I highlight the following statements from the text: "He realized that the Lord his God must be adored in the man," and "We should also remember that our Lord and God alone must be adored." We may consider these affirmations to be an early reference to *mia proskynesis*, although the Council of Ephesus was still to take place, some 70 years later. Indeed, the eighth anathema of Cyril of Alexandria in his third letter to Nestorius (November 430), condemns those who do "venerate the Emmanuel with one adoration and glorify him with one praise" (DS 259).[14]

With regard to Christian anthropology, one ought to underline Hilary's paraphrase of the text of Genesis 3, and its elaboration for catechetical-pedagogical purposes, for example,

> The devil had enticed Adam with food and led him from the glory of paradise to the place of sin – to the region of the forbidden tree. And he had corrupted him with ambition for a divine name by promising a future similar to that of the gods.

This theme will be re-visited in a brief excursus in the concluding pages of this study, by means of the episode of the theft of the pears by the young Augustine. From a soteriological point of view, one can highlight the following phrases or lines from Hilary's text: "With the devil overcome by the man, his head now being crushed...." This is a clear reference to the *proto-evangelium* in the third chapter of Genesis, and – in the long run – to the paschal mystery of our Lord.

Chromatius of Aquileia and His Use of *Sensus Plenior*

The Church Fathers were particularly familiar with the texts of Scripture. They knew them at the tips of their fingers. On several occasions they departed from the literal sense of a biblical text – namely, the meaning intended by the original inspired author, writing for a specific audience, in a particular socio-historical situation and using a specific literary genre – and started to read it differently, by applying it to a new context. In other words, a text starts to be read, interpreted and to be explained in a totally different context. One of the ways this has taken place is through what is called *sensus plenior*, literally the fuller sense. *Sensus plenior* refers to the way that biblical texts, especially from the Old Testament, acquire a meaning that transcends the original literal sense, as intended by the original inspired author. Such a meaning, namely, the meaning intended by the principal author, God, emerges in the light of later events marking the history of salvation. This can be witnessed in what a late fourth-century Church Father, Chromatius of Aquileia (d.407), stated in his *Tractates on the Gospel of Matthew*.

In the text, below, quoted from the mentioned work by Chromatius, this study will demonstrate how this Church Father takes five texts from the Old Testament. He finds the *sensus plenior* of these five texts in the Gospel passage of Matthew 4. Four of these texts are from the Psalms, while the fifth is from the Book of Job. Chromatius writes:

> David also prefigures this rejection of temptation when he speaks of the Lord, saying, 'No evil shall befall you, no scourge come near your tent' (Ps 91:10 NRSV). No sin of diabolical scourge could come close to the body of the Lord. Therefore, the Lord withstood temptations from the enemy that he might restore victory to humankind. He thereby made sport of the devil, according to what David also proclaimed: 'Leviathan that you formed to sport in it [i.e. the sea]' (Ps 104:26). And again: 'He will crush the oppressor [*in Chromatius, the false accuser*] (Ps 72:4). And also: 'You crushed the heads of Leviathan; you gave him as food for the creatures of the wilderness' (Ps 73:14). In the book of Job, the Lord declared that this Leviathan would be made sport of and caught in this temptation, saying, 'You will draw out Leviathan with a fish-hook' (Job 40:24).
>
> (*Tractate on Matthew*, 14.5: CCL 9a, 255)[15]

As has been just observed in this text, Chromatius does not soar in high theological altitudes, nor does he present any practical applications to his readers or listeners. He simply explores a possible *sensus plenior* of five Old Testament texts and claims to find it in Mt 4:11, namely, "Then the devil left him, and suddenly angels came and waited on him." The connection that Chromatius devises is, in my opinion, too stretched from the point of view of contemporary biblical scholarship.

Gregory the Great and His Pastoral Method

Another commentary on the text which is being zoomed upon is that found in *Homily* 16 by Pope Gregory the Great (540–604)[16] who seeks to make a comparative presentation between the temptations addressed to Jesus, the new Adam and the temptations which the first Adam faced. This homily by the Bishop of Rome was delivered on 4 March 591 at the Basilica of St John Lateran. It was the first Sunday of Lent. With regard to the third temptation, the sixth-century Father affirms:

> He [i.e. the Devil] tempted him [i.e. Jesus] by an avaricious desire for high position when "he showed him all the kingdoms of the world, saying, 'I will give you all these if you will fall down and worship me'." But the Devil is overcome by the second man in the same way as he boasted of overcoming the first man. He exits our heart at the same juncture where he first made his earliest inroads.
>
> (PL 76:1135–1136)[17]

From this text, it is easily evident that Gregory the Great successfully makes a very clear comparison between the Fall, as described in Genesis 3, and the Matthean text being investigated. While the first Adam succumbed to the Serpent's evil suggestions and misused his liberty, the second Adam was victorious in resisting Satan. Gregory then goes on to stress the power of God's word and the importance of patience as a Christian virtue. In fact, he states:

> When the Lord was tempted by the Devil, he answered him with the commands of sacred Scripture. By the Word that he was, he could have easily plunged his tempter into the abyss. But he did not reveal the power of his might, but he only brought forth the precepts of Scripture. This was to give us an example of his patience, so that as often as we suffer something from vicious persons we should be aroused to teach rather than to exact revenge. Consider how great God's patience is, how great our impatience. When we are provoked by some injury or threatened harm, or moved to rage, we seek revenge as far as possible. When we are unable to obtain it, we make our threats. But the Lord endured the Devil's opposition, and he answered him with nothing except words of meekness.
>
> (PL 76:1135–1136)[18]

In this text, Gregory – in his typically pastoral style – advises his listeners to act appropriately. The example given by Jesus in his third temptation serves as a guide and model to Christians when they find themselves in difficult situations which possibly lead them to act rashly and unlovingly. The text affords us with a glimpse of Gregory's character and his pedagogy. As in countless other texts from his very vast *corpus* of writings, Gregory the Great is keen to suggest practical directives to individuals from all walks of life. It is evident from his many works that this Church Father showed deep psychological insight, and the advice he gave is useful today as it was in his time. Basing himself on Scripture and on classical authors, Gregory manifests a deep knowledge of the human person and seeks to share his profound thoughts on many themes in a direct, concise and incisive manner. Gregory's pastoral convictions are clearly revealed in his *Regula pastoralis*: *ars est artium regimen animarum*.[19]

In his commentary on Mt 4:8–11, he clearly displays a pragmatic approach that is sensitive to the daily experiences of Christians when faced by adversity. Relying upon the wisdom of Scripture, he is quick to adapt the biblical text with an open mind and heart to the faithful. Keeping in mind the above-mentioned shining adage he proposes in his *Regula pastoralis*, Gregory's truly pastoral attitude is characterised by *tranquillitas animi*, *moderationis gratia*, *honesta cura* and *decoris consideratio*. This is clearly evident in the text we have studied where he calmly elaborates a useful application that Christians could adopt in their daily life experiences.

Furthermore, in accordance to the third part of his *Regula*, Gregory proposes – in the text we have studied – a very practical suggestion. The directive which he proposes reveals his deep psychological insights which are useful today as much as they were in his time. The shepherd of souls who *bene vivens* must know *qualiter doceat* according to the personal circumstances of those whom he is advising. The magnanimous advice he gives is based on natural law, enlightened by divine revelation and wisely adapted with open-mindedness, clarity and pastoral solicitude.

A Brief Excursus and Some Concluding Reflections

Unfortunately, Augustine (354–430), the great Doctor of Hippo, does not delve into the text which has been the object of this study. It would have been very interesting to read into his interpretation of the text in Matthew's Gospel. In a text from his *Confessions*, he narrates about his own temptation to steal. He states: "I lusted to thieve… I stole that of which I had enough, and much better. Nor cared I to enjoy what I stole, but joyed in the theft."[20] Here, he describes the theft of the pears from a neighbour's orchard, his and his friends' intention not being to eat the pears, since they stole out of sheer love of evil only. Augustine and his friends "took huge loads, not for… eating, but to fling to the very hogs."[21]

The episode just mentioned from the *Confessions* demonstrates that Augustine's pleasure lay, not in eating the pears, but in the wickedness of the act itself: "For when gathered [the pears], I flung them away, my only feast therein being my own sin, which I was pleased to enjoy."[22] Elsewhere, Augustine says: "My heart… having no temptation to ill, but the ill itself. It was foul, and I loved it; I loved to perish, I loved mine own fault, not that for which I was faulty, but my fault itself."[23] He describes himself as having "loved a sin for its own sake."[24] Although unrelated to the fourth chapter of Matthew's Gospel, these texts demonstrate the powerful force exerted upon the young Augustine by the temptation to steal. In these texts, is the mature Augustine "re-creating" Adam's sin, when he looks back with introspection at the evil in which he was enveloped? A useful comparison can be made with the prodigal son (Lk 15:11–32) who also fed the swine. The conclusions, in my opinion, are self-evident. The young Augustine, overcome by temptations, can be likened to the prodigal son who distanced himself from his father, and who eventually returned to the fold in his long-postponed conversion.

Since his earliest childhood experiences, Augustine was confronted with bubbling temptations, and so, the dilemma between good and evil. Knowing too well what human beings really are – from his wide spectrum of experiences – Augustine is certain that an unending battle between good and evil is present even in the young child. The opening book of the *Confessions* and the beginning of the second attest to this tension or struggle, most probably, a projection on the part of Augustine. This tension continues to unfold in Augustine's encounter and subsequent closeness to the Manichaeans.

This research has offered a modest attempt to focus on the patristic reading of the text of Mt 4:8–11. Readers can observe a discernible difference not only in styles, but also in emphasis. Seasoned scholars, as well as the man-in-the-street, witness to how different patristic texts have sought to read into four intriguing verses from the Gospel of Matthew. The temptations of Jesus, both at the Synoptic strata, as well as at contemporary Christological studies, remain fundamental to a proper and balanced comprehension of the Christian life. The experience which Jesus Christ underwent in the desert is a powerful and prophetic set of gestures and options which have inspired Christians of all ages and milieu. We have been able to observe the genuine attempt made by different patristic authors to elaborate upon a biblical text, principally with pedagogical and catechetical intentions. The historical-salvific dimension of the four verses we have studied from the wider Matthean pericope has been articulated in a variety of ways by some of the Church Fathers.

At the same time, we can also note, in some cases, the general theological debate in the background, as in the case of Hilary's text. In the case of the brief texts from Athanasius, we can catch a glimpse of the search for a more radical lifestyle by some Christians who were leaving the comfort of the cities to the austerity of a life of sacrifice and penance in the desert. In the case of the text from the *Opus Imperfectum*, one appreciates the logical reasoning used by the author, while in the text from Chromatius of Aquileia, one encounters the awareness of a *sensus plenior* of some Old Testament passages as realised in Matthew's Gospel. Gregory the Great offers his listeners practical applications and clear guidelines based on the scriptural passage we have studied. In all these examples, we have been able to appreciate a variegated use of Scripture – an experience that has been not only interesting to observe, but also enriching, intuitive and thought-provoking. The relevance of the Church Fathers to contemporary society has been vindicated once again.[25] As we have been able to appreciate, the text remains a pivotal point of reference for the committed behaviour of Christians in this post-modern era, as it has been for the past twenty centuries.

Notes

1 Henri de Lubac, *Paradoxes* (Paris: Livre Français, 1946), 68: "Mais comment retrouver le christianisme sinon en remontant à ses sources, en tâchant à le ressaisir dans ses époques de vitalité explosive?"

2 Henri de Lubac, Preface, in AA.VV., *Les chemins vers Dieu*, Lettres Chrétiennes 11, intro., choice of texts by France Quéré-Jaulmes – Adalbert-G. Hamman (Paris: Grasset Editions du Centurion, 1967), 7.

3 Adalbert-G. Hamman, *La vie est un long jour de fête* (Paris: Brepols, 1995), 242.

4 Adalbert-G. Hamman, *Les racines de la foi* (Paris: O.E.I.L, 1983), 12.
5 The English translations of the patristic texts presented in this study – with the exception of those by Gregory the Great and Augustine – are found in Manlio Simonetti, ed., *Ancient Christian Commentary on Scripture: New Testament,* Vol. 1a. *Matthew 1-13* (Downers Grove, Illinois: InterVarsity Press, 2001). Hereafter: Simonetti, *Ancient Christian Commentary on Scripture*, 1a.
6 Its authorship was for centuries wrongly attributed to John Chrysostom, a misconception first refuted by Erasmus in 1530. Some candidates for its authorship include an Arian priest in Constantinople named Timothy; Maximinus, an Arian bishop who accompanied the Goths; and Anianus of Celeda. It exhibits a mildly Arian Christology and represents the sometimes confusing theology that permeated Christianity in its formative centuries. It was well regarded into the Middle Ages in spite of its theological deficiencies, but fell out of widespread study after Erasmus' critique. See https://en.wikipedia.org/wiki/Opus_Imperfectum (accessed 16.8.2018). Cfr also Manlio Simonetti, "Opus imperfectum in Matthaeum," in Angelo Di Berardino, ed., *Dizionario patristico e di antichità cristiane*, II (Casale Monferrato: Marietti, 1994), col.2489–2490.
7 Simonetti, *Ancient Christian Commentary on Scripture*, 1a, 62.
8 A proposition stated or assumed for subsequent reasoning, especially, one of the two propositions in a syllogism from which the conclusion is drawn.
9 Simonetti, *Ancient Christian Commentary on Scripture*, 1a, 63.
10 Literally, speaking under the guise of something else. A point-by-point interpretation that goes beyond what a narrative says on the surface to find deeper and further links with reality, e.g. the allegory of the vine in Is 5 and Ps 80.
11 Simonetti, "Opus imperfectum in Matthaeum," 2489–2490.
12 Author's translation of text as consulted in Santino Raponi, "Cristo tentato e il Cristiano. La lezione dei Padri," *Studia Moralia* 21 (1983): 229.
13 Hilaire de Poitiers, *Commentaire sur l'Évangile de Matthieu 1-13*, Sources Chrétiennes 254 (Paris: Cerf, 1978). English translation: Simonetti, *Ancient Christian Commentary on Scripture*, 1a, 63.
14 Walter Kasper states: "From the fact that the subject is one, it follows that we do not worship Jesus' humanity as if it were a different subject *hos hetepon hetepo* only together with the Logos, but that both are glorified in one single worship *mia proskynesis* (DS 259). Walter Kasper, *Jesus the Christ* (Tunbridge Wells: Burns and Oates, 1976), 236.
15 Simonetti, *Ancient Christian Commentary on Scripture*, 1a, 64.
16 Cfr Grégoire le Grand, *Homélies sur l'Évangile*, Livre I, Sources Chrétiennes 485 (Paris: Cerf, 2005), 345–359.
17 Simonetti, *Ancient Christian Commentary on Scripture*, 1a, 62–63.
18 Ibid., 63.
19 Cfr Gregory the Great, *Liber Regulae Pastoralis*, I.1: Grégoire le Grand, *Règle Pastorale*, I, Sources Chrétiennes 381 (Paris: Cerf, 1992), 128.
20 *Confessiones* II,4,9. The following English translation has been used: *The Confessions of St Augustine*, transl. by E.B. Pusey (London: Heron Books, 1962).
21 Ibid.
22 Ibid., II,6,12.
23 Ibid., II,4,9.
24 Ibid., II,7,15.
25 A future research on the same theme intends to explore texts from Theodore of Mopsuestia, Ephrem of Nisibis and Jerome. Cfr Ephrem de Nisibe, *Commentaire de l'Évangile concordant ou Diatessaron*, Sources Chrétiennes 121 (Paris: Cerf, 1966), 95–103; Saint Jérome, *Commentaire sur saint Matthieu*, Vol. I, Sources Chrétiennes 242 (Paris: Cerf, 1977), 97–100.

Bibliography

Augustine. 1962. *The Confessions*, transl. by E.B. Pusey. London: Heron Books.

Grégoire le Grand. 1992. *Règle Pastorale*, I, Sources Chrétiennes 381. Paris: Cerf.

Grégoire le Grand. 2005. *Homélies sur l'Évangile*, Livre I, Sources Chrétiennes 485. Paris: Cerf.

Hamman, Adalbert-G. 1983. *Les racines de la foi*. Paris: O.E.I.L.

Hamman, Adalbert-G. 1995. *La vie est un long jour de fête*. Paris: Brepols.

Hilaire de Poitiers. 1978. *Commentaire sur l'Évangile de Matthieu 1–13*, Sources Chrétiennes 254. Paris: Cerf.

Kasper, Walter. 1976. *Jesus the Christ*. Tunbridge Wells: Burns and Oates.

Lubac, Henri de. 1946. *Paradoxes*. Paris: Livre Français.

Raponi, Santino. 1983. 'Cristo tentato e il Cristiano. La lezione dei Padri', *Studia Moralia*, 21, 209–237.

Simonetti, Manlio. 1994. 'Opus imperfectum in Matthaeum', in Angelo Di Berardino, ed., *Dizionario patristico e di antichità cristiane*, II. Casale Monferrato: Marietti. 2489–2490.

Simonetti, Manlio, ed., 2001. *Ancient Christian Commentary on Scripture: New Testament*, Vol. 1a. *Matthew 1–13*. Downers Grove, IL: InterVarsity Press, 2001.

5 Defending the Scriptural Legitimacy of *Ousia* Language

St. Athanasius and Basil of Ancyra

Gheorghe Ovidiu Sferlea

Introduction

According to Socrates of Constantinople, of the more than 300 bishops who attended the Council of Nicaea, only five were found to brave the overwhelming consensus of the others. Of these, Eusebius of Nicomedia and Theognis of Nicaea signified shortly after being sent into exile that they were now willing to approve the document, including anathematisms, and asked Emperor Constantine for permission to return to their sees.[1] However, they were not the only ones who had difficulty in accepting the Nicene definition. Eusebius of Caesarea recounts in detail in a letter composed just after the end of the council his own doubts and reservations concerning the Creed that, "under the pretext of adding a single word", the bishops would formulate and ratify. That word was *homoousion*. Eusebius eventually put his signature on the Nicene Creed, yet not before having asked for clarification and having been assured by Emperor Constantine himself that the term was not to be understood in a materialistic sense. Indeed, it did not imply division or partition in God's essence (*ousia*).[2]

Hostility toward the Nicene definition would only grow in the coming years, especially after Constantine's death. While the situation was complex, Marcellus of Ancyra and his rather modalist views on Trinitarian theology were prone to become a major factor in the process of contestation.[3] Though he had not many reasons to be happy with the Nicene settlement, which apparently, he did not even sign personally, Marcellus nonetheless provided the opponents of Nicaea with a promising angle of attack. As the creed of 325 looked ineffective in face of the neo-Sabellian danger, the search for a new definition of faith had to be considered open once again. Thus, the anti-Nicene front sought to advance a rather subordinationist agenda under the guise of an assertive and increasingly well-articulated anti-modalist rhetoric. A milestone in implementing this project was the Council of Antioch, 341. New criticism of *homoousion* was quite soon to emerge, as a significant number of bishops, though not a majority came to discover that not only was the term theologically flawed, but it was not scriptural either.[4]

DOI: 10.4324/9781003273592-5

The present paper aims to examine two answers to the criticism according to which *ousia* language has no scriptural basis. One of these comes from St Athanasius and was formulated for the first time in his opuscule *On the Decisions of the Council of Nicaea*. The second belongs to an anti-Nicene who is none other than the successor of Marcellus. Basil of Ancyra was an opponent of Athanasius and was actively involved in the conciliar attempts to articulate a non-Arian alternative to Nicaea. It is therefore interesting to observe how the internal dialectic of the anti-Nicene opposition led Basil to defend the terminology of *ousia* in a manner that bears similarities to that of St. Athanasius.

St Athanasius' *De Decretis*

Some scholars believe that the most plausible context for writing *De decretis* was provided by the council of Sirmium in 357, which launched an explicit attack on the legitimacy of using categories such as *substantia* or *ousia* in theology.[5] This criticism may not have been official though, and therefore an earlier dating, closer to the beginning of the 350s, is at least equally plausible.[6] Whether or not the challenge was official, Athanasius reports in the first paragraph that certain bishops of anti-Nicene persuasion, whom he calls "Arians", were contesting the use of unscriptural terms in a Church faith document: "Why did the Fathers at Nicaea use terms not in Scripture, 'from the essence' and 'same in essence'?"[7]

In his answer, Athanasius feels the need to clarify, among other things, how these formulae were introduced in the final text, a story that contrasts with that provided by another eyewitness to the events, Eusebius of Caesarea. While the latter claims that the initiative came from the emperor, St Athanasius attributes it to the bishops.[8] Both "from the essence" and "same in essence" emerged as a last resort solution. The fathers would have preferred sticking to scriptural texts to reject Arian errors, but the opponents proved skilled enough to twist in their favor all scriptural testimonies that were brought forth against them. The fathers were thus forced to change the approach and to attempt to concentrate the meaning of those scriptural texts, which ended up with the two formulae making their way into the creed.

At the heart of debates were expressions indicating Son's origin "from God" (as opposed to the Arian "from nothing").[9] To Arius' sympathizers, such language applied in equal proportion to the Son and to creatures: they all could be said to come from God, without any of them being entitled to claim a genuinely divine status on that basis. The fathers then resorted to the formula "from the essence of the Father", which was meant to clarify the expression "from God" in a way apt to radically distinguish between the Son and creatures. As for the assertion of the Son being "like the Father", the Arians were also quick to argue that such "likeness" applied just as well to humans as a result of a moral effort. And once again the fathers had to make clear that there was more than likeness between the Father and the Son. The latter had, in fact, to be conceived of as "inseparable from Father's essence", and that was indeed something very different from a moral affinity acquired progressively through effort.[10]

After this historical account setting the context for the litigious formulae, the question of their theological legitimacy must be addressed. Are those formulae covered by the testimony of the Scriptures? Is it allowed at all to speak of God by resorting to philosophical categories such as "essence (*ousia*)"? As regards the second question, Athanasius notes, a ready observation can be made: opponents of the Nicene definition have themselves coined technical terms such as "from nothing", "from the will" or "mutable".[11] Those opponents would no doubt argue that while the terms are not exactly to be found as such in Scripture, they are legitimate nonetheless, for they only serve to encapsulate the meaning of scriptural phrases, at least according to an interpretation of their own. Athanasius feels entitled then to claim an equal right on the behalf of the Nicene creed. Even though Scripture nowhere literally speaks of God's "essence", many passages indicate that the connection between the Father and the Son must be situated at the most important level. Athanasius' answer develops in two steps. First, a series of scriptural expressions are listed, speaking of a special, unique relation between the Father and the Son. A metaphysical presupposition is stated in a second time: this connection cannot be accidental, for in that case, the consequence would be a denial of God's simplicity. It must, on the contrary, be of the order of *ousia*. If God the Father is to be conceived as simple, and the Son is "proper" and inseparable from Him, then one must understand Him as belonging to the Father's very being.

Athanasius fairly admits that the Nicene formulae cannot be found *expressis verbis* in the Scriptures. The careful reader cannot however get stuck in such narrow-minded literalism, as the anti-Nicenes would demand, for the content of those formulae can easily be recognized in many places that testify to a special closeness between the Father and the Son:

> even if the expressions are not in so many words in the Scriptures, yet, as was said before, they contain the sense of the Scriptures, and expressing it, they convey it to those who have their hearing unimpaired for religious doctrine.[12]

If one takes a look at which those Scriptures more precisely are, a strong predomination of the fourth Gospel is immediately obvious: "If God were your Father, you would love Me; for I proceeded forth from the Father" (Jn 8, 42); "Not that anyone has seen the Father, save He who is from God, He has seen the Father" (Jn 6, 46); "I and My Father are one" (Jn 10, 30); "The Only-begotten Son which is in the bosom of the Father, He has declared Him" (Jn 1, 18); "I in the Father and the Father in Me" (Jn 10, 38; 14, 10–11). The last expression is especially significant, for it is equivalent to saying "I am from the Father, and inseparable from Him".[13] The quoting of these texts is not surprising, as they often appear in Athanasius' polemic.[14] It is new that they are used to biblically root and justify the Nicene expressions "from the essence" and "same in essence", hardly mentioned in his anti-Arian *Orations*.

At this moment, an additional point is introduced into the argument. When saying "from God" or "from the Father", what level of divine reality do the terms "God" and "Father" indicate in these expressions, Athanasius asks. The referent could be conceived as a thing "around God", that is something only accidentally related to His essence (ὡς ἐν τῇ οὐσίᾳ τὸ συμβεβηκὸς). Or, otherwise, these terms could indicate God's ontological very intimacy, what he is, *i.e.* his "being" proper. But the first cannot be a valid choice, for it would imply God to be subject of composition, made up of *ousia* and various non-essential properties. Therefore, one must embrace the second possibility, for God has no parts. Divine simplicity is a metaphysical premise that St Athanasius holds for tacitly accepted by all sides. Thus, if God is conceived to be simple and if He is confessed as being, according to *Ex* 3: 14–15 ("I am He who is... I am the Lord God"), when it is said about the Son that he is "from God" or "from the Father", it is said "in more explicit but equivalent language" that He is "from the essence of the Father".[15]

The category of essence (*ousia*) does not first appear at this point. Mention of it has been made already in paragraph 13, where several scriptural texts emphasizing the distinction between the Son and creatures are quoted: *Ps* 2, 7: ("You are My Son, this day have I begotten You"), *Prov* 8, 25. ("The Lord says of Himself in the Proverbs 'Before all the hills He begets me'"), *Jn* 1, 3 ("All things were made by Him") and *Jn* 1, 18 ("The Only-begotten Son, who is in the bosom of the Father, He declared Him"). "Son" and "creature" are notions sharply distinguished in all these texts. An unambiguous conclusion must be drawn:

> If then son, therefore not creature; if creature, not son; for great is the difference between them, and son and creature cannot be the same, unless His essence be considered to be at once from God, and external to God.[16]

This argument will become prominent in Basil of Ancyra. But the use of *ousia* is not further discussed or justified.

One might be surprised that in a text meant to defend the theological decisions of Nicaea, so (relatively) little space is given to the key formulae "from the essence" and "same in essence", in fact, three paragraphs. This however clearly reflects a personal assessment. In Athanasius' estimate, objections against Nicene formulae are for the most part but pretence and evasions. His opponents' real problem lies with the deep theological orientation of the creed, that is confessing and securing Son's genuine divinity.

For Athanasius, this confession is pervasive in the Scriptures, and the use of biblical texts in *De decretis* appears as massive as in his previous anti-Arian works. Scriptures proclaim time and again Christ's genuine sonship, eternity and divinity. That is also the meaning of the contested formulae. Seen from such a perspective then, those formulae are fully scriptural, even when they cannot be literally derived from a particular passage of the Scriptures.

At the end of *De decretis*, Athanasius appends the text of Eusebius of Caesarea's *Letter to the Church of Caesarea*. This is an apologetic text in which Eusebius seeks to prove that his eventual acceptance of the Nicene creed does not mean renouncing the faith he always confessed and preached before his flock. It is thus noteworthy that Eusebius takes the pain to discuss every important difference between the confession of faith he had presented before the bishops in Nicaea to clear himself of the charge of heresy, and the final text made up by the majority. There is however one significant omission. Regarding the sequence "true God from true God" not a single word is to be found in his scrutiny. Of course, Eusebius could simply have considered the sequence unimportant. While such an explanation cannot be dismissed from the outset, one would suspect Eusebius' passing over this particular detail to betray a much more serious concern. It is not difficult to imagine why. Despite its apparent unsophistication or, perhaps, precisely because of it, the formula "true God from true God" is perfectly balanced as to counter and forestall any kind of ontological subordination of the Son to the Father[17] – a principle that Eusebius entertained – and was most likely intended to do so. In addition, it could hardly have been criticized for being too technical or for not having scriptural testimonies to bring on its behalf (*cf. Jn* 1, 1; *Jn* 20, 28; *Jn* 14, 6).

Explaining that a "true God" could mean less than a "true God" may have looked too bold an exercise even for such an accomplished writer as Eusebius. Attacking the sequence head-on just after having signed the text containing it was equally complicated. The most convenient way to deal with it was to simply skip it. It appears to have been anything but an innocent omission on his part. Eusebius was indeed aware as to what the title "true God" could signify, for he had emphatically rejected its application to the Son in a letter to Euphration of Balanea, probably written a few years before Nicaea: "even though the Son himself too is a God, yet he is not true God. For there is one and unique true God, the reason being there is no one to precede him".[18] Athanasius has knowledge of this letter because he briefly mentions the point in *De synodis*.[19] And he also reports in *De decretis* that his opponents hold, following Eusebius and his fellows, "that the Son is not true God".[20]

The conspiracy of silence initiated by Eusebius appears to have functioned remarkably well during the next decades. Eastern councils continued to call the Son "God", but never "true God".[21] This is a striking fact, suggesting that these councils did not simply intend removing scripturally unwarranted terminology, but rather freeing themselves completely from the theological orientation of the Nicene creed, which this expression perhaps best encapsulates. A language of ambiguity was instead cultivated and favored, especially during the 350s, in a hopeless attempt to retrieve the theological innocence of before 325. But the disruptive emergence of heteroousians marks the beginning of a crisis that would lead to the end of this project. One of those highly alarmed by this new theological strain was Basil of Ancyra, to whom we may now turn our attention.

Basil of Ancyra's *Letters*

At the end of the 350s, Basil of Ancyra emerges as the leading figure of the Homoiousian party, assisted by Eustathius of Sebaste and George of Laodiceea. Before that, Basil was part of the alliance seeking to find an alternative to the Nicene formula of faith by defining the Son as being "like (*homoios*)" the Father.[22] Basil shared with the Homoians a negative assessment of Nicene *homoousion*, which he rejected for being modalistic or "sabellian". For Basil, this problem must have been all the more relevant as he was appointed to Ancyra precisely because he was deemed capable to do away with the theological legacy of his predecessor, Marcellus.

Following the Homoian narrative, Nicaea did not secure a solid confession of the Son's divinity, but rather left the doors wide open to Marcellus' heresy. Accordingly, the Homoians did not style themselves as promoting a view of the Son that was, *mutatis mutandis*, not very inconsistent with Arius', but as merely trying to avoid a neo-Sabellian twist within Christian theology, with the unpleasant, yet necessary price of throwing away the Nicene definition altogether. However, Basil became increasingly dissatisfied with the overall evolution of Homoian theology as well.

Basil's personal theological position emerged in reaction to Homoian unwillingness to admit that the Son's likeness to the Father is "in all things (*kata panta*)", as the synod of Antioch in 345 had declared.[23] Without such qualification, the Homoian formula remained exposed to an overtly subordinationist interpretation. And, whatever the tactical reasons of Homoian reluctance may have been, Aetius and Eunomius were quick to seize the opportunity of pressing the Homoian stance to its logical conclusion. To put it simply, they pointed out that if the Son is not to be declared "like" the Father in essence (*ousia*), as Homoians tacitly agreed, he must then be considered as "unlike" (*anhomoios*) or, even better, "different in essence" (*heteroousios*) from the Father and thus, strictly speaking, as a "creature" and a "thing made". The truth of Homoian theology, at least in the eyes of Aetius and Eunomius, appeared to be Heteroousianism.

Aetius and Eunomius did not shake Basil's conviction that Nicaea ought to be replaced. Yet their radical interpretation managed at least to expose a liability in the Homoian formula. It was plain enough that, taken in itself, this formula contained no guarantee against such unacceptable Arian stridencies as professed by Heteroousians. Therefore, Basil tried to fix the breach open into the Homoian theology by resorting to *ousia* language in order to qualify the nature of the Son's likeness to the Father. Basil's formula was eventually to be that the Son was "like in essence (*homoios kat'ousian*)" to the Father. However, the bishops assembled in Sirmium decided in 357 that such terminology was neither scriptural nor reverent.[24] It was an unambiguous attack against Nicaea, but also against Basil's formula, who quite ironically found himself in a position similar to that of Athanasius.

Basil's answer came in two letters, the earliest of which was written in the spring of 358, proceeding from a small gathering of bishops at Ancyra before Easter. The second was drafted in the summer of the following year, in response to a document known as the "Dated Creed", issued in Sirmium in May 359. After having been a matter of some dispute, the authorship of the second letter, which is perhaps a "little treatise", was recently restored to Basil and will be accepted as such hereafter.[25]

In the first letter, Basil makes clear from the beginning that his perspective is Trinitarian: "Our faith is in a Father, a Son and a Holy Spirit". Two further principles are then laid down. The first is that names such as "Father" and "Son" ought to be taken seriously in what they indicate about divine generation: "a father always begets a son like himself". The second is that Christian faith in "a Father, a Son and a Holy Spirit" is not a faith in "a creator and a creature, for 'creator and creature' are one thing but 'father and son' are another, since these two concepts differ in meaning".[26] Both these arguments are also to be found in Athanasius, but in favor of *homoousion*.

In the next paragraph, the term *ousia* comes out again in a slightly modified version of the first principle: "for every 'father' is understood to be the father of an essence like his". The analogy of human generation is often used by Basil, and so is the category of *ousia*, much more often than in Athanasius. At this point, no further explanation is proposed, except that "the 'Father' does not mean the Father of an activity but of an essence like himself, whose subsistence corresponds with a particular activity".[27] Later, when he discusses the theme of Son as Wisdom, he expands the idea. If the Father is not wise by participation in wisdom, he must be himself wise, that is "himself an essence, without compounding". One would perhaps expect an argument coming somewhere close to Athanasius's appeal to divine simplicity, but Basil continues:

> The Wisdom which is the Son is an essence (*ousia*) begotten of the essence of the Wise, which is Wisdom. The Son will subsist as an essence like the essence of the wise Father, from whom the Son originated as Wisdom.[28]

It might be surprising, but the text quite clearly suggests that Basil does not have in mind a unified, indeed unique divine *ousia*, shared by the Father and the Son. Rather, being an *ousia*, Father begets another *ousia* that is "like" his, namely, the Son. Two *ousiai* appear to be implied in this passage, for each is said to "subsist" as an *ousia* in its own right. The first begets the former, which ensures a close similarity between them. Nonetheless, they are still two distinct *ousiai*.

Leaving Trinitarian implications aside for the moment, is the terminology of *ousia* scripturally grounded? Basil does not directly address the question in this first letter. He is above all concerned with demonstrating the special way in which the Son is Father's unique and true Offspring, without common measure with creatures that are sometimes also called God's "sons". The latter are "loosely and equivocally so called", whereas the Son is "Son of God" in a proper sense, that is "in the essential likeness of the Father whose Son he is called".[29] A correct understanding of this point is crucial in Basil's eyes for distinguishing between Christianity and Jews or Greeks.[30] Several scriptural texts are quoted and briefly explained, all indicating the Son's essential likeness to the Father. Son's essential likeness to the Father is for Basil a logical consequence of his having been begotten from the Father's *ousia*. *Prov* 8, 22 and 25, for instance, are testimonies to this. So, Basil holds, "if anyone, on hearing the Son's, 'He created me', and, 'He begets me', does not take 'begets me' literally and as a reference to essence, but says that 'He begets me' means the same as 'He created me', thus denying that the Son is by the two terms as the perfect [begotten] without passion, confessing that he is a mere creature and not a Son", that person deserves to become anathema.[31]

Other texts quoted to substantiate the same argument are *Jn* 5, 26 ("As the Father hath life in himself, so hath he given to the Son to have life in himself")[32] and *Phil* 2, 7 ("Who, being in the form of God, thought it not robbery to be equal with God, but made himself of no reputation, and took upon him the form of a servant, and was made in the likeness of men"). *Phil* 2, 6–7 is an important testimony, for it helps Basil make several points. First, together with Rm 8, 3, it contains a literal reference to the concept of "likeness", Basil's watchword. *Phil.* 2, 7 is taken to also have "essential" implications. Basil's reading is original. He admits that the sequence "in the likeness of men" refers in its plain sense to the Son's incarnation, but he also holds that it *a fortiori* indicates Son's likeness to the Father. If by His begetting from the Virgin, an act that was not natural to Him, the Son was brought to the likeness of men, how much more His immaterial and passionless generation from the Father, which was according to His nature, vouchsafed Him essential likeness to the Father? In addition, *Phil.* 2, 7 makes clear that the Son was made in the likeness of the essence, not in the identity, a polemical allusion to the Nicene *homoousios*.[33]

Basil's second letter comes in the wake of the council that took place in the spring of 358 at Sirmium. The council was dominated by his former allies, the Homoians, who again decided to put under ban any reference to *ousia* in Christian theological discourse. The challenge cannot be ignored any longer. Therefore, Basil abruptly begins his reply: "It is plain that the term, 'essence' does not appear in the Old and the New Testaments, but the sense of it is to be found everywhere". However the first and the sole example is the text of *Ex* 3, 14. Basil is aware of Paul of Samosata's condemnation in the previous century and holds that the term *ousia*, contained in *Ex* 3, 14, was meant to emphasize Son's real and distinct reality, against Paul's and Marcellus modalistic tendencies, which reduced the Son to a "verbal expression and utterance", on the basis of an erroneous reading of *Jn* 1, 1, and thus "refused to say 'Son of God'". On what ground *Ex* 3, 14 also applies to the Son, Basil does not explain, but simply presupposes the fact: "now the Son also is 'He Who is'".[34]

After having briefly exposed the doctrines of the Neo-Arians and then defended the use of the expression "three *hypostaseis*" by the Easterners as "an acknowledgment of the subsistent, real individualities of the persons",[35] the next step in Basil's argument is to bring into discussion biblical texts that are proofs of the Son's likeness to the Father. *Col* 1, 15 proclaims the Son to be "the image of the invisible God", which means that "the Son is like the Father".[36] Other testimonies are those already discussed in the previous *Letter*, mainly *Rom.* 8, 3 and *Phil.* 2, 6–7.

Instead of Conclusion: Basil, the Neo-arians and Nicaea

Basil's second *Letter* closes on a polemical note. Targeting the Neo-arians, he deliberately confuses them with the Homoians in attributing to the first the manoeuvres that ended up with the interdiction of the term *ousia* on the ground of its unscriptural origins. In Basil's estimate, the Neo-arians would have benefited from such a move, for they would have been able to keep speaking about Son's likeness in will and activity to the Father while observing a telling silence on the most important aspect, *i.e. ousia*. Basil also attacks them for the hypocrisy of rejecting *ousia* as unbiblical while using the titles of "ungenerate" and "generate" instead of the names of "Father" and "Son" revealed by the Lord.[37] It is certain however that the ban imposed at Seleucia came from the Homoian majority and was likely directed not only against Nicaea and the Homoiousians, but also against Aetius and Eunomius. It may well be that the Neo-Arian interpretation of Homoian apophaticism about God's *ousia* was perceived as a much more serious threat to the Homoian project, for it undermined the narrative according to which a non-Arian, non-Nicene and non-Sabellian theology of the Son was indeed possible and desirable. This seems to have been the objective of a majority of Eastern bishops at least from Antioch (341) onwards. This was also Basil of Ancyra's objective.

Prima facie, it could be tempting to regard Basil's theological stance as an opening towards the Nicene *homoousion*. This however was most probably the opposite of what he wanted to achieve. Despite the initial hopes of St Athanasius, Basil did not intend to get closer to, let alone to retrieve Nicaea, but rather to remain true to the original Homoian intuition. Yet, within the new context, the Son's genuine likeness could only be preserved if *ousia* was openly included in it, against the Neo-arian *heteroousion*. By arguing that the Son is "like in essence" to the Father, Basil thought that the sound middle-way between the extremes of Sabellianism (Nicaea included) and Arianism was well secured and the core of the Homoian project would, in the end, be saved from the bleeding inflicted by the Heteroousian attack. His attempt did not prove successful.

Of course, explaining Basil's failure is a matter of some speculation. Political and ecclesiastical circumstances are likely to have played their part. Here only some brief observations about his theological achievement can be attempted. Did Basil's case for the essential likeness contain enough warranties to preclude a Heteroousian conclusion? It is at least allowed to recall that, although his both *Letters* are directed primarily against the Heteroousians, when speaking about the Son's essential likeness to the Father he always has in mind two *ousiai*, and he is most probably implying the Holy Spirit being the third.[38] This is a crucial point. How are these three *ousiai* to be conceived? They are numerically distinct. Each subsists and exists as a separate *ousia*. Qualitatively, they are very similar, yet not identical.[39] Indeed, the Father's is the ungenerate *ousia*, whereas the Son's is the generate.[40] Nor are these equal. Only one *ousia* is rightly called "the God", and that is Father's. The Son's is simply "God". And only one *ousia* possesses divinity with full sovereignty, and that is again Father's.[41] While Basil would have pointed to the overwhelming extent of their likeness, it seems that Eunomius could still have had grounds to make the point of their (to some extent) unlikeness. To put the matter otherwise, Eunomius could still have claimed that, on his opponent very terms, the Son's *ousia* is of a different constitution or, if one prefers, "nature"[42] than the Father's. So even following Basil's statements, it was possible to infer that the Son was, strictly speaking, *heteroousios*.

Basil's failure as a leader for the Homoiusians was sometimes attributed to his political inability.[43] It has been also pointed out that he lacked a clear distinction between *ousia* and *hypostasis* as the Cappadocians would soon manage to establish.[44] Such regret might be better suited for Athanasius though. Leaving aside the question of whether one can discover in Basil of Ancyra grounds to read him as a Cappadocian *manqué*, it must be recalled that for him maintaining a certain measure of ontological subordination between the Son and the Father was not thought to be the problem, as it arguably was for St Athanasius and the Cappadocians, but the solution. The solution, that is, apt to prevent Trinitarian theology from collapsing either into Sabellian confusion or into tritheism. Basil is part of a tradition that sought to secure a distinct and permanent identity for the Father, the Son and the Holy Spirit by ontologically grading them.[45] His *Letters* bear testimony to the fact that he carried with him both the strengths and the shortcomings of that tradition.

Notes

1 Socrates of Constantinople, *Historia ecclesiastica* I.VIII.31–34. For a recent account of the council, see Davin M. Gwynn, "Reconstructing the Council of Nicaea", in *The Cambridge Companion to the Council of Nicaea*, ed. Young Richard Kim (Cambridge: Cambridge University Press, 2021): 90–119.
2 Athanasius, *De decretis Nicaenae synodi* 33, 7. See also 33, 12–13.
3 On Marcellus and his significance in fourth-century debates, see Joseph T. Lienhard SJ, *Contra Marcellum. Marcellus of Ancyra and Fourth-Century Theology* (Washington, D.C.: The Catholic University of America Press, 1999), and Sara Parvis, *Marcellus of Ancyra and the Lost Years of the Arian Controversy* (Oxford: Oxford University Press, 2006).
4 For the Nicene and post-Nicene debates, illuminating accounts are to be found in Parvis, *Marcellus of Ancyra and the Lost Years of the Arian Controversy*, 38–252, and *eadem*, "The Reception of Nicaea and *Homoousios* to 360", in *The Cambridge Companion to the Council of Nicaea*: 225–254. See also Lewis Ayres, *Nicaea and Its Legacy: An Approach to Fourth-Century Trinitarian Theology* (Oxford: Oxford University Press, 2004): esp. 84–166; Thomas Kopecek, *A History of Neo-Arianism* (Cambridge, MA: The Philadelphia Patristic Foundation, 1979); and Khaled Anatolios, *Retrieving Nicaea. The Development and Meaning of Trinitarian Doctrine* (Grand Rapids, MI: Baker Academic, 2011): 58–86.
5 For instance, Uta Heil, "Schriften gegen Eusebianer und Homöer: 3.5. De *decretis Nicaenae synodis*", in *Athanasius Handbuch*, ed. Peter Gemeinhart (Tübingen: Mohr Siebeck, 2011): 211.
6 Thus Lewis Ayres, "*Athanasius*" Initial *Defense* of the Term *homoousios*: Rereading the *De Decretis*', *Journal of Early Christian Studies* 12.3 (2004): 338, situates *De decretis* in 353. A very recent case for 353 is made by Parvis, "The Reception of Nicaea and *Homoousios* to 360": 245–246.
7 Athanasius, *De decretis* 1,1: ἀγράφους λέξεις, τὸ ἐκ τῆς οὐσίας καὶ τὸ ὁμοούσιον; English translation by John Henry Newman, in *Nicene and Post-Nicene Fathers*, Second Series, Vol. 4, ed. Philip Schaff and Henry Wace (Buffalo, NY: Christian Literature Publishing Co., 1892), slightly altered. Newman's version will be reproduced hereafter.
8 Athanasius, *De decretis* 33, 7 (Eusebius's testimony) and 20, 3–6 (Athanasius' testimony). For the introduction of *homoousios* in the Creed of Nicaea, see Mark J. Edwards, "Alexander of Alexandria and the *Homoousios*", *Vigiliae Christianae* 66.5 (2012): 482–502.
9 Athanasius, *De decretis* 19, 1–5.
10 Athanasius, *De decretis* 20, 5: οὐ μόνον ὅμοιος, ἀλλὰ καὶ ἀδιαίρετός ἐστι τῆς τοῦ πατρὸς οὐσίας.
11 Athanasius, *De decretis* 18, 1.
12 Athanasius, *De decretis* 21, 2–3.
13 Athanasius, *De decretis* 21, 4.
14 For instance, *Orationes contra Arianos* I, 4, 56; II, 12, 22, 33; III, 5, 55 *etc.*
15 Athanasius, *De decretis* 22, 1–5.
16 Athanasius, *De decretis* 13, 5–6.
17 I cannot but join the observation made by Mark J. Edwards, *Catholicity and Heresy in the Early Church* (London: Ashgate, 2002): 132.

> It might be said that the Nicene article 'true God from true God' invests the Son with every attribute that scripture and logic predicate of the Father, and the reticence of Eusebius in his letter to Caesarea suggests that he found this a more intractable element than the *homoousion*".

18 *Athanasius Werke* III.1, 5 (= *Urkunde* 3,3): ἐπεὶ καὶ αὐτὸς θεὸς μὲν ὁ υἱός, ἀλλ' οὐκ ἀληθινὸς θεός. εἷς γὰρ ἐστι καὶ μόνος ἀληθινὸς θεὸς διὰ τὸ μὴ ἔχειν πρὸ αὐτοῦ τινα. Eusebius's letter was dated by Hans-Georg Opitz to *ca.* 318, and is only fragmentarily extant.

19 Athanasius, *De synodis* 17, 3: ὁ δὲ ἀπὸ Καισαρείας τῆς Παλαιστίνης Εὐσέβιος γράφων πρὸς Εὐφρατίωνα τόν ἐπίσκοπον οὐκ ἐφοβήθη φανερῶς εἰπεῖν ὅτι 'ὁ Χριστὸς οὐκ ἔστιν ἀληθινὸς θεός'.

20 Athanasius, *De decretis* 6, 1–2.

21 The one exception is the text composed by the Westerners at Serdica (343), but it is doubtful whether this text had ever been intended as a "creed". See Parvis, *Marcellus of Ancyra and the Lost Years of the Arian Controversy*, 236–239.

22 On Basil and the Homoiousians, see Winrich Löhr, *Die Entstehung der homöischen und homöusianischen Kirchenparteien: Studien zur Synodalgeschichte des 4. Jahrhunderts* (Bonn: Wehle,1986), and *idem*, "A Sense of Tradition: The Homoiousian Church Party", in *Arianism After Arius. Essays on the Development of the Fourth Century Trinitarian Conflicts*, ed. Michel Barnes and Daniel H. Williams (Edinburgh: T&T Clark,1993): 81–100. See also Timothy D. Barnes, "*A Note* on the Term *Homoiousios*", *Zeitschrift für Antikes Christentum* 10 (2006): 276–285, and Mark DelCogliano, "George of Laodicea: A Historical Reassessment", *Journal of Ecclesiastical History* 62.4 (2011): 667–692.

23 Athanasius, *De synodis* 26, VI, 1--3. "Like in all things" to the Father is close to Eusebius of Caesarea's stance at least from the 330s. See for references and discussion Mark DelCogliano, "Eusebian Theologies of the Son as Image of God before 341", *Journal of Early Christian Studies* 14.4 (2006): 459–484.

24 Athanasius, *De synodis* 28, 6.

25 See Xavier Morales, "Basil of Ancyra's Treatise on Faith: Confirming the Authorship", *Vigiliae Christianae* 72.1 (2018): 71–92.

26 Epiphanius, *Panarion* 73.3, 1–3; Engl. transl. Frank Williams, Epiphanius of Salamis, *Panarion* (Brill: Leiden, 2013). Williams's translation will be reproduced with minor changes hereafter.

27 Epiphanius, *Panarion* 73. 4.

28 Epiphanius, *Panarion* 73. 6, 8.

29 Epiphanius, *Panarion* 73.5, 5–7.

30 Epiphanius, *Panarion* 73.5, 3:

> But the church has believed that God is not only a creator of creatures —Jews and Greeks understand this—but is also the Father of an Only-begotten. He possesses not only his creative activity whereby he is understood to be a creator, but a generative activity peculiar and unique to himself, whereby we understand him to be the Father of a unique Offspring.

31 Epiphanius, *Panarion* 73.11, 1.

32 Epiphanius, *Panarion* 73.7, 6–7.

33 Epiphanius, *Panarion* 73.8, 8 and 9, 6–7.

34 Epiphanius, *Panarion* 73.12, 1.

35 Epiphanius, *Panarion* 73.16, 1.

36 Epiphanius, *Panarion* 73. 17, 1.

37 Epiphanius, *Panarion* 73. 19, 1 *sq*.

38 Epiphanius, *Panarion* 73.73.3.3; 73.7.6; 73.10.9; 73.11.3; This is a point already noticed by scholars. See for instance Xavier Morales in his '"*Introduction*"' to Athanase d'Alexandrie, *Lettre sur les Synodes. Synodale d'Ancyre. Basile d'Ancyre, Traité sur la foi, ed. and trans.* Annick Martin, and Xavier Morales, SC 563 (Paris: Cerf, 2013): 109–110.

39 Epiphanius, *Panarion* 73.9.7:

> For, I say again, as he was not brought to identity with men in the likeness of men and of sinful flesh, but, for the reasons given, became like the essence of the flesh, so, by being made like in essence to the Father who begot him, the Son will not bring his essence to identity with the Father, but to likeness to [him].

40 Epiphanius, *Panarion* 73.8.7.

41 Epiphanius, *Panarion* 73.9.5:

> As he was 'like' the flesh in being flesh and subject to the passions of the flesh, and yet was not the same, in the sense that, as God, he is not 'the form' of 'the God' but the form of 'God', and 'equal', not to 'the God' but to 'God'. Nor does he with full sovereignty like the Father. For as he was not to sin a man, and yet behaved tike a man, 'For whatsoever the Father doeth, the Son also doeth'.
>
> Cf. ibidem10.4.

42 Basil also says the Son is "like in nature" to the Father. See Epiphanius, *Panarion* 73, 19, 5: "And in understanding a Son of God to be God, we also understand the said Son of God to be of like nature (ὅμοιον ... κατὰ τὴν φύσιν) with Him whose Son he is understood to be." *Cf. ibidem* 9, 6.

43 *E.g.* Mark DelCogliano, "George of Laodicea: A Historical Reassessment' Reassessment", *Journal of Ecclesiastical History* 62.4 (2011): 687–690.

44 Tikhon Alexander Pino, "Like Us in All Things but Sin: Basil of Ancyra and the *Homoiousion*", *Journal of Early Christian Studies* 27.1 (2019): 93: "Thus, even if he has not arrived at a distinction between substance and person, he is nevertheless attempting to juggle the simultaneous unity and difference in Father and Son."

45 See Jonannes Zachhuber, "Basil and the Three-Hypostases Tradition. Reconsidering the origins of Cappadocian theology", *Zeitschrift für Antikes Christentum* 5.1 (2001): 65–85.

Bibliography

Ancient Sources

Aetius, Syntagmation, ed. and trans. Lionel R. Wickham, 'The Syntagmation of Aetius the Anomean', *Journal of Theological Studies* (n. s.) 19.2 (1968): 540–549.

Athanase d'Alexandrie, *Lettre sur les Synodes. Synodale d'Ancyre. Basile d'Ancyre, Traité sur la foi, ed. and trans.* Annick Martin, and Xavier Morales, SC 563 (Paris: Cerf, 2013).

Athanasius Werke: ——— I. *Die Dogmatischen Schriften*, ed. Martin Tetz (*Epistula ad episcopos Aegypti et Libyae*, Karin Metzler, Dirk Uwe Hansen, Kyriakos Savvidis, Berlin: De Gruyter, 1996; *Orationes* I *et* II *contra arianos*, Karin Metzler, Kyriakos Savvidis, Berlin: De Gruyter, 1998; *Oratio* III *contra arianos*, Karin Metzler, Kyriakos Savvidis, Berlin: De Gruyter, 2000).

——— II. *Die Apologien*, ed. Hans-Georg Opitz (*De Decretis*, *De Sententia Dionysii*, *Apologia de fuga sua*, *Apologia secunda*, *Epistula encyclica*, *De morte Arii*, *Epistula ad monachos*, *Historia arianorum*, *De Synodis*, *Apologia ad Constantium*, Berlin: De Gruyter, 1935–1941).

——— III. *Urkunden zur Geschichte des arianischen Streites* 318–328, ed. Hans-Georg Opitz (Berlin: De Gruyter, 1934–1935).

Basile de Césarée, *Contre Eunome* suivi de Eunome, *Apologie, ed. and trans.* Bernard Sesboüe, Georges-Matthieu de Durand, and Louis Doutreleau, SC 299 and 305 (Paris: Cerf, 1982–1983).

Epiphanius of Salamis, *Panarion*, ed. Karl Holl, GCS 37 (Leipzig: Hinrichs Verlag, 1933); trans. Frank Williams, NHMS 63 and 76 (Leiden: Brill, 2008–2013).

Eunomius of Cyzicus, *Apology*, ed. and trans. Richard P. Vaggione, in Eunomius, *The Extant Works* (Oxford: Clarendon Press, 1987).

Socrates de Constantinople. *Histoire ecclésiastique, livre I*, trans. Pierre Périchon, and Pierre Maraval, SC 477 (Paris: Cerf, 2004).

Secondary Literature

Anatolios, Khaled, *Retrieving Nicaea. The Development and Meaning of Trinitarian Doctrine* (Grand Rapids, MI: Baker Academic, 2011).

Ayres, Lewis, *Nicaea and Its Legacy: An Approach to Fourth-Century Trinitarian Theology* (Oxford: Oxford University Press, 2004).

Ayres, Lewis, '*Athanasius*' Initial *Defense* of the Term *homoousios*: Rereading the *De Decretis*', *Journal of Early Christian Studies* 12.3 (2004): 337–359.

Behr, John, *The Formation of Christian Theology, Vol. 2: The Nicene Faith* (Crestwood, NY: St. Vladimir's Seminary Press, 2004).

Barnes, Timothy D., '*A Note* on the Term *Homoiousios*', *Zeitschrift für Antikes Christentum* 10 (2006): 276–285.

Behr, John, *The Formation of Christian Theology, Vol. 2: The Nicene Faith* (Crestwood, NY: St. Vladimir's Seminary Press, 2004).

DelCogliano, Mark, 'Eusebian Theologies of the Son as Image of God before 341', *Journal of Early Christian Studies* 14.4 (2006): 459–484.

DelCogliano, Mark, 'George of Laodicea: A Historical Reassessment', *Journal of Ecclesiastical History* 62.4 (2011): 667–692.

DelCogliano, Mark, 'The Literary Corpus of George of Laodicea', *Vigiliae Christianae* 65.2 (2011): 150–169.

Edwards, Mark J., *Catholicity and Heresy in the Early Church* (London: Ashgate, 2002).

Edwards, Mark J., 'Alexander of Alexandria and the *Homoousios*', *Vigiliae Christianae* 66.5 (2012): 482–502.

Gwynn, David M., ('Reconstructing the Council of Nicaea', in Young Richard Kim (ed.), *The Cambridge Companion to the Council of Nicaea* (Cambridge: Cambridge University Press, 2006): 90–119.

Heil, Uta, 'Schriften gegen Eusebianer und Homöer: 3.5. D*e decretis Nicaenae synodi*', in Peter Gemeinhart (ed.), *Athanasius Handbuch* (Tübingen: Mohr Siebeck, 2011): 210–214.

Kopecek, Thomas, *A History of Neo-Arianism* (Cambridge, MA: The Philadelphia Patristic Foundation, 1979).

Lienhard, Joseph T. *SJ*, *Contra Marcellum. Marcellus of Ancyra and Fourth-Century Theology* (Washington, D.C.: The Catholic University of America Press, 1999).

Löhr, Winrich, *Die Entstehung der homöischen und homöusianischen Kirchenparteien: Studien zur Synodalgeschichte des 4. Jahrhunderts* (Bonn: Wehle, 1986).

Löhr, Winrich, 'A Sense of Tradition: The Homoiousian Church Party', in Michel Barnes, Daniel H. Williams (ed.), *Arianism After Arius. Essays on the Development of the Fourth Century Trinitarian Conflicts* (Edinburgh: T&T Clark, 1993): 81–100.

Morales, Xavier, *La théologie trinitaire d'Athanase d'Alexandrie* (Paris: Institut d'Etudes Augustiniennes, 2006).

Morales, Xavier, *Introduction* to *Basile d'Ancyre, Traité sur la foi*, 107–114.

Morales, Xavier, 'Basil of Ancyra's Treatise on Faith: Confirming the Authorship', *Vigiliae Christianae* 72.1 (2018): 71–92.

Morales, Xavier, *Introduction to Basile d'Ancyre, Traité sur la foi, ed. and trans.* Annick Martin, and Xavier Morales, SC 563 (Paris: Cerf, 2013): 107–114.

Parvis, Sara, *Marcellus of Ancyra and the Lost Years of the Arian Controversy* (Oxford: Oxford University Press, 2006).

Parvis, Sara, 'The Reception of Nicaea and *Homoousios* to 360', in Young Richard Kim (ed.), *The Cambridge Companion to the Council of Nicaea*, (Cambridge: Cambridge University Press, 2021): 225–255.

Pino, Tikhon Alexander, 'Like Us in All Things but Sin: Basil of Ancyra and the *Homoiousion*', *Journal of Early Christian Studies* 27.1(2019): 85–97.

Zachhuber, Jonannes, 'Basil and the Three-Hypostases Tradition. Reconsidering the Origins of Cappadocian Theology', *Zeitschrift für Antikes Christentum* 5.1 (2001): 65–85.

6 Questioning St. Gregory of Nyssa's Anthropology and Theory of Sexuality in *On the Making of Man*

Florin Toader Tomoioagă

Introductory Remarks

St. Gregory of Nyssa's commentary on man's creation is a well-known and much-debated topic in the field of Patristic theology. His anthropology, scattered in different ascetical, philosophical, and dogmatic works, is interpreted and reinterpreted by modern scholars in surprisingly different and contradictory ways. The reason behind this passionate and often harsh debate is, on one side, the rise of interest for the writings of the Cappadocian Father starting with the beginning of the last century, and on the other side, the permanence of the anthropological theme. Many prophetical (and likely prescient) voices advocate that the twenty-first century will be the century of anthropology in theological research and beyond. We ourselves witness this happening, with the contemporary social and bio-ethical challenges addressing the modern and pre-modern essentially Christian worldview and definition of the human being. Although St. Gregory's epoch was primarily the century of Christology, the topic of the human being was also central – precisely because the Logos became man and therefore the Fathers of the Church had to shape a Christological anthropology. Then and now, in order to answer adequately to the three most important philosophical questions – "What can I know? What ought I to do? What may I hope?" – one must first answer the serious question: "What is the human being?" A fresh look at the Bishop of Nyssa's thought on this topic is theologically challenging, intellectually demanding, and will deepen the significance of the questions for our own world now.

One of the most controversial aspects of his thinking is the way St. Gregory pictures the human condition, especially the human body and sexuality. There is a general agreement among scholars that in the Gregorian writings human sexuality and reproduction are non-essential for the definition of man as *imago Dei*, despite their own respective positive or negative evaluation of this vision. According to the Bishop of Nyssa, human sexuality is secondary – accidental for human beings and intended by God only through the perspective of Adam and Eve's fall from paradise. He imagined that if the primordial man had not fallen, he wouldn't have needed sexual

DOI: 10.4324/9781003273592-6

reproduction for the perpetuation of the human race, but would have had an angelic-like way of multiplication. Therefore, human sexuality is only emergency equipment adapted by God to man's actual lapsarian condition. This view, one must recognize, is highly problematic.

But what is most striking in the Orthodox and non-Orthodox scholars' examination of these aspects of the Gregorian thinking is the fact that both sides don't seem to be aware of the consequences it has on Orthodox anthropology and ethics. Apart from being a simple matter of theological speculation, it influenced, mediated through another great Patristic writers such as St. Maximus the Confessor, not only the anthropology of Eastern Christianity but also its believers' *modus vivendi*. Rightly, Protestant and Catholic scholars mention the hypothetical character of St. Gregory's speculation about the origins of the human sexuality, a character otherwise explicitly and humbly recognized by the author.[1] The problem appears when the St. Gregory's Orthodox interpreters, neglecting the hypothetical character of these assumptions postulated mainly in the work *On the Making of Man*, shape a whole anthropology and ethics without a critical interpretation of these ideas. The purpose of my paper is to analyze St. Gregory of Nyssa's view of human nature – especially in terms of its distinction between male and female – and to gesture towards its implications for Orthodox anthropology.

The Doctrine of Man's Double Creation and the Origin of Human Sexuality – Classical and Contemporary Interpretations

The so called "doctrine of man's double creation" in St. Gregory of Nyssa implies two different moments in the creation of man: the first one is the intention of God to create the human being (Gen.1:26) and the second one is the accomplishment of this intention (Gen.1:27). Between the two moments, there is a difference. While in Gen.1:26 God intends to create human beings "in our image, in our likeness", in the next verse (Gen. 1:27) "God created mankind in his own image... man and female he created them". The last part of the verse, which states the sexual differentiation of the humankind is apparently a new element added to the human being. The "divine image" is concretely bestowed upon the human being as "man and female". Here, St. Gregory notices a gap, which is coherent with his pleading in favour of the monastic life (virginity) as a return to the pure "image" and overcoming the sexual differentiation. In this section of the study, I focus on the academic evaluation of some fragments from the *On the Making of Man* in this direction.

In every Patristic author's anthropological thinking, the interpretation of Genesis 1:26–27 is essential because it reveals human being's origin, condition, and meaning. This is also true in the case of St. Gregory. The great dilemma he tries to elucidate is how man is spiritually made in the image of God and simultaneously, at the biological level, shares with the animals their condition. Gerhart B. Ladner noted that

> these two verses (Genesis 1:26 and Genesis 1:27) form the hub around which, for him, the body-mind relationship turns. They define the Archimedian point from which he tries to move the great dilemma between man's spiritual image-likeness to God and his involvement in the irrational tangles of this world.[2]

In Christian spirituality, especially of the East, the beginning is often a revelation of the end: whether we speak about the creation of the world, of man or of his paradisiacal state, the fulfillment of creation brought by Christ's Resurrection in the world is partially a restoration (although always more than that) of the beginning, when all creation and human being were designed to be in harmony with God.

In *On the Making of Man*, Fr. John Behr identifies three "aetiological passages" – texts that deal with the origin of human division into male and female. He writes:

> The burning question for Gregory in these passages is how human beings, who now exist in misery, can be called like God, Who exists in blessedness; for although Scripture asserts that humankind was created in the image, there is clearly no similarity between humankind's present existence and that of God (*HO*16.3–4, 180bd).[3]

The main issue is the contradiction between the idealistic beginning of human existence stated by Scripture and the misery, pain, suffering, and disharmony that sequently affect it. St. Gregory tries to save the dignity of man by fulfilling the gaps offered by the elliptic language of the Scripture. As we will see, such an endeavour is worthy but risky.

Commenting on Genesis 1:26–27, St. Gregory states in a well-known passage:

> We must, then, examine the words carefully: for we find, if we do so, that that which was made 'in the image' is one thing, and that which is now manifested in wretchedness is another. 'God created man,' it says; 'in the image of God created He him'. There is an end of the creation of that which was made 'in the image': then it makes a resumption of the account of creation, and says, 'male and female created He them.' I presume that everyone knows that this is a departure from the Prototype: for 'in Christ Jesus,' as the apostle says, 'there is neither male nor female.' Yet the phrase declares that man is thus divided.[4]

Interpreting the creation narrative of Genesis, St. Gregory tries to explain what seemed to be an inner contradiction of the biblical text. God created human beings in His image, but in reality such a generic being does not exist; concretely, it is either man or woman. Here is the apparent logical contradiction: since the Divine is asexual, and we were made in His image, what could be the origin of the human division into male and female? Moreover, since "there is neither male nor female... in Christ", why human being is thus divided? (Gal. 3:28), The Bishop of Nyssa tries to imagine an appropriate answer to these seemingly dilemmatic statements of the Bible. But in this passage, he transforms St. Paul's moral argument (different peoples, social categories or men and women are equals in Christ) into an ontological arguments ("the image" presupposes a pure human being, neither male nor female).

Marc Cortez summarizes and explains the above passage in this way:

> In other words, God first declares his intention to create beings in his image (v. 26), an intention that finds its creative fulfilment in the first half of the following verse. But the narrative continues with the addition of 'male and female he created them', something not mentioned in the expression of divine intent. To Gregory, this suggests that the verse contains two logical moments in creation: (1) God's determination to create humans in his image and (2) the addition of sexual differentiation to that original creative vision.[5]

The first logical moment corresponding to Genesis 1:26 and to the first part of verse 27 coincides with a virtual creation of all humankind. In his interpretation, St. Gregory follows and yet modifies Philo of Alexandria, who states in *De opificio mundi* that the creation of man according to Genesis 1:26 "was an ideal, a generic, a typical creation, and that man thus created is an intellectual being only, incorporeal, sexless, immortal by nature".[6] For St. Gregory, in contrast, the whole of humanity is contemplated by God in the beginning, and thus virtually created. In his words,

> the entire plenitude of humanity was included by the God of all, by His power of foreknowledge, as it were in one body, and that this is what the text teaches us which says, 'God created man, in the image of God created He him'.[7]

Commenting on the passage from *HO*16, 7, Jean Daniélou offers its classical interpretation: the division of the sexes in male and female was superadded while "mortality, sexuality, all biological life is strange to the true 'nature' of man".[8]

St. Gregory continues his explanation of the human being's compound nature by integrating the intelligent/rational element and the irrational one:

> While two natures – the Divine and incorporeal nature, and the irrational life of brutes – are separated from each other as extremes, human

> nature is the mean between them: for in the compound nature of man we may behold a part of each of the natures I have mentioned– of the Divine, the rational and intelligent element, which does not admit the distinction of male and female; of the irrational, our bodily form and structure, divided into male and female: for each of these elements is certainly to be found in all that partakes of human life.[9]

Hans Urs von Balthasar comments that here "Gregory of Nyssa's approach, according to which God created the consequences of disobedience – sensuality, and especially sexuality – along with human nature, in his foreknowledge (κατὰ πρόγνωσιν) of sin",[10] influenced St. Maximus the Confessor. He notices that "in the anthropology of Gregory of Nyssa, the sexual organs are both a (precreated) consequence of sin and a means of limiting the self-destructive tendencies of creation and providing for the continuity of the human race".[11] If this is the case, the definition of the human being is highly questioned. Man is finally something else that what he/she was supposed to be according to God's "ideal" project.

But Fr. John Behr proposes a different reading of St. Gregory's statements, apart from the classical one belonging to Jean Daniélou and Hans Urs von Balthasar. Quoting the above passage, *HO* 16, 9, he affirms that:

> Gregory, commenting on Gen. 1.26–27, is speaking in an unambiguously prelapsarian context; there is not even a hint of considerations pertaining to a Fall, even one that is as yet only divinely foreseen. Humankind, the image of God, was created male and female, which has no reference in the Archetype, but is part of its 'community and kinship' (κοινωνίαν... συγγένειαν) with irrational animals. Although, following the order of Gen. 1.27, humankind's 'community and kinship' with the irrational animals is described as succeeding their creation in the image of God, there is no sense of it being 'economic,' nor is it limited to the function of procreation – it is simply the 'particular characteristics of human nature' (τῆς ἀνθρωπίνης φύσεως τὰ ἰδιώματα) as distinct from the divine Nature. This addition is a necessary part of humankind's medial position, essential to their divinely ordained function, and therefore, unquestionably prelapsarian.[12]

Fr. John Behr is right here: in a clearly non-lapsarian context, St. Gregory affirms that the human being was created as a mixture of spiritual and material elements, corresponding to the image of God and to the nature of animals; since the divine Archetype is sexless, the division of the human being into male and female, in this context, is morally neutral and is similar to that of the animals. Fr. Behr's general aim in his article "The Rational Animal: A Rereading of Gregory of Nyssa's De hominis opificio" is to demonstrate that the sexes were not created in view of the fall and that the only way of multiplication of human beings is the one generally known, *i.e.*

in asexual manner. As interpreted by Fr. Behr, the angelic-like mode of multiplication suggested by St. Gregory means nothing else that the prevalence of reason/spirit over sensation and sensuality – a position contrary to the classical interpretation.

However, in this text, St. Gregory does not present the full picture of the origins of human sexuality, as John Behr presupposes. The Cappadocian Father gradually develops the subject, which receives its full answer in *HO* 17, 4–5. While Fr. John Behr invites us to read *On the Making of Man* Chapter 17, 4–5 through this prism, this fragment (*HO* 16, 9) must be understood as an incomplete statement that receives full elaboration in Chapter 17.

Here is the explanation of the cause that is the origin of human sexuality, in the first aetiological text:

> ...perceiving beforehand by His power of foreknowledge what, in a state of independence and freedom, is the tendency of the motion of man's will – as He saw, I say, what would be devised for His image the distinction of male and female, which has no reference to the Divine Archetype, but, as we have said, is an approximation to the less rational nature.[13]

Here, St. Gregory suggests that God created the distinction of male and female foreseeing the fall. Sexuality is linked to the fall. This text of St. Gregory and other similar passages are hard to reconcile with Fr. Behr's denial that sexuality was added as an "economic measure".

In the second aetiological passage, the Bishop of Nyssa develops his earlier statements. He reiterates the idea of man's double creation, asserting that sexuality was added by God in mind with Adam and Eve's (future) disobedience and fall from Paradise. God's intention was to bestow upon humanity an angelic way of life; accordingly, had the primordial man not fallen, he would have had an angelic-like manner of reproduction; but foreseeing the forefathers' fall and the peril that the human race would not be able to perpetuate, God fashioned human sexuality similar to that of animals as a solution fitted to their (future) lapsarian state. St. Gregory states:

> ... He Who brought all things into being and fashioned Man as a whole by His own will to the Divine image, did not wait to see the number of souls made up to its proper fullness by the gradual additions of those coming after [here, of course, it is about the virtual simultaneous creation of the *pleroma* of all souls, of all humanity in the image of God[14]]; but while looking upon the nature of man in its entirety and fullness by the exercise of His foreknowledge, and bestowing upon it a lot exalted and equal to the angels, since He saw beforehand by His all-seeing power the failure of their will to keep a direct course to what is good, and its consequent declension from the angelic life, in order that the

> multitude of human souls might not be cut short by its fall from that mode by which the angels were increased and multiplied – for this reason, I say, He formed for our nature that contrivance for increase which befits those who had fallen into sin, implanting in mankind, instead of the angelic majesty of nature, that animal and irrational mode by which they now succeed one another.[15]

Eugenio Corsini notes that the distinction of the sexes by God was "surajoutée" to the image from the very beginning, "justement dans la prévision du péché qui aurait empêché le mode dereproduction prévu pour les homes".[16] It is, therefore, a "modification" of the original plan of God "mais tout cela s'est passé – si l'on peuts'exprimer ainsi en parlant de Dieu – sur le plan théorique et nonsur le plan pratique, comme s'il était revenu sur son oeuvre et l'avaitmodifiée".[17] Despite Corsini's statements, the implicit danger of this vision ishard to miss: sexuality is an necessary "compromise" made by God in order to allow man's multiplication on the Earth, not an organic component of the human being. This state is somehow unnatural for the human being – not because he/she was not created as such as a sexual being, but because God had something else in His "mind" while contemplating an ideal creation of the human being. The correcting "solution" of this state is almost suggested here through the invocation of the angelic life: celibacy.

In the opening part of the above-quoted passage and in other Gregorian passages, some people may read the first creation through the Origen's lens, as a real pre-existence of the souls before their embodiment. This is not the case. Following Jean Daniélou, *The Brill Dictionary of Gregory of Nyssa* explains that

> It must however be noted that, in Gregory, the first creation does not refer to the real preexistence of an archetypical human being in the world of ideas, but indicates the intentional preexistence of the totality of human beings in the divine mind.
>
> (J. Daniélou, 62)[18]

Between the first and the second creation, there is a great difference not only temporally but ontologically. Indeed, the first one is outside time and ideal, irrespective of man's fall, while the second one is in time – in history – taking into account the possibility of man's fall (although not necessarily fated or unavoidable). In conclusion, *The Brill Dictionary of Gregory of Nyssa* writes:

> The first creation of the human *pleroma* is thus distinct from the creation of the historical Adam, in which the distinction of the sexes is found, without however sin being present, since this was before the fall, and grace preserved the first parents.[19]

Indeed, the distinction of the sexes is not related in Nyssa to the actual fall of man because is prior to it; still, the fall is determinant for this distinction, although it has not happened yet. This view gives the impression that the creation and the fall happened in the same moment – in other words, they coincide.

Fr. John Behr glosses the above-quoted text from *HO*17, 4:

> Such a fall from this angelic state, and the mode of increase appropriate to it, to the level of animals, would have curtailed the completion of the human race, for human(kind) (at this stage of Gregory's explanation) would have had no essential kinship with the animals. So God implanted the bestial mode of succession in human nature, a mode which is suited to the state of those in sin, those who no longer look to the good, even though human(kind) has not as yet fallen. But God's own providential act, implanting 'the bestial and irrational mode of succession' in human nature, does not make human beings bestial. Rather it is their own inclination to the merely material that renders human beings truly bestial.[20]

According to Fr. Behr, the animal mode of succession is fitted to the humankind lapsarian state, but man's freedom produces the fall into materiality (sensuality, instincts) and renders him truly bestial. He tries to prove that by the expression "that mode by which the angels were increased and multiplied", St. Gregory is not speaking about an asexual multiplication, but by one marked by the power of reason over the irrational part of man. In Behr's view, "sexuality itself...is explicitly stated to be the only means of human increase".[21]

For the former Dean of St. Vladimir's Orthodox Seminary, there is an unanswered question in the Gregorian work, although it is raised:

> The question which Gregory's veiled thought in *HO*17.4–5 raises, but does not answer clearly, is whether, prior to their inclination to the material, their *epistrophe*, human beings would have multiplied using the dynamics of the irrational mode of increase implanted by God in their nature but in a mode appropriate to their rational, or 'angelic' dignity, or whether any utilization of these irrational dynamics already constitutes an *epistrophe* so that humans would have multiplied in paradise using other means. Gregory's comments on the angelic mode of increase, in the first part of Chapter 17, and the third aetiological passage, in Chapter 22, give clearer indications of his enigmatically couched thought.[22]

The whole demonstration of St. Gregory is that a return to the "original" man, angelic-like and undifferentiated sexually, is possible because this was the first man God had in His mind before creation.[23] The Cappadocian

Father has neither a "veiled thought", nor an "enigmatically couched thought" in *On the Making of Man.* He clearly affirms an angelic, alternative way of man's reproduction, had he not fallen. We will explore it in the next section of the article, dealing with Chapter 17.

The Definition of Human Sexuality from an Eschatological Perspective

Not only the beginning of human history but also its end, as it is presented by the Bible, serves to shape St. Gregory's original anthropology. This is due to the fact that the beginning (the creation) and the end (the resurrection) correspond in his thinking. The end is a restoration of the primordial state of the universe and, therefore, of humankind. Thus, St. Gregory tries to bridge the apparent gap between the idea of man created in the image of God and man's division into male and female by appealing to eschatology. There he finds the solution to the following question: how man's multiplication on the Earth would have been had humanity not fallen? The answer is simple: similar to that of the angels. It is inspired by the Lord's answer to the Sadducees regarding the woman of many marriages: "for in the resurrection," He says, "they neither marry, nor are given in marriage, neither can they die any more, for they are equal to the angels, and are the children of God, being the children of the resurrection" – cf. Mt. 22:30–31, Lk. 20:35–36 and by Saint Paul's affirmation that in Jesus Christ, "there is neither male nor female" (Gal. 3:28). Corroborating the eschatological condition of the human being which lacks the necessity of sexual reproduction and affirms the irrelevance of male or female' status in Christ, the Cappadocian Father concludes that the angelic life must have been the original intention of God for humans. He postulates that:

> Now the resurrection promises us nothing else than the restoration of the fallen to their ancient state; for the grace we look for is a certain return to the first life, bringing back again to Paradise him who was cast out from it.[24]

Had man not fallen, he would have had a similar manner of multiplication to that of the angels, i.e. sexless and beyond human understanding. This idea is developed in a fragment in which St. Gregory answers the objections of his opponents which hold that the primordial sin was a chance for humanity's increase in number, and therefore was a positive thing:

> Yet while, as has been said, there is no marriage among them, the armies of the angels are in countless myriads; for so Daniel declared in his visions: so, in the same way, if there had not come upon us as the result of sin a change for the worse, and removal from equality with the angels, neither should we have needed marriage that we might

> multiply but whatever the mode of increase in the angelic nature is (unspeakable and inconceivable by human conjectures, except that it assuredly exists), it would have operated also in the case of men, who were 'made a little lower than the angels', to increase mankind to the measure determined by its Maker.[25]

For Fr. John Behr, the term "marriage" used in this biblical and Gregorian context has a specific, negative significance. It doesn't have the generally accepted meaning, but denotes the human attempt to overcome physical death through reproduction – through children. Thus he writes that

> Gregory retains the sense of the term 'marriage' as it is used by his opponents: a means of succession impelled by the fear of death, a distortion of the proper use of our irrational and animal nature by a mind which has itself become impassioned, subject to irrational fears, bestial. This is also the sense of Christ's answer to the Sadducees: equal to the angels and so no longer dying, the children of the resurrection will have no need for a marriage governed by the necessity of succession to the point of submerging the personal ('word-bearing') element within marriage—marrying seven times for the sake of descendants. This is the context of Gregory's answer: 'neither should we have needed [such] marriage that we might multiply.' Gregory does not attempt to redefine 'marriage,' but does firmly assert that there was another mode in which the human race might have increased.[26]

One must recognize that Fr. Behr's interpretation is inappropriate. "Marriage" in Mt. 22:30–31, Lk. 20:35–36, and in this Gregorian passage is a means of perpetuating human life on the earth; the term does not have depreciative connotations, connected to the fear of death or the irrational, animal nature of man, as in Fr. Behr's interpretation. If this forced interpretation fails, the whole argument of Fr. Behr fails; and it fails indeed, because from St. Gregory's perspective, marriage is seen as the normal mode of multiplication for human beings while its opposite, the angelic mode of multiplication, would have been adequate if the man would have not fallen.

There is a third aetiological passage in *HO*22, 2, 3, 4. After analyzing it, Fr. J. Behr concludes:

> Human beings never had the possibility to multiply in the way that the angels do, but rather they could have increased in a *manner* (τρόπος) similar to the angels, employing their medial nature, partaking in both the rational and irrational, in a properly human manner. It therefore remains within human beings' own determination whether to use this kinship with the irrational in an angelic, that is, rational, truly human

> or 'word-bearing' manner, or to overturn this order by becoming truly, or merely, bestial, and so limit their use of their sexuality to the bestial need, for instance, to provide succession or any of the other perversions dreamt up by the 'evil husbandry of the mind' (*HO*18.4, 193b) in its impassioned attachment to the irrational.[27]

But actually, in this fragment, Fr. Behr applies contemporary Orthodox anthropological teaching to St. Gregory's understanding of sexuality. It spiritualizes it. He reads St. Gregory from a contemporary perspective and thus "corrects" him. It is true that "Human beings never had the possibility to multiply in the way that the angels do"[28] and that they use their sexuality in a bestial way. But St. Gregory specifically affirms that the sexual multiplication of human beings is borrowed from the animal nature and is strange to the true nature of human beings:

> since we may be sure that, if He had bestowed on man, before imprinting on our nature the distinction of male and female, the power for increase conveyed by this utterance, we should not have needed this form of generation by which the brutes are generated.[29]

In the quoted article, Fr. John Behr affirmed a few pages before:

> In this perspective, when Gregory speculates about the possibility of human generation in an 'angelic mode,' he is not suggesting that human beings could have multiplied in paradise by means of an asexual, angelic reproduction. Rather, he is hinting at the possibility, once the mind is free from passion and vice, for a restored use of human sexuality, an exercise of sexuality under the full autonomy of reason, in an angelic mode, in which the human being fulfills its purpose in creation of uplifting and integrating the life of the body and the senses with reason and the divine.[30]

But as we noticed above, sexuality itself is an afterthought of God, in view of the fall and, in Nyssa, the discussion is above its passionate or impassionate character. The problem lies elsewhere. Marriage and sexuality are opposed by St. Gregory to an angelic way of multiplication, although, understanding the negative implication of such a view on anthropology, John Behr tries to deny this opposition.

Martin Cortez notes that

> Gregory's understanding of the human person is framed by three theological loci: the *imago Dei,* the incarnation, and the resurrection. And it is not difficult to see why, since all three loci introduce challenging questions about what means to be human.[31]

His view is contrary to that of John Behr. Summarizing the different hermeneutical approaches of St. Gregory's thinking, Martin Cortez reaches the following conclusions:

> Although Gregory does not unpack every step in his thinking, the logic appears to move something like this:

1 The *imago Dei* is what is most essential to being human.
2 The *imago Dei* is fundamentally about human persons participating in and manifesting God's goodness, which includes all of his divine attributes.
3 God does not include sexual differentiation as one of his good attributes.
4 Therefore, sexual differentiation is not a part of the *imago Dei.*
5 Therefore, sexual differentiation is not a part of essential humanity.[32]

St. Gregory confirms the above summary of his thinking. In *HO*18.1 he states that the irrational and passional character of the human life has its cause in its kinship with animal life:

> For I think that from this beginning all our passions issue as from a spring, and pour their flood over man's life; and an evidence of my words is the kinship of passions which appears alike in ourselves and in the brutes; for it is not allowable to ascribe the first beginnings of our constitutional liability to passion to that human nature which was fashioned in the Divine likeness; but as brute life first entered into the world, and man, for the reason already mentioned, took something of their nature (I mean the mode of generation), he accordingly took at the same time a share of the other attributes contemplated in that nature; for the likeness of man to God is not found in anger, nor is pleasure a mark of the superior nature; cowardice also, and boldness, and the desire of gain, and the dislike of loss, and all the like, are far removed from that stamp which indicates Divinity.[33]

The preceding passage follows *HO*17, 4, where, as we have noticed, St. Gregory clearly affirms that sexuality was added to make possible human reproduction in the perspective of Adam and Eve' fall from the angelic way of life. The passage opens with a revelatory question, which the Cappadocian Father tries to answer in the whole treatise *HO*: "how it was that after the making of His image God contrived for His work the distinction of male and female".[34]

The correspondence between the primordial state of the human being and its eschatological state implies not only that the passions but also the afflictions that characterize us are superadded to it:

> we will say that the Resurrection is '*the reconstitution of our nature in its original form*'. But in that form of life, of which God Himself

> was the Creator, it is reasonable to believe that there was neither age nor infancy nor any of the sufferings arising from our present various infirmities, nor any kind of bodily affliction whatever. It is reasonable, I say, to believe that God was the Creator of none of these things, but that man was a thing divine before his humanity got within reach of the assault of evil; that then, however, with the inroad of evil, all these afflictions also broke in upon him.[35]

In reality, the afflictions – "coats of skins" – are the result of the passions and will be removed at the Resurrection:

> Just so our nature, becoming passional, had to encounter all the necessary results of a life of passion: but when it shall have started back to that state of passionless blessedness, it will no longer encounter the inevitable results of evil tendencies. Seeing, then, that all the infusions of the life of the brute into our nature were not in us before our humanity descended through the touch of evil into passions, most certainly, when we abandon those passions, we shall abandon all their visible results (…) when we have cast off that dead unsightly tunic made from the skins of brutes and put upon us (for I take the "coats of skins" to mean that conformation belonging to a brute nature with which we were clothed when we became familiar with passionate indulgence), shall, along with the casting off of that tunic, fling from us all the belongings that were round us of that skin of a brute; and such accretions are sexual intercourse, conception, parturition, impurities, suckling, feeding, evacuation, gradual growth to full size, prime of life, old age, disease, and death.[36]

Gerhart B. Ladner summarises these apparently disparate ideas in a single note:

> God according to Genesis 1:27 gave man a mortal and bisexual body because He foresaw how he would act and because He knew that under these circumstances mortality and sexuality would have a remedial function; but neither Adam nor any man had or has to do evil. Only when Adam and Eve actually committed sin did the inferiority of man's bodily constitution make its appearance, symbolized in Holy Scripture by the χιτῶνες δερμάτινοιof Genesis 3:21. As far as its relation to evil is concerned, the body was and is only an instrument and it can be an instrument also of good. In Paradise, before the fall, the body was in full unison with the highest part of the soul, and, after its resurrection, it will again be in harmony with the spirit. On earth the ascetic way of life mystically anticipates man's return to Paradise and must, therefore, tend toward spiritualization of the body and thus toward re-assimilation to God.[37]

The antidote to the fall of human beings into passions is, naturally, within St. Gregory's frame of thinking, the life of virginity. Virginity reverses the process of death, which begins through man's coming into existence by means of lust and passions:

> The physical bringing of children into the world—I speak without wishing to offend—is as much a starting-point of death as of life; because from the moment of birth the process of dying commences. But those who by virginity have desisted from this process have drawn within themselves the boundary line of death, and by their own deed have checked his advance; they have made themselves, in fact, a frontier between life and death, and a barrier too, which thwarts him. If, then, death cannot pass beyond virginity, but finds his power checked and shattered there, it is demonstrated that virginity is a stronger thing than death; and that body is rightly named undying which does not lend its service to a dying world, nor brook to become the instrument of a succession of dying creatures.[38]

For someone who decides to live a virgin life, "conception is no more an iniquity, nor child-bearing a sin", because the birth is a spiritual one, not of the will of the flesh but of God.[39]

Generally, St. Gregory seems not only to underestimate the role of sexuality, but sees it as an emergency equipment adequate to man's fallen state. In order to soften such a harsh conclusion and the consequences that it has on human existence, Marc Cortez explains the "nonessential" character of sexuality contextually, as a relative concept:

> The fact that Gregory view biological sexuality as 'nonessential', however, does not entail the conclusion that it is unimportant. Much of what shapes our identities as human persons is nonessential in the same way. For example, my relationship with my wife is nonessential (I would still have been human without it) yet fundamentally important (it is now an irreplaceable aspect of my particular identity). And Gregory presents biological sexuality in much the same way. Neither does the nonessential nature of biological sexuality mean, for Gregory, the loss of any enduring significance for sexuality in the eschaton. As we have seen, his theology has resources for maintaining that resurrected persons will still be shaped by the material realities of the present body. Just as Macrina will always be marked by having-been-scarred, so I will always be shaped by having-been-male, even as my identity continues to be reshaped and transformed eternally as well. Sarah Coakley thus rightly observes that Gregory has an 'eschatologically oriented theory of gender', though only through an eschatological vision that is thoroughly Christological as well.[40]

The problem, from my point of view, with this "eschatologically oriented theory of gender", is its relationship with the beginning. The creation and the eschatology speck to each other, therefore, if sexuality is only a "safety device", a divine "compromise", human life and history were never intended as such by God, and not because of the fall, but because human being should have never been man and woman. If this idea was indeed in Gregory's mind, one must recognize that it changes the whole picture of human life, history and civilization.

Conclusion

This paper reviewed a few of the main academic readings of St. Gregory's view of human sexuality. These readings, as we see, are different and sometimes divergent. Against a traditional reading, based on Jean Daniélou and Hans Urs von Balthasar, Fr. John Behr proposes a different perspective in an attempt to reconcile contemporary Orthodox understanding of sexuality with that of the Cappadocian Father. But irrespective of how he is interpreted today, St. Gregory was very influential on the anthropology of the Eastern Church, especially as mediated by St. Maximus the Confessor. The Cappadocian Father received his classical interpretation in the work of Jean Daniélou and Hans Urs von Balthasar, and their conclusions are generally accepted in modern and contemporary Orthodox theology, apart from a few distinct voices.

Gerhart B. Ladner strives to prove the inner coherence of St. Gregory of Nyssa's anthropological ideas, which "hinge on the question whether or not believed that it could have been meaningful for man, the spiritual image of God, to have a body even without sin".[41] He concludes that Gregory of Nyssa "saves the dignity of the body as well as that of the mind", because "if... man's creational body was close to spirit, the Gregorian doctrine of the resurrection of the bodies is not inconsistent with his anthropological system".[42] Certainly, he doesn't save the dignity of human sexuality. According to the same author, "Gregory's whole anthropology is directed toward the overcoming of corporeality as it exists in man after the fall".[43]

When taking into consideration *Gen. 1: 26–27*, St. Gregory and his interpreters are basically trying to answer the question: "What is the human being?" The subtle change of perspective brought by the idea that sexual differentiation was introduced into human nature only as a "safety device"[44] in the view of the fall has tremendous implications.

First of all, it changes the definition of the human being, considering it less that the humans God intended to create if man had not fallen.

Second, it changes the goal of the human life. The first implication changes the answer to the question: "What ought I to do?" If God's intention irrespective of the fall was to create a sexless being, the goal of human life must then be celibacy – as a return not only to the paradisiacal state, but also to the model first man intended by God.[45]

In the third place, it blames human sexuality and considers it a necessary evil in the perspective of spiritual life; it reduces it to a purely utilitarian meaning.

In the fourth place, human society, civilization, and history are marred not mainly because of the fall, but because human life itself is different from what God intended for the human beings. Accordingly, *The Brill Dictionary of Gregory of Nyssa* states this fragile balance between the valorization of creation in Nyssa and its connexion with original sin:

> "The sensual forces are nevertheless neutral, and the 'animal' body is also a good creation of God—as well as the 'image' of the image of God in the soul. The positive valorization of corporeality is however obscured through the idealist conception of matter, space and time (*diastema*) in which concrete history appears as a consequence of sin."[46]

As a conclusion, it is a dangerous working thesis to start with in Christian life generally, and in spiritual life particularly. Although in the Orthodox theology this thesis is widespread, it is not a *dogma*. It could be considered only a *theologoumenon*, i.e. an acceptable theological opinion for some Patristic authors or theologians, while disputable for others. Orthodox anthropology should not lay its foundations on this Gregorian hypothesis.

Notes

1 Gerhart B. Ladner, "The Philosophical Anthropology of Saint Gregory of Nyssa", *Dumborton Oaks Papers*, 12 (1958): 93.
2 Ibid., 83.
3 John Behr, "The Rational Animal: A Rereading of Gregory of Nyssa's De hominis opificio", *Journal of Early Christian Studies*, 2 (1999): 233.
4 St. Gregory of Nyssa, "On the Making of Man", XVI, 7, *Nicene and Post-nicene Fathers of the Christian Church*, second series, vol. V, Schaff Philip (Editor), translated by William Moore and Henry Austin Wilson (New York: Charles Scribner's Sons, 1917), 405.
5 Marc Cortez, *Christological Anthropology in Historical Perspective: Ancient and Contemporary Approaches to Theological Anthropology* (Grands Rapids, MI: Zondervan Publishing House, 2016), 46.
6 Gerhart B. Ladner, "The Philosophical Anthropology", 81.
7 St. Gregory of Nyssa, "On the Making of Man", XVI, 17, 406.
8 Jean Daniélou, *Platonisme et théologie mystique: essai sur la doctrine spirituelle de saint Grégoire de Nysse* (Paris: Éditions Montaigne, 1944), 61.
9 St. Gregory of Nyssa, "On the Making of Man", XVI, 9, 405.
10 Hans Urs von Balthasar, *Cosmic Liturgy. The Universe According to Maximus the Confessor*, translated by Brian E. Daley (San Francisco, CA: S.J., Ignatus Press, 2003), 187. PG 91, 1104AB. For a general account of Balthasar's view on Gregory's anthropology, see Hans Urs von Balthasar, *Présence et pensée* (Paris: Beauchesne, 1952, 1988), 25–29, 47–52.
11 Hans Urs von Balthasar, *Cosmic Liturgy*, 191.

12 John Behr, "The Rational Animal", 235–236.
13 St. Gregory of Nyssa, "On the Making of Man", XVI, 14, 406.
14 Gerhart B. Ladner, "The Philosophical Anthropology", 83.
15 St. Gregory of Nyssa, "On the Making of Man", XVII, 4, 407.
16 Eugenio Corsini, "Plérôme humaine et plérôme cosmique chez Grégoire de Nysse", *Écriture et culture philosophique dans la pensée de Grégoire de Nysse*, M. Harl, Editor (Leiden: Brill, 1971), 121.
17 Eugenio Corsini, "Plérôme humaine", 121.
18 *The Brill Dictionary of Gregory of Nyssa*, Lucas Francisco Mateo-Seco and Giulio Maspero (ed.), translated by Seth Cherney (Leiden, Boston, MA: Koninklijke Brill NV: 2010), 43.
19 *The Brill Dictionary of Gregory of Nyssa*, 43.
20 John Behr, "The Rational Animal", 239.
21 Ibid., 243.
22 Ibid., 240.
23 Eugenio Corsini arrives at a different conclusion: "L'état idéal de l'homme parfait, totalement selon l'image, privé de sexe, est une abstraction gratuite, parce que Grégoire n'en parle nulle part: l'unique état de perfection qu'il connaît est celui des premiers parents dans le paradis" ("Plérôme humaine", 122).
24 St. Gregory of Nyssa, "On the Making of Man", XVII, 2, 407.
25 Ibid.
26 John Behr, "The Rational Animal", 241.
27 Ibid., 244–245.
28 Ibid., 244.
29 St. Gregory of Nyssa, "On the Making of Man", XXII, 4, 412.
30 John Behr, "The Rational Animal", 224.
31 Marc Cortez, *Christological Anthropology*, 33.
32 Ibid., 48.
33 St. Gregory of Nyssa, "On the Making of Man", XVIII, 1, 407–408.
34 Ibid., 4, 407.
35 St. Gregory of Nyssa, "On the Soul and the Resurrection", *Nicene and Post-nicene Fathers of the Christian Church*, second series, vol. V, Schaff Philip (Editor), translated by William Moore and Henry Austin Wilson (New York: Charles Scribner's Sons, 1917), 464.
36 Ibid., 464–465.
37 Gerhart B. Ladner, "The Philosophical Anthropology", 93.
38 St. Gregory of Nyssa, "On the Virginity", XIII, *Nicene and Post-nicene Fathers of the Christian Church*, second series, vol. V, Schaff Philip (Editor), translated by William Moore and Henry Austin Wilson (New York: Charles Scribner's Sons, 1917), 359.
39 Ibid., 360.
40 Marc Cortez, *Christological Anthropology*, 55.
41 Gerhart B. Ladner, "The Philosophical Anthropology", 87.
42 Ibid., 91.
43 Ibid., 89.
44 Peter Brown, *The Body and Society. Men, Women and Sexual Renunciation in Early Christianity* (London, Boston, MA: Columbia University Press, 1988), 295.
45 For a detailed discussion on St. Gregory's influence on marriage and it's evaluation in the contemporary Orthodox theology, see Tomoioagă Florin Toader, "St. Gregory of Nyssa's View on the Origin of Human Sexuality in Orthodox Contemporary Anthropology", *Teologie și viață*, 1–4 (2019): 97–113.
46 *The Brill Dictionary of Gregory of Nyssa*, 556–557.

Bibliography

Behr, John, "The Rational Animal: A Rereading of Gregory of Nyssa's De hominis opificio", *Journal of Early Christian Studies*, 2 (1999): 219–247.

Brown, Peter, *The Body and Society. Men, Women and Sexual Renunciation in Early Christianity* (London, Boston, MA: Columbia University Press, 1988).

Corsini, Eugenio, "Plérôme humaine et plérôme cosmique chez Grégoire de Nysse", *Écriture et culture philosophique dans la pensée de Grégoire de Nysse*, M. Harl, Editor (Leiden: Brill, 1971).

Cortez, Marc, *Christological Anthropology in Historical Perspective: Ancient and Contemporary Approaches to Theological Anthropology* (Grands Rapids, MI: Zondervan Publishing House, 2016).

Daniélou, Jean, *Platonisme et théologie mystique: essai sur la doctrine spirituelle de saint Grégoire de Nysse* (Paris: Éditions Montaigne, 1944).

Gregory of Nyssa, St., "On the Making of Man", XVI, 7, *Nicene and Post-nicene Fathers of the Christian Church*, second series, vol. V, Schaff Philip (Editor), translated by William Moore and Henry Austin Wilson (New York: Charles Scribner's Sons, 1917).

Gregory of Nyssa, St., "On the Soul and the Resurrection", *Nicene and Post-nicene Fathers of the Christian Church*, second series, vol. V, Schaff Philip (Editor), translated by William Moore and Henry Austin Wilson (New York: Charles Scribner's Sons, 1917).

Gregory of Nyssa, St., "On the Virginity", XIII, *Nicene and Post-nicene Fathers of the Christian Church*, second series, vol. V, Schaff Philip (Editor), translated by William Moore and Henry Austin Wilson (New York: Charles Scribner's Sons, 1917).

Ladner, Gerhart B., "The Philosophical Anthropology of Saint Gregory of Nyssa", *Dumborton Oaks Papers*, 12 (1958): 59–94.

The Brill Dictionary of Gregory of Nyssa, Lucas Francisco Mateo-Seco and Giulio Maspero (ed.), translated by Seth Cherney (Leiden, Boston, MA: Koninklijke Brill NV: 2010).

Tomoioagă, Florin Toader, "St. Gregory of Nyssa's View on the Origin of Human Sexuality in Orthodox Contemporary Anthropology", *Teologie și viață*, 1–4 (2019): 97–113.

von Balthasar, Hans Urs, *Cosmic Liturgy. The Universe According to Maximus the Confessor*, translated by Brian E. Daley (San Francisco, CA: S.J., Ignatus Press, 2003).

von Balthasar, Hans Urs, *Présence et pensée* (Paris: Beauchesne, 1952, 1988).

7 Philo and Ambrose on Genesis 25 as Slavery in Passions

Victor Yudin

Introduction

Philo of Alexandria (c. 20 BC 50 AD), followed by Ambrose of Milan (c. 340 397 AD), uses the Old Testament story of Esau and Jacob (*Genesis* 25) in order to revise the Stoic interpretation of enslavement into passions, by providing it with a further religious insight.

In fact, the Stoics did not fight slavery which was widely spread throughout Antiquity. Starting with their founder Zeno, they perceived slavery as a key allegory for the explanation of their moral philosophy. The major part of their ethical doctrine was dedicated to the examination of passions. They had an extremely negative perception on passions considering them to be a source of evil.

According to the Stoics, the meaning of human life is in the struggle against passions, since humanity in general, and each individual in particular, indulging into passions, becomes their victim. True slavery consists in the power of passions over a human being. On the contrary, true freedom consists in ἀπάθεια (liberation from passions). Only a wise man is really free from passions, whereas a fool is enslaved by them. The wise men are rare, whereas most people are enslaved by passions on different degrees, since they ignite each other with their emotional state: e.g. anger at another person naturally causes his anger, thereby both parties wage a war with each other. Gradual liberation from passions by means of ἀταραξία – detachment – is a long process of rational discernment.[1]

This moral theory significantly influenced the Hellenistic period of the Old Testament (especially in Alexandria), as well as Christianity which soon followed. Early Philo of Alexandria wrote two works on this subject in the Stoic fashion: (1) *Every virtuous person is free*,[2] and (2) *Every vicious person is a slave*. Eusebius of Caesarea lists both these treatises among the authentic Philo's writings.[3] The second of these works has not been preserved, but since this pair was composed as an exercise on the standard Stoic subject matter, it is still possible to reconstruct some of the ideas from this treatise.[4]

Curiously, the Old Testament exegesis, which Philo was so famous for, is practically absent in *Probus*. Nevertheless, his comments on one peculiar

DOI: 10.4324/9781003273592-7

passage are especially valuable because they hardly fit into Philo's Jewish habitual discourse. This passage is about the story of the two sons of Isaac – Esau and Jacob. Philo claims that since by nature Jacob was temperate, and Esau intemperate, their father implored the Lord to make his eldest son a slave to the younger, as otherwise he would inevitably become a slave to his own passions instead. Surprisingly, Philo reads this prayer into the biblical text although it is absent there.

I think that Philo deliberately distorts the content of the biblical passage about Isaac and his sons Jacob and Esau in order to present the passage in a Stoic spirit.[5] To do this, he applies his oratorical skills, which he learns in the process of writing this treatise. He does this in order to prove that Stoicism itself comes from the Jewish religion. However, he claims that essentially they come down to the same teaching.

It is possible that this projection of one teaching onto another constitutes the beginning of an allegorical method of interpreting Scripture. It was introduced and later spread in Christianity through the Alexandrian school of biblical exegesis. The key idea of this method is that Scripture should not always be taken literally, instead often it says one thing, but it means something else on a much deeper level.

A few centuries later, in his letters to Simplicianus, Ambrose of Milan followed Philo in his *Genesis* 25 interpretation, this time within the Christian framework. Our paper aims to figure out the original character of this interpretation, taking into account Philo's Stoic background to his exegesis.

To understand our statement, we suggest the following two parts of our discussion. First, we will demonstrate how Philo distorts the biblical text about two brothers in order to turn it into the foundation of Stoicism (1). Then, we will show how this and similar interpretations made their way into the exegesis of some of the church fathers, such as Ambrose of Milan (2).

Philo's Search for Stoicism in Scripture

In *Probus*, Philo is engaged in an exercise in oratorical technique, the purpose of which is to argue in favor of Stoic wisdom *Every good person is free*. Philo does an excellent job of explaining the meaning of this idiom on the basis of a large amount of material mainly from Greek and Roman antiquity.[6] However, in order to provide his reasoning with a universal character, Philo also turns to Persian, Indian and Jewish sources, despite the fact that these are few in his treatise. He uses only five quotes from the Old Testament, of which the most original is his interpretation of a passage we are dealing with in our paper. According to Philo, this significant passage represents the beginning of Stoicism, since Zeno of Kition as the founder of the Stoic school, learned his wisdom from the Jewish Scripture. To prove this unusual statement, Philo subtly alters the content of this passage, turning it into a philosophical text, which it is certainly not. Let us see how Philo delivers on this task.

Philo on Slavery to the Passions in the Story of Jacob and Esau (*Genesis* 25)

As a preliminary remark, Philo makes a basic observation concerning slavery, namely, that there exist two kinds of it: slavery of the body and slavery of the soul.[7] Most people view the first type of slavery as the only one. Nevertheless, it is precisely the bondage of the soul, which is enslaved to the passions tormenting us, that interests us. In *Probus* 57, Philo refers to a key biblical text that helps to understand what bondage of the soul actually means.[8]

> We may well suppose that the fountain from which Zeno drew this thought was the law-book of the Jews, which tells us of two brothers, one wise and temperate, the other incontinent, how the father of them both prayed in pity for him who had not attained to virtue that he should be his brother's slave. He held that slavery, which men think the worst of evils, was the best possible boon to the fool; because the loss of independence would prevent him from transgressing without fear of punishment, and his character would be improved under the control of the authority set above him.[9]

This interpretation is quite unique and original. Philo's main ideas in this text are as follows:

a Zeno of Kition borrowed his Stoic doctrine from the Jewish law. He did this on the basis of a biblical story about two brothers, one of whom was reasonable (σώφρων), and the other was intemperate (ἀκόλαστος, ἄφρων).

b The essence of this story is as follows: although the father of two sons had an equal affection for them, still he prayed (εὔχεται), that the intemperate should serve (be a slave) the temperate.

c For most people, slavery (δουλεία) is considered the worst thing that can happen to a person. However, in this case, slavery – for an intemperate brother is the best possible solution. On the one hand, the loss of power over himself (independence) (αὐτεξούσια) will lead to the situation when he will not be able to commit misdeeds without fear of punishment. On the other hand, his character (τὸ ἦθος) will improve under the supervision of his temperate brother who takes care of him (προστασία).

At the face value, Philo cites a stunning example of Stoic wisdom from Scripture. According to his explanation, we find a story in the Bible in which a certain father of his two sons behaves like a real Stoic who understands the deadly danger of passions, since they are the source of every evil. Being a good father, he wishes to protect his children from these destructive passions. On the one hand, the father sees that one of his two sons is by nature intemperate, and therefore is not capable of coping with his passions on his own. On the other hand, his other son is temperate by nature, and therefore easily copes with any passions that may attack him.

This raises the problem because the eldest son receives in accordance with Jewish tradition the rights of the first-born son. This means that after the death of their father, he will become the head of the family. All other family members, including his brother, must obey him as they used to obey their father. In anticipation, the father decides to go against his tradition: he transfers the rights of the first-born from the elder brother to the younger (in fact, both were born together, as one appeared from the mother's womb earlier, whereas the other followed him, holding his brother's foot). First, the father does this for the sake of his family, otherwise an intemperate man (even if his son) might inflict suffering to the rest. If you let this happen no one can help him anymore. Second, if so he also turns the other family members into servants of his passions: nominally he will be the family's boss, but in fact his passions rule over him and the others. Thus, unbridled passions will rule the family, starting with its head.

Moreover, Philo states that the father makes this paradoxical decision out of pity and compassion (λαβὼν οἶκτον) for his intemperate son. He does not want him to suffer in the grip of passions. According to Philo, the father gives him into slavery to his brother (ἵνα δουλεύσῃ τῷ ἀδελφῷ), so that his brother would take decisions instead of him. His temperate brother (σώφρων) will be able to conquer not only the passions which confront him personally, but also the passions of his family, since he is called to take care of them. Obviously, the father, as a true stoic, understands that the reason provides with the strength to conquer passions, whenever they may arise: potentially, in himself or really in another person. After all, only a reasonable person is truly dispassionate (ἀπαθής). That is why he is also responsible for the others. The temperate brother, having received responsibility from his father, will gradually help his intemperate brother to improve his unruly character, which is mostly made up of distractive habits (τὸ ἦθος). With such a limitation to his power, the intemperate brother also can no longer commit a mischief without fear of punishment, as he would as the head of the family.

And now let's turn to the biblical text that Philo uses,[10] and check how adequate his above paraphrase is. Thus:

> 21 Isaac prayed to the Lord on behalf of his wife, because she was childless. The Lord answered his prayer, and his wife Rebecca became pregnant.
> 22 The babies jostled each other within her, and she said, "Why is this happening to me?" So she went to inquire of the Lord.
> 23 The Lord said to her, "Two nations are in your womb,
> and two peoples from within you will be separated;
> one people will be stronger than the other, and the older will serve the younger".[11]

It seems to us that there are a number of serious discrepancies between this text and Philo's interpretation mentioned above. Let us have a closer look into these discrepancies.

First, Philo does not mention the names of the main characters. This concerns not only the two sons (Jacob and Esau), but also their father (Isaac) let alone their mother (Rebecca). I suspect that Philo does this on purpose, as he paraphrases many details of *Genesis* 25: 21–23, while significantly altering its content. Obviously, he is thoroughly familiar with this text.

Second, Philo causes a certain confusion hoping that the reader would mix up certain biblical stories in his mind. If Philo had not paraphrased this text so close to the original, then one would think that we are talking yet about another family from *Genesis*, where the father had two sons, one of whom was reasonable, and the other was not. Surely, this story is about Adam and his two sons Cain and Abel.[12] Surprisingly, Philo implies a certain projection of one text onto another, since in fact, it was Cain who turned out to be truly unreasonable by the fratricide he committed. On the contrary, in the case of Esau and Jacob, Esau ultimately turned out to be not so much an unreasonable a servant of the passions as Philo suggests. Ultimately, he forgives Jacob and accepts him, even though this happens many years after the latter's return.[13] Throughout the years of his preceding life, Esau remained his family's head and reasonably coped with this challenging task. In what sense, he then can be considered a servant of the passions is unclear. It also turns out that Isaac's prayer for the request of the slavery of an intemperate son to a reasonable one does not come true, since Isaac never becomes Jacob's slave.

Third, the Bible does not say anything about Isaac's prayer. This does not mean that it is a complete fiction. In fact, this prayer is a compilation of thoughts contained in the biblical story, but on other occasions. The story does present Isaac's prayer but in connection with Rebecca's infertility.[14] It also says that the Lord heard Isaac's prayer,[15] yet concerning Rebecca's sterility, and not the primacy of the younger over the elder. It also states that the Lord made the younger rule over the elder.[16] However, the Lord does this not thanks to Isaac's prayer, but in response to Rebecca's request.[17]

Fourth, Philo assumes that Isaac preferred Jacob to Esau, while he shows pity for Esau: since he, being a father, loves him too. Nevertheless, he decides to give him into slavery to his temperate son, who will take care of his brother. Contrary to this, the biblical text explicitly says that Isaac loved Esau, whereas Rebecca loved Jacob.[18] As a hunter, Esau was a typical male figure, who impressed Isaac, while Jacob lived in tents and helped his mother with the housework.

Finally, their father (Isaac) could not know about the real character of his sons, since the Lord decided to give one in servitude (alternatively, to slavery) to the other when they were still in the womb. At that moment, their father could not possibly know the gender of his children, let alone their character. Besides, the Scripture nowhere says that the character of the brothers was formed before their birth (by nature), as Philo appears to claim. Their characters were formed during their adolescence, or more likely, when they became young men. Esau sells his birthright for lentil stew when he comes home from the hunting.[19] Obviously at this point, he was no longer a child.

Fifth, in the biblical passage two verbs are used side by side – ὑπηρετέω and δουλεύω. The repetition is typical for Semitic versification, when the main form repeats what was said before with a slight difference in order to emphasize the main idea. Here too, the difference between these two verbs is stressed. What exactly these notions mean still needs to be figured out. In Greek, the concepts of "servitude" and "slavery" (ὑπηρέτησις and δουλεία) differ only contextually (that is, they are interchangeable). The biblical passage speaks of servitude, not necessarily about slavery. The elder brother will serve the younger, not the elder brother will be the younger's slave. In his interpretation, Philo unambiguously reads slavery into this passage, since he goes on explaining the meaning of slavery. He argues that δουλεία (according to a common sense) is the greatest evil that can happen to someone. On the contrary, servitude can by no means be the greatest evil, and even less so, an evil according to a common sense.

So, it becomes obvious that Philo deliberately changes the content of the biblical text,[20] turning it into a basic text of the Stoic ethical doctrine. Let us see if this is the exceptional case with his *Probus* exercise.

In his later work *Legum allegoriarum*,[21] dedicated to the development of an allegorical method of biblical exegesis, Philo returns to the story of the two brothers:

> Once again, of Jacob and Esau, when still in the womb, God declares that the one is a ruler and leader and master but Esau is a subject and a slave. For God the maker of living beings knows well the different pieces of his handiwork, even before he has thoroughly chiseled and consummated them, and the faculties which they are to display at a later time, in a word, their deeds and experiences... And so when Rebecca, the soul that awaits on God, goes to inquire for God He tells her in reply: "Two nations are in thy womb, and two peoples shall be separated from thy belly, and one people shall be above the other people, and the elder shall serve the younger". For in God's judgment that which is base and irrational is by nature a slave, but that which is fine character and endowed with reason and better, is princely and free. And this is not only when either is full-grown in soul, but even if their development is still uncertain.[22]

In contrast to the above interpretation, here Philo makes a number of clarifications that bring his interpretation closer to the original. First, he calls all the main characters by their names: father and mother (Isaac and Rebecca) as well as their two sons (Esau and Jacob). Second, he draws attention to the fact that it is not Isaac, but Rebecca who is perplexed about her babies' fight in her belly. The Lord explains to her that two nations are fighting in her womb, of which the larger will serve the smaller. Philo even provides us with an exact quotation of the biblical text from the Septuagint's Greek translation.[23]

However, Philo immediately connects this biblical quote to his own interpretation, which is essentially a repetition of the ideas from his *Probus*.[24] That one who is base and irrational by nature (φύσει), is already a slave and therefore he must serve the other one who is endowed with reason, and thereby is free. God makes his decision even before someone's birth: he perfectly knows his creations and therefore chooses the one who will serve the other.

However, what is lacking in this latter interpretation, is Isaac's prayer to make the elder son into his younger brother's slave, since the former is intemperate while the latter is temperate. It was this "prayer of Isaac" that became a foundation for Philo's Stoic interpretation. Since it is absent in this text, you get an impression that it is no longer Isaac but the Lord is a Stoic. Such an idea is surely absurd but curiously it seems to be an ultimate Philo's position.

Ambrose's Usage of Philo's Stoic Interpretation of *Genesis* 25

Philo's interpretation of *Genesis* 25 significantly influenced Ambrose's interpretation of the text about two brothers. Ambrose comes back to it on several occasions. Curiously, he follows Philo's ideas without referring to his source. At the same time, he retains Philo's Stoic interpretation, passing it off as authentically Christian. He achieves this result by means of specific Christian terminology, which is neither found in Philo nor in the biblical passage under the scrutiny.

I have divided this part into two sections: (3.1.) Stoic influence of Philo's interpretation of *Genesis* 25 in Ambrose's *Letter to Simplicianus*; (3.2.) Certain presence of Philo's Stoic interpretation of *Genesis* 25 in other Ambrose's works. Let us proceed to our examination.

Stoic Influence of Philo's Interpretation of Genesis 25 in Ambrose's Letter to Simplicianus

Ambrose of Milan discusses the biblical story of Isaac and his two sons in three of his writings: *Letter to Simplicianus* (7), *Letter to Orontianus* (20), and *On Jacob or the Blissful Life* (17–20).[25] Throughout these writings (especially in the first one), he faithfully follows Philo's ideas, converting them to Christian identity due to the specific Christian terminology he chooses to apply.

The first of these works is dedicated to the Stoic double motto *Every virtuous person is free*, as well as *Every vicious person is a slave*. In many respects, his treatment is a faithful reception of Philo's ideas from *Probus*, and possibly also from the other lost twin treatise on this topic. Curiously, Ambrose does not mention Philo's name anywhere. This would be considered as plagiarism nowadays, but in antiquity, there were other ideas concerning the importance of quotes and imitation. Philo too uses certain biblical stories without indicating the names of the characters, e.g. in the story of Isaac and his two sons. The purpose of such a treatment may still differ. Philo does this in order to provide a Stoic character to the biblical story, whereas Ambrose does so in order to present Philo's Stoic discourse as authentically Christian.

Thus, Ambrose presents Philo's reasoning in response to Simplicianus' request to explain to him the meaning of "slavery" in Paul's expression *You have been bought with a price, do not become slaves of men.*[26] Ambrose tells Simplicianus that our freedom is in Christ only, and it consists in the knowledge of wisdom. In order to understand what wisdom and freedom imply, Ambrose quotes unnamed philosophers (apparently Stoics) who assert that *every virtuous person is free*, while *every bad person is a slave.* Ambrose takes over the proceeding discourse to discuss Philo's ideas.

Following Philo, Ambrose argues that there are two types of slavery[27]: one is slavery of the body and the other is slavery of the soul.[28] He is not interested in the first type of slavery in favor of the second type. The latter one concerns the slavery in the passions or, as he formulates elsewhere, a bondage to sin.

In view of the discussion above, only a sage can be free, while a sage is only someone who follows Christ. Further Ambrose continues his examination of *Genesis* 25 with a discussion on wisdom.

> Let us consider the source of that philosophy from which the patriarchs drew their wisdom and learning... 7. Did not Jacob, that source of all wisdom, who by reason of his wisdom was preferred to his elder brother, pour an abundance of this reasoning into the hearts of all?[29]

It should be noted right away that Ambrose does not repeat Philo's main deviation from Scripture, namely, "the father's prayer" with the request to make one son (Esau) a slave of another (Jacob). Unlike Philo, Ambrose also calls the main characters by name. Nevertheless, He repeats most of the elements of Philo's interpretation, introducing certain Christian insertions.

Following Philo, Ambrose argues that Scripture is the source of all philosophy. As we have already discussed, Philo is referring to various philosophers, such as Heraclitus, Plato, and Zeno of Kition. Although Ambrose does not mention any philosophical system in particular, it is clear that he follows Philo's reasoning. Since he gives the same biblical example about Isaac and his two sons, he probably means the philosophical doctrine of the Stoics (*ista philosophia*), which Zeno, if to believe Philo, learned from this story. In addition, Ambrose speaks of Jacob as the source of all wisdom, obviously drawing a prophetic parallel with Christ, whom apostle Paul perceives as the source of all freedom, knowledge and wisdom.

> Although the devoted father felt a father's affection for both his sons, he judged each differently... He bestowed grace on one and pity on the other, grace on the wise and pity on the foolish.[30]

Following Philo, Ambrose speaks of Isaac's deep affection for both his sons.[31] However, Scripture tells us about Isaac's preference for Esau. Further, Ambrose switches to the Christian terminology of grace (*gratia*), which the father bestows on the wise son, and compassion (*misericordia*) on the foolish. This attitude appears as an expression of equal affection for both sons. Yet, neither pity nor grace is mentioned in *Genesis* 25. Philo is the only author who speaks of the father's pity for his intemperate son, while Ambrose imitates it with a similar notion (*misericordia*). Yet by using the notion of grace Ambrose imposes his Christian understanding onto this already unusual interpretation. The parallel of Isaac (whose name is omitted) with Christ is clearly traceable. After all, only God is a real father, capable of bestowing grace. Moreover, he does it so "for granted", as what the Latin word *gratia* actually means.

Further, Ambrose explains what exactly these grace and pity consist of:

> Because he (Esau) could not rise to virtue by means of his own resources, or make any advance on his own initiative, (Isaac) gave him the blessing of serving his brother, of being his slave, showing that folly is worse than slavery, which would be a remedy for him, because a fool cannot rule himself, and if he does not have someone to control him, he will be destroyed by his desires.[32]

According to Ambrose, Isaac feels pity or, more accurately, compassion for Esau, because as a fool, he is not able to live on his own, but will inevitably run into trouble by his passions. In such a state, he does not have the strength of returning to virtue by means of his own efforts. Knowing that folly is worse than slavery, the wise father delivers his son into slavery to his brother on the account of his parental blessing. He is convinced that slavery is a blessing for Esau, since he needs the control and correction on the part of a wise man.

> After due deliberation the devoted father made him his brother's slave so that he would be guided by the other's prudence... So he put a yoke on the foolish one as on an unruly man, and he denied freedom to one who he decreed must live by his sword. He put his brother over him so that he might not sin by his temerity, but that, being subject to his authority and limitations, he might come to repentance.[33]

Ambrose continues to impose Christian meaning onto this passage, emphasizing freedom from sin and the need to repent. The alteration of the vocabulary from the "passion" in the case of Philo to "sin" (*peccatum*) and further liberation from it by means of "repentance" (*paenitentia*) signifies a transition from a Stoic framework to a Christian one. The father protects his son not from passions only, but ultimately from sin. He admits one brother into slavery by the another, who will rule him by means of discretion. Finally, the wise instruction may lead him to repentance (*paenitentia*). Understandably, repentance does not point to abstract sinfulness but to really committed sins. Thus, his task is in protecting him from sin and the dangers which it brings about.

Further, Ambrose distinguishes between two sorts of actions: by necessity and by free will.

> Slavery, you see, draws a distinction (some are weak of necessity though strong of purpose, because that is more beautiful which is done not of necessity but willingly), and so he put on him the yoke of necessity and later secured for him the blessing of willing subjection.[34]

Ambrose discusses two types of servitude: one by necessity, the other by free deliberation. The first type of servitude coincides with the first type of slavery presented by Philo, as the slavery of the body is also a bondage under compulsion. The other kind of servitude, as a servitude in accordance with one's will, is not actually slavery, since it favors freedom. Ambrose believes that both types of slavery perfectly apply to Esau, since thanks to compulsory slavery, Esau may change his character and freely accept his condition.

Here, Ambrose again follows Philo, as both appear to assert that a person can be a slave in a body, but free in his soul.[35] As we remember Philo provides an interesting case of Diogenes, who was taken into slavery by the pirates and sold on the market. Immediately after the purchase, he began to tell his owner how to behave.[36] A few paragraphs later Ambrose comes down to a similar biblical example of Joseph, who was also sold into slavery to Egypt, but ruled Egypt as a lord.[37] Esau is also an example, as Ambrose argues that the same person can be a slave in the body first, but gradually turn into a free person in his spirit.

These reflections lead Ambrose to the following conclusion:

> *Natura* does not make a man a slave but folly does. Esau was born free but became a slave...[38]

These two sentences elegantly express the essence of Stoic ethics. It consists of the following: when a person lives by nature, he lives wisely. When he indulges into passions, he loses his independence by becoming their slave. This is exactly what happens to Esau: at first he was free (by nature), but becomes a slave to his passions and detaches himself from nature. To free him from this slavery, his father delivers him into bondage to his prudent brother. Note that Ambrose's explanation contradicts Philo's reading in claiming that Esau was intemperate by nature already in his mother's womb. Therefore, his father out of pity for his son was forced to ask God in prayer to deliver his poor intemperate son into slavery to his temperate brother.

Obviously, such an interpretation contradicts not only Scripture but likewise the Stoic doctrine, since the assumption of Esau's intemperance by nature implies a nature's imperfection, which contradicts their doctrine.[39] The Stoics believed that passions are the product of human activity as well as a poor use of one's power to deliberation. Curiously, Ambrose's correction to Philo's ideas matches both Scripture and the Stoic philosophy.

Certain Presence of Philo's Stoic Interpretation of *Genesis* 25 in Other Ambrose's Works

In *De Jacob vel vita beata*, Ambrose again returns to the theme of the father (Isaac) and his two sons (Esau and Jacob). The title of the work suggests a detailed discussion of our passage. The work's subtitle *De... vita beata* perceives Jacob as a happy man, while his life appears as an example for others. The meaning of Jacob's happiness lies precisely in his temperate character, which leads him to a life free from passions (ἀπάθεια). Such a passion-free life is presented as a happy life. Paradoxically, Jacob becomes an embodiment of the Stoic ideal.

He also tries to lead his brother to a similar happy life. Curiously, in *De Jacob* Ambrose tones down the discourse on slavery, replacing it with the idea of servitude.[40] For instance:

> Nevertheless, Esau brought it about by his demands and entities that he did receive a blessing, but such a blessing as was in agreement and correspondence with the earlier one, namely that he should serve his brother. Indeed the one who could not command and rule the other ought to have served him in order to be ruled by the one who was more wise. It was not the role of the holy patriarch to deliver his own son to the ignoble state of slavery.[41]

In this passage, Ambrose gets rid of Philo's main idea of slavery, which he originally uses in his *Letter to Simplicianus*. There he is outspoken in his position on Esau's slavery to Jacob: the latter rules the former *by his sword*, implying that if necessary Jacob must be ready to use violence against his intemperate brother. On the contrary, here Ambrose says *neque enim fuit Patriarchæ sancti, ut filium suum degeneri conditioni servitutis addiceret....*[42] Thus, he completely rejects a slavery of one brother to another. Instead, Ambrose suggests servitude as the novel ideal for their incongruous relations.

Both brothers receive their father's blessing. However, Esau receives a blessing to serve his brother, while Jacob receives a blessing to rule his brother. According to Ambrose, both these blessings are two sides of the same blessing of the holy patriarch. It is not so much striking that Isaac is called a patriarch, which is a standard protocol, but the "holy patriarch" (*Patriarchæ sancti*), thereby shifting to a Christian perception of the biblical story, since it is common in Christianity to emphasize the holiness of certain figures of the Old Testament.

Unfortunately, in this text, Ambrose does not explain the intriguing distinction between slavery and servitude, although he clearly makes the point of their difference. The Septuagint translation of *Genesis* 25:23 about "the service of the greater people to the lesser", in principle, admits either of these two possibilities, while Philo favors the idea of slavery. Obviously, in *De Jacob* Ambrose gradually departs from Philo's interpretation of the biblical text in a nuanced way.

Yet, even here one can trace comparisons typical for Philo, for instance, from Solomon that a fool cannot be trusted with his decisions, because he is fully unpredictable and changes like the moon.[43] Another allegory, this time of a Stoic nature that arrived from Philo to Ambrose concerns a ship losing control without a captain at the helm. Indeed, a fool who is trying to get control of his life is similar to such a ship. In fact, he is ruled by a storm raging in the sea of passions.

> But since he had two sons, one without moderation and the other moderate and wise, in order to take care for both like a good father, he placed the moderate son over the son without moderation, and he ordered the foolish one to obey the one who was wise. For the foolish man cannot of his own accord be a disciple of virtue or preserve in his intent, because the fool changes like the moon. Isaac was right to deny Esau freedom to make his own choices: else he might drift like a ship in the waves without a helmsman.[44]

In *Letter to Orontianus*, Ambrose further comments the story of Isaac and his two sons, this time using his allegorical method of exegesis to its utmost range.[45] Ambrose believes that the eldest son represents the folk of Israel, while the younger one represents Christianity. The first receives the father's blessing, while the second receives his love. On the one hand, love is also a blessing, yet it is a blessing of faith and true freedom, the meaning of which is revealed in Christ only. On the other hand, the blessing of Esau represents the Jewish folk as it is the blessing according to the law which is hard, if not harsh at times.

Here the theme of the father and two of his sons takes over to the New Testament insight of the prodigal son story,[46] which Ambrose treats in his *Exposition on the Gospel of Luke*.[47] There as much as here, he finds a parallel with two nations – Jewish and Christian, the first of which receives the blessing of servitude to the second, while the second receives the blessing of love.

In three of his works, in which Ambrose comments on the Old Testament story concerning the father and his two sons, he resorts to Philo's interpretation to different degrees. Philo tends to reduce the meaning of this passage to the Stoic ideas. The main insight behind this interpretation is that although the father has equal affection for both his sons, still he delivers the eldest son into slavery to the younger. The father does it so in order to free his son from the slavery of his own passions that tend to destroy him at any point. At the same time, Ambrose gets rid of the most inconsistent element of Philo's interpretation, namely, of the so-called "prayer of Isaac" concerning the father imploring the Lord to give one son into slavery to another while they were still in their mother's womb. Ambrose correctly understands that this "prayer" is not only absent from Scripture, but also distorts the Stoic doctrine of nature. Philo seems to vigorously defend this doctrine presenting it as an authentic biblical teaching.

Finally, Ambrose clothed his rendering of Philo's interpretation in a shell of Christian terminology, using the key concepts of "sin" (*peccatum*), "repentance" (*paenitentia*), "grace" (*gratia*), "saint" (*sanctus*), etc. Thereby he shifts the discussion upon a different Christian level. Being faithful to Philo's allegorical method of biblical exegesis, Ambrose perceives the brothers as a symbol of the Jewish and Christian folks, while identifying the freedom from slavery in the voluntary service to Christ.

Conclusion

In *Probus* as Philo's early work on the Stoic theme, the author resorts to oratorical manipulation of certain biblical texts in order to convince the reader that all wisdom originates in Jewish law. This applies not only to Stoic philosophy, the founder of which was Zeno of Kition, but also to other philosophers, such as Heraclitus and Plato.

To prove the Jewish origin of Greek philosophy, Philo applies various tricks of oratorical technique: e.g. rendering the information which fits into his fiction, while avoiding talking about what does not.

A striking example of this approach is his interpretation of *Genesis* 25 concerning Isaac and his two sons Esau and Jacob. Philo not only keeps silent about the names of the main characters, but also claims that, although the father loves both sons equally, still goes to implore the Lord to make his intemperate son (Esau) a slave to the temperate one (Jacob). Thus, Philo portrays Isaac as a Stoic sage who understands the meaning of slavery, namely, that it is better to be in bondage to your loving brother than a slave to your own passions, destroying everyone around. What is peculiar is that several elements of Philo's presentation of the biblical story (such as "the father's prayer about his sons" as well as his equal affection for them) are simply not found in Scripture. Paradoxically, Philo is busy inventing a "Stoic Bible".

Curiously, Ambrose of Milan borrowed Philo's interpretation and devoted one of his works (*Letter to Simplicianus*) to a detailed analysis of the Stoic wisdom *Every virtuous person is free*. In this treatise, the story of Isaac and his two sons occupies an important place. Here, Ambrose meticulously follows Philo's ideas (for instance, speaking about the father's equal affection for both his sons), while never mentioning his source. Ambrose discusses this passage in the framework of the Stoic doctrine of passions which produce and destroy the folly, while the wise carefully avoids all passions.

However, Ambrose's main achievement is his application of Christian terminology upon the Stoic idioms so cleverly constructed by Philo. Instead of using the key notion "passions" Ambrose talks about "sin" (*peccatum*) which inevitably strikes a fool. Only by the means of "grace" (*gratia*), bestowed by the "holy" (*sanctus*) patriarch Isaac, his temperate son (Jacob) will gradually lead his intemperate elder brother (Esau) to "repentance" (*paenitentia*).

Later, in a *Letter to Orontianus*, Ambrose uses Philo's method of allegorical exegesis, arguing that Esau prophetically represents the Jewish people, while Jacob represents the Christians. The elder son will serve the younger, this is to say, the Christians will take over the Jews becoming the true people of Israel, since the true wisdom consists in a free service to Christ.

Notes

1 Nussbaum, M.C., *Therapy of desires. Theory and practice in Hellenistic ethics*. Princeton, NJ. 1996. P. 363.

2 *Quod omnis probus liber sit*, infra *Probus*.

3 Eusebius of Caesarea, *Ecclesiastical History* II, xviii, 6–7. A century later, Jerome in his list presented in *De viris ilustribus* (11), which is based on Eusebius, omits mentioning *Probus*. This shows a tendency of not appreciating the Stoic influence upon Philo.

4 Despite the fact that *Quod omnis probus liber* sit is one of the most famous paradoxes of the Stoics, their works on this topic have not survived. Three treatises with the analysis of this text belong - one to an eclectic (Cicero), another to a Jew (Philo) and the third to a Christian (Ambrose). M. Petit, *Introduction* to Philon d'Alexandrie, *Quod omnis probus liber sit*, in *Les œuvres de Philon d'Alexandrie*, 28. Cerf, Paris. 1974. P. 75. We deal with the last two authors in our current contribution.

5 *Genesis* 25:21–23.

6 An excellent examination of the work's structure is in M. Petit, *Introduction* to Philon d'Alexandrie, *Quod omnis probus liber sit*, in *Les oevres de Philon d'Alexandrie*, 28. Cerf, Paris. 1974. Pp. 29–34.

7 *Probus* 17.

8 ἔοικε δὲ ὁ Ζήνων ἀρύσασθαι τὸν λόγον ὥσπερ ἀπό πηγῆς τῆς Ἰουδαίων νομοθεσίας, ἐνῇδυοῖν ὄντοιν ἀδελφοῖν, τοῦ μὲν σώφρονος, τοῦ δ᾽ ἀκολάστου, λαβών οἶκτον ὁ κοινός ἀμφοῖν πατήρ τοῦ μὴ ἐπ᾽ἀρετήν ἥκοντος εὔχεται, ἵνα δουλεύσῃ τῷ αδελφῷ, τὸ δοκοῦν μέγιστον εἶναι κακόν, δουλειάν, ἀγαθὸν τελεώτατον ὑπολαμ βάνων ἄφρονι, τὸ μὲν αὐτεξούσιον ἀφῃρημένῳ πρὸς τὸ μὴ σὺν άδείᾳ πλημμελεῖν, ἐκ δὲ τῆς τοῦ προεστῶτος προστασίας βελτιωθησομένῳ τὸ ἦθος.

Probus 57.1–57.7. Philo, *Quod omnis probus liber sit*, in *Philonis Alexandrini Opera quae supersunt*. Ed. L. Cohn, P. Wendland. Vol. VI. Berolini. 1915. P. 16.

9 Philo of Alexandria, *Every good man is free*, in *Philo in ten volumes*, IX. Translation F. H. Colson. London, Cambridge, MA. 1967. P. 43.

10 21ἐδεῖτο δὲ Ισαακ κυρίου περὶ Ρεβεκκας τῆς γυναικὸς αὐτοῦ, ὅτι στεῖρα ἦν· ἐπήκουσεν δὲ αὐτοῦ ὁ θεός, καὶ ἔλαβεν ἐν γαστρὶ Ρεβεκκα ἡ γυνὴ αὐτοῦ. 22ἐσκίρτων δὲ τὰ παιδία ἐν αὐτῇ· εἶπεν δέ Εἰ οὕτως μοι μέλλει γίνεσθαι, ἵνα τί μοι τοῦτο; ἐπορεύθη δὲ πυθέσθαι παρὰ κυρίου, 23καὶ εἶπεν κύριος αὐτῇ Δύο ἔθνη ἐν τῇ γαστρί σού εἰσιν, καὶ δύο λαοὶ ἐκ τῆς κοιλίας σου διασταλήσονται·καὶ λαὸς λαοῦ ὑπερέξει, καὶ ὁ μείζων δουλεύσει τῷ ἐλάσσονι. *Gen* 25.21.1 - 25.23.5. Translation LXX. *Septuaginta*. Ed. A. Rahlfs. Stuttgart. 1935. P. 263.

11 *Genesis* 25:21–23, NIV.

12 *Genesis* 4:16.

13 *Genesis* 32.

14 *Genesis* 25:21a. Isaac prayed to the Lord on behalf of his wife because she was barren...

15 *Genesis* 25:21b *...the Lord answered his prayer and his wife Rebecca became pregnant.*

16 *Genesis* 25:23b *...and the older will serve the younger.*

17 *Genesis* 25:22 *The babies jostled each other within her, and she said Why is this happening to me? So she went to inquire of the Lord.*

18 *Genesis* 25:28.

19 *Genesis* 25:29–34.

20 *Genesis* 25:21–13.

21 *Legum allegoriarum* 3.88–104.

22 Philo, *Legum allegoria*, in *Loeb Classical Library*, Harvard. Tr. Colson and G. H. Whitaker. 1929. P. 165.

23 *Genesis* 25:23.

24 *Probus* 57.

25 *De Jacob vel vita beata.*

26 1 Cor. 7:24.

27 *Epistola* 7:24. The English translation is in Saint Ambrose, *Letters*. Translated by M. M. Beyenka, in *Fathers of the Church*. New York. 1954.

28 *Slavery is twofold, one of the body, and the other of the soul* – Ambrosius, *Epistula* 7:24 and *Probus* 17.

29 Ambrosius, *Epistola* 7.6–7. *Nonne etiam fons ille disciplinarum omnium Iacob ubertatem disputationis huius omnium pectoribus infudit qui sapientiae merito praelatus est frtri seniori?* Sancti Ambrosii opera. Pars X. *Epistolae et acta*. Tom I. Ed. O.Faller. *Corpus Scriptorum ecclesiasticorum latinorum*. Vol. 57. Vienna, 1968 (Infra CSEL 57). P. 46.

30 Ambrosius, *Epistola* 7.7. *Denique pater pius, qui inter duos filios adfectu enim necessitudine fertur, meritis autem iudicia formantur -, cum divideret alteri gratiam, alteri misericordiam, sapient gratiam, insipienti misericordiam...* CSEL 57. P. 46.

31 *Isaac loved Esau..., but Rebecca loved Jacob.* 25:28.

32 Ambrosius, *Epistola* 7.7. *...quia ad virtutem se propriis viribus erigere non poterat nec spontaneum gressum adtollere, benedixit eum, ut serviret fratri suo et esset ipsius servus, ostendens ita deteriorem esse servitude insipientiam, ut remedio, ei servitus sit, quia stultus regere se non potest, et nisi moderatorem habet, praecipitatur propriis voluntatibus.* CSEL 57. P. 46.

33 Ambrosius, *Epistola* 7.8. *Diligens ergo pater et consulens, servum eum fratri suo fecit, ut eius regeretur consilio...* CSEL 57. P. 46.

34 Ibid.

35 *Probus* 17.
36 *Probus* 120.
37 *Epilstola* 7, 9, 190.
38 Ambrosius, *Epistola* 7.9. *Nec igitur natura servum facit, sed insipientia, nec manumission liberum, sed disciplina.* CSEL 57. P.47.
39 Peter Garnsey explains this inconsistency by the influence of Aristotle on Philo. In *Politics* (1287b37-41), Aristotle recognizes the existence of slavery by nature, believing that some people were born slaves, others free. Everyone must accept the status in which he was born and is. According to Philo, Esau was born a slave, while Jacob was born free, so both should take this as granted. Garnsey, P., *Ideas of slavery from Aristotle to Augustine.* Cambridge. 1996. P. 162.
40 11. Et ipse tamen ut benediceretur cogendo elicuit et impetravit; sed eam benedictionem, quæ cum superiore congrueret et conveniret, ut serviret fratri suo. Etenim qui imperare non poterat, el alterum regere, servire debebat, ut a prudentiore regeretur. Neque enim fuit Patriarchæ sancti, ut filium suum degeneri conditioni servitutis addiceret... *De Jacob et vita beata* II, 3.11. PLM XIV. P. 619.
41 Ambrose, *De Jacob et vita beata*, in *Loeb Classical Library*, Harvard. Tr. M.P. McHugh. 1972.
42 *It was not the role of the holy patriarch to deliver his own son to the ignoble state of slavery...* Saint Ambrose. *Letters.* Translated by M. M. Beyenka, in *Fathers of the Church.* New York. 1954. p. 71.
43 *Sirah* 27:11.
44 *sed ut bonus pater, cum duos haberet filios, unum intemperantem, prudentem et sobrium alterum, quo utrique consuleret, intemperanti præfecit sobrium, et insipientem prudenti statuit obedire; quia insipiens non potest voluntarius virtutis esse discipulus, nec perseverare in studio, quia stultus sicut luna mutatur: merito que ei libertatem proprii negavit arbitrii, nel velut navis in fluctibus sine gubernatore fluilaret... De Jacob et vita beata* II, 3.11. Sancti Ambrosii Mediolanensis, *De Jacob et vita beata* II, 3.11. *Patrologia Latina*, Ed. J.-P. Migne. XIV. Paris. 1845. p 619.
45 *Letter to Orontianus* 20: 4–6.
46 *Luke* 15:1-32. Cf. Ambrose de Milan, *Traité sur l'Evangile de S. Luc.* Introduction, texte et notes par G. Tissot. *Sources Chrétiennes* 63. Cerf. 1956; *Ancient Christian Commentary on Scripture. New Testament III. Luke.* Ed. A. A. Just Jr. Illinois: InterVarsity Press. 2003. 248–249.
47 *Exposition on the Gospel of Luke* 7.

Bibliography

Ambrose, *De Jacob et vita beata*, in *Loeb Classical Library*, Harvard. Tr. M.P. McHugh. 1972.

Ancient Christian Commentary on Scripture. Old Testament II. Genesis 12–50. Ed. M. Sheridan. Westmont, IL: InterVarsity Press. 2002.

Ancient Christian Commentary on Scripture. New Testament III. Luke. Ed. A. A. Just Jr. Westmont, IL: InterVarsity Press. 2003.

Colson, F.H., *Introduction to Quod omnis probus liber sit*, in *Philo in ten volumes*, IX. London, Cambridge, MA: Harvard University Press, 1967.

Garnsey, P., *Ideas of slavery from Aristotle to Augustine.* Cambridge. 1996.

Nussbaum, M.C., *Therapy of desires. Theory and practice in hellenistic ethics.* Princeton, NJ. 1996.

Petit, M., *Introduction* to Philon d'Alexandrie, *Quod omnis probus liber sit*, in *Les oevres de Philon d'Alexandrie*, 28. Paris: Cerf. 1974.

Philo, *Quod omnis probus liber sit*, in *Philonis Alexandrini Opera quae supersunt*. Ed. L. Cohn, P. Wendland. Vol. VI. Berolini. 1915.

Philo, *Legum allegoriarum*, in *Loeb Classical Library*, Harvard. Tr. Colson and G. H. Whitaker. 1929.

Philo of Alexandria, *Every good man is free*, in *Philo in ten volumes*, IX. Translation F. H. Colson. London, Cambridge, MA: Harvard University, 1967.

Philon d'Alexandrie, *Quod omnis probus liber sit*. Introduction, texte et notes par M. Petit, in *Les oevres de Philon d'Alexandrie*, 28. Paris: Cerf, 1974.

Saint Ambrose. *Letters*. Transl. M. M. Beyenka, in *Fathers of the Church*. New York. 1954.

Sancti Ambrosii opera. Pars X. *Epistolae et acta*. Tom I. Ed. O. Faller, in *Corpus Scriptorum Ecclesiasticorum Latinorum*. Vol. 57. Vienna, 1968.

Sancti Ambrosii Mediolanensis, *De Jacob et vita beata* II, 3.11. *Patrologia Latina*, Ed. J.-P. Migne. XIV. Paris. 1845.

Septuaginta. Ed. A. Rahlfs. Stuttgart: Deutsche Bibelstiftung, 1935.

8 Wealth and Power

A Personal Meditation on Luke 18:18–25 {With Short Pastoral and Patristic Comments}

Nicu Dumitrașcu

Introduction

The subject of "eternal life", of "eternity", has always been an exhaustive human preoccupation, regardless of how it has been variously understood. It takes up an important place in people's mindset. Some imagine that it will be the ideal place to receive their rewards for sufferings in this life. Others see it as a radical change of all that exists here and now, in the present. If here we are "condemned" to suffering, deficiency, pain, mockery, and sometimes even death, in the beyond all these will be no more. The hope of these people consists of the life eternal coming as soon as possible, so that they can get away from all the bad things that are happening to them. Others feel indignant about why the Saviour places so many obstacles in front of those who *are* rich, but who still wish to inherit eternal life. Some Christians consider that they must sell all and follow Him, fully conforming to the disciples' example (see Acts 4.32–37). Others have no problem with using various means to gather riches, unrestrictedly, in the belief that all such are "the blessings of God". In this confused and ambiguous context, we wish to analyze our chosen passage, hoping we can offer a few biblical reflections regarding these problems, especially in the context of the secularization of contemporary society.

The Context of the Meeting Between Jesus and the High Official

The episode in Luke 18:18–25 is part of a larger context, which begins in Chapter 9.51 and ends with the meeting between Jesus and Zacchaeus, described in Chapters 19.1–19.10. This sizeable segment of text is Luke's description of the Saviour's activity during his journey to Jerusalem. Here, we can see that, through the teaching that Jesus gives to his disciples and the people, the accent falls upon the relationship between man and material possessions. In the following, we wish briefly to cover the central ideas that can be found in the key sections of the segment that we have marked, regarding material possessions.

In Chapters 9–10, Luke describes the disciple's calling and mission, at the centre of which we repeatedly find the comparison between material

DOI: 10.4324/9781003273592-8

gains and the gains received by following Jesus (9.3, 61; 10.1–11, 25–42). In Chapters 14.1–14.24, we read how the Saviour suggests that benevolence and compassion for the needy are important characteristics of His Kingdom. In the following passage (14.25–35), Jesus talks about self-denial, about forsaking material possessions and even family, in order to become part of His Kingdom. Chapter 15, the chapter of "the lost things", ends with the description of a "lost son" who has wasted his father's material possessions. Through the reconciliation of the father with the son, the ending of the chapter shows what (or who) are, in fact, the true possessions. This parable shows how the divine joy does not compare with the joy given by possessions and can also stand for the reconciliation of God with the sinner who confesses his sins.[1]

In Chapter 16, Jesus directly addresses His disciples (16.1), but it seems that the Pharisees were nearby and could hear what He said (16.14). The idea that Jesus conveys in this passage concerns enrichment by unjust wealth while totally neglecting the needs of the poor. The Saviour's words especially concern the Pharisees who loved money (16.14–16) and were part of a corrupt society in which the strong dominated and the weak and poor were thrown out. However, the starting point of this passage is to draw attention to the way in which rich people *are* able to serve the expansion of the Kingdom of God by using their money in the right way. Luke suggests that it does not matter how much you possess, as long as you follow Christ with a clean heart and self-denial. Continuing the journey to Jerusalem, Chapter 17 offers teachings regarding the consolidation of the disciples' faith and about the way of discipleship. Chapter 18, the chapter containing questions about everlasting life, consists of two episodes: the first is about a Pharisee and a tax collector (18.9–14), and the second is about Jesus' meeting with the rich young man. Both episodes point out that "the attachment to material possessions poses a large obstacle in the way of living an authentic life with God".[2] In Luke's opinion, the problem of abuses arising from material wealth seems to be resolved by the later example he gives in 19.1–10, where he describes how Jesus meets Zacchaeus, the rich chief of the tax collectors (19.1–2). All tax collectors had money but, considering his position, Zacchaeus would have been excessively affluent and this makes the meeting all the more significant. We are told that the encounter completely changed Zacchaeus. He pledges to give half his wealth to the poor and, in reparation for all his acts of injustice while accumulating his riches, he will give fourfold to those individuals he has wronged.

The message that Luke wants to convey here implies that the coming of Jesus is the same thing as the coming of the Kingdom of God, which is, itself, the coming of the salvation announced from the very beginning of the Gospel (1.69).[3]

In this context of the exploration of the relationship between the Kingdom of God and material possessions, lies the text that we are considering for our study. We will now proceed to the exegetical and pastoral meditation upon Luke 18:18–25.

The Goodness of Jesus and the Temptation of Deception

The section under discussion describes the meeting between Jesus and a *rich* ruler. (It will be noted later that, immediately prior to this meeting, Jesus had blessed some little children, despite the disciples' insistence that the children should not be allowed to go to Christ.) Although it is most likely that Luke follows Mark's text very closely, Luke calls the person who comes to Jesus with questions about eternal life, a "ruler"[4] unlike Mark, who just says it was a "man" (Mark 10.17). As a ruler and rich, we can understand that he was an influential man in society, known for his rigorous piety. Yet, he had no religious service.[5]

When the high official approaches Jesus with his question, he addresses Him in an unnatural way: not as Teacher, as people usually addressed Him, but as *Good Teacher.* This can be understood as part of a rhetorical strategy[6] because this mode of address was unknown to the Jews. There is no place in the Talmud where someone has addressed a Rabbi in this way.[7] In the whole of creation, only the *Law* was considered purely *Good,* by the Teachers of Law. They believed that every letter of the Law was a living creature, having its own distinctive role in the creation of the world. Moreover, they even had a sort of superstition about the value of Law, close to idolatry, because some of them claimed that God himself is subject to the Law.[8] Therefore, it should have been impossible for someone to address a Teacher, even if he was one who did great things, with this appellation *Good Teacher.* It was almost a sacrilege.

Is it possible that the leading man has worked out that he is in front of the Law Giver Himself? Had he intuited the true identity of the Teacher before him? It is very unlikely. It's more probable that, arrogantly, he uses a little trick: wanting to gain Jesus' favour from the outset. The addition of the word *Good* was a strategy to flatter Jesus into giving the answer he wanted. But the Saviour notices this deliberately misleading attitude of His questioner and rejects it gently, telling him: "Why do you call Me good? No one is good except God alone" (v.19).[9] He did not ask that because *He is not really good* but because, on another occasion mentioned by Matthew, Jesus referred to himself as "gentle and humble in heart" (11, 29). He did not deny Himself nor deny His own divinity, but He just tried to make this high official understand his error and realize that his mode of address was not the right one. Of course, the ruler did not believe that he was addressing a divinity, but a wise man. From Him he sought, by the ordinary means of this world, to gain favour and to find out which is the best and fastest way to reach the Kingdom of Heaven. Similarly, the Saviour wanted to clarify things in advance. The Kingdom of Heaven or eternal life is not like this world. For the children of the Kingdom, the worldly principles of relationships in society are no longer valid.[10]

The ruler then asks his question, "What am I to do to possess eternal life?" It is similar to that of the Samaritan in Chapter 10.25 and is a basic soteriological question. It does not refer to a reward for something in this world, but to the eternal life that follows the condition of being a son of God.[11]

Therefore, Jesus rejects the flattering attitude and servile and manipulative behaviour of the high official, but He does understand it, as such behaviour was common to the society to which he belonged. The message of this initial dialogue is that whoever wants to be part of the Kingdom must abandon any kind of adulation, because it implies dishonest and untruthful behaviour. It becomes even more dangerous in someone who is holding a higher position in society: in politics, business, or even in the Church.

For any leader, even if he is Mayor, Minister, Congressman, or Head of State, the difference between flattery and eulogy is often difficult to define. Eulogy is welcome when it is realistic and given with honesty, while flattery is an undeserved tribute. But flattery is pleasant and inviting and insinuates itself little by little within the human soul.

Metropolitan Bartholomew said in one of his discourses:

> "When you praise someone, it means that what you say about him is true. You tell a man that he is wise because God really gave him such a quality. But when you say to someone that he is wise but he is really mediocre, or that he is talented in a particular field but he is not, then you lie, because what you say does not really define him. You make him believe what he is not and flatter him, because you praise him more than he deserves. By granting him attributes that he does not possess, but which he would wish to posses, you cause him to slip into a kind of egomania, which is more dangerous even than conscious selfishness. While egoism implies an exaggerated attitude for personal interests, egomania goes further, namely to an overestimation of personal value. Not only with His life example, but also with His word, Jesus teaches us to run from people's praise and from the abyss of vainglory. He encourages us to do good deeds without saying them aloud in front of our fellows and to consider them as our natural duty to God.
> (Matt. 6: 2, 6, 17–18)." [12]

The leader we are talking about may have been told repeatedly that he is clever, blessed with gifts like no other and even good looking, and that may explain why he can no longer distinguish between what is true and what is false. It is a two-dimensional lie. He, who flatters, is not only lying to the man to whom he has assigned qualities that do not belong to him but to himself, also. Flattery is a sin because he who flatters inoculates the man he is addressing with pride and arrogance, meaning that he is attempting to ruin his soul and his heart.

As the Saviour, Jesus' first concern was to not succumb to flattery.

Sadness or Sourness of Wealth

To leave no doubt as to the criteria by which a man can be saved, Jesus replies to the high official's question by repeating five[13] of the ten commandments from the Decalogue: "Do not commit adultery, Do not murder, Do not steal, Do not give false evidence, Honor your father and mother" (v. 20).

Adherence to these commandments would show a person's righteousness. Therefore, when He is asked about the inheritance of eternal life, Jesus answers with questions based on the Old Testament Law, which, for the Jews, was the will of God. In other words, said the Lord Jesus, whoever wants to inherit eternal life must live a righteous life, according to the justice of God.[14] Eternal life is justice and righteousness, because God is justice and righteousness. Those who want to have eternal life must live their life according to the Law of God, because it is this alone that defines the people of God regarding ethics and social relationships. These requirements that God has for the earthly life are, according to the Bible's words, the way to eternal life.[15]

Not without irony, the high official is quick to answer Jesus saying that he has kept all of the commandments from his youth (v. 21). Once again, we see the deceit of this man who, though he knew what he ought to do, asks only for the sake of the question. The man who stood in front of Jesus was not sincere.[16] If he knew the answer, why did he still ask? He wanted to show everyone that by following the prescriptions of the Law, in letter rather than in spirit, he had won the right to hope for eternal life. He really only wants a public authentication certificate! Being a great man of society, he was used to being recognized as an authority by others and he believed that the rules by which the earthly world operates are not different from those in the celestial world.

He declares that, "he has from his youth lived a God–fearing and pious life".[17] However, what is lacking in him is the positive side of our nature, which drives us to contribute to our neighbour's good, and for this purpose, to sacrifice our own.[18]

To this kind of behaviour, the Saviour responds with the example of the children from the previous passage. Children are the best symbol of purity, meekness of spirit, humility and modesty. In Christ's teaching, the Kingdom of God is for those who become like children. The Kingdom of God is characterized by humility, modesty and purity rather than power, wealth or social status. The contrast that Jesus presents consists of the fact that these children, who appear to have nothing, actually have everything; and this young man, who has so many riches, has lost everything. The Kingdom of God is full of paradoxes. When we are concerned with this worldly life, our eyes are turned to our present but this is not as He wants it to be. When we turn to ask God about the life everlasting, He draws our attention to Himself, the true eternal life.

In the light of the rich official's answers, Jesus becomes more radical and tells him that he still lacks one thing. He must sell all his material possessions and, what the money he receives for them, he must give to the poor. Thus, he will collect treasures in heaven. When that is done, he ought to leave everything behind and follow Jesus (v. 22). In other words, keeping the commandments is important and necessary to enter the Kingdom of Heaven, but if you really want to be perfect *you have to deny everything that restricts your freedom to follow Christ*. The Kingdom is present with Jesus and entry into the fellowship with him is entry into salvation.[19]

Perfection is more than the inheritance of eternal life. Many scholars take the view that Jesus was indicating that a further commandment or duty, additional to the Law, is a prerequisite to eternal life.[20] Perfection requires perfect measures. The action Jesus demands must somehow transcend the commandments.[21]

To put it differently, whoever wants to be perfect has to take a radical decision. Anyone who decides to renounce material possessions all his life becomes a monk, enters a monastery and takes monastic vows of chastity, poverty and unconditional obedience. He swears in front of the altar that he will not possess personal wealth. Everything belongs to the monastic community to which he belongs.[22] But those who have a family also have some obligations in this respect. The family man cannot live like a monk. He must work, earn and save wisely for himself and his family. Within the family is increased responsibility – one for another – and by exercising this responsibility, man manifests himself as a person within whom shines the image of God.[23]

In the Eastern faith, it is believed that perfection is won through a continuous struggle with the temptations of this passing world. But the high official of the Gospel was not ready for such a step, though perhaps he had come before Jesus with some hope or belief that everything is negotiable: including perfection. However, when he heard Jesus' exhortation, the high official was saddened and went out without saying a word (v. 23). Why was he sad? Because wealth is like a drug and, even though you know that it is not good for you, you cannot give it up. It has become an idol.[24]

Wealth dictates how you live. It steals your power of decision. It makes you a slave. It takes away your freedom. *That is why* the high official *was sad*: because he knew that the delusionary lure of money and fortune is even stronger than the desire for freedom. Man is created free by God and with a desire for communion and communication, but wealth constrains his idea of freedom and brings separation.[25]

Wealth Is Not a Sin in Itself but Is Dangerous for Salvation

Jesus then speaks to His disciples saying: "How hard it is for those who have money to enter the Kingdom of God! It is easier for a camel to go through a needle's eye than for a rich man to go into the Kingdom of God" (v.24–25). Jesus was not against wealth itself. Do not forget that He had rich friends. Lazarus was not a poor man, since he prepared very expensive feasts for many guests. Joseph of Arimathea and Nicodemus were also rich people. Consequently, we must conclude that He despised neither them nor their wealth.

And the most obvious example is Zacchaeus, who was not just rich, but as the chief of tax collectors, would have been extremely rich (Luke 19:1–10). Jesus went to have lunch in his house, despite of all the existing prejudices of that time regarding the publicans. Working in the finance system, these Jewish civil servants were administering the taxes for the invaders, the Roman Empire, and did not hesitate to make their incomes illicitly. The commonly held view is that tax collectors were fraudulent, demanding more from the population than was due and lining their own pockets with the excess. If the Roman authorities demanded records, it would have been easy for the collectors to modify any receipts in their own favour. Because they worked for the enemy, and because people knew how they acquired their wealth through theft and fraud at the expense of the poor and defenseless, they were treated as sinners.[26] People were shocked that Jesus came into the house of a publican, and not just any publican, but the chief of those who were robbing them.

Jesus enters the house of Zacchaeus because He knew that he will recognize his own fault and, bravely, not stand by but take affirmative action. Zacchaeus wants to give back what he has taken unjustly and return it to those he has oppressed. He says, "I shall give half of my possessions to the poor, and if I have extorted anything from anyone, I shall repay four times as much" (Luke 19:8). In other words, Zacchaeus not only recognizes his sin, but he is also willing to repair the injustice that he carried out and even with great generosity.[27] In the moment of conversion, his attitude towards money has been completely changed. One may take Zacchaeus and the rich ruler as examples of how individuals either succeed or fail to receive the Kingdom.[28]

We might have expected Jesus to go on to say, "And what are you going to do with the other half? How did you know so well to appreciate how much and what you ought to keep?" But He does not say that. He does not tell Zacchaeus to give all his wealth to the poor, but leaves it up to him to decide how much he obtained illicitly. Jesus shows him trust and then forgiveness based on his decision to become an honest man.[29]

Since ancient times, money has been an instrument of civilization because it facilitates trade. Money itself is neither good nor bad; man gives it its moral value. However, it carries in it a bad germ. Because of a certain habit, it may become a vice. This is why it should be avoided. St. Basil the Great says avarice itself is characterized by a constant concern to turn everything into gold.[30]

"When you are touched by the fever of enrichment, you think only of gold. You dream about it when you are sleeping and it is on your mind when you are awake".[31]

The greater the wealth, the more terrible is the desire or lust for enrichment. And if lust for enrichment is born, the real purpose for money disappears, namely, just reward for honest work. There is no sin if a man, wisely and with intelligence, invests his financial resources in a particular business to prosper and get rich. But if, in his work, he is using unfair means, taking money from illicit business, deceiving both his employees and business partners, then he commits a major sin.[32]

So, Jesus *is not opposed to wealth itself* or to the rich people who honestly acquire their wealth and care for the poor. However, He is against those who, through deceit and fraud, corruption and threats, collect huge treasures for themselves to the detriment of the poor and defenseless.[33]

When Jesus talked about treasures in heaven (v. 22), he was thinking of *our good deeds*, which are the true *spiritual wealth*. Any good deed is like a *spiritual gold coin* that you have stored up in heaven. Over time, they will be a deposit for your soul when it enters the Kingdom of Heaven. It is not only God's mercy which opens the gate into the Kingdom of Heaven, but also the good deeds which we do during our earthly life. If a man stores up his treasure on earth, then his heart and soul will stay there. But if he stores up his treasure in heaven, then the gates of heaven will be opened for him. For where the treasure is, there will be man's heart and soul.

Therefore the radicalism of Jesus regarding the difficulties encountered by a rich man who wants to enter the Kingdom of Heaven (v. 25) is fully justified. Jesus' attitude is admirably outlined by St. Basil the Great, who says that the rich man cannot hope that by earning wealth he will redeem the sins he has committed, because wealth has not a redemptive function in the Christian sense. The rich take their reward only during their earthly life. After their death, they will not take anything with them other than the injustices they have committed and these will not help them but rather they will condemn.[34]

Wealth, Power and Ministry as Perfect Application of Jesus Words

There is often a very close connection between wealth and power. Rich people often possess considerable influence, while those who are powerful frequently become rich. A man, who possesses wealth and properties (such as media institutions and real estate), will have connections in all fields of life and employees whose lives depend on his decisions. *Thus, because he is rich, he has power.* Likewise, a man who holds high political and administrative functions – with the power of decision and influence in the highest spheres of civil society – *can become wealthy* by using his business skills and intellectual potential. In other words, there is a kind of inter-dependence between wealth and power, noting that, once acquired, they can each make a master into a slave.

Typically, excessive wealth makes you lose your internal balance and believe that everything is permitted. You believe that nothing is impossible when you have enough money. Wealth is delusory, giving you the feeling that you hold all the power and control, whereas actually you are just a tool, without will and without freedom, acting under the impulse of purely material interests.[35] Moreover, you have the feeling that all your decisions are unbeatable and you are always right. You do not accept criticism, contradiction or defeat. You love to be beloved and you start to believe that everyone owes you respect and appreciation. You are convinced that you are above, better and cleverer than others, and the higher you climb the political or social ladder, the more you need them to bring you more honours and to be more submissive to you. Your rationality is in darkness. Your conscience is perverted and your value system reverses its hierarchy. In short, you turn into someone whose heart no longer belongs to Him.

The high official from the Gospel was part of the elite society of his time.[36] He had money and power and acted accordingly. We do not know how he got them, but we realize how difficult it is for him to be separated from them.

He addresses Jesus as he is used to being addressed himself. He had servants who would have done anything to get into his good graces. The same happens today with rich people, who have not only money and wealth, but power over others. Those who are serving these people know very well that it is risky to misrepresent their words or to question their judgment. They fear them because they have money, connections in all fields and can influence any decisions. For them, laws are changed, suspended or made no longer applicable following various pretexts. Here's why our high official thought he would get an answer which would fully satisfy him. He believed that the age-old successful formula, practiced by the rich and powerful of his time, would prevail: as do so many such men of our own times.

By contrast, Jesus was a *true* leader, stronger and richer than anyone else, but *His power was defined as ministry* and his wealth as renunciation. He brings into this world a different kind of relationship between people; one that the high official from the Gospel does not understand. What is most sad, is that the ruler does not want to try to understand, but simply refuses. He felt that his social status allowed him a special treatment in accordance with the attitudes of his time. The relationship between people was a distorted one, wherein one type of person was expected to dominate the other. Jesus comes to replace this materialistic way of thinking with a spiritual or sacerdotal one.

The materialist example par excellence, which reflects the worldly balance of power even in social democratic systems, is found in the political sphere. Normally, under democracy, "people power" should perfectly fit within the moral parameters of the Gospel: where the biggest and strongest must serve those numerous and defenseless. Because political leaders are elected by the people, they are representatives of the people and lead in their name. Their duty is to be *servants of the people*. In other words, their mission is not to receive honours, or to make a fortune, in ways more or less illicit, but to serve. It is worth noting that the word *Minister* means *servant* (ὑπηρέτης *in Luke 1:2*). This term is used for "priests" in religious language because the priest is the *servant* of God and of his believers. This is the duty that Christ requires. And He gives himself as an example. He says that the Son of Man came into the world not to be served but to serve, to be the servant of all (Mark 10:45). However, what Minister remembers every day that he must serve the people? How many congressmen, once in government, remember that their primary duty is to try to solve the problems of those who chose them? Unfortunately, rather, they often consider themselves entitled to dictate to the people or, at best, to ignore them.[37]

The message of "service" is exactly what Christ the Saviour brought into the world. In the Gospel according to Mark, we can read how this message is taken up in answer to a request from two of his own disciples. The two brothers, James and John, Zebedee's sons, desire to sit at His right and left when He will sit on the throne of the Kingdom of Heaven. Jesus answers by telling them that they know not what they say. He tells them that their relationship must not be one of domination but one of ministry, saying, "If anyone wants to be great among you he will be your servant, and if anyone wants to be first among you he will be the slave of all" (Mark 10: 43–44). His meaning is further developed by His use of the word *among* rather than *above*. I suggest that these words anticipate, at least in principle, the relationship between people today in a democratic society. I say "in principle" because, in reality, even in today's democratic societies, there are inevitable hierarchies. Sadly, if leaders think in terms of "above" rather than "among" each other, then the notion of power – and perhaps the desire for it – is automatically induced. Likewise, the dehumanizing nature of power, as with wealth, lures men into a system wherein the Gospel standards of morality are found only in the letter of the Law and not in the spirit of the act.

The two words, *ministry* and *service*, define a single reality. The legacy our Saviour Jesus Christ left us is to *serve one another*. Each of us is a *gift* from God and our duty is to acknowledge each other as His gift. Regardless of the field in which we work – in education, in health, in public office or in the Church, we have to be aware that through our work, done with fervour and conscience, we are expected to put ourselves in the service of others. This is the definition of interpersonal communion that God wants from us.[38]

Conclusions

The two concepts of *wealth* and *power* can either corrupt each other, when deprived of Christ's support, or they can support each other and be transformed into ministry, when employed in the service of God and our neighbours.

Wealth and power enslave a person because they occupy his mind with worries of their loss. By such limiting thoughts, they make the individual their slave.

God has given people material goods from His most great kindness and, consequently, we can imitate Him, showing our love for our fellows (1 Corinthians 11:1; Ephesians 5:1–2).

The Rich could show their love for the Poor through their material acts of mercy, and the Poor could show theirs to the Rich by acts of spiritual prayer. Thus, they will appear together at the Supreme Judgment.

Notes

1 John Gillman, *Possession and the Life of Faith: A Reading of Luke-Acts* (Minnesota: The Liturgical Press, 1991), 80–81.

2 Gillman, *Possession and the Life of Faith*, 85.

3 John Nolland, *Luke 18: 35–24:53 (WBC)*, vol. 35c (Dallas: Word Books, 1993), 908.

4 Darrell L. Bock, *Luke 9:51–24:53 (BECNT)*, (Grand Rapids, Michigan, Baker Academic, 1996), 1476. The author suggests that the terminology of Luke is important, because, in his writings, when he uses the word "ruler", he refers to the Pharisees, a group that had a good reputation, as it is known.

5 L. Bock, 1476.

6 Usually, this kind of addressing someone was used, in certain situations, for good people, but in no way was it used for God. See I. Howard Marshall, *The Gospel of Luke (NIGTC)* (Grand Rapids, MI: The Paternoster Press &William B. Eerdmans Publishing, 1978), 684.

7 John W. Wenham, "Why Do You Ask Me About The Good? A Study of the Relation between Text and Source of Criticisme: Short Studies", *New Testament Studies* 28.1 (1982): 116–125.

8 Léonce de Grandmaison, Jésus Christ, sa personne, son message, ses preuves, "*Verbum Salutis*", *I* (Paris: Gabriel Beauchesne, 1930), 287–288.

9 Jesus' declaration regarding the fact that only God is good emphasises the unicity of His holiness and justice, a declaration that we can frequently find in the Old Testament (1 Cronici 16.34; 2 Cronici 5.13, Ps. 34.8; 106.1; 118.1; 136.1 etc. See L. Bock, 1478.

10 Fowl connects the question the ruler raised to Jesus to the claim about entering the kingdom (eternal life) as a child. (Stephen Fowl, "Receiving the Kingdom of God as a Child: Children and Riches in Luke 18.15ff', *New Testament Studies* 39 (1993): 153–158.

11 L. Bock, 1476.

12 Bartolomeu Anania (Metropolitan of Cluj), The leading man. Listened from http://www.crestinortodox.ro/predici-audio-mp3/i-p-s-bartolomeu-anania/ips-bartolomeu-anania-tanarul-bogat-134078.html (accessed 20.05.2020)

13 Luke Timothy Johnson, *The Gospel of Luke (Sacra pagina)*, vol. 3 (Minnesota: The Liturgical Press, 1991), 278. The author suggests that the commandments that the Lord Jesus reminds are a combination of those in Deuteronomy 6.5 and Leviticus 19.18.

14 L. Bock, 1476.

15 John Nolland, *Luke 18:35–24:53 (WBC) vol. 35c* (Dallas: Word Books, 1993), 887.

16 This must be taken as an oriental way of talkink since we find a number of western scholars who agree that the ruler was sincere in his confession. He comes to Jesus with a vital question about eternal life affirming he has been a careful observer of the commandments since his youth (Ezra P. Gould, *A Critical and Exegetical Commentary on the Gospel according to St. Mark* (Edinburgh: T. & T. Clark, 1907):191; Walther Zimmerli, "Die Frage des Reichen nach dem ewigen Leben", *Evangelische Theologie* 19 (1959): 96; Julius Schniewind, *Das Evangelium nach Markus (Das Neue Testament Deutsch*, 1 (Gottingen: Vandenhoeck &Ruprecht, 1958: 103).
17 David Peter Seccombe, *Possessions and the Poor in Luke – Acts* (Studien zum Neuen Testament und seiner Umwelt, B.6 (Linz: Albert Fuchs, 1982), 121.
18 Gould, 191.
19 Seccombe, 124.
20 For details see Seccombe, 121–123.
21 Josef Ernst, J., *Das Evangelium nach Lukas (Regensburger Neues Testament)*, (Regensburg: Verlag, 1977), 501.
22 Hierotheos (Vlachos) of Nafpaktos, *Monahismul Ortodox ca viață profetică, apostolică și martirică [Orthodox monasticism as a prophetic, apostolic and martyric life]* (Craiova: Metropolitan of Oltenia Press, 2005), 22–26.
23 Irineu Pop, "Învățăminte morale și sociale în opera Sfântului Vasile cel Mare, necesare activității preoților în vremea noastră [Moral and social ideas in the writings and activity of Saint Basil the Great]" *Studii Teologice* 3–4 (1985): 282–283.
24 Charles Cranfield, "Riches and the Kingdom of God St. Mark 10, 17-31", *Scottish Journal of Theology* 4 (1951): 302–313.
25 Daniel Dayuch, "Chrysostom's unveiling of a new ethos. The social-action teaching in his four sermons on Luke 16:19-31", in N. Dumitrașcu (ed.) *Theology and Society* (Oradea: University Press, 2007), 27–28; 32–33, 41.
26 Robert O'Toole, *The Unity of Luke's Theology: An Analysis of Luke-Acts* (Good News Studies 9), (Willmington/Delaware: M. Glazier, 1984), 129.
27 O'Toole, 132.
28 Stephen Fowl, "Receiving the Kingdom of God as a Child: Children and Riches in Luke 18.15ff", *New Testament Studies* 39 (1993), 157.
29 Dayuch, 37.
30 S. Basilii Magni, *Patrologia Cursus Completus. Seria Graeca* (PG), ed. J. P. Migne, Paris, 1857, vol. 31, Homilia in divites, 296 B-C.
31 Theodor Damșa, "Wealth and Poverty in the Light of the Homilies of Saint Basil the Great", *Mitropolia Banatului* 4–6 (1979), 304–305.
32 S. Basilii Magni, Homilia II in Psalmum XIV, PG. vol. 29: 265 B.
33 This social injustice has always existed. Poverty, deprivation, suffering and misery have always been in the world, in all times and all peoples. At the end of the fourth century, Asterius of Amasea harshly condemns the way rich people acquired their wealth on account of the sufferings of the poor. Roman dignitaries were stealing from soldiers' incomes, they judged unjustly, and emptied the communities' storehouses to increase their fortunes. The rich who had a large harvest threw the surplus into the sea, and the poor would die of hunger. The rich were sleeping in luxurious palaces, and the poor who had no two beams to make a roof, were sleeping in the garbage like pigs. (Nestor Vornicescu, "Combaterea nedreptăților sociale în cuvântările episcopului Asterie al Amasiei [Combating social injustice in the speeches of Bishop Asterius of Amasea], *Studii Teologice* 7–8 (1958): 455).
34 S. Basilii Magni, Homilia in Psalmum LXI, PG. Vol. 30, 480C.

35 Ioan Bria, "Mission and Secularization in Europe", *International Review of Mission* 77 (1988): 117–130.

36 The term in Luke is ἀρχός, which most probably means a leader in the synagogue. It is again the rich Jew in the sense the one who has the grace of God in abundance and does not want to share it with the gentiles, who were poor of grace.

37 Nicu Dumitrașcu, "Despre o ierarhie incertă a valorilor în societatea românească. Teama de a ne asuma public propria identitate [About an uncertain hierarchy of values in Romanian society. The fear to assume in public our own identity]", in D. Vanca and T. Tia (eds) Invasion of Non-Values in a Multi-Media Society (Alba Iulia: Reîntregirea Publishing House, 2010), 305–317.

38 Theodor Damian, "Aspecte ale teologiei darului în sinteza părintelui Stăniloae [Aspects of Gift Theology in the Synthesis of Father Staniloae]", *Glasul Bisericii* 5–8 (1999): 25–34.

Bibliography

Bartolomeu, A. 2007, *The Leading Man*. Listened from http://www.crestinortodox.ro/predici-audio-mp3/i-p-s-bartolomeu-anania/ips-bartolomeu-anania-tanarul-bogat-134078.html

Basilii Magni, S. 1857, *Patrologia Cursus Completus*. Seria Graeca (PG), (ed. J.P. Migne), Paris, vol. XXIX, Homilia II in Psalmum XIV, 265 B.

Basilii Magni, S. 1857, *Patrologia Cursus Completus*. Seria Graeca (PG), (ed. J.P. Migne), Paris, vol. XXX, Homilia in Psalmum LXI, 480 C.

Block, Darell L. 1996, Luke 9:51–24:53 (BECNT), (Grand Rapids, Michigan, Baker Academic).

Bria, I. 1988, "Mission and Secularization in Europe", *International Review of Mission*, 77 (305), 117–130.

Cranfield, C.E.B. 1951, "Riches and the Kingdom of God St. Mark 10, 17-31", *Scottish Journal of Theology*, 4, 302–313.

Damian, T. 1999, "Aspects of gift theology in the synthesis of Father Staniloae", *Glasul Bisericii*, 5–8, 25–34.

Damșa, T. 1979, "Wealth and Poverty in the light of the Homilies of Saint Basil the Great", *Mitropolia Banatului*, 4–6, 304–305.

Dayuch, D.A. 2007, "Chrysostom's unveiling of a new ethos. The social-action teaching in his four sermons on Luke 16:19-31", in N. Dumitrașcu (ed.) *Theology and Society*, 24–43 (University of Oradea Publishing House, Oradea).

de Grandmaison, L. 1930, *Jesus Christ, sa personne, so message, ses preuves*, Verbum Salutis, I, Paris, 287–288.

Dumitrașcu, N. 2010, "About an uncertain hierarchy of values in Romanian society. The fear to assume in public our own identity", in D. Vanca and T, Tia (eds.) *Invasion of non-values in a multi-media society*, 305–317 (Reîntregirea Publishing House, Alba Iulia).

Ernst, J. 1977, *Das Evangelium nach Lukas (Regensburger Neues Testament)*, Regensburg, 501.

Fowl, St. 1993, "Receiving the Kingdom of God as a Child: Children and Riches in Luke 18.15ff", *New Testament Studies* 39, 153–158.

Gillman, J. 1991, *Possession and the Life of Faith: A Reading of Luke-Acts* (Minnesota: The Liturgical Press).

Gould, E.P. 1907, *A Critical and Exegetical Commentary on the Gospel according to St. Mark* (Edinburgh: T&T Clark).
Johnson, Luke Timothy. 1991, *The Gospel of Luke (Sacra pagina)*, vol. 3 (Minnesota: The Liturgical Press).
Marshall, I. Howard. 1978, *The Gospel of Luke (NIGTC)* (Grand Rapids, MI: The Paternoster Press &William B. Eerdmans Publishing).
Nolland, John. 1993, *Luke 18: 35–24:53 (WBC)*, vol. 35c (Dallas: Word Books).
O'Toole, R.F. 1984, *The Unity of Luke's Theology* (Good News Studies 9), Delaware (SUA), 129–135.
Pop, I. 1985, "Moral and social ideas in the writings and activity of Saint Basil the Great", *Studii Teologice*, 3–4, 282–283.
Schniewind, J. 1958, *Das Evangelium nach Markus (Das Neue Testament Deutsch, 1)*, Gottingen, 103.
Seccombe, D.P. 1982, *Possesions and the Poor in Luke – Acts* (Studien zum Neuen Testament und seiner Umwelt, B.6), Linz.
Vlahos, I. 2005, *Metropolitan of Nafpaktos, 2005, Orthodox monasticism as a prophetic, aposthlic and martyr life*, 22–26 (Craiova: Metropolitan of Oltenia Publishing House).
Vornicescu, N. 1956, "Combating social injustice in the speeches of Bishop Asterius of Amasea", *Studii Teologice* 7–8, 455.
Wenham, John W. 1982, "Why Do You Ask Me About The Good? A Study of the Relation between Text and Source of Criticisme: Short Studies", *New Testament Studies*, 28.1.
Zimmerli, W. 1959, "Die Frage des Reichen nach dem ewigen Leben", *Evangelische Theologie*, 19, 90–97.

9 "Love Whoever Hates You and Persecutes You" The Reception of the Mount Sermon in a Fourth-Century Anonymous Work

Pablo Argárate

Introduction

The *Ktābā dmasqātā*[1] or Liber Graduum (LG) is a *collection of 30 discourses* or *mēmrē* (M) from an anonymous author, preceded by a prologue written by the Syrian editor of the work. It was not until 1719 that the LG is mentioned in the manuscripts of the Vatican. Kmosko found it in 1901 within the manuscripts of the British Museum, edited, and published it in 1926 with an extensive introduction ("Praefatio"), a Latin translation, and a dossier on the development of Messalianism.[2] Kmosko's work will strongly determine the directions of research for many years. In addition, he mentioned in the introduction, three key areas, namely, the date of the LG, its relation to the Messalian movement, and the Diatessaron as its underlying biblical text.

In Kmosko's edition, the text takes 460 columns of the Patrologia Syriaca. About the *author* of the LG, states the editor that he wished to remain anonymous and that nothing is known about his life and time. He holds only to traditions that consider the author to be one of the last disciples of the Apostles. The editor assumes that he was one of the first teachers who wrote in Syriac. He also calls him "Blessed" (*tubana*). It is clear therefore that even the editor of the LG does not know much about the author. Almost all experts now agree on a deliberate *anonymity*. The author regards himself as a charismatic interpreter of the Bible. Furthermore, the content of the work shows that the writer is a spiritual leader of a pre-Christian monastic community in a time of change.[3]

The *date* of the LG is today fixed in the second half of the fourth century with the *terminus ante quem* of 400.[4] It has to be *placed* in the Persian Empire in Mesopotamia, Adiabene in what is today northern Iraq.[5] More precisely, in a hilly region with frost in winter, in the vicinity of the Roman Empire.

The various *mēmrē* are diverse regarding extension and genre. While M 19 is the longest, M 6 is the shortest *mēmrā*. There is usually no continuity among the different pieces. R. Kitchen suggests the following *structure*: (a) basic commands (M 1–9); (b) advanced perfection (10–24); (c) last period

DOI: 10.4324/9781003273592-9

and salvation of the righteous (25–30). According to the *genre*, the LG is a rule for the community, with long biblical stories, sermons, treatises on the controversy over the role of the contemporary church and also about sexuality and marriage, brief oppositions between righteous and perfect, and justification and encouragement of the spiritual ministry of the righteous.[6] Above all, Kitchen sees the LG as a "sect-canon", which serves the needs of the community.[7]

Regarding *reception and impact* of the LG, they are almost non-existent. The fundamental distinction between the righteous and perfect occurs only in Philoxenos of Mabbug, however, in a different context. The *community* of the LG appears as an isolated, short-lived, and localized phenomenon. It will not survive the internal and external conflicts and violent upheavals. On the one hand, this form of Christianity is strongly rooted in the archaic characteristics of the Syrian Church. On the other hand, it remains an unsolved mystery. Nevertheless, the LG is one of the most ancient works which has come to us from ancient Syriac literature devoted to the subject of spiritual life and asceticism. As such it is a very precious source and witness to the very archaic spirituality of Christianity in Mesopotamia. It unfolds a pneumatic mysticism, characteristic of archaic Syrian spirituality indigenous to Mesopotamian Christianity. Indeed, this manifestation of an enigmatic form of Christianity puzzled scholars since the publication of Kmosko's edition of the *Ktābā dmasqātā*.

Among many features, it is the profusion and variety of *religious groups* portrayed throughout its 30 *mēmrē*, which particularly drew attention to our anonymous work. Along with some more traditional forms such as the leaders of the community, the priests, the "sick" and the "children", some mysterious sorts of Christian enter into the picture like the group of "faith" and that of "love". Nevertheless, the most frequent and consistent ones are the *Upright* (or righteous) and the *Perfect*. This distinction is closely associated with that one between major and minor commandments or between corporal and spiritual ministries. The origin of the separation between Perfection and Uprightness is traced by the LG to the very origins. Adam, created in Perfection, by failing to keep God's commandments fell from that state and Uprightness, which was sanctioned until the coming of Christ, who would manifest in himself the true nature of Adam and Perfection.

The *LG* portrays this *Perfection* in a rather negative way, by denying the features of Uprightness.[8] Whereas the upright live in the world and care for it, working, possessing, and getting married, the Perfect are characterized by radical renunciation of the world (they "fast to the world"), neither working nor marrying nor having any tie with that world. On the contrary, they closely follow Christ by taking up his cross in complete poverty and lowliness. And in doing so, according to the *LG*, they have succeeded in acquiring the status that Adam had in paradise before the fall.[9] Their functions within the community comprise teaching to all the new life and the distinction between major and minor commandments. However, repeatedly the LG places the hallmark of Perfection in unlimited love and forgiveness, in the footsteps of the Jesus' Sermon on the Mount. The Perfect are thus required to love and forgive all, without distinction: women, heretics, pagans, sinners, and even their own murderers.[10]

The *quest for perfection* builds without any doubt the centre of the *LG*. From its very outset, already in the first paragraph of M 1, Perfection and Uprightness are brought into relation with the commandments of the Lord. These fall into two major categories: major and minor commandments. Furthermore, this distinction is closely related to that, which separated between Perfection and Uprightness. Indeed M1 begins by summarizing its topic:

> In which can be found an exposition of the commandments, showing for what purpose each single one has been given and to whom, why our Lord Jesus Christ gave major and minor commandments, and how one can distinguish Perfection from Uprightness, and that through the major commandments one becomes Perfect and through the minor ones Upright.[11]

At this juncture, the author identifies the rationale of the *LG* as teaching the fundamental discernment between both types of commandments. In fact, the major commandments constitute the topic of M 2,[12] where the author rehearses a long list of exhortations taken from the New Testament, mostly from the Gospel, and especially from the Sermon on the Mount/Plain. Curiously, among these, there is no mention of love of God, but chiefly love of Christ, love among the disciples, and even to the enemies. In addition, it is worth noting that in the *LG* the major commandments do not primarily refer to the Decalogue but to the new Law proclaimed by Christ.[13]

Love to God is addressed in a general sense,[14] referred as one of "the great commandments in the Torah", on account of their object. These are even called "the two great commandments of love",[15] which are at the same time.[16] One ought to point out here the variations in the rendering of these commandments. Traditionally couched as "Love the Lord your God with all your heart and with all your strength and with all your soul and with all your mind",[17] following the biblical text, it also appears as: "Love the Lord your God more than yourself and your neighbor as yourself".[18] In addition, this love to God is required to be deep and "with everything you have",[19] even loving "God more than yourself".[20]

Nevertheless, this love to God does not appear usually without reference to the *love to the neighbours*.[21] These are interpreted in a broad sense and entail "all people" or, expressed in another way, "all descendants of Adam".[22] It is this love to all fellow humans, which takes the central position in the *LG*. The quest for perfection is thus deeply linked to love, more than to ascetical renunciation.

Turning our attention to the *biblical realm*, the *text* underlaying the LG is in first place the Diatessaron,[23] while the Pauline corpus appears to be based on a pre-Peshitta form. Besides the canonical books, we find references to Sirach, the Acts of Thekla, the Didache, the Shepherd of Hermas, and the Gospel of Thomas.

A basic feature of the LG can be seen in its *strong biblical approach.*[24] Although it is not primarily an exegetical work, it is full with more than 1,200 quotations from the Bible.[25] In addition to this, there are countless allusions and ultimately the whole horizon of thought of the work is biblical.

The exegesis of the LG is the subject of several studies. Here, we have to mention the studies by Louf,[26] Strothmann,[27] Kowalski,[28] Juhl,[29] Bettiolo,[30] and Kitchen.[31] The attention of scholars, as is particularly the case with Kowalski, focuses on the first three chapters of Genesis, namely the state before and after the Fall. Additionally, Corbett believes to have found in "call for a holy war" of Deuteronomy the basic symbolic structure, upon which is the *LG* based.[32] However, despite this structural significance, the biblical main reference is, in my opinion, to be placed in the Sermon on the Mount, as I will discuss below.

In dealing with the Bible, the LG shows a *double attitude*. On the one hand, one may say that the LG is faithful to the integrity of the biblical story, being insofar in line with the Antiochene exegesis.[33] On the other hand, however, a certain "targumic" freedom from the text cannot be overlooked.[34] In this regard, we can see a certain *eisegesis*[35] that functions as a legitimation of the institution of the Upright and Perfect.[36] In this context, we have to see M 9 and M 19. While the former presents a real catena of texts, it is the important M 19, which has given the title of the whole work.

Mēmrā XIX

Mēmrā 19 is the longest of the entire LG. Its significance is not only given by its contents that I will later analyze but also by its reference to steps and ascent that eventually made from this anonymous work the "Book of Steps".

Although it is quite challenging to provide a general structure and organization of our book it is clear that the first *mēmrē* offers the first approach. As already exposed, M 1 has the title of "*On the distinction between the major commandments, for the perfect, and the minor commandments, for the upright*". Indeed, this serves not only as a description of the first M, but constitutes meanwhile a programmatic presentation of the entire book. From the very beginning, the author establishes a clear distinction within the community at which he is addressing his work. Perfect and Upright are served by different classes of commandments, i.e. major and minor. In other words, it is through these different commandments, that one attains either of these states. To a great extent, the entire message of the LG is summarized here. On the basis of this fundamental distinction, the LG will address either this or other group (or even some other[37]). In this vein, M2 addresses those who wish to be perfect. M3 establishes another distinction based on the prior one between physical and spiritual ministry. In fact, it reflects that distinction of M1, this time from another perspective. M 4–7 focuses on those who have not attained perfection. M4 and M5 are to great measure parallel since based upon Pauline imagery they refer to the sick and infant, who are fed by vegetables and milk. M7 following upon this deals finally with the commandments for the upright. From the very outset, it is clear that the LG proposes different categories of Christians and provides for that a biblical support, i.e. the diverse commandments. At the end of M7, among many other passages, this is clearly stated:

> God desires that all people should live. For this [reason], he gave major and minor commandments so that all might endeavor according to their strength. With the major ones, one becomes Perfect and with the minor ones, one becomes an Upright one.[38]

It is this discernment, which constitutes the content and title ("On the Discernment of the Way of Perfection") of our M19. In addition to this, we discover here the emergence of another key concept: "way".

This *mēmrē* is *structured* in the following way: After a relatively short introduction on the distinction between road and paths (paragraphs 1–8), the bulk of the chapter (paragraphs 9–34) provides a highly significant contraposition of biblical passages drawn almost exclusively from the New Testament. As it has been done in prior *mēmrē*, this contraposition aims at presenting the core of the biblical message. In effect, 25 (24) sets of relatively short biblical texts.[39] While the road is almost exclusively designed as "the road of perfection",[40] the other element of the contraposition is "the path(s) that deviate from that road". The superiority of the road over the paths is apparent. This is why the author of the LG feels obliged to briefly explain why the minor commandments or paths have been promulgated. In the conclusion (paragraphs 35–40), the author backs to the introduction by underscoring again the superiority and in the meantime the necessity of undertaking the road, while stating the temporal character of the paths.

Relevant for our present study is the *use of biblical texts* within the *mēmrē*. With the only exception of two Old Testament passages, interestingly situated at the beginning and end of the lists, all the other texts proceed from the New Testament, chiefly the Synoptics (no reference to John) and the Pauline letters (included Hebrews) and only one mention of the book of Acts. Besides this concentration upon the New Testament, we can observe the *centrality of some passages* that come again on different occasions as it is especially the case of Phil 2:3: "Consider every person better than yourself".[41]

I have already pointed out the significance of the concept of road, which is opposed to the multiple paths. It was also stated that this couple is connected to the one that distinguishes between major and minor commandments. The Road of Perfection is one of the so-called major commandments, while the paths are the minor ones.

First of all, we have to begin by stating that the *distinction between road and paths* has no biblical basis. On the contrary, both concepts appear usually in parallel, mainly in Isaiah (2:3; 26:7; 30:11; 40:3; 43:16) but also in the Synoptics in reference to John the Baptist and the Messiah (for instance Mt 3:3 that quotes Isa 40:3[42]). Especially interesting is Isa 2:3:

> And many peoples will come and say, 'Come, let us go up to the mountain of the Lord, To the house of the God of Jacob; That He may teach us concerning His ways and that we may walk in His paths.' For the law will go forth from Zion and the word of the Lord from Jerusalem.

Its relevance is due not only by the reference to road and paths and having both in plural, but also because of the image of the "mountain of the Lord". This text is, nevertheless, never alluded in the *LG* nor are the concepts of road and paths opposed. On the contrary, they appear to be a parallel expressions. Lastly, another couple comes here referring, also in parallel, the eschatological revelation of God by his law/will. In any case, significant for us is here that the author of the *LG* cannot refer to the Scriptures as support for his distinction between road and paths.

In the ancient culture (biblical and extra-biblical), the *images of road and of path* are very well known and design moral conduct and options based on personal freedom in shaping the own life. In the Synoptics, we have in addition the reference to the way or road "of life" (Mt 7:14), which is connected to a narrow gate. The LG quotes this text. However, "life" as a goal of the road is opposed to "perfection": "But listen to what our Lord said, 'The road that leads to life is narrow'; but how much more narrow is that [road] that leads to Perfection and to the greater glory?"[43] In the *LG*, therefore, there is no mention of the gate and the road leads not to life but to perfection, while the paths are said to conduct to "places of life". Besides this, the image of LG is not of walking but mainly of ascending a steep road on a mountain that leads to the "city of the saints". To some extent, it could be drawn into parallel with Moses ascent, however, with different nuances. Gregory of Nyssa's *Vita Moysis* moves in this direction. Perhaps closer is the later seventh-century *Scala Paradisi*. Nevertheless in LG, there is no mention of a ladder, as it is the case of the work of John Climacus.

Regarding the *paths*, we cannot avoid noticing a certain ambiguity. Almost all the biblical passages referring to the path are introduced by stating from them that they "deviate from the straight road". Their function is therefore clearly negative. In two passages, there is, nevertheless, an attempt of reverting this to some extent by affirming that these paths are God's will. In effect, they "are not despicable, but our Lord and his preachers made them deviate from that great road because of the infant and the sick".[44] The same is expressed almost at the end of the *mēmrē*: "Because of this [the infants and the ill] our Lord and his preachers prepared for them paths...".[45] In this vein, the paths appear to be a concession to weakness and have only a temporary value and eventually they inevitably have to lead to the road. Nevertheless, it is apparent that, in most of the cases, it is exactly the opposite of what occurs and they end up preventing people from taking up the road.

The topic of the road and paths has led us – already from the very title – to the concomitant subject of the different kinds of *commandments*. While the images of the road and paths are mostly concentrated on M 19,[46] the distinction of commandments pervades the entire LG.

The significance of the commandments (*mitzvuot*, *entolai*) in the Bible does not need to be underscored. Due to its relevance and in the meantime its number, already in the sacred texts, we find the quest for finding some kind of order and hierarchy within a large amount of commandments. While the Decalogue takes a crucial place in biblical revelation, this "ten words" or commandments are not in any way the unique systematization of God's commandments. In fact, besides the key function of the ten words of the Sinai, we observe throughout the Bible, constant efforts of reducing God's commandment to a manageable number and, in the same way, to establish, which are the fundamental of all these series. Tradition will soon regard in the *Sh^ema* the crucial mandate and in the meantime attitude of Israel towards its Lord. Love of the neighbour (Lv 19:18) will soon take a second place to the *Sh^ema*. In this context, Jesus himself provides this answer in Mt 22, Mk 12, Lk 10 when he is asked about which of all the commandments are the most important. In this statement of Jesus, the New Testament is a witness to the ongoing question of the relevance of the commandments and its structure and hierarchy. In other words, a distinction between many commandments needs to be established. This requires, however, certain hermeneutical criteria that ground the distinction and hierarchy.

In this sense, Jewish tradition, and as such also reflected in the New Testament, provides a certain precedent and basis for the LG's distinction between major and minor commandments, although without using its explicit terminology.

Within this context of systematization of the commandments, the LG acknowledges the key function of *Jesus Christ as the definitive interpreter of Scriptures*:

> Look, the apostle said, 'He made the first and last Testaments one Testament. He eliminated the law of the commandments, which were not necessary by his won commandments so that in both of these testaments of which he had made one Gospel, he might create people anew... For he took these major commandments of the Old Testament, these upon which hung the whole power of the Law and the prophets,

> and fixed them in the New Testament and gathered all of its power, the first and the last and placed them in a single New Testament...[47]

In the *set of 25 pairs of biblical texts*, which constitute the centre of M 19, major commandments can be reduced to an unlimited love that forgives and reaches sinners, the ones who hate, offend, and even murder us. This had been previously stated in M 11:

> For a person will never rise above that [commandment], ... nor will he attain Perfection, unless he approaches that [commandment], 'Forgive him seventy times seven' and 'Think of him as better than you.'

Unlimited love makes the heart pure. Ascetical elements such as not possessing anything, fasting, or even not marrying, although present within the major commandments, have only the preliminary function of enabling perfect love. On the contrary, every kind of limitation refers to the minor commandments, addressed to those who are not capable so far of going beyond any boundary. In this sense, major commandments regard *the other as a mysterious presence of God that needs to be acknowledged and venerated*. Within this context, one can understand how the precept of loving "your neighbor *as* yourself" can be considered by the *LG* as being a minor commandment. In fact, the Gospel, concentrated in the Sermon of the Mount, requires as the often-quoted passage of Phil 2:3 states, considering everybody better than oneself.

When the author of the LG has to explain the *rationale for the minor commandments*, his answer refers almost always to a concession to the weakness and their transitory value. These commandments are provided mostly for the infant, the immature, the sick, and the feeble. In this sense, these minor commandments are described as *spiritual milk* to the *solid food* of the major commandments. There are few passages, however, where the minor commandments are addressed to the dissolute, the stiffed-necked and corrupt,[48] or the wrong-doers and offenders. Interesting to note is that the LG regards the leaders and rulers of the community as incapable of perfection mainly due to their duty of judging and punishing the guilty ones. On this basis, as long as they carry out their duty they are not able to accomplish the unlimited love towards sinners and, by this, of attaining perfection.

Having distinguished from the very beginning major from minor commandments as a key criterion and rationale for the *LG* and manifested the significance of the major commandments, the *LG* goes yet even beyond, by maintaining the possibility – and to some extent even the requirement – of *transcending those major commandments*. Moreover, this is explicitly linked to love.

"If one is prepared to try, it will prove possible not only to surpass the minor commandments for the sake of love, but even the major ones".[49]

This transcendence of major commandments is the special topic of M16, which deals "about how a person may surpass the major commandments in love". And this is explained through texts drawn from the Gospels, chiefly from the Sermon on the Mount.[50] In a paradigmatic passage, the author renders even in a clearer fashion what is meant with transcending those commandments:

> Again he said to you: 'Love your brother more than yourself. From here you shall understand what is love – whoever will put himself in the place of his friend. If my love is true for you, offer yourself in place of your brothers.' However, if you love the evil ones, your despisers, more than yourself, you are much greater than he who [only] loves his neighbor more than himself and his despiser as himself. In this way, you will greatly surpass the major commandments and be glorified with our Lord... Kiss the feet of your betrayers, and look, you will surpass one who [only] washes the feet of his betrayers.[51]

This passage clearly transpires Christian maximalism, linking Perfection to love to the enemies and murderers. The Sermon on the Mount and its logic appear at the core of the *LG* rather than the Call to Holy War.[52] Indeed, I would like to draw the attention to its usage of the first part of the section immediately following the beatitudes in Lk 6:27–28. In five places, the *LG* refers to this passage expressed by the conjunction of the three verbs, i.e. bless, love, and pray, however, with some variants. While the text of Luke presents four verbs, *LG* always omits "do good", placing "bless" before "love", and connecting "love" with those who "hate", and replacing "those who abuse you" by "those who [harm and] persecute [and deals harshly with] you".[53] As a result, the opposition between love and hate is stronger. In addition to this, the *LG* introduces the topic of persecution that was not explicitly present in the New Testament text.[54] This evidently has its own purpose in addressing the persecutions taking place in the community.[55] In the highly significant M19, which opposes roads and paths, the author holds:

> The Perfect road is this, 'Bless him who curses you and love him who hates you, and pray for whomever harms you and persecutes you'.[56]

The relevance of this passage lies in identifying these three attitudes with the perfect road, i.e. with Perfection. In some other places, alongside the above-mentioned three verbs, forgiveness appears as well.[57] Another significant passage in the same *mēmrē*, conflating texts from Matthew and Luke, states in an even more persuasive fashion:

> This is the Perfect road: If you love only the one who loves you and you greet only your brothers, what is your righteousness? Because even

> tax-collectors and heathen and sinners act in this way. But love whoever hates you and persecutes you, and your peace will increase toward the good and the evil, and you shall be imitating the Father in heaven who makes his sun rise[58] and his rain fall upon them equally.[59]

Conclusions

The *LG* interprets the Bible against this background of the fundamental distinction between major and minor commandments – already present in the title of M1 – which provides the key instrument for presenting the different ways of perfection and uprightness, under the images of the road and the paths. It is not clear that this constitutes, as Kitchen has suggested, a presupposed agenda in interpreting the biblical texts.

Although to some extent the *LG* is moving in the direction of the later Antiochene school there is no full identification, first of all since the *LG* precedes it. Its analysis while fully respecting text and context turns often into *eisegesis* and reading into the texts its main intuitions, i.e. the distinction between perfection and uprightness.

The Syriac *LG* is to be situated rather in the history of reception and interpretation of the Sermon on the Mount. Within this context, it remains almost unparalleled in reflecting Jesus' uncompromised maximalism and radicalism.

> Therefore, when we have climbed these steps and have rooted up sin and its fruits from the heart, then we will be filled with the Spirit, the Paraclete, and our Lord will dwell in us completely. We will eat freely from that tree of life that is our Lord, from which we were deprived by the transgression of the commandments; and then, we will be able to love and be merciful to all people, even our murderers, and be able to pray with love for all people and for our murderers. When we [are able to have] mercy upon and love everyone in this way, including our murderers, our heart being pure, then we will increase in Perfection and live according to that great, acceptable, and perfect will of our Lord.[60]

The *LG* acknowledges therefore the centrality of scriptures in the life of Christian communities. It is these scriptures that shape the community. In doing this, the author of the *LG* seeks in the meantime for the centre of scriptures, of divine revelation, and finds this in Jesus' message of universal and unlimited love. This is the deepest revelation of the mystery of God, of the Father's heart and will. The radicality of that message is not watered down in the *LG*'s understanding of perfection. This cannot be reduced to asceticism or even to mysticism, but requires a dynamism that goes beyond any limitation.

Perfects and Perfection in the *LG* require indeed an extreme asceticism[61] that entails the full renunciation of the world in all its forms. Nevertheless, the goal of this tremendous asceticism is having received the Spirit, the configuration with the humble and suffering Christ and his all-embracing love.[62] In this *imitation Christi*, we become servants not only of the good but especially of the evil ones, the enemies, and even their own murderers,[63] Perfects are called not only to imitate Christ, but also, in doing so, to an *imitatio Patris*, by reflecting upon the world the deep mystery of God – like God's sun – the unlimited compassion of the Father, who does not distinguish between saints and sinners.

Notes

1 For a *status quaestionis* see Pablo Argárate, "Das *Ktābā dmasqātā*. Forschung und Bedeutung des syrischen Liber Graduum," in *Bibel, Byzanz und Christlicher Orient: Festschrift für Stephen Gerö zum 65. Geburtstag*, (Orientalia Lovaniensia Analecta 187, eds. Emmanouela Grypeou, Alexander B Toepel, Timothy Sailors and Dmitrij Bumazhnov (Leuven: Peeters, 2001), 239–258. Another publication attempting to cover the most relevant issues regarding our book, Christian S. Heal and Robert A. Kitchen, eds, *Breaking the Mind: New Studies in the Syriac "Book of Steps"* (Washington, DC: The Catholic University of America Press, 2014).

These are the chapters contained in it: Robert A. Kitchen, "Disturbed Sinners: The Pursuit of Sanctity in the Book of Steps"; Brian Colless, "Adelphios of Edessa as Author of the *Liber Graduum* and Messalianism"; John Corbett, "The Ascetic Life as Holy War: The Biblical Basis of the *Book of Steps*"; Jeff Childers, "A Broken Mind: The Path to Knowledge in *Liber Graduum*"; Martien Parmentier, "The *Liber Graduum/Book of Steps* on Magic"; René Roux, "Biblical Exegesis in the *Book of Steps*"; Geoffrey Greatrex, "The Romano-Persian Frontier and the Context of the *Book of Steps*"; Timothy Pettipiece, "Parallel Paths: Tracing Manichaean Footprints along the Syriac *Book of Steps*"; Pablo Argárate, "Perfects and Perfection in the *Book of Steps*"; Kelli Bryant, "You Are What You Eat: Dietary Metaphors in the Syriac *Liber Graduum*"; Tera Harmon, "Falling from the Path of Perfection: Sin in the Syriac *Liber Graduum*"; Kyle Smith, "A Last Disciple of the Apostle: The 'Editor's' Preface, Rabbula's *Rules*, and the Date of the *Book of Steps*"; Gregory Kessel, "A Previously Unknown Reattributed Fragment from Memra 16 of *Liber Graduum*"; Matthias Westerhoff, "Did the Author of the *Book of Steps* Understand Paul?"; Kristian S. Heal "Repentance in the *Book of Steps*"; David Taylor, "Future Directions in the Study of the Book of Steps"; Sergey Minov, "Marriage and Sexuality in the Book of Steps"; Thomas Kollamparampil, "Hidden Work of the Heart in the Liber Graduum"; Aryeh Kofsky und Serge Ruzer, "Reading the Ascetic Ideal into Genesis 1-3: Hermeneutic Strategies in *Liber Graduum* 21". See also David J. Lane, "The Book of Grades or Steps," *The Harp* 14 (2001), 81–88.

2 Michael Kmosko, ed., *Liber Graduum*. Patrologia Syriaca I,3 (Paris: Firmin-Didot, 1926). An English translation is provided in *The Book of Steps. The Syriac Liber Graduum*, Cistercian Studies 196, trans., intr., notes Robert A. Kitchen and Martien F. G. Parmentier (Kalamazoo, MI: Liturgical Press, 2004). This is the translation used in my study. In referring to the LG, I provide *mēmrē*, paragraph, and page of this translation.

3 Robert A. Kitchen, "Becoming Perfect: The Maturing of Asceticism in the Liber Graduum," *Journal of the Canadian Society for Syriac Studies* 2 (2002), 31.
4 Vgl. Kmosko, *Liber Graduum.* Praefatio, CXLIX–CLX.
5 A different position is expressed by Lionel Wickham, "Teaching about God and Christ in the Liber Graduum". In *Logos. Festschrift für Luise Abramowski* zum 8. Juli 1993, ed. Hans Brennecke. *Beihefte* zur *Zeitschrift* für die *neutestamentliche Wissenschaft* 6 (1993), 488: "The work probably comes from the fourth century; its milieu is West, rather than East, Syria".
6 Kitchen, *Becoming Perfect*, 31.
7 Robert. A. Kitchen, "The Gattung of the Liber Graduum, Implications for a Sociology of Asceticism". In *IV Symposium Syriacum, 1984: Literary Genres in Syriac Literature (Groningen, Oosterhesselen 10-12 September),* (Orientalia Christiana Analecta 229), (Rome: Pont. Institutum Studiorum Orientalium, 1987), 175.
8 This has lead to the belief that the *LG* might be addressed to the Upright rather than to the Perfect, this being more of a theological category. See Kitchen, The Gattung of the Liber Graduum, 181:

> The Just, who undoubtedly are the majority of the *LG* community, are more concretely described and are the principal audience of the *LG*. The Perfect are not as clearly defined and in fact, represent more a school, not an individual. Its function as a canon for the community was the purpose for writing.

9 See Aleksander Kowalski, *Perfezione e Giustizia di Adamo nel Liber Graduum*, Orientalia Christiana Analecta 232 (Rome: Pont. Institutum Studiorum Orientalium, 1989); Gary A. Anderson, *The Genesis of Perfection: Adam and Eve in Jewish and Christian Imagination* (Louisville: Westminster John Knox Press, 2001), and Robert A. Kitchen, "Syriac Additions to Anderson: The Garden of Eden in the Book of Steps and Philoxenus of Mabbug," *Hugoye Journal of Syriac Studies* 6,1 (2003), 1–47, https://doi.org/10.31826/hug-2010-060103.
10 See Pablo Argárate, "Perfects and Perfection in the *Book of Steps*", in Heal and Kitchen *Breaking the Mind.*
11 I, 1 (7).
12 II, 1 (13):

> Now let us expound the major commandments, through which a person is made Perfect; that is to say, those commandments that were given by our Lord and his apostles to the Perfect, and distinguish them from the 'vegetables and milk'.

13 And also by the apostles. II, 1 (13).
14 VII, 13 (74): "Then, let us deeply love our God and love and honor every person so that we may inherit the kingdom"; 79: human persons "should treat one another well and love their Creator".
15 IX, 3 (90): "Sometimes the Lord cast them down even below Uprightness, [the stage] that fulfills these two great commandments of love, because Uprightness does not curse or harm anyone."
16 XI, 1 (113) "When the Law says, 'Love the Lord your God more than yourself and your neighbor as you' you should say, 'This commandment is mine'."
17 XXX, 26 (360).
18 XI, 1 (113).
19 Instead of "with all your soul".

20 XXII, 23 (270–271): Know this, my friends, that all the beauty of the virtuous commandments, which you find in the Law or in the prophets, that is their sense, these commandments, which are called *iota* as our Lord said,

> You shall love the Lord God and the people who are all descendants of Adam, who are your neighbors, relatives, and family'. Therefore let us fulfill the Gospel and the *Iota*, which are one testament by which people conduct themselves in a new way.

21 XXX 26 (360): "and love your neighbour as yourself."
22 XXII, 23 (271).
23 Alfred Rücker, "Die Zitate aus dem Matthäusevangelium im syrischen 'Buche der Stufen'," *Byzantinische Zeitschrift* 20 (1932): 342–354.
24 In this way states Kitchen: "Virtually all his illustrations and allusions are biblical – with the exception of Memra Six...". Kitchen and Parmentier (transl.), The Book of Steps, lxiii. On the general biblical preaching in Syria, see Hughes Oliphant Old, *The Reading and Preaching of the Scriptures in the Worship of the Christian Church*. vol. 2: *The Patristic Age* (Grand Rapids, MI: Baker, 1998), 247–295. Also L. Wickham, *Teaching about God and Christ*, 487:

> The work is certainly learned in its scriptural exegeses and wealth of biblical quotations especially from the gospels and the Pauline corpus inclusive of Hebrews (without Revelation, 2 Peter, Jude and the small Johannines, though James is not cited either).

25 See Matthias Westerhoff, "Zur Paulus-Rezeption im Liber Graduum: der Apostel als Vorbild". In *Syriaca. Zur Geschichte, Theologie, Liturgie und Gegenwartslage der syrischen Kirchen*, 2. Deutsches Syrologen-Symposium (Juli 2000, Wittenberg), Studien zur orientalischen Kirchengeschichte Bd. 17, ed. Martin Tamcke (Münster: LIT Verlag, 2000), 254:

> Der LG entfaltet keinen Gedanken ohne Berufung auf die Heilige Schrift und hie insbesondere auf 'alles was unser Herr und er Apostel (...) ihren Jüngern befohlen haben' (5,5 [108]). Die Herrenworte entstammen der Bergpredigt und der Spruchtradition der Synoptiker insgesamt, weniger dem Johannesevangelium.

26 André Louf, "Une ancienne exégèse de Phil. 2, 6 dans le *K^{e}taba d^{e}Masqata* (Livre des degrés)" *Studiorum Paulinorum Congressus Internationalis Catholicis*, AB 17-18, Rome 1963, II, 523–533.
27 Werner Strothmann, "Jesus-Sirach-Zitate bei Afrahat, Ephraem und im Liber Graduum". In *A Tribute to A. Vööbus. Studies in Early Christian Literature and Its Environment, Primarily in the Syrian East*, ed. Robert H. Fischer (Chicago, IL: Lutheran School of Theology at Chicago, 1977), 153–158.
28 Kowalski, *Perfezione e Giustizia*, 183–200.
29 Diana Juhl, *Die Askese im Liber Graduum und bei Afrahat. Eine vergleichende Studie zur frühsyrischen Frömmigkeit*, Orientalia biblica et christiana 9 (Wiesbaden: Harrassowitz, 1996).
30 Paolo Bettiolo, "Scritture e cristianesimi nella Siria tra II e IV secolo," *Cristianesimo nella storia* 19,3 (1998), 479–481.
31 Robert A. Kitchen, "Making the Imperfect Perfect: The Adaptation of Hebrews 11 in the 9th Memra of the Syriac Book of Steps," In *The Reception and Interpretation of the Bible in Late Antiquity. Proceedings of the Montréal Colloquium in Honour of Charles Kannengiesser, 11-13 October 2006 (The Bible in Ancient Christianity)*, eds. L. DiTommaso and L. Turcescu (Leiden: Brill, 2008), 227–251.

32 John H. Corbett, "They Do not Take Wives, or build, or Work the Ground: Ascetic Life in the Early Syriac Church," *Journal of the Canadian Society for Syriac Studies* 3 (2003), 16–17:

> Semeio-structural analysis will clearly demonstrate how the Call to Holy War (with its associated themes of standing up, ascetic warfare, fasting and the single life—together, of course with the messianic banquet and the bridal chamber) generates the fundamental symbolic structure underlying the complex text of the Book of Steps.

33 Cf. Robert A. Kitchen "Slouching towards Antioch: Biblical Exposition in the Syriac Book of Steps". In *Syriac and Antiochian Biblical Interpretation for the 3rd Millennium*, ed. Robert D. Miller (Piscataway, NJ: Gorgias, 2008), 29.

34 Cf. A. Kowalski, *Perfezione e Giustizia*, 192: "Come abbiamo già osservato a proposito dell'AT, nel LG la Scrittura, pur conservando tratti facilmente riconoscibili della tradizione testuale siriana, viene trattata in un modo abbastanza libero, parafrastico, si potrebbe dire 'targumico'".

35 *The Book of Steps. The Syriac Liber Graduum*, lxiv.

36 See Peter Nagel, "Die "Märtyrer des Glaubens" und die "Märtyrer der Liebe" im syrischen Liber Graduum," In *Religion und Wahrheit. Religionsgeschichtliche Studien. F.S. Gernot Wießner zum 65. Geburtstag*, ed. Bärbel. Köhler (Wiesbaden: Harrassowitz, 1998), 129: "Aus diesem hermeneutischen Ansatz [d.h. der Unterscheidung zwischen kleinen und großen Geboten] resultiert eine Zwei-Stufen-Lehre: die erste Gruppe der Gebote gilt 'den Gerechten', die zweite den 'Vollkommenen'. Alle weitere Unterscheidungen sind diesem Grundsatz untergeordnet oder erscheinen als dessen Folge".

37 See particularly XXX.

38 VII, 21 (80).

39 In some cases, several passages appear convoluted.

40 On two occasions in different order the adjective "straight" is added to this description. XIX, 17 (194): "straight and Perfect road"; XIX, 20 (195): "Perfect and straight road".

41 Also, in II, 6 (18); V, 2 (46).4 (48).11 (53); VIII, 5 (85); XI, 4 (116).5 (117); XIX, 9 (191); XXX, 14 (352). There are, however, some variants in the rendering of the text. For instance, V, 11 (53) is: "Regard your neighbor better than yourself"; XI, 4 (116): "Consider your brother better than yourself"; XI, 5 (117): "Think of him as better than you", or even XXX, 14 (352), in an expanded way and in plural: "Take up the illness of the sick and consider everyone as better than yourselves."

42 Here the road is rendered in singular, while path appears in plural.

43 XIX, 3 (185).

44 XIX, 2 (184).

45 XIX, 35 (205).

46 And to some extent XX.

47 XIX, 7 (188).

48 XIX, 24 (199).

49 II, 41 (20)

50 XVI, 388–389 (159–160). The same takes place in 393–396 (161–162).

51 XVI, 396 (162).

52 J. Corbett, "They Do not Take Wives," 16–17.

53 Luke 6:27–28: "But I say to you that listen, Love your enemies, do good to those who hate you, bless those who curse you, pray for those who abuse you."

NT LG
Love – enemies bless – curse

Do good – hate
Bless – curse love – hate
Pray – abuse pray – (harm) persecute (deals harshly)

54 Although it was somehow present as closing element in the previous Beatitudes, there is no explicit mention of persecution there. Nevertheless, this connection is made in Mt 6:43 "You have heard that it was said, 'Love your neighbor and hate your enemy.'"

55 See Shafiq Abouzayd, "Violence and Killing in the Liber Graduum," *Aram* 11–12 (1999–2000), 451–465 and Robert A. Kitchen, "Conflict on the Stairway to Heaven. The Anonymity of Perfection in the Syriac Liber Graduum," In *Symposium Syriacum VII*, Orientalia Christiana Analecta 256, ed. René Lavenant (Rome: Pontificum Institutum Orientalium, 1998), 211–220.

56 XIX, 12 (192). See also II, 2 (14): "Love him who hates you, bless him who curses you, pray for the one who harms you and persecutes you" and XXX, 2 (341):

> Bless whoever curses you and love whoever hates you, and pray for whoever persecutes you and deals harshly with you. Have in your mind to become like lambs for the slaughter, just as it is written, 'Because of you, our Lord, we die everyday and have become like sheep for the slaughter'.

57 XVII, 7 (173):

> These and such like them are the sufferings: If you bless whoever curses you and love whoever hates you and pray for whoever persecutes you and forgive whoever does you wrong 70 times seven in one day, all this because our Lord said, 'Never be angry against one who sins against you'.

58 Instead of Kitchen's "shine".

59 XIX, 508–509 (204).

60 XX, 7 (216).

61 For asceticism in the *LG* see Kitchen, *Becoming Perfect*, 30–43 and Juhl, *Die Askese*.

62 See Antoine Guillaumont, "Situation et signification du « Liber Graduum » dans la spiritualité syriaque", *Symposium Syriacum 1972*. Orientalia Christiana analecta 197 (Rome: Pontificalum Institutum Orientalium Studiorum, 1974), 313:

> Les vertus du parfait sont avant tout l'humilité, le pardon, la douceur. Il s'applique à faire la paix parmi les hommes, à les enseigner avec humilité, à les corriger s'il le faut, mais en s'abstenant de les juger: aussi bien il s'estime inférieur à tous les hommes, bons ou pécheurs.

63 Argárate, *Das Ktābā dmasqātā*, 257:

> Aus den 30 Mēmrē resultiert ein faszinierendes Bild einer asketisch charismatisch geprägten Gemeinde. Mitten in den verschiedenen und sogar komplexen Verfolgungen werden die Christen aufgerufen, ihren leidenden, armen und gedemütigten Herrn nachzuahmen. Auf diesem Weg werden sie durch die steigernde Präsenz und Wirksamkeit des Geistes zu einer mystique pneumatique bewegt. Ziel des Weges ist die Stadt Gottes, der Garten von Eden, die Wiedererlangung des verlorenen Paradieses.

Bibliography

Abouzayd, Shafiq, "Violence and Killing in the Liber Graduum." *Aram* 11–12 (1999–2000): 451–465.

Anderson, Gary A., *The Genesis of Perfection: Adam and Eve in Jewish and Christian Imagination*, Louisville: Westminster John Knox Press, 2001.

Argárate, Pablo, "Das *Ktābā dmasqātā*. Forschung und Bedeutung des syrischen Liber Graduum." In *Bibel, Byzanz und Christlicher Orient: Festschrift für Stephen Gerö zum 65. Geburtstag*, Orientalia Lovaniensia Analecta 187, edited by Emmanouela Grypeou, Alexander B Toepel, Timothy Sailors and Dmitrij Bumazhnov, 239–258. Leuven: Peeters, 2001.

Bettiolo, Paolo, "Scritture e cristianesimi nella Siria tra II e IV secolo." *Cristianesimo nella storia* 19, 3 (1998): 479–481.

Corbett, John H. "They Do Not Take Wives, or Build, or Work the Ground: Ascetic Life in the Early Syriac Church." *Journal of the Canadian Society for Syriac Studies* 3 (2003): 16–17.

Guillaumont, Antoine, "Situation et signification du «Liber Graduum» dans la spiritualité syriaque." In *Symposium Syriacum 1972. Orientalia Christiana analecta 19*, edited by Ignatius Ortiz de Urbina, 311–322, Rome: Pontificalum Institutum Orientalium Studiorum, 1974.

Heal, Christian S., and Robert A. Kitchen, eds., *Breaking the Mind: New Studies in the Syriac "Book of Steps"*, Washington, DC: The Catholic University of America Press, 2014.

Juhl, Diana, *Die Askese im Liber Graduum und bei Afrahat. Eine vergleichende Studie zur frühsyrischen Frömmigkeit*. Orientalia biblica et christiana 9, Wiesbaden: Harrassowitz, 1996.

Kitchen, Robert A., "The Gattung of the Liber Graduum, Implications for a Sociology of Asceticism." In *IV Symposium Syriacum, 1984: Literary Genres in Syriac literature (Groningen, Oosterhesselen 10–12 September). Orientalia Christiana Analecta* vol. 229, 173–182, Rome: Pont Institutum Studiorum *Orientalium*, 1987.

Kitchen, Robert A., "Conflict on the Stairway to Heaven. The Anonymity of Perfection in the Syriac Liber Graduum." In *Symposium Syriacum VII, Orientalia Christiana Analecta* 256, edited by René Lavenant, 211–220, Rome: Pontificum Institutum Orientalium, 1998.

Kitchen, Robert A., "Becoming Perfect: The Maturing of Asceticism in the Liber Graduum." *Journal of the Canadian Society for Syriac Studies* 2, 1 (2002): 38–52. https://doi.org/10.31826/jcsss-2009-020106.

Kitchen, Robert A., "Syriac Additions to Anderson: The Garden of Eden in the Book of Steps and Philoxenus of Mabbug." *Hugoye Journal of Syriac Studies* 6, 1 (2003): 1–47. https://doi.org/10.31826/hug-2010-060103.

Kitchen, Robert A., "Making the Imperfect Perfect: The Adaptation of Hebrews 11 in the 9th Memra of the Syriac Book of Steps." In *The Reception and Interpretation of the Bible in Late Antiquity. Proceedings of the Montréal Colloquium in Honour of Charles Kannengiesser, 11–13 October 2006 (The Bible in Ancient*

Christianity), edited by L. DiTommaso and L. Turcescu, 227–251, Leiden: Brill, 2008.

Kitchen, Robert A., "Slouching towards Antioch: Biblical Exposition in the Syriac Book of Steps." In *Syriac and Antiochian Biblical Interpretation for the 3rd Millennium*, edited by Robert D. Miller, 53–79. Piscataway, NJ: Gorgias, 2008.

Kmosko, Michael, ed., *Liber Graduum. Patrologia Syriaca* I, 3, Paris: Firmin-Didot, 1926.

Kowalski, Aleksander, *Perfezione e Giustizia di Adamo nel Liber Graduum*, Orientalia Christiana Analecta 232, Rome: Pont. Institutum Studiorum Orientalium, 1989.

Lane, David J., "The Book of Grades or Steps." *The Harp* 14 (2001): 81–88.

Louf, André, «Une ancienne exégèse de Phil. 2, 6 dans le K^e*taba* d^e*Masqata* (Livre des degrés)» *Studiorum Paulinorum Congressus Internationalis Catholicis*, AB 17–18, Rome 1963: 523–533.

Nagel, Peter, "Die "Märtyrer des Glaubens" und die "Märtyrer der Liebe" im syrischen Liber Graduum." In *Religion und Wahrheit. Religionsgeschichtliche Studien. F.S. Gernot Wießner zum 65. Geburtstag*, edited by Bärbel. Köhler, 127–142, Wiesbaden: Harrassowitz, 1998.

Old, Hughes Oliphant, *The Reading and Preaching of the Scriptures in the Worship of the Christian Church*. vol. 2: *The Patristic Age*, 247–295. Grand Rapids, MI: Baker, 1998.

Rücker, Alfred, "Die Zitate aus dem Matthäusevangelium im syrischen 'Buche der Stufen'." *Byzantinische Zeitschrift* 20 (1932): 342–354.

Strothmann, Werner, "Jesus-Sirach-Zitate bei Afrahat, Ephraem und im Liber Graduum." In *A Tribute to A. Vööbus. Studies in early Christian Literature and Its Environment, Primarily in the Syrian East*, edited by Robert H. Fischer, 153–158, Chicago, IL: Lutheran School of Theology at Chicago, 1977.

The Book of Steps. The Syriac Liber Graduum. Translated, introduced and annotated by Robert A. Kitchen and Martien F.G. Parmentier, Cistercian Studies 196, Kalamazoo, MI: Liturgical Press, 2004.

Westerhoff, Matthias, "Zur Paulus-Rezeption im Liber Graduum: der Apostel als Vorbild." In *Syriaca. Zur Geschichte, Theologie, Liturgie und Gegenwartslage der syrischen Kirchen. 2. Deutsches Syrologen-Symposium (Juli 2000, Wittenberg)*, vol 17 of *Studien zur orientalischen Kirchengeschichte*, edited by Martin Tamcke, 253–259, Münster: LIT Verlag, 2000.

Wickham, Lionel, "Teaching about God and Christ in the Liber Graduum." In *Logos. Festschrift für Luise Abramowski* zum 8. Juli 1993, edited by Hans Brennecke, 486–498. *Beihefte zur Zeitschrift für die neutestamentliche Wissenschaft*, no. 6, Berlin: De Gruyter, 1993.

10 Theological Principles in the Formation of the Biblical Canon According to Athanasius' Thirty-Ninth Paschal Letter

Gunnar af Hällström

Introduction

Today the Bible is a book. It is conveniently referred to as "the Bible." Even though there are differences among the Christian denominations concerning the precise contents of the Bible, there is no need to correct the name of the Big Book. The situation was different, however, in Athanasius' days. There was not one book, but Scriptures, in the plural. Easily a modern theologian applies an anachronistic approach to the Bible in the patristic era – since it was not there yet.

True, there were some attempts to form a bible, a single, holy book. Or rather, to form a collection of Holy Scriptures with clear enough limits in order to be considered one single entity. Among the first such attempts, Canon Muratori is mentioned. This list of authoritative books was published for the first time as late as 1740. It was composed in Latin, possibly in Rome. The date of its composition is not quite clear, but according to most scholars it derives from the late second century or beginning of the third. The reason for this dating is the fact that it seems to claim that it was written soon after the episcopacy of "pope" Pius I (140–155). It is well-known that the beginning of the list is lacking, and therefore the Gospels of Matthew and Mark are not mentioned. Further, it is known that the list explicitly excludes the Shepherd of Hermas from the canon, but seems willing to accept a pseudo-epigraphical apocalypse, the (Greek) apocalypse of St. Peter. It is not accepted by everybody, Canon Muratori says, indicating that there was a discussion going on in the church concerning the New Testament canon. In practice, Canon Muratori counts with three categories of books claiming to be Holy Scripture: those accepted by the church, those rejected by the church, and useful Christian literature that could be read privately but should not be read publicly in the church.

A few decades later Origen of Alexandria discussed the problem of canonicity. The best-known passage on this topic is extant in the Ecclesiastical history of Eusebius (HE VI 25), but Origen comments on the biblical canon in a number of other texts as well.[1] As the scholar he is, he deals very

DOI: 10.4324/9781003273592-10

accurately with the question. The *conditio sine qua non* is that a book, in order to be canonical, has to be inspired by the Holy Spirit. The Church recognizes the inspiration and includes the book in question within the biblical canon. However, in Origen's view, there may be inspired books that do not belong to the canonical ones. The Shepherd of Hermas, for example, Origen believes to be divinely inspired, but he does not dare to claim canonicity for it.[2] He thinks his own conviction is not enough. He accepts the fact that there are different opinions concerning the canonicity of certain books. There are those who regard the Acts of Paul as genuine. Origen notes this, but the canonicity is not thereby accepted or rejected within the church. On the other hand, 2 Peter and 2–3 epistles of John are disputed by some. Origen is honest enough to mention this, but he does not doubt the canonicity of those texts. The literary style of the Epistle to the Hebrews is too sublime for the apostle Paul, but their theology is Pauline.[3] That is enough for Origen: he treats the Hebrews as canonical. There are, in the end, three categories of writings claiming canonicity: genuine, false, and mixed.[4] In this respect, Origen's attitude is much the same as that of Canon Muratori. In addition, both of them reveal that there was a discussion concerning canonicity going on in the church. The discussion went on in Rome as well as in Alexandria. The problem of canonicity was recognized, and the solutions to it were similar though not identical.

The author of Canon Muratori is not known. Origen, for his part, was a highly influential person, but also very controversial. None of the two owned authority enough to settle the problem of canonicity. A council might have had the authority needed. However, as far as we know, no such council took place earlier than the latter half of the fourth century.

The Council of Laodicea included a list of canonical books in its 60th canon.[5] Unfortunately, the dating of the council is far from certain. The years 363–364 are often proposed, with a tolerance of about 20 years in both directions. The 60th canon is particularly difficult to date. It is lacking in many Greek manuscripts and in all Latin translations. Under these circumstances, it must be concluded that not even this council enjoyed authority enough to fix the problem of canonicity. The opinion frequently stated by scholars that Athanasius of Alexandria was decisive in the formation of the biblical canon still stands. He had the authority needed.

Athanasius (296–373) was, and still is, an authority both in the East and in the West, and well-known in both quarters since he lived in both parts of the Empire. In his Paschal Letters, 45 all in all, he announced the date of the Easter celebration for the current year. This procedure was needed, since Easter was not one of the festivals celebrated on a fixed date. The 39th letter, being the Paschal letter of the year 367, served the same purpose as the other letters, but it offered a list of the biblical books as well. The parishes, preparing to celebrate the most important of the Christian feasts, got an additional gift in this first-ever authoritative list of biblical books. Athanasius was the first one to speak of biblical books as canonical, in Greek "*kanonizomena*." Origen had used the term "*homologoumena*" in the same meaning, but there is a difference in the nuances. "*Kanonizomena*" is a legal term, indicating a normative status, whereas "*homologoumena*" is ecclesiastical, more democratic in nature: it indicates that the people of God accepts the writing in question as a normative one.

A serious problem is attached to the text of the 39th Epistle of St. Athanasius: a huge part of the Greek original is lost.[6] It contains about two pages in a modern print, half of that being occupied by the list itself, and about one page containing comments on it. The passage on the date of the Easter celebration is missing. The Syriac and Coptic versions are extant, but even they are not complete.[7] Also in them, pages and passages are occasionally missing. The Coptic translation corresponds fairly well with the Greek original; thus it can be considered a reliable translation. The following comments are based primarily on the Greek fragment, with some additional details from the Coptic version.

The main question that the present article wishes to answer is not "what books were included?" but rather "why is the biblical canon such an important issue?" Did the fourth-century church really need such a listing of books? Scholars sometimes make a distinction between a practical canon, used in the lectionaries containing liturgical readings, and a legal canon, fundamental for the formation and defense of doctrine. As for Athanasius, what was the purpose of his list?

Antiheretical Target

The most central principle in Ep. 39 is the antiheretical principle. The very first sentence in the Greek text is about heretics, and the last sentence mentions the heretics, too. It is obvious, though not always explicitly said, that the biblical canon was needed because of the heretics. Since they exist, the Church needs a list. More precisely, a canon was needed, Athanasius says, since the heretics wrote "*apocrypha*," secret books. The believers read not only apostolic writings, nor were they always content with reading only edifying texts written by acknowledged church leaders. They also read religious books containing harmful teaching. The list which Athanasius presented defined what could be read by all and at any point of time, privately and publicly. His list was meant to be legally binding, as far as a church leader could oblige his flock. The heretics are thus the reason for Athanasius' choice of the term "*kanonizomenoi*." This being so, it seems that those scholars are right who claim that Marcion of Sinope with his reduced New Testament canon was one of the reasons why the church once started considering the number of gospels, as well as the content of the biblical canon in general.[8] A strong enough enemy compelled the Church to defense and counter-attack, by presenting a list of canonical books. Reference to philosophy, church tradition, and the ministry, though they provided a useful defense in many other cases, were not particularly helpful in a situation where Christians were reading heretical literature and referring to it.

Who were those heretics that indirectly gave cause to the present-day biblical canon? In the Greek text, they are neither named nor described. In the Coptic text, two heresies are mentioned, but unfortunately in another context than the biblical canon. The two heresies attacked by Athanasius are the Melitians (also called Meletians) and the Arians. They are not explicitly said to be the heretics that composed apocryphal books. However, toward the end of the Coptic Letter 39, the Melitians are mentioned again in bypassing. Here, Athanasius says that he has heard, that is, not experienced himself, that heretics and Melitians in particular boast about apocryphal books. He does not say, however, that the Melitians themselves had written those scriptures, but he may have meant that.[9] As far as we can see, the Arians, also mentioned among the heretics, argued for the inferiority of the Son using biblical, not apocryphal writings. Being Athanasius' principal opponents, "heretics" without further characteristics could reasonably be understood as the Arians. There is, however, no support for such an identification. As for the Meletians, there is hardly any indication in the early Christian sources before Athanasius that they would have used apocryphal books. Athanasius claims that the heretics he discussed did so. The fact that the Arians and Melitians had a certain kind of agreement particularly in Egypt explains why Athanasius mentioned them both together,[10] but not why they are combined with apocryphal scriptures. He was deeply offended by both groups and accused them of almost any offence. The Melitians deny Christ, he says, they are apostates, dogs, characterized by wickedness.[11] It is, therefore, not very surprising that he accuses them of reading false writings also. Seen from a historical perspective, most of his accusations against them lack foundation. This can be said also in the light of the compromises the catholic church had made with regard to the Melitians in Egypt. It is likely that the accusation concerning the Melitians' attitude toward the apocrypha lacks credibility, too. The Melitian church used to be an *ecclesia martyrum*, a persecuted group where martyrdom was highly esteemed. In such an environment, visions and revelations were frequent.[12] Such spontaneous phenomena, however, do not match Athanasius' description of heretics writing deliberate forgeries and providing these with titles referring to ancient heroes in order to increase the authority of these writings.

The canons of the synod of Laodicea, relatively contemporary with Athanasius' Paschal Letter, provide a clue as to who the heretics were. The clue is, admittedly, not very decisive. Among the heretics mentioned in the 8th canon of the synod, the Phrygians are mentioned. It is not indicated that these were the cause of the list of canonical books appearing 52 canons later. But some church fathers used to accuse the Montanists of producing "innumerable books" (bibloi apeiroi, Hippolytus)[13] and claiming canonical authority for them. This claim is easy to understand, since the Montanist

Phrygians produced prophecies, uttered in the name of God or Christ or the Holy Spirit. Such revelations from above were extremely authoritative. They were, according to the catholic opponents, regarded among the Phrygians to be beyond all criticism. In addition, their prophecies could be used in the same way as canonical writings, that is, they were read in connection with the church liturgy.[14] Unfortunately, it is not possible to declare that the heretics mentioned by Athanasius were Montanists. But they seem to have represented a similar, or parallel, phenomenon in their attitude toward holy scripture. As it happens, Canon Muratori mentioned the Montanists, too, and rejected them. The rejection is relatively polite. The Montanists are not called heretics, it is just that the "number of the prophets is complete." There is, consequently, no place for Montanist prophecies. The language used by Athanasius against his opponents is much harder. The heretics were called "dead" by Athanasius. They cannot have been just slightly misled, innocent churchgoing people. They were definitely outsiders from Athanasius' point of view.

A more likely candidate than the Montanists is the Gnostics, not least since Egypt was the cradle of numerous Gnostic teachers. Already in the Early Church, they were famous for writing their own gospels, letters, and apocalypses, influenced by their theological conviction. It is easy to understand why Athanasius, so strongly propagating for the true incarnation of Christ, could get strongly upset from their religious literature. These writings were formally close to the New Testament books but theologically miles away from the thought of Athanasius. According to him, "the whole design and tendency of Holy Scripture" is to inform mankind about the divinity of the Saviour and his Incarnation.[15]

Athanasius provides two examples of apocrypha written by heretics. In the Coptic text, we are told that misled people referred to some apocryphal writings written by or about such Old Testament characters as Enoch and Isaiah. Neither Arians nor Melitians wrote such books. In Jewish and Jewish-Christian circles, these two were important figures, however.[16] But Athanasius is referring to apocrypha written only recently. Thus, the ancient Ascension of Isaiah and The Testament of Moses do not fit the description. Thus, these well-known texts do not come into consideration.

Pastoral Concern

In the short Greek text containing the list of canonical books, there are numerous references to a certain group of believers, referred to by Athanasius as the "*akeraioi*," the simple believers. Because of them, we are told, a list of books was needed,[17] even more so, the list is absolutely necessary (*anagke*). These are the ones that may be led astray by the apocryphal books produced by the heretics. Who were these simpletons? First, they got a surprisingly high mark from Athanasius for their spiritual life in other respects than their reading habits. The only negative statement about them is that they were easily deceived. They are characterized by holiness (*hagiotes*) and simplicity (*haplotes*).[18] This implies that far from being secularized or half-hearted nominal Christians, they were exemplary believers. The notion of simplicity contains two aspects: either the heart is simple (undivided, that is, totally engaged) or the intellect is simple (naïve, stupid). Or both heart and intellect are naïve. In Athanasius' city, Alexandria, these simple believers were present already in Clement's and Origen's times.[19] Both these Alexandrians attested to the fact that these were easily deceived by heretics. Consequently, when they found a book pretending to be holy scripture but was not, they were deceived, according to Athanasius. The titles of these false scriptures were similar to those of the biblical books. Athanasius used the word *homonymia,* homonym, referring to these writings, thus it was impossible to judge from the names whether they were genuine or not. In other words, there must have been names such as "the Gospel according to NN," "the Letter of the apostle NN," and "the Revelation of NN." As we already suggested, such writings existed among the Gnostics. They were, in fact, a trademark of Gnosticism. In the list of suspects, the Gnostics take, therefore, one of the first places. This is admittedly convenient, since the Gnostics were notoriously difficult to define. In by-passing it should be noted that, according to Athanasius, in his days the ordinary Christian could and should read! There can be no reading of heretical literature unless there is literacy. Origen testified to this more than a century earlier. He fought a constant war against "the friends of the letter," "*amici litterae,*" a group represented foremost by the church-attending simpletons.[20] Their exegesis was erroneous, but they were capable of exegesis. John Chrysostom, in his numerous admonitions to his audience to read the Bible at home, testified to literacy among these people as well. The quality of this literacy is another matter, and need not be discussed here.

Athanasius takes a pastoral attitude toward the ordinary, simple Christians. He states that he wrote down the list because of them. Can this piece of information be trusted? Too often the church fathers claimed that they were writing because of the simpletons, when most Christians needed spiritual guidance. Let us take Origen's *Contra Celsum* as an example. The attack launched by Celsus could cause anxiety among uneducated ordinary believers, we are told.[21] Only the uneducated ones? Anyone who has read *Contra Celsum* can realize that the discussion is certainly not meant for simple Christians. On the contrary, in order to defend Christianity Origen more or less sacrificed the uneducated multitudes of Christians and defended the philosophically minded advanced Christians. The uneducated functioned as an excuse for writing. Athanasius may have acted similarly. In theory, Athanasius presented the list of canonical books because of the simpletons. However, the church as a whole needed it. Athanasius himself suggested this when writing that he presented the list because of the "*anagke kai khresimon tes ekklesias*" the necessity of the whole church. If a modern parallel is accepted: many bookshops, when not church owned, are offering a remarkable variety of religious literature. New Age, different types of meditation, astrology, fundamentalist writings, and bishops' official reports, here they can be found side by side. Some books are theologically close, others very far from traditional Christianity. Athanasius wished to give guidance in the complex world of religious literature.

Classes of Religious Writings

In Athanasius' Paschal Letter, three kinds of religious writings can be traced. First, there are the books characterized as "*theopneustoi*," usually translated "inspired." The word was, as is well-known, used already in 2 Tim. 3:16, referring to writings that Christians should read. The church fathers knew an active meaning of the word also, in English perhaps best rendered by "divinely breathing" or "inspiring." This meant that the reader, not only the author, of such a text will be inspired by God. In Ep. 39, Athanasius used the word in its passive sense. Thereafter Athanasius presents an interesting version of apostolic succession in the form of biblical succession. In this text, not the office of a bishop, but the Scriptures passing on through a series of handing-overs guarantees authentic Christianity. Athanasius' view is Christocentric: the starting point is the words of Jesus Christ. His words continue in the words of the apostles, and from them the next generation of Christians receive them. Thus, not even the apostle Paul, much less Athanasius himself may be called a teacher. Both have received their religious knowledge from Jesus Christ. This way the high age of the canonical Scriptures is illustrated, and their authenticity guaranteed. Nothing may ever be added or removed from the list, Athanasius claims, in a statement that reminds of Revelation 22:19 (and Deut.4:2). Differing from the Apocalypse, Athanasius refers the prohibition to all biblical writings, not to the text of one particular book.

Second, Athanasius mentions books called "Apocrypha." They are more or less homonymous with the genuine biblical books, but Athanasius does not provide their names explicitly. They pretend old age, but they are written only recently. Probably they are not identical with the New Testament Apocrypha published e.g. by Hennecke and Schneemelcher. These are relatively harmless and populistic presentations of miraculous deeds by Jesus Christ and the apostles. The apocrypha Athanasius is talking about are "poison." This probably means that they rejected central Christian doctrines – to judge from Athanasius' vehement reaction. The badly preserved Gospel of the Ebionites, and the Gospel of Hebrews, for example, would match the description. They could be regarded "poison" because of their anti-Athanasian Christology. Athanasius does not mention theses writings, though.

Finally, there are the mixt writings.[22] "But for greater exactness I add this also, writing of necessity; that there are other books besides these not indeed included in the Canon, but appointed by the Fathers to be read by those who newly join us."[23] In the Coptic text, Athanasius mentions seven such books: The Wisdom of Solomon, the Wisdom of the Son of Sirach, Ester, Judith, Tobit, Didache, and the Shepherd of Hermas. Such an intermediate category was mentioned in all the lists of canonical books we have discussed. Canon Muratori dealt with three classes, also there the Shepherd of Hermas being an example of non-canonical but useful reading. Origen distinguished between three classes as well: *homologoumena, amfiballomena (mikta)*, and *notha*. Athanasius reached the same conclusion: there is a category of religious writings that is not (necessarily) divinely inspired, nor is it in the list of canonical books. However, they contain some edifying material. In *Contra paganos*, Athanasius expressed the same thought: "*The holy and inspired scriptures are sufficient, but there are many other writings by our blessed teachers produced for the same purpose (piety and truth). Those who study these will know how to interpret the scriptures.*"[24] There were, then, more than the seven books listed by Athanasius among the works worth reading. This third class consisted of pastoral, that is, edifying literature, written by trusted persons.

Salvation through Genuine Scriptures

Early Alexandrian theology was a theology of the Logos. Even so, the emphasis given by Athanasius to the Scriptures is astonishing. "We have the Holy Scriptures, which are sufficient to instruct us perfectly," Athanasius states in the Coptic text. And, referring to the multitude of religious texts, he asks: "What do the spiritual Scriptures lack that we should seek after in these empty voices of unknown people?" "Unbedingter Biblizismus" is an expression used for this attitude. Athanasius' concept of the Scriptures is not one that creates a tension between Christ and the Bible, the person, and the book. On the contrary: the written word is an extension, or even actualization, of the Logos incarnate. In the Gospels, Christ promised to bring water to the thirsty, and even more, salvation to the sinner. His words to the Samaritan woman on this topic are well-known (John 4), and so are his words on the last day of the Suckot (Tabernacles) festival in John 7:17: "If anyone is thirsty let him come to me." Athanasius transferred these words to the Scriptures.[25] In other words, what the Incarnate Logos was to people in Jesus' days, the Scriptures are now. This being so, in his 39th Epistle Athanasius even ventures an expression such as "*pros soterian grafas,*" Scriptures giving salvation. Confronted with such an expression the "secret" of Athanasius' list of canonical books begins to be revealed. A person reading the wrong literature risks spiritual death. A person reading canonical, inspired, Christ-containing texts will find salvation. The problem of canonicity is therefore not a theoretical one. It is a soteriological issue and thereby the most central one.

Conclusion

Canon Muratori and Origen made it clear that the biblical canon was a much-debated topic. Firm opinions were uttered. Neither revealed the identity of those who held a certain writing genuine or not genuine. They just indicated that "some" regarded a book canonical, others not, though the word "canonical" itself was not yet in use. Written records concerning the debate are not extant, we only have the information that different opinions existed. The list of Athanasius was also part of a discussion of some sort, since "true brethren" had asked the Alexandrian bishop to compose it. With Athanasius, the development reached a point where alternative lists of canonical books no longer were an option. The Alexandrian bishop listed without hesitation all acceptable books, and these should be regarded legally binding. Nothing could or should be added or removed.

All three early Christian lists of canonical books admit the existence of three categories of writings. By accepting an intermediate group between genuine writings and forgeries, they allow that Christians may read other books than biblical ones. It is a bit strange that this intermediate group was recommended to catechumens, at least as far as the deuterocanonical scriptures are concerned. During earlier centuries some people found Christian faith by reading, reading not any useful Christian books, but genuine biblical texts. This holds true concerning many of the second-century apologists, for example. Athanasius recommended that believers read their Bible first and last. There one can meet Christ and through him salvation.

Athanasius does not provide arguments in favor of his list. He sees no reason to defend it. He presupposes that the books included in the canon are agreed upon. He himself has not made up the list, he got it from his predecessors. Ultimately these scriptures derive from Christ himself and his apostles. Thus, they are both authoritative and, also important, ancient indeed. Though the discussion was first and last about the New Testament, which was endangered by the production of modern forgeries, Athanasius' arguments apply also to the Old Testament. According to him, Christ is found there, too.

The second category of books, the modern forgeries, constitutes a threat to salvation, therefore they should not be read at all, in particular not by the simple believers. The mixed writings in the third group can be used with caution. There is no discussion as to whether also pagan literature could be read by advanced believers. This question was discussed by Basil the Great. In his "Exhortation to Youths as to how they shall Best Profit by the Writings of Pagan Authors," Basil gives a cautious permission to consult edifying non-Christian texts in addition to Christian ones. Basil's treatise is hard to date, but it should be relatively contemporary with Athanasius' 39th Letter. The Cappadocian Father spoke about "poison" in pagan texts, but he also recognized the sweet taste of "honey" present at least in some of them. By admitting an intermediary category of edifying books Athanasius prepared the way for a solution to the problem concerning non-Christian literature, but he himself did not deal with the problem. Edifying text may be read, that was Athanasius' conclusion. Basil went one step further by admitting that regardless of the religion of the author, useful works could be read.

Athanasius concluded his discussion concerning the biblical canon by referring to the present time of the liturgical year. Easter was approaching. According to 1 Cor. 5:8, the old leaven and all sort of wickedness should be removed and a new one used instead. In the same way, the false scriptures (though they were not old!) should be rejected and the canonical scriptures taken in use. The Easter celebration can begin.

Notes

1 See Origen's Commentary on St. John's Gospel 13, 17 and Homilies on Joshua 7, 1.
2 Commentary on the Romans 10, 31.
3 In Eusebius He VI 25.
4 Commentary on St. John 13, 17.
5 A translation of the canons into English can be found in The Nicene and Post-Nicene Fathers, second series, vol. XIV.
6 The original Greek text, edited by P.-P. Joannou, is available in *Fonti: Discipline generale antique, vol.1.1, Grottaferrata (*Rome) 1963. A translation into English can be found e.g. in The Nicene and Post-Nicene Fathers, series two, volume four.
7 These texts are available in English in D. Brakke, *Athanasius and the Politics of Asceticism*. Oxford: Clarendon Press, 1995.
8 "Markion, dessen "Kanon" die Entwicklung überall vorwärts treiben musste", von Campenhausen, Die Entstehung der christlichen BIbel. Tübingen: J.C.B.Mohr 1968, p. 160; more in detail pp. 174–177, p. 175 in particular: "Der erste christliche Kanon bleibt in jedem Fall seine eigenste Schöpfung, bei der ihm kein Kirchenmann und kein Gnostiker vorangegangen ist." It is probably right to say with Wilhelm Schneemelcher that Marcion was not the creator of the NT. canon, but promoted its formulation. –Die Entstehung des Kanons des NT und der christlichen Bibel. *Theologische Realenzyklopädie* 6 p. 38.
9 D. Brakke, Canon Formation and Social Conflict in 4th Century Egypt. *Harvard Theological Review* 87:4 (1994) p. 411 claims that there is "some plausibility" in Athanasius' statement that Melitius wrote apocrypha. But he seems to prefer the interpretation that Melitians used but did not write such texts, p. 413.
10 As for Arians and Melitians in Egypt, see L. W. Barnard, Athanasius and the Meletian Schism in Egpyt. *The Journal of Egyptian Archeology* 59 (1973): 181–189.
11 Barnard, Athanasius and the Meletian Schism, 185–186.
12 D. Brakke has, correctly, noticed this, Canon Formation and Social Conflict in 4th Century Egypt, *HTR* 87:4, 399.
13 Refutatio 8.12.
14 This is evident from Tertullian in his Montanist period, e.g. *De anima* 9.4.
15 Against the Arians 214–215. I owe this reference to T. Winter, *Salighetens källor*. Turku 2009, 33.
16 Rowan Williams, *Arius. Heresy and Tradition*. Grand Rapids, MI and Cambridge: Eerdmans, 2002, 41 draws attention to a certain Hieracas who used

extra-canonical literature, *Ascensio Isaiae* in particular. This Hieracas caused considerable trouble to the Alexandrian diocese.

17 Thus also James Ernest, *The Bible in Athanasius of Alexandria*. Leiden: Brill, 2004, 339.

18 These two characteristics, simplicity and holiness, are not grammatically connected to any subject in the sentence. They are, however, mentioned as the reasons why the simple believers are deceived. Athanasius refers to St. Paul 2 Cor.11:3 without explicitly quoting him, where both simplicity and holiness are mentioned as characteristics of believers that run the risk of being deceived by the "serpent."

19 For further information, see Gunnar af Hällström, *Fides Simpliciorum according to Origen of Alexandria*. Diss. Helsinki, 1984.

20 af Hällström, *Fides Simpliciorum* according to Origen of Alexandria, 46–51.

21 *Contra Celsum* Preface.

22 It is impossible to accept the opinion of Wilhelm Schneemelcher, according to whom Athanasius abandoned Origen's division of religious literature into three classes by rejecting the middle category. See "Die Entstehung des Kanons des Neuen Testaments und der christlichen Bibel. *Theologische Realenzyklopädie* 6, 44. He admits, though, somewhat inconsistently that Athanasius placed Didache and Hermas in a special group of their own.

23 Letter 39:7, the Greek text. The translation is from The Nicene and Post-Nicene Fathers, series two, vol. 4, 552.

24 *Contra Paganos*, Preface.

25 This is so in Ep. 39. In Ep. 44, however, Christ is the one bestowing refreshing drink to those thirsty.

Sources

Kirchhofer, Johannes, *Quellensammlung zur Geschichte des neutestamentlichen Kanons bis auf Hieronymus*, pp. 7–9. Zürich 1844. Online version: www.bible-researche.com/athanasius.html.

Joannou, Pericles-Pierre, *Fonti: Discipline generale antique (IVe-IXe s.)*. Grottaferrata/ Rome, 1963.

Translation of Greek version into English: *Nicene and Post-Nicene Fathers*. Series two, volume four. Grand Rapids, MI: Eerdmans Publishing Company, 1957.

Translation of the Coptic version into English: Brakke, David, *Athanasius and the Politics of Asceticism*, 326–332. Oxford: Clarendon Press, 1995.

Literature

Barnard, Leslie William, Athanasius and the Meletian Schism in Egypt, *The Journal of Egyptian Archeology* 59 (1973): 181–189.

Bokedal, Tomas, *The Scriptures and the Lord. Formulation and Significance of the Christian Biblical Canon*. Diss. Lund: Lund University Publications, 2005.

Brakke, David: Canon Formation and Social Conflict in 4th C. Egypt. Athanasius of Alexandria's 39th Festal Letter. *Harvard Theological Review* Vol. 87, 4 (1994): 395–419.

Brakke, David, *Athanasius and the Politics of Asceticism*. Oxford: Clarendon Press, 1995.

Campenhausen, Hans Freiherr von, *Die Entstehung der christlichen Bibel*. Tübingen: J. C. B. Mohr, 1968.

Ernest, James D., *The Bible in Athanasius of Alexandria*. Boston, MA/Leiden: Brill, 2004.

Hällström, Gunnar af, *Fides Simpliciorum according to Origen of Alexandria*. Diss. Helsinki: Societas Scientiarum Fennica, 1984.

Schneemelcher, Wilhelm, Die Entstehung des Kanons des Neuen Testaments und der christlichen Bibel. *Theologische Realenzyclopedie* 6, article "Bibel III."

Williams, Rowan, *Arius, Heresy and Tradition*. Grand Rapids, MI and Cambridge: Eerdmans, 2002.

Winter, Tuisku: *Salighetens källor*. En studie i Athanasios av Alexandrias 39:e påskbrev. Unpublished thesis pro gradu. Åbo, 2009.

11 Augustine's Approach to Scriptural Interpretation

Carl Séan O'Brien

Introduction

The most striking characteristic of Augustine's approach to scriptural interpretation is the level of generosity he displays towards differing readings of others on the same quest for truth. Indeed, it is already noteworthy that he conceives of divergent opinions in this manner, rather than presenting them as the conflicting views of opponents which would be more typical of the period. This contrasts sharply with the attitude of many other Church Fathers (such as Basil).[1] This chapter analyzes Augustine's approach to scriptural interpretation against the background of his conception of divine love and charity as outlined in *Confessiones* 11–13 and *De Doctrina Christiana*, along with a case study of his exegesis of *Genesis*.[2] Both aspects are interlinked in Augustine, since God's very act of creation is an act of divine love.[3] In fact, several key Augustinian concepts are revealed through his approach to Scripture, such as his attitude to translations of the Bible, as well as to the acquisition of knowledge (since this can also influence the manner in which we approach Scripture), along with his presentation of a method for critical textual interpretation.

Augustine's methodology of scriptural exegesis betrays an intrinsic tension between the inherent stability of the Bible (as a written work and as an authoritative corpus) and the interpretative flexibility of dialogue (since Augustine envisages Scripture as a living voice and denies the possibility of any single reader achieving a universalizing interpretation). God permits multiple interpretations of the same passages of Scripture (*Confessiones* 12.18.27; 12.31.42), which is in itself an act of divine love; it is even possible for scriptural meaning to surpass the signification that Moses himself intended. Despite this, Augustine presents a vivid image of the ideal exegete in *De Doctrina Christiana* as a learned reader (2.8.12; 2.13.20), highly competent in languages, working from the most accurate texts (3.1.1). For those unable to conduct scriptural interpretation in this manner such as recently baptized "infants", those who are competent, such as Augustine as bishop, will serve as their "books" (*Sermon* 227). Augustine's role as a preacher, then, is informed both by pastoral and pedagogical concerns,

DOI: 10.4324/9781003273592-11

since Scripture presents us with a path both to love and to wisdom. He outlines a framework in which scriptural interpretation should take place as a mechanism for combating heresy, while minimizing the extent to which rival readings should form the source of conflict through arguing for a multiplicity of possible interpretations. In the course of outlining this framework, he subsumes rhetoric and pagan wisdom more generally as tools of Scriptural exegesis.

The Modes of Scriptural Interpretation and Love and Charity

Augustine not only reflects the validity of the traditional four modes of scriptural interpretation: literal (historical), figurative, allegorical (moral) and anagogical (mystical), but even goes beyond this to posit a multitude of meanings in the text.[4] Given all the possible modes of scriptural interpretation, this raises the question of when we should apply the necessary mode. The overriding rule is that of charity: a range of interpretations may all be regarded as true provided that they reflect the twofold aspect of love for God and for one's neighbour. The aim of Scripture is to impart love and charity and scriptural interpretation should lead us along the path to attaining both of these:

> Therefore whoever thinks to himself that he understands the divine Scriptures or any given amount of them, but with such an interpretation that does not build up the twin love of God and of neighbour does not understand them yet.
>
> (*doctr. chr.* 1.36.40; cf. *doctr. chr.* 1.35.39)[5]

This twin love functions both as the prerequisite and as the measure for accurate scriptural interpretation: Augustine is willing to accept that an interpreter, who might fail to capture the author's meaning precisely and yet does so in a manner that reinforces this twofold love, has committed an error, but still achieves the desired result (*doctr. chr.* 1.36.41). This example clarifies the charity which Augustine extends towards those with differing interpretations, while simultaneously exemplifying the significance of the pedagogical aspect: the errant interpreter should be corrected for his own good (to avoid repeated errors, since he will have difficulty harmonizing other scriptural interpretations with his original, false opinion, *doctr. chr.* 1.37.41).

However, Augustine does provide concrete guidance: if the text – taken literally – leads to a charitable interpretation there is no need to apply the figurative mode. At *doctr. chr.* 3.16.24, Augustine supplies the example of "if your enemy is hungry, give him bread to eat" which can be taken literally while the conclusion "for you will heap burning coals on his head" (*Proverbs* 25.21–22; *Romans* 12.20)[6] must be taken both figuratively and charitably (not as a figurative allusion to somehow harming an enemy in any way).[7]

Augustine employs allegorical interpretation to attempt to harmonize inconsistencies in Scripture. For example, the image of a serpent is used both negatively (in his temptation of Eve) and positively in the admonition to be wise like serpents (*doctr. chr.* 3.25.36).[8] Perhaps the most elaborate example of Augustine's allegorical interpretation of Scripture is his reading of the divine creation of the world in *Genesis* as an account of God's reshaping of the sinful soul (*conf.* 13.12.13). In addition to the allegorical method, Augustine mentions other techniques which can be used to resolve ambiguities, such as paying attention to grammar, punctuation or pronunciation (*doctr. chr.* 3.2.2), along with knowledge of word forms.

Augustine's adoption of the notion of figurative interpretation consists of a text bearing a range of meanings, rather than a single true meaning (which necessarily excludes other productive ways in which to read the text).[9] Reading Scripture with only one meaning in mind places too tight a restriction on the wisdom it contains and ignores its depths.

> For just as a fountain in a confined space is more copious and it supplies more streams across a more extended space than any one of those brooks, which after drawing from the same fountain after a great interval, in this way the account of your dispenser [Moses], though brief in its account, but destined to serve many as the basis of discussions, gushes forth rivulets of truth from which, on these topics, each of us may draw the truth he can, this man this truth and another man a different truth, though circling around in more circuitous discourse.
>
> (*conf.* 12.27.37)[10]

The key notion here is that of the interpreter doing his best to uncover the truth (rather than attempting to lay claim to intellectual supremacy). Assuming that one alone has access to the truth leads one to the sin of arrogance and is a form of closed-mindedness that Augustine repeatedly opposes: no interpreter can definitively argue that his interpretation was the one intended by Moses (*conf.* 12.24.33). Since Scripture is divinely inspired it can contain truths that lie beyond the understanding of individual interpreters, while exegetical commentaries can hit upon truths that even surpass the express intentions of the commentator. The astute reader might even find a line of interpretation in Augustine which goes beyond what he intended, but which is still true.

The Role of Language and Textual Criticism in Scriptural Interpretation

Augustine also has a text-critical approach towards establishing the most authoritative version of Scripture (consultation of the most authoritative texts, i.e. the oldest manuscripts, and in the case of variants amongst these texts following the most widespread or most ancient reading.[11] One of the fundamental precepts which Augustine applies to his interpretation of the Scriptures is that they are never wrong (even if they record immoral deeds or if they may at times appear to be in conflict, this is due to issues of translation). The solution is to elucidate one passage of Scripture by drawing on another passage[12]: this approach is based upon his understanding that all of Scripture is in harmony.

> If something discordant comes up there [in Scripture], it is not permissible to say that the author of this book does not express the truth, but either the codex is erroneous or the translation errs or you do not understand.
>
> (*c. Faust.* 11.5)[13]

Augustine supplies the example of the apparent conflict of the description concerning the visit to Christ's tomb in Matthew, who describes the angel as sitting on the rolled-back stone and Mark who mentions the angel inside the sepulchre – this might simply refer to two separate angels[14] or to one of the evangelist's gaps in memory, but it is clear that the writer of Holy Scripture could not deceive (*Letters* 28): "Each of the Evangelists believed that it was necessary to recount what they were recounting in the order in which God had wished to bring it to his remembrance while examining these matters" (*cons. Ev.* 2.21. 51).[15]

The tension between interpretative flexibility and scriptural stability is reflected in Augustine's remarks on the closing of the canon, dividing religious texts into a group of authoritatively stable ones and those which are useful, but open to refutation:

> But who does not know that the sacred canon of Scripture, both of the Old and of the New Testament, is enclosed within its own limits and that it is placed before all the other subsequent letters of the bishops... however, the other letters of the bishops which have been composed or are being composed after the establishment of the canon, may be refuted if there is anything in them which accidentally diverges from the truth.
>
> (*De Baptismo contra Donatistas* 2.3.4)[16]

The ideal interpreter will read both canonical and non-canonical texts, but be more cautious in relation to the non-canonical texts, only reading them subsequently "so that they do not occupy a weak mind beforehand" (*doctr. chr.* 2.8.12).[17] In order to determine whether Scriptures are canonical or not, the interpreter will follow a similar method to that advocated by Augustine in the case of evaluating the respective authority of the manuscript, first paying attention to the number of catholic churches that accept the text as canonical and amongst those churches privileging those with greater authority (determined by whether they were the seat of an apostle and the recipient of epistles).[18] More authority attaches to the original text than to the translation (*ciu.* 15.13) – this will allow the exegete to rectify the problems caused by "the infinite variety of Latin translations" (*doctr. chr.* 2.11.16). A similar attitude should be applied to the evaluation of the material contained within the canonical books with the greatest attention paid to instructions for attaining a sanctified life, commencing with the simpler passages before progressing to the more obscure.

One accomplishment that Augustine repeatedly stresses as being necessary for competent scriptural interpretation is in-depth study of the relevant languages:

> A great cure against the ignorance of proper signs is acquiring knowledge of languages. And men of the Latin language, whom I have now undertaken to teach, have need of two other languages for acquiring knowledge of the divine Scripture, Hebrew and Greek, so that they may revert to the original versions, if the infinite variety of the Latin translators raises doubt in them.
>
> (*doctr. chr.* 2.11.16)[19]

Interestingly, Augustine's expectations (for others) exceed his own abilities here: he, by his own admission, never mastered either Greek or Hebrew (although this does raise the question of how seriously we should take Augustine's claims concerning his own limitations). He admits this himself at *doctr. chr.* 4.31.64:

> In these four books I have attempted to depict myself not as I am, for I am lacking in many ways, but the sort of person I ought to be who devotes himself to labour in sound, that is Christian, teaching, not only for himself, but even for others.[20]

Augustine does acknowledge that it is not always possible to achieve the requisite linguistic competence, in which case he suggests consulting with those who speak the original language or consulting and comparing a range of translations (*doctr. chr.* 2.14.21), Furthermore, he confesses the limitations of his knowledge when he admits he is unaware of whether the lack of ornamentation in Scripture is the result of the deficient translation or the decision of the original authors (though he is still convinced of the beauty of the original version, *doctr. chr.* 4.20.41).

Augustine clarifies why he does not consider the Latin translations to contain the same degree of accuracy as the Greek:

> For the scriptural translations from the Hebrew language into Greek are possible to count, but the Latin translators are not by any means.

> For in the first period of the faith if a Greek manuscript came into the hands of anyone, to whom it seemed that he had knowledge of either language, *be it ever so little*, he dared to translate it.
>
> (*doctr. chr.* 2.11.16, my emphasis)[21]

In this, he follows in a long tradition of regarding the Septuagint as being the product of divine inspiration and equal in authority to the Hebrew[22]: "For it is said by all the more knowledgeable churches that the translators enjoyed the presence of the Holy Spirit to such an extent that amongst so many men there was a single mouth" (*doctr. chr.* 2.15.22), though this voice is the one most calculated to be "fitting for the Gentiles".[23]

The ability to compare multiple translations also helps to shed light on the more obscure passages (*doctr. chr.* 2.12.17).[24] Indeed, many of Augustine's examples of mistranslation focus on correcting Latin texts (cf. *doctr. chr.* 2.13.19); this is not solely the result of greater familiarity with the language, but a consequence of the high value he places upon the Septuagint. In fact, Augustine presents the Septuagint translation as the result of an act of cosmopolitanism accomplished by Ptolemy II Philadelphus which opened these sacred texts up to the world, whereas previously he claims (with a certain amount of anti-Jewish polemic) that the jealousy of the Jews had kept them hidden.[25] Amongst the Latin versions, he favours the (Vetus) Itala, although he subordinates this to the authority of the Septuagint (*doctr. chr.* 2.15.22). However, in this regard, Augustine does not simply follow tradition blindly. At *doctr. chr.* 4.7.15, for example, he departs from the Septuagint translation, since he finds its reading more obscure (though even here he does not criticize it, attributing its impenetrability to its figurative nature) and opts instead to follow Jerome's Vulgate:

> Not, however, following the Septuagint translators, who even in their translation were guided by the Holy Spirit and who seem to have said this in another manner in order to direct the mind of the reader to the examination of the spiritual sense, for which reason some passages are ever more obscure on account of being more figurative, but I shall follow the translation from Hebrew into Latin of the presbyter, Jerome, who is completely competent in both languages.
>
> (*doctr. chr.* 4.7.15)[26]

In general, though, Augustine has numerous reservations with regard to the readings which Jerome introduces, does not see him as enjoying the same level of inspiration as the translators of the Septuagint (which is equivalent to that granted to the Old Testament authors) and notes the rejection of Jerome's Vulgate by the congregation at Oea (Tripoli) when it was read in place of the traditional text.[27]

Augustine outlines his own lack of competency in Hebrew, when highlighting the difficulty of mastering the necessary linguistic skills for scriptural interpretation, but points out that this alone is still insufficient for ascertaining the truth behind the text; this claim paves the way for the broader education he advocates for the exegete.

> And if he [Moses] speaks in the Hebrew language, he should strike my senses in vain and he should never touch my mind, however, if he were to speak in Latin, I would know what he said. From where would I know whether he spoke the truth? If I would know this, would I know it from him? For within me, in the inward residence of my thoughts, neither Hebrew nor Greek nor Latin nor a foreign language without the help of the mouth and tongue, without the clatter of syllables, truth would tell me "he speaks the truth".
>
> (*conf.* 11.3.5)[28]

Augustine distinguishes between the plain and obscure parts of Scripture and draws upon this distinction to offer a solution to uncovering the truth behind the more obscure passages: almost everything can be extracted from the plainer passage and applied to the more difficult passage. The same technique can be applied by drawing on knowledge of pagan texts: "However, those who know the tropes perceive them in the sacred texts and use their knowledge considerably to understand them. But it is not fitting here to entrust them to those unacquainted with them..." (*doctr. chr.* 3.29.40).[29] While there appears to be a certain amount of condescension exhibited in Augustine's response here, this is belied by the open attitude to teaching which he expresses at *doctr. chr.* 4.9.23 (and Augustine gives the grounds that he does not wish to appear to be teaching grammar as his reason for avoiding this style of teaching here).

Pedagogical Aspects

The elements of charity and the pedagogical aspects both shape the framework in which Augustine approaches Scripture in *De Doctrina Christiana*.

> ...if only one insists that the hearer or collocutor does not lack either the desire for learning or the mental capacity that he might be able to receive it in whatever manner it might be made known and the one who teaches should pay less attention to teaching eloquently than to teaching clearly.
>
> (*doctr. chr.* 4.9.23)[30]

Augustine would rather accept a barbarism than better Latin which does not clarify the sense (*doctr. chr.* 3.3.7). His purpose in laying out the rules for scriptural interpretation, as he makes clear in the Preface, is that students of Scripture "may profit not only by reading others who have laid open the mysteries of the divine Scriptures, but by themselves also opening up the mysteries to others" (*doctr. chr.* prol. 1).[31] Since each word of Scripture transmits the divine truth, it can only be expounded following the precepts which Augustine himself outlines in *De Doctrina Christiana.*

Diligent reading of Scripture by an "alert reader" (*doctr. chr.* 2.13.20) is particularly important, since it is a lazy and careless reading of Scripture which is the originator of heresy (along with the excessive pride of believing that one's false interpretation is, in fact, the only correct one, cf. *conf.* 12.25.34):

> But those who read without purpose are ensnared by many twisting obscurities and ambiguities replace one signification for another and in some places they cannot discover even a reasonable interpretation; some phrases are so obscure as to cover the signification in most thick darkness. I do not doubt that this was divine forethought so that pride might be suppressed through labour and intellect might be renewed by mental aversion, which generally counts as worthless what is easily discovered.
>
> (*doctr. chr.* 2.6.7–8)[32]

Similarly, at *Confessiones* 12.1, and again in Augustine's discussion of the Psalms, Scripture represents a promise made by God to us: we only need to ask for the wisdom necessary to interpret Scripture and we shall be granted it: "For certain mysteries of the Scriptures are closed up not in order to deny them, but that they might be opened up to those who knock" (*Enarrationes in Psalmos* 93.1).[33]

For Augustine scriptural interpretation is also closely connected with his role as a teacher. The bishop, as the expounder of Scripture, can even be identified with it, as Augustine claims: "We are your books. Therefore pay attention" (*Sermon* 227).[34] For Augustine, there is a distinction between the mode of understanding Scripture (*modus inueniendi*, the subject of the first three books of *doctr. chr.*) and the mode of communicating it (*modus proferendi*). McCarthy notes that it is difficult to maintain a separation of both modes, given the level of orality inherent in Biblical interpretation at the time.[35] For Augustine, the act of interpreting Scripture merges with the act of communicating it, since the whole purpose of Scripture is to compensate for our mortality and to lead us to a virtuous life, i.e. one marked by love and charity. The act of Biblical education merges with the bishop's role in employing Scripture as an exhortation to virtue. Bishops, however, are fellow students (*En. In ps.* 126.3), though they utter their teachings with understanding, unlike certain types of birds which give voice to words they do not understand (*En. In ps.* 18(2).1). In having the humility to recognize their role as fellow students, the bishops are differentiated from the Platonic philosophers who believe that their learning raises them above other men, like actors upon the stage (cf. *conf.* 7.9.14).

Despite Augustine's charitable attitude, he is far from naïve, illustrated by the rhetorical strategy he adopts. First, he anticipates polemical attacks from his opponents ("Before I begin the work it seems to be best to respond to those who will object to it or who would object to it, if I did not placate them in advance", *doctr. chr.* prol. 1).[36] Second, he attributes this disagreement to the ignorance of his opponents; they have failed to understand the rules of scriptural interpretation (*doctr. chr.* prol. 2.); he also attacks the arrogance of those who have a good grasp of Scripture, but who feel that they are beyond the need for a regulated framework, since – according to their own claims – they interpret with divine inspiration. Augustine positions himself as someone with far greater expertise in relation to his opponents, by suggesting that his rules of interpretation are equivalent to him pointing with his finger to an obscure star, which some of his opponents cannot see, while others cannot even see his finger. Part of the reason why Augustine is so accommodating when it comes to the theories of others is that he regards Scripture as too complex to be fully understood by any single person (*doctr. chr.* 3.37.56).

Augustine outlines seven steps which lead to wisdom: (1) fear of God, (2) piety, (3) knowledge (4) resolution, (5) counsel, (6) purification of heart, (7) termination (*doctr. chr.* 1.7. 9).[37] Fear of God ensures that we approach the study of Scripture with the right frame of mind since it destroys our pride: Augustine previously attributed an excessive love for one's own opinion as a cause of error in Scriptural interpretation (*doctr. chr.* 1.37.41). This suppression of pride is reinforced by the second stage, piety, which allows us "rather to think and to believe that what is written there, even if it is concealed, is better and more true than anything which we could know by ourselves" (*doctr. chr.* 2.7.9)[38] Knowledge orients the mind of the interpreter towards what Augustine has already clarified as the purpose of Scripture, love of God, by reminding the reader that he has been affected by the love of temporal things and drawn away from divine love.[39] While the remaining steps are of great significance in Augustine's understanding of how religious salvation is to be attained, he himself does not relate them so closely with the actual process of scriptural interpretation, so detailed analysis of them need not concern us here.

In keeping with Augustine's previous career as a teacher of rhetoric, he is particularly open to the use of pagan sources, if it can help explain Scripture:

> For we should not refuse to learn letters on the grounds that they report that Mercury was their devisor, nor since they have dedicated temples to justice and to virtue...should we therefore abandon justice and virtue. No, indeed, let every good and true Christian understand that wherever he may find truth it belongs to his Lord.
>
> (*doctr. chr.* 2.18.28)[40]

Truth belongs to God and those who lead a Christian life even if they articulate it with a script written by others. A solid general education, such as in history, natural science or grammar can also assist with the interpretation of Scripture (*doctr. chr.* 2. 28.42 cf. 2.29.45; 3.29.40). History is significant since it allows us to understand the cultural context of Scripture, with different ethical standards in the Mosaic texts (such as polygyny, though he still suggests that this can be interpreted allegorically) and that of the Gospels.[41]

Augustine's motive behind this intellectual openness is neither innocent nor random, but rather part of a typical Christian move to appropriate Platonic Philosophy for the Christian tradition. In Augustine's reconstruction (which he borrows from Ambrose), it is not that the Christians drew upon Platonism, but rather that during Plato's time in Egypt he learned the wisdom of the prophet Jeremiah so

> he [Ambrose] showed that it is much more probable that Plato was saturated by Jeremiah in our literature, so that he might be able to teach and to write those views which are justly praised...reflecting on the time in this way it is much more credible that they [the philosophers] learned from our literature whatever good and true things they said, than that the Lord Jesus Christ learned from Plato (*doctr. chr.* 2.28.43).[42]

Actually, Augustine obfuscates here somewhat, since by his own admission the dates (i.e. Plato's anteriority to Christ) would indicate the reverse to be the case. Augustine does not particularly trouble himself with the ethics of such appropriation:

> those called philosophers and chiefly the Platonists, if they have said what is true and commensurate with the faith, not only should we not turn away from it, but we should even assert a claim to it from those who possess it unjustly.
>
> (*doctr. chr.* 2.40.60)[43]

According to Augustine's understanding, Christians are justified in appropriating pagan learning, since they are more suitably equipped to make better use of it and this follows in the tradition of Moses who appropriated Egyptian wisdom (*doctr. chr.* 2.40.61). Augustine finds further Biblical justification for the Christian appropriation of pagan philosophy in the Israelite removal of gold and silver objects from Egypt at the command of God in order to place them in the service of Christ.

De Doctrina Christiana combines an outline Augustine's rules for scriptural interpretation (Book 3) with an examination of the role of rhetoric in Christian teaching (Book 4), an example of the combining of the classical and Christian traditions. In fact, Augustine expressly connects both elements when he notes that the primary aim of rhetoric is to teach (*doctr. chr.* 3.12.27). Rhetoric becomes subordinated to Christian teaching and indeed the purpose of studying rhetoric is to become a more effective teacher, although even this will not be sufficient to win over the most intransigent opponents. Scripture itself serves as a model of the various rhetorical styles to be emulated such as Paul's subdued, temperate (*doctr. chr.* 4.20) and majestic styles (*doctr. chr.* 4.24). Admittedly, Scripture does not supply a model for the use of harmony or ornamentation (*doctr. chr.* 4.20.41), but this is to be found in Ambrose (*doctr. chr.* 4.21.48) and Augustine authorizes adding harmony, provided that this does not obscure the truth of the passage. If a preacher lacks the necessary eloquence he can simply learn a sermon composed by someone else and deliver it:

> For the one who steals carries off that which belongs to another, but the word of God is not foreign to those who obey Him and rather it is the one who speaks well but lives badly who speaks the words that belong to another.
>
> (*doctr. chr.* 4. 29.62)[44]

Scripture is to be lived, not simply form the subject of discussion. Augustine notes that his own original attempt to study the Scriptures failed because he was initially disappointed that they lacked the eloquence of Cicero (*conf.* 3.4.8).

In many ways, Augustine's appropriation of rhetoric for the Christian tradition can be read as an anti-rhetorical act.[45] Rhetoric is undermined since it derives its authority not from its own station, but through its claim to expound a written text (though one which most Christians would have been familiar with via the bishop's sermons, rather than through direct reading). In *Confessiones* 9, Augustine sees his role as a *venditor verborum* ("seller of words") to be at odds with Christianity, leading ultimately to his resignation as a professor of rhetoric.[46] Indeed at *doctr. chr.* 4.2.3, Augustine appropriates rhetoric for service to the truth (i.e. the Christian faith). Preaching may require rhetorical skill, but it transcends purely rhetorical activity. The preacher cannot simply memorize his homily verbatim, but should pay attention to the response of the congregation – he should repeatedly discuss the same topic in a variety of ways, until the audience show that they have understood; the preacher should then immediately proceed to another topic (or end the discourse).[47] In this manner, scriptural exegesis is subordinated to didactic aims, not employed for the purposes of self-aggrandizement (as is so often the case with rhetoric). The exegesis should be done with a view to forestalling future objections and with the aim of anticipating future objections (*doctr. chr.* 4.20.39). In this context, Augustine draws a distinction between speaking wisely (i.e. closely adhering to the precise words of Scripture) and speaking eloquently (i.e. following the guidelines prescribed by the rhetorical tradition, but not necessarily expounding Scripture accurately),[48] a distinction which also applies to the authors of the sacred texts themselves (*doctr. chr.* 4.6.10). Naturally, by speaking wisely, Augustine means a command of Scripture that goes beyond mere understanding and citation, but which entails an understanding that itself implies a serious commitment to uncover the truth contained within: "However, a man speaks more or less wisely to the extent to which he makes progress in Holy Scriptures, I do not say by reading and memorizing them, but by understanding them well and investigating carefully into their meaning" (*doctr. chr.* 4.5.7).[49] The preacher's eloquence comes rather from the virtuous manner in which he leads his life, rather than his choice of words.[50] The eloquence of the Scriptures goes beyond the so-called eloquence of the rhetorical tradition which relies upon ornamentation and manipulation of the emotions. By contrast, Scripture achieves true eloquence since the manner in which it expresses truth could not be expressed in any other way (*doctr. chr.* 4.6.9). This echoes Philo's comments at *Mos.* 2.37–40, where the *Septuagint* translation is conducted with mathematical accuracy so that it could not be better expressed in any other way, although conversely each word of Scripture can be expounded in a manifold manner, Aug. *doctr. chr.* 12.19.27).

The aim of reading Scripture is to move beyond a need for it as a support for the virtuous life, but it is still required to lead others to this point: "Therefore a man relying upon faith and hope and charity and holding on to them firmly does not require the Scriptures except to teach others" (*doctr. chr.* 1.39.42). The central role of teaching in Augustine's understanding of Scripture's purpose is intrinsically connected with his overarching principle of charity: the preacher's teaching of Scripture is to be understood as an act of charity. The existence of Scripture is a testament to human weakness just as much as the Incarnation is. Scripture perfects us in charity, while the Incarnation allows us to understand creation.[51]

As a rhetorical exercise, Scriptural interpretation is subject to all the vices of sophistry: love of disputation for its own sake (rather than as a means to uncover the truth), the urge to show off, love of deceit (*doctr. chr.* 2.31.48) and pride in one's specialized knowledge (although Augustine admits the necessity of a certain amount of specialized knowledge in order to understand the figurative significance of various allusions in Scripture).[52] Disputing about words according to Augustine only harms the preacher's audience (*conf.* 12.18.27). It is still possible that an interpreter may fail to capture the truth originally intended by the author and yet this interpretation may also be true. Amongst the manifold range of truths found in Scripture no single interpreter can uncover the full range (*conf.* 12.24.33).

In keeping with Augustine's views regarding the Christian appropriation of pagan wisdom, true opinions are not the property of the interpreters who uncover them, but belong to everyone (*conf.* 12.25.34). This view, however, is not solely applied to support Augustine's open-minded approach to the use of non-Christian wisdom, but intrinsically bound up with the charitable framework within which he views scriptural interpretation. The genuine interpreter should both feel pleasure at the correct understanding of the text (even if he is not the originator of this particular line of thought) and ownership of the correct interpretation since "all the lovers of the truth hold it in common" (*conf.* 12.25.34).[53] Love of the false interpretation merely because it is one's own is the very opposite of the charitable approach that should be applied to Scripture. Since Scripture was intended for the use and enjoyment of all,[54] there is no place for partisan or schismatic approaches that attempt to appropriate Biblical truth and claim it for themselves. Likewise, no one should claim exclusive knowledge of the opinions of Moses (since his text is capable of bearing numerous meanings, *conf.* 12.31.42) – it is even designed so that those who cannot initially understand do not reject it due to their lack of comprehension (*conf.* 12.26.36). Augustine uses this as the model for his own account – he wishes to be clear enough that anyone can understand his interpretation, but not in such a way that the views which he puts forth might exclude alternative (true) interpretations (*conf.* 12.31.42).

Augustine criticizes views that are not the result of a genuine attempt to uncover the truth behind Scripture, but based upon rashness and arrogance (*conf.* 12.25.34). The counterpart to the proud intellectual, who exults in his sophisticated scriptural interpretation while simultaneously losing sight of the actual purpose of scripture (*conf.* 7.9.13), is supplied by Augustine's own mother, Monica, who is in possession of Christian truth. In *Confessiones*, this appears to be treated more positively, than in early works (like *De Ordine*, where the simplicity of this religious experience is implied to be inferior).[55] That he re-evaluates this earlier stance is clear when he notes that it is simply the authority of the Church which guarantees the veracity of the Gospels: "Indeed, I would not have believed the Gospels if the authority of the Catholic Church had not moved me" (*Contra Epistolam Manichaei Quam Vocant Fundamenti* 5.6).[56]

Augustine's Exposition of *Genesis*

Augustine's exegesis of *Genesis* forms an interesting case study of his approach to Scripture. First, he does not attempt to explain every aspect of the mystery of creation,[57] which conforms to his view that Scripture can be the object of multiple levels of interpretation and one single teaching or one single interpreter cannot uncover the various levels of truth that it contains. The difficulty of expounding *Genesis* 1–3 is illustrated by the regularity with which he returned to the text over the course of his career and by the fact that he never completed his volume on the literal interpretation of *Genesis*.

Second, his reason for approaching the text, at least initially, in *De Genesi Contra Manichaeos* was to combat the Manichaean attacks on the Christian account of creation. Augustine's extensive Platonizing in this text in his attempt to find a response is particularly noteworthy, but I shall concentrate here on the manner in which he presents Manichaean attacks as the result of an incorrect (and negatively motivated) reading of Scripture; i.e. the Manichaean errors result from approaching Scripture with a false mindset. The Manichaeans concentrate their criticism particularly on the *Genesis* account of the fourth and seventh days. The issue with the fourth day is that this is when the sun is created, so that there would have been no way of marking the three previous days (*Gn. adu man.* 1.14.20). The Manchiaean objection to the account of the seventh day is that God should have no need for resting and that this is contradicted by *John* 5.17 where Christ states "my Father is working until now" (*Gn. adu. Man.* 1.22.33).[58] In contrast to the false claims of the Manichaeans that the New Testament contradicts the Old, Augustine sees the New Testament as representing the fulfilment of the Old Testament.[59] In line with the charitable attitude he adopts towards Scripture, he presents himself as attempting to correct and educate the Manichaeans, rather than engaging in a polemic against them.

Essentially, the Manichaean attack originates from one simple error – they comment on Scripture without either knowing it adequately or having a significant grounding in the rules for scriptural interpretation which Augustine would later outline in *De doctrina Christiana*: "the greater the extent to which we enter into Scripture and accustom ourselves to them, the more we come to know their modes of expression" (*Gn. adu. Man.* 1.9.15).[60] Since the Manichaeans read the creation account within the mythical framework associated with their own religion, they do not understand how to read Scripture correctly (*DGCM* 1.1.2). They assume that the text should be taken literally, whereas the descriptions of human things must be transferred to the divine (*Gn. adu. Man.* 1.14.20). Since God's nature lies beyond language, it can be misleading to read Scripture directly. For example, the reference to God resting on the seventh day actually refers to the rest God will grant us in return for our good works (*Gn. adu. Man.* 1.22.34). The point of the creation narrative is not to present a myth, as the Manichaeans mistakenly think, but rather to outline the manner in which God's will unfolds, both in the course of creation, as well as in Scripture. In order to be able to understand this unfolding of God's will, as revealed in Scripture, one needs to approach it with the right frame of mind, i.e. that of charity, which the Manichaeans in their conviction that they have found errors in the Biblical account, have failed to do. For Augustine, it is a classical case of focusing on Scripture's rhetorical forms, but failing to understand its wisdom.

Conclusion

Augustine essentially views the existence of Scripture as an act of mercy granted by God to compensate for human weakness. Even those who follow Augustine's demanding programme of language acquisition, study and textual analysis will not manage to exhaust the full range of scriptural meanings. The existence of Scripture is an act of divine love and the right approach to reading the Bible is from the perspective of love and charity. This helps to clarify the particular attention which Augustine pays towards expounding the *Genesis* narrative over the course of his career: both from the perspective that Scripture, just like creation, represents the unfolding of the divine will, and that both are acts of divine love. Augustine's exegesis of Scripture is informed by other branches of learning: Platonism, history, numerology and rhetoric, yet all of these are subordinated to the search for the truth. His willingness to draw upon pagan learning reveals a certain open-mindedness, which is reflected by the tolerance he displays towards alternative interpretations of Scripture.

Scriptural interpretation, for Augustine, is characterized by a pedagogical approach, though Augustine positions himself less as a teacher and more as a fellow student. This stance allows him to highlight many of the worst aspects associated with Scriptural interpretation: the arrogance of those who feel that they are beyond any guidance, who assume that their readings alone must be the correct one and who polemicize against their opponents; traits typical of the worst features of rhetoric, a branch of study which Augustine both subordinates to the service of Christianity and undermines by devaluing eloquence in relation to clarity. Despite his open mindedness, Augustine is determined that scriptural interpretation should take place within a prescribed framework, since misreading the sacred text is the basis of heresy. In all this, Augustine identifies the process of scriptural interpretation as the path to wisdom, the truth and the virtuous life.

Notes

1 See for example *Eun*.
2 For a general overview of *De Doctrina Christiana*, see Harrison (2006). Louth (1989), Camargo (1998) and Stock (2017) are also helpful.
3 For an account of the interaction between pagan and Christian approaches to the generation of the world, see O'Brien (2015).
4 Fletcher (1985), 60; Cf. Horn (2014), 140; *conf.* 12.27.37, discussed below; cf. *conf.* 12.18.27.
5 Quisquis igitur Scripturas divinas vel quamlibet earum partem intellexisse sibi videtur, ita ut eo intellectu non aedificet istam geminam caritatem Dei et proximi, nondum intellexit. Unless otherwise noted, translations are my own.
6 Trans. ESV.
7 Cf. the comprehensive discussion at Williams (2001), 69.
8 The idea is that the serpent protects its head and, as Christians, we should protect our head, Christ.
9 Cf. Weele (1985), 15–18.
10 Sicut enim fons in parvo loco uberior est pluribusque rivis in ampliora spatia fluxum ministrat quam quilibet eorum rivorum, qui per multa locorum ab eodem fonte deducitur, ita narratio dispensatoris tui sermocinaturis pluribus profutura parvo sermonis modulo scatet fluenta liquidae veritatis, unde sibi quisque verum, quod de his rebus potest, hic illud, ille illud, per longiores loquelarum anfractus trahat.

11 *c. Faust.* 32.19.
12 Williams (2001), 62.
13 Ibi si quid velut absurdum moverit, non licet dicere: Auctor huius libri non tenuit veritatem: sed, aut codex mendosus est, aut interpres erravit, aut tu non intellegis.
14 *cons. Ev.* 3.24.63.
15 unusquisque evangelistarum eo se ordine credidit debuisse narrare, quo voluisset Deus ea ipsa quae narrabat eius recordationi suggerere in eis duntaxat rebus...
16 Quis autem nesciat sanctam Scripturam canonicam, tam Veteris quam Novi Testamenti, certis suis terminis contineri, eamque omnibus posterioribus episcoporum litteris ita praeponi ... episcoporum autem litteras quae post confirmatum canonem vel scriptae sunt vel scribuntur... licere reprehendi, si quid in eis forte a veritate deviatum est ...Cf. the discussion at Deems (1945), 189.
17 ne praeoccupent inbecillem animum.
18 Augustine supplies an account of the Scriptures which he himself regarded as canonical at *doctr. chr.* 2.8.13.
19 Contra ignota signa propria magnum remedium est linguarum cognitio. Et latinae quidem linguae homines, quos nunc instruendos suscepimus, duabus aliis ad Scripturarum divinarum cognitionem opus habent, hebraea scilicet et graeca, ut ad exemplaria praecedentia recurratur, si quam dubitationem attulerit latinorum interpretum infinita varietas.
20 ... ago, quod in his quattuor libris non qualis ego essem, cui multa desunt, sed qualis esse debeat qui in doctrina sana, id est Christiana, non solum sibi sed aliis etiam laborare studet, quantulacumque potui facultate disserui.
21 Qui enim Scripturas ex hebraea lingua in graecam verterunt, numerari possunt, latini autem interpretes nullo modo. Ut enim cuique primis fidei temporibus in manus venit codex graecus et aliquantulum facultatis sibi utriusque linguae habere videbatur, ausus est interpretari.
22 Cf. Philo, *Mos.* 2.37–40; *Fug.* 54.
23 Qui iam per omnes peritiores Ecclesias tanta praesentia Sancti Spiritus interpretati esse dicuntur, ut os unum tot hominum fuerit.
24 Augustine's example is *Isaiah* 58:7, alternatively translated as "*Et domesticos seminis tui ne* despexeris" ("and do not look down upon the domestics of your seed") and "*Et carnem tuam ne* despexeris" ("and do not look down upon your flesh") as reciprocally clarifying the correct meaning (kinsmen). He also supplied two translations of *Isaiah* 7:9, along with mistranslation of the Greek word ὀξύς (sharp/swift) as sharp rather than swift at *Rom.* 3:15 or μόσκος (calf) for μοσχεύματα (tree shoots) at *Wisdom* 4:3.
25 *doctr. chr.* 2.15.22.
26 Non autem secundum *Septuaginta* interpretes, qui etiam ipsi divino Spiritu interpretati, ob hoc aliter videntur nonnulla dixisse, ut ad spiritalem sensum scrutandum magis admoneretur lectoris intentio, unde etiam obscuriora nonnulla quia magis tropica sunt eorum, sed sicut ex Hebraeo in Latinum eloquium presbytero Hieronymo utriusque linguae perito interpretante, translata sunt.
27 *Epistola* 71.
28 ...et si hebraea voce loqueretur, frustra pulsaret sensum meum nec inde mentem meam quidquam tangeret; si autem Latine, scirem quid diceret. Sed unde scirem, an verum diceret? Quod si et hoc scirem, num ab illo scirem? Intus utique mihi, intus in domicilio cogitationis nec Hebraea nec Graeca nec Latina nec barbara veritas sine oris et linguae organis, sine strepitu syllabarum diceret: "Verum dicit".

29 Quos tamen *tropos* qui noverunt agnoscunt in Litteris sanctis eorumque scientia ad eas intellegendas aliquantum adiuvantur. Sed hic eos ignaris tradere non decet...

30 si tenet auditorem vel collocutorem discendi cupiditas nec mentis capacitas desit, quae quoquo modo intimata possit accipere; non curante illo qui docet quanta eloquentia doceat, sed quanta evidentia. This stress on the clarity of Scripture and scriptural exegesis, even if it comes at the expense of eloquence, is also part of a long tradition, cf. Basil, *hex.* 6.2.24–28.

31 ut non solum legendo alios qui divinarum Litterarum operta aperuerunt, sed et aliis ipsi aperiendo proficiant.

32 Sed multis et multiplicibus obscuritatibus et ambiguitatibus decipiuntur qui temere legunt, aliud pro alio sentientes; quibusdam autem locis quid vel falso suspicentur non inveniunt, ita obscure dicta quaedam densissimam caliginem obducunt. Quod totum provisum esse divinitus non dubito, ad edomandam labore superbiam et intellectum a fastidio renovandum, cui facile investigata plerumque vilescunt.

33 Regularly numbered 94 in English editions. Sicut intentissime audivimus, cum psalmus iste legeretur; ita intente audiamus, cum revelat Dominus quae hic dignatus est opacare mysteria. Ad hoc enim clauduntur quaedam sacramenta Scripturarum, non ut denegentur, sed ut pulsantibus aperiantur.

34 Codices vestri nos sumus. adtendite ergo... Actually Augustine began preaching before his consecration as a bishop.

35 Cf. McCarthy (2007), 332, n. 13.

36 Quod antequam exordiar videtur mihi respondendum esse his qui haec reprehensuri sunt aut reprehensuri essent, si eos non ante placaremus.

37 The seven rules of Tichonius (*doctr. chr.* 3.36.52–3.37.56).

38 ... cogitare potius et credere id esse melius et verius quod ibi scriptum est, etiam si lateat, quam id quod nos per nosmetipsos sapere possumus.

39 Cf. *doctr. chr.* 1.33.37.

40 Neque enim et litteras discere non debuimus quia earum repertorem dicunt esse Mercurium, aut quia iustitiae virtutique templa dedicarunt... propterea nobis iustitia virtusque fugienda est. Immo vero quisquis bonus verusque Christianus est, Domini sui esse intellegat, ubicumque invenerit veritatem...

41 Despite this Augustine is adamant that Lot's incest with his daughters should not be taken literally. Gilmore (1946), 150.

42 probabilius esse ostendit quod Plato potius nostris Litteris per Hieremiam fuerit imbutus, ut illa posset docere vel scribere quae iure laudantur? ... Ita consideratis temporibus fit multo credibilius istos potius de Litteris nostris habuisse quaecumque bona et vera dixerunt, quam de Platonis Dominum Iesum Christum...

43 Philosophi autem qui vocantur, si qua forte vera et fidei nostrae accomodata dixerunt, maxime Platonici, non solum formidanda non sunt, sed ab eis etiam tamquam ab iniustis possessoribus in usum nostrum vindicanda.

44 Qui enim furantur, alienum auferunt, verbum autem Dei non est ab eis alienum, qui obtemperant ei; potiusque ille dicit aliena qui, cum dicat bene, vivit male.

45 Schaeffer (1996), 1133.

46 Cf. Tell (2010), 385. Tell links Augustine's views to a rejection of a specifically Manichaean form of rhetoric rather than rhetoric tout court.

47 *doctr. Chr.* 4.10.25.

48 *doctr. Chr.* 4.5.7–8.

49 Sapienter autem dicit homo tanto magis vel minus, quanto in Scripturis sanctis magis minusve profecit, non dico in eis multum legendis memoriaeque mandandis, sed bene intellegendis et diligenter earum sensibus indagandis.

50 Marshall (1992), 9.
51 Williams (1989), 141.
52 An example of this is the significance of numerology or allusions to specific plants.
53 ...quoniam in commune omnium est veritatis amatorum.
54 Augustine regularly draws a distinction between uti und frui.
55 Rist (1994), 56.
56 Ego vero Evangelio non crederem, nisi me catholicae Ecclesiae commoveret auctoritas.
57 Cf. Cavadini (2017), 151.
58 Trans. ESV.
59 Rist (1994), 298. Cf. *Gn. adu. Man.* 1.22.33.
60 Quantum accedimus in Scripturis et in eis assuescimus, tantum nobis locutiones earum innotescunt.

Bibliography

Primary Sources

Augustinus, Aurelius, *Opera Omnia*, vols. 1–11, 1841–1967, Paris: Migne.

Secondary Literature

Camargo, M. "Non solum sibi sed aliis etiam. Neoplatonism and Rhetoric in Saint Augustine's *De doctrina Christiana*", *Rhetorica: A Journal of the History of Rhetoric* 16 (1998), 393–408.

Cavadini, J. C. "*Creatio ex Nihilo* in the Thought of Saint Augustine" in G. A. Anderson and M. Bockmuehl (eds.) *Creatio Ex Nihilo. Origins, Development, Contemporary Challenges*, University of Notre Dame Press, 2017, 151–171.

Deems, M. M. "Augustine's Use of Scripture", *Church History* 14 (1945), 188–200.

Fletcher, P. "Augustine and the Pleasures of the Text", *CEA Critic* 48 (1985), 56–61.

Gilmore, A. A. "Augustine and the Critical Method", *Harvard Theological Review* 39 (1946), 141–163.

Harrison, C. "*De Doctrina Christiana*", *New Blackfriars* 87 (2006), 121–131.

Horn, C. *Augustinus*. Munich: Verlag C. H. Beck, 1995, 3rd edition, 2014.

Louth, A. "Augustine on Language", *Literature and Theology* 3 (1989), 151–158.

Marshall, D. G. "Making Letters Speak: Interpreter as Orator in Augustine's *De Doctrina Christiana*", *Religion and Literature* 24 (1992), 1–17.

McCarthy, M. "We Are Your Books: Augustine, the Bible and the Practice of Authority", *Journal of the American Academy of Religion* 75 (2007), 324–352.

O'Brien, C. S. *The Demiurge in Ancient Thought. Secondary Gods and Divine Mediators*. Cambridge University Press, 2015.

O'Brien, C. S. "The Platonism behind Basil's Trinitarian Theology" in F. Lauritzen and S. Klitenic Wear (eds.) *The Byzantine Platonists: From Plotinus to Bessarion (284-1453)*, Steubenville: The Catholic University of America Press/Franciscan University Press, 2021, 14–31.

Rist, J. M. *Augustine. Ancient Thought Baptised*. Cambridge University Press, 1994.

Schaeffer, J. D. "The Dialectic of Orality and Literacy. The Case of Book 4 of Augustine's *De doctrina christiana*"; *PMLA* 111 (1996), 1133–1145.

Stock, B. The *Integrated Self. Augustine, the Bible and Ancient Thought*. Philadelphia: University of Pennsylvania Press, 2017.

Tell, D. "Augustine and 'the Chair of Lies': Rhetoric in the *Confessions*", *Rhetorica: A Journal of the History of Rhetoric* 28 (2010), 384–407.

Weele, M. V. "Augustine and Interpretation in *On Christian Doctrine* and the *Confessions*", *CEA Critic* 47 (1985), 13–21.

Williams, R. "Language, Reality and Desire in Augustine's *De Doctrina*", *Literature and Theology* 3 (1989), 138–150.

Williams, T. "Biblical Interpretation" in E. Stump & N. Kretzmann (eds.) *The Cambridge Companion to Augustine*, Cambridge University Press, 2001, 59–70.

12 The Doctrine of Love in Saint's Gregory the Great Commentaries on the *Song of Songs*

Adina Voichița Roșu

Song of Songs – General Considerations. The Allegorical Interpretation. Sources of the Work

A book as rich as the *Song of Songs,* one of the oldest pastoral works in the history of the universal literature, has always provoked the interest of the Christian exegetes, but also of all researchers in the humanist, philosophical, social fields, by the magnitude of its idealistic, spiritual and cultural dimensions. Among the Fathers of the Church, Gregory the Great comments on the doctrine of love from the *Song of Songs*, marking its wonderful depth and influence, but also its imperfections. However, we intend to highlight all of them, by analyzing the text from the point of view of the idealistic, spiritual, but also the stylistic valences.

In *the Dictionary of Spirituality*, Robert Gillet emphasizes the "extreme importance"[1] of *the Song of Songs* for the development of the Christian spirituality, in the Patristic era. In addition, the author adds, this influence

> is not limited to becoming an abundant source of spiritual life referring to thoughts and wishes; it extends also to expressions and enriches the language of spirituality in a singular way. In accordance with the action of *the Epistles* of Saint Paul and his teachings on the Church, wife of Christ, this spiritual terminology is established by borrowing the most common means of expression to the images and vocabulary suggested by the relationships of the human husbands, as the most apt to express the ineffable appreciation of God in his relations with his creature and also by translating the mutual impulses of love that unites them. The Middle Ages will only have to develop and systemize this work of assimilation, not adding anything essential.[2]

In the patristic literature, the manner of exegesis that the Fathers adopted in their commentaries on *the Song of Songs* is the allegorical (with the exception of Theodore of Mopsuestia who states about *the Song of Songs* that is a work without a secretly understood meaning),[3] as in the entire Holy Scripture appears the image of the matrimonial union to describe either the

DOI: 10.4324/9781003273592-12

union between God and his people, in the time of the Old Law, or the union of Christ with the Church within the framework of the New Covenant. Among the Fathers who commented on *the Song of Songs* is also mentioned Gregory the Great, Pope of Rome in 590,[4] named *gloriosissimus praefectus urbis*.[5] The arguments of Saint Gregory the Great made in the work *Commentaries on the Song of Songs* certifies that this poem is one of the oldest biblical revelations of the divine love, as is conceived by the Holy Scripture.

Following the teachings of Tradition, Gregory the Great values the allegory of the steps that the soul must ascend to God ("Ups into his heart he put", Ps, 83.6), in order to emphasize the need for man to move from a language "in accordance to body" to one "in accordance to spirit".

Since the beginning of the work *Commentaries on the Song of Songs*, Saint Gregory the Great emphasizes that the interpretation of the subject approached in the poem, the complexity of the meanings, cannot be understood without an adequate interpretation, essential for establishing the meaning, this being the allegorical (mystical), because "the allegory is set to the disposition of the soul which is far away from God, as a machine that wants to lift it towards God": "Allegoria enim animae longe a deo positae quasi quandum machinam facit, ut per illam leuentur ad deum".[6] The term *machina* has been widely used in Latin literature. It is found to be used strictly in the military field, but also in the civilian. Starting from there, it had many figurative meanings. Saint Gregory the Great frequently uses it. Here, the allegory is the "machine" that lifts toward God, "a kind of lifting device, which, misused, could crush us instead of lifting us from a spiritually point of view".[7] Elsewhere the term *machina* used by Saint Gregory the Great represents the remorse (*Mor.*, I, 48) or the power of love (*Mor.*, VI, 58).[8] Further, Saint Gregory the Great emphasizes that, in order to animate and provoke our heart toward the divine love, *the Song of Songs* went so far as to use the simple terms of human love.

The language of bodily and earthly love, says Gregory the Great, expresses the limited love that should stimulate the love for God:

> *quia, dum membra corporis nominat et sic ad amorem vocat, notandum est quam mirabiliter nobiscum misericorditer operatur, qui, utcor nostrum ad instigationem sacri amoris accenderet, usque ad turpis amoris nostri verba distendi. Sed, unde se loquendo humiliat, inde nos intellectu exaltat: quia ex sermonibus huius amoris discimus, qua virtute in divinitatis amore ferveamus.*[9]
>
> For it is worth noting the wonderful and humble way in which it acts upon us when it mentions the parts of the body and thus invites to love, which goes so far as to use the language of our vulgar love, to inflame our heart and to provoke it to the sacred love. But from where it is humbled by word, from there the spirit inflates us: because from the sayings of this love we learn by what virtue we must burn into the divine love.

Allegory, in the sense that Gregory gives here, plays a purely instrumental and transitory role. The golden rule is precisely to shatter without delay the outer shell of *the word*, to clear it of its literal, own, and human meaning, and to invest it with a new, figurative, and divine meaning. This is the exegetical procedure that Gregory adopts throughout the commentary and which allows him to keep his thinking at a good distance from the erotic vocabulary of *the Song* and to guide his listeners from the outward appearance of the words to the inner intelligence. The pure look of the heart is the only one that opens the way to the deepest mysteries of God. *The Song* appears to us as a poem of God's tenderness for man, the love *story* that awakens man's intelligence to spiritual intelligence to whisper to him *the ineffable* language of contemplation.

The treatise of Saint Gregory the Great reveals the rich human, Christian, and pastoral experience. His mentality resembles to the very religious state of mind of several psalmists of the era, the era when the *Song of Songs* was born. It is worth noting that this book is not called "*Song*" but "*The Song of Songs*". This situation is also found in the Old Testament, said Gregory the Great, where there are holy things and holy things among the holy things, sabbaths and sabbaths of the sabbaths, as there are in the Holy Scripture songs and songs of songs: "Nec uacue adtendendum est, quod liber iste non 'canticum' sed 'canticum canticorum' vocatur. Sicut enim in veteri testamento alia sunt sancta et alia sancta sanctorum, alia sabbata et alia sabbata sabbatorum, ita in scriptura sacra alia sunt cantica et alia cantica canticorum".[10]

The composition of the text, the whole of exegetical ideas and processes, allows one to guess at first sight elements of doctrine and themes already highlighted in the previous tradition. Thus, we can recognize four sources that inspired the reflection of Gregory the Great: Origen, Saint Augustine, Aponius and even his own writings, *Morales*.[11]

Saint Augustine's influence was felt throughout his entire work, Saint Gregory the Great being a "great disciple" of his, whom he attended with the greatest pleasure and admiration.[12] The commentary prologue develops several themes whose content is revealed as being fundamentally related to Augustine's theology: the theme of the human's fall who is predestined to blindness, a prey of wrongdoing and error, the theme of the mystery of God who is not revealed in the Scriptures except to those who know how to undertake their study with humility and ardor, the theme of the search by *mens*, the term used by Saint Augustine to refer to the higher faculty of the soul.

Even from the prologue of the commentary, Saint Gregory's perspectives on the double dimension, letter, and spirit, place his exegesis in the purest Augustinian descendance. Among the verses commented by Saint Gregory, some of them come back several times in the Augustinian texts. Saint Augustine quoted from the *Song of Songs* and commented on several verses in his work, which allows us to find, among his lines, the interpretation he gave to this biblical poem. The texts of Saint Gregory and Saint Augustine present in their content close links, such as the common use of some terms. For example, for the two authors, the black color symbolizes the darkness of ignorance where the pagans were cast before their coming to faith. Both rely on the text of Saint Paul in *Ephesians* 5,8.

The second name we need to mention in the inventory of the sources of the commentary of Saint Gregory is that of Aponius. The only work that tradition has kept bearing his name has remained little known: more precisely, it is a commentary on the Song. This text presents common features with the comment of Saint Gregory the Great. Researcher Johannes Witte has shown that Aponius lived at the end of the fourth and early fifth centuries, and the date when his commentary was conceived, is between 405 and 415. At the end of his work, Witte points out with a few parallel texts the connection between Aponius and Gregory.[13] For Gregory and Aponius, *the Song of Songs* symbolically describes the marriage of Christ with the Church. In identical terms, the two authors rely on the thought of Saint Paul.

Following in the footsteps of Aponius and, like him, referring to Saint Paul, Gregory presents the royal chamber of the Groom as a place that opens the penetration of the most hidden mysteries.

In the commentary on *the Song* 1, 3, Aponius and Gregory meet within the same line of interpretation: the image of the widespread perfume illustrates the progressive spread of the name of God in the world, starting from the mystery of the Embodiment. By this, they are different from Origen and Augustine, for whom the widespread perfume symbolizes the spread of the name of Jesus through the Gospel and preaching.

To both, the body of Christ (*incarnationis mysterium – diuinitas incarnata*) is the vessel from which the name of God, the perfume of the divine knowledge (*innotescere*), escapes.

Aponius assimilates *greges sodalium* with the heretical sects, with the herds of false companions who have poisoned the doctrine and who continue to invite the Bride to their table to attract her toward wrongdoing.

Saint Gregory reiterates the same ideas, but from a more temperate perspective. The Groom cannot wait and rest, but only in the heart of those who live "in a burning faith" and who cultivate "the green grass of virtues".[14]

The third source that reveals itself in the depth of the commentary is Saint Gregory himself, reminding of *Morales* about Job, which he wrote during his stay in Constantinople.

The theme of man's blindness through the original sin, in order to be fundamentally Augustinian, is reiterated in the commentary through borrowed formulas from *Morales*.[15]

By the time Gregory writes, the line of interpretation he adopts is already classic. Indeed, we notice the same elements to Augustine and before him to Origen.

Thus, for the three authors, self-knowledge begins with recognizing the image of God in every human being. In addition, Gregory's dependence on

Augustine and Origen remains uninterrupted throughout the exegesis of the verse. Each of them interprets the biblical text in the sense of warning the believers against the pagan practices and the deeds of the corrupt vicars.

In other passages in the commentary, Gregory elaborates his reflection by being as freely inspired from *Morales*.

Gregory proves to be the heir of Origen by his way of understanding the meaning of Scripture, but also by some details of exegesis.

Saint Gregory interpreted the biblical poem by referring directly and even with some insistence to the texts of Origen, by the translations of Jerome and Rufin.[16]

Commenting on the first verse of *the Song*, Gregory explains, in Origen's manner, that the arrival of the Groom in person comes to crown a long wait, initially nourished by the succession of messengers.

For Gregory and for Origen, the wine, which is similar to the breasts of the Groom, is assimilated with the knowledge of the law and the prophets.

The divine word recorded in the sacred texts is always offered to man under the double dimension of letter and spirit. The Pauline antinomy, evoked by Gregory, becomes the key to his interpretation on *the Song*. "The letter kills"[17] because it tends to close man in the categories of a world that the original sin has polluted to the depths, turning it away from God; it is nothing more than the favorite symbol of the exteriority in which the mistake attracted the fall of Adam.

The believer will begin on his way from the exteriority in which he was scattered to the interiority that will render him the original union with God only in the movement of the letter toward the spirit.

Gregory's meditation on *the Song* becomes at this point particularly clear. Thus, here is the biblical book that sheds light in its most vivid contrasts on the double letter and spirit dimension of the Scripture.

The Symbolism of the Groom and the Bride

Gregory the Great exposes the translation of the most important theme of *the Song* and develops the symbolism of the Groom and the Bride: the divine love, our soul in ascension toward God, the thresholds that the soul has to pass, the old and new world – the discrepancies between Jews and Christians, between the heretics and the righteous people of the Church, themes that have been resumed mostly from by his predecessors.

Gregory the Great takes from Origen the clarification regarding the title, as well as the symbolism of the Groom (the Lord) and the Bride (the Church),[18] remembering the songs of honor of the Old Testament, of which *the Song of Songs* represents the song of union that is sung at the wedding of the Groom and the Bride:

> *Canticum veroconiunctionis cum deo hoc estcanticum, quod in nuptiis sponsi et sponsae canitur, id est Canticum canticorum.*[19]

"Indeed, the Song is that of union with God, this is the song that is sung at the wedding of the Grooms and Brides, meaning *the Song of Songs*".

The expression of the mutual love of Christ – the Groom and the Church – the Bride dominates the entire *Commentary* of Saint Gregory.

The bride is, at the same time, the individual soul which seeks the traces of the Groom on the paths of virtue and who will not see her desire fulfilled only in a meeting where the human will make a place for the divine (*Mor. 27: 4*).

The content of the commentary is presented as a summary of the Gregorian doctrine.

We note the variety and richness of the themes that Gregory addresses in this short text. It is important, therefore, in reading the commentary, to keep in mind certain passages from Gregory's other works in order to understand the density he wished to give here to his thinking and to better capture the full extent of it.

Ever since the first lines of the prologue, Gregory has sought to synthetically describe the conditions of the dialogue between man and God. From the original sin, the present life opens to humanity as a painful path of exile. Being deprived of the goods of paradise, blinded in his heart by the very custom of unbelief, at this point, the man sank into the carnal in which he locked himself with accents of divine language and spiritual intelligence.

In this perspective, Gregory presents *the Song of Songs* as the biblical book that leads the believer to the highest degree of contemplation. It is the poem whose "secret is only penetrated by the mind capable of revealing the hidden meanings",[20] the song of accompanying God that surpasses all the other songs of the Bible, the holy book that ends, in the relation of God–man, the master–servant dialectics, to be seen Father–son, to inaugurate the much more intimate and unexpected Bride–Groom relationship. Finally, *the Song of Songs* is the book that comes to complete and crown Solomon's work, after *Proverbs* and *Ecclesiastes*. In the Song, it is true, beyond the moral and the natural life, "the contemplative life is presented, whose arrival we desire, as well as the vision of the Lord in person...".[21]

For Gregory, the *Song of the Songs* is, first and foremost, the spiritual song that celebrates "the holy union between the Groom and the Bride", whose figures shine with all the brilliance in Christ and in the Church: "The bride is, in fact, the Church itself in its perfection; The Groom is the Lord". Like the Old Covenant, *the Song* sang the love of Yahweh for Israel – the Bride, in the same way that it now exalts the love that God bears in Christ for the Bride – Church.[22]

The unstoppable joy that the Bride feels sensing the charms of the Groom is valorized by Gregory in a purely histological sense. He seeks to demonstrate, through the play of comparisons suggested in the biblical text, the eminent superiority of Christ – the Groom concerning the gifts and promises revealed to the Bride in the Old Testament by "the science of the law and the science of the prophets".[23] The kisses that the Bride now exchanges with him overwhelm her with the ineffable gifts of the divine knowledge, before which any human science or wisdom is nothing but vanity.

The relationship of Christ – the Groom and the Church-Bride does not exhaust only through it the entire symbolic richness of the *Song of Songs*. As Gregory tries to prove, this essential relationship finds its perfect expression in the mystical relationship that unites the individual soul with Christ – the Groom.

The Song must be read as a parable that suggests to the soul the mysterious realities of the contemplative life: "… in *the Song of Songs* is presented the contemplative life that we want to come and the vision of the Lord in person".[24]

The Christian is thus surrounded by the beneficial atmosphere of the engagement of Christ with the Church, and even he is invited to join in the joy of the Bride, to the extent that the Groom considers accompanying himself individually. In this case, the name and privileges of the Bride must be taken into consideration for the individual soul. The Church includes all its members in the relationship it maintains with Christ, but they do not all vibrate equally intense to the joy of the union with the Groom. For this reason, undoubtedly, the scenario from *the Song* features two main characters surrounded by two categories of figures: the young people who accompany the Bride and the groups of companions who accompany the Groom the faithful soul will have to first of all "know itself",[25] to watch with vigilance the inner guard, to sit with discernment to listen to masters and vicars in discovering the Word of God together with them and in learning their lessons regarding the demanding laws of conversion and the spiritual progress.

Only with this price will the Soul-Bride come to pass from the outside of the sensitive world where sin holds it toward the interiority of the contemplative life where the Groom will overwhelm it "with the touch of his inner grace".[26]

For Saint Gregory the Great, in the same note to the whole tradition, the wife (sponsa)[27] is above all, the Church. In the 10th paragraph of the work *Commentaries on the Song of Songs*, the husband is God and the wife is the Church in its perfection, the angels being companions of the husband (sodales), then those who follow them (adulescentulae). Nevertheless, the sum of these various categories represents the wife: all together are the wife, because all together are the Church.[28]

The sources of the *Commentaries* of Gregory the Great are the teachings of Augustine, the books of Aponius, the exegesis of Origen. The beginning of *the Commentaries* is the call to our own knowledge in order to be able to get rid of the blindness, ignorance, and unworthiness of man after the fall into sin:

> *Postquam a paradise gaudiis expulsumest genus humanum, in istam peregrinationem vitae praesentis veniens caecum cor ab spiritali intellectu habet. Cui caeco cordi si diceretur voce divina: «Sequere deum»*

> *vel «Dilige deum» sicut ei in lege dictum est, semel foris missum et per torporem insensibilitatis frigidum non caperet quod audiret. Idcirco per quaedam enigmata sermo divinus animae torpenti et frigidae loquitur et de rebus, quos novit, latenter insinuat ei amorem, quem non novit.*[29]

After humanity has been expelled from the happiness of paradise, entering the pilgrimage of the present life, it has a blind heart in terms of spiritual intelligence. If the divine voice would say to this blind heart: "Follow God" or "Love the Lord," as was told to it in the law, once exiled, cold, and stuck up in sensitivity, it would not understand what it would hear. Also, through the enigmas that the divine discourse addresses to the soul which is stung by the cold and starting from the realities that it knows, it sneaks to it, the love that it does not know.

Starting from the same mystical relationship *soul-God*, the statement made by His Excellency Archbishop Bartholomew of Cluj, in the book *the Poetry of the Old Testament*, it is worth to be mentioned. He mentions that the ideas of the Gregory of Nyssa were continued by Pope Gregory the Great and these were later taken over by the Eastern asceticism and mysticism, specifying that

> in this human-divine bridal engagement it is not about the still impure soul, haunted by passions, as it is in the phase of shunning of passions, but of the one that has entered the higher stage of contemplation, now consumed by the longing for the supreme knowledge and the perfect union. In this respect, spiritual grounds will be drawn from *the Song of Songs* by many Fathers who have studied Philokalia, such as Maximus the Confessor, Nikitas Stithatos, John Climacus, Elias Ecdicus, Simeon the New Theologian, Gregory of Sinai, the Patriarch Callistus.[30]

If a man knows himself, he knows that he was created in the image of God and therefore he must be worthy of Him and not act in the image of the evil. The soul can rise when the senses are at heights. The Kiss from *Prologue*:

> Kiss me with the kiss of his mouth!
> Your endearment is better than wine
> and it's the fragrance of your ointments
> sweeter than anything that it's fragrance[31]

It represents, says Gregory the Great, the peak of the feeling to which the soul can ascend: "the kiss of his mouth is the fullness of the inner peace itself: when we will be with Him, we will have nothing more to know" (ad quam cum pervenerimus, nihil remanebit amplius, quod quaeramus).[32]

Wine signifies the knowledge of the Law and the Prophets. Wife, the Church is fed more by preaching the embodiment than by learning the Law:

"Plus enim nos nutriuit incarnationis praedicatio quamlegis doctrina. Dicat ego: meliora sunt ubera tua super uinum".[33]

"For the preaching of the Embodiment, has fed us far more abundantly than the learning of the Law. So, the Wife says: Your breasts are better than the wine".

Throughout the entire commentary the fragrances, smells, aromas, and balms are all symbols of love: "unguenta Domini virtutes sunt, unguentum Domini Spiritus Sanctus fuit".[34] That is why Saint Gregory the Great says in the 21st paragraph that the wine poured out, is the unseen Deity who becomes visible through the embodiment: "unguentum effusum nomen tuum".[35] "Your name is a wide-spread anointing perfume". The perfume poured refers to the kenotic act, the draining of the divine glory of Christ (cf. Philippians 2: 6–7). The verb εκκνωθέν shows the entirely emptying of the whole container, of its content.

At the same time, Gregory the Great describes the thresholds that the soul must gradually pass: "Primus ergo aditus domus istius porta fidei, secundus prouectus ascensus spei, tertius latitude caritatis, quartus iam perfectio caritatis ad cognitionem secretorum dei".[36]

"The first entrance of this house is therefore the door of faith, the second stage of the journey are the steps of hope, and third, this endless extension of love for the knowledge of the mysteries of God".

Love in Commentaries on the Song of Songs

First, we can discern what the love described in *the Song of Songs* is for Gregory the Great. It is closer to *the Agape* than to *the Eros*. Love is celebrated by a language that sometimes hurts our taste and our decency. But, like the bolder terms used by the prophets, these images, explainable by an outdated civilization, less refined and perhaps even less pharisaical than ours, are to some extent neutralized by the very pure atmosphere of the exigency and waiting for the moral conversion in which we are permanently involved. Despite the symbol of marriage and the imitated expressions from the love poetry of the time, the love of which *the Song of Songs* speaks, is much different from the *Eros* of Plato, opposed to the *Agape* in an exaggerated way.

The word ἀγάπη, characteristic to the language of the New Testament, especially to the vocabulary of Saint Paul and Saint John, is mentioned ten times in *the Song of Songs*. It is important to note that the term ἀγαπάω is almost exclusively biblical.[37]

The meaning of the word ἀγάπη expresses the Christian love, in the sense of understanding, closeness, sympathy, friendship, and soul nobility.

Defining this love, in its essence, is a very difficult thing because this love is such a rich reality, its content being above our mind and very difficult to be rationally defined, as Saint Paul said: "is outside all knowledge"(*Eph.* 3:19). Compared to *the Eros* of paganism, which represents the elevation of man toward God, *Agape* the Christian love is at its origins a descent of God toward man, so that man in turn can rise toward God.[38]

Ἀγάπη is not only the descent of God toward man, but also man's effort to meet and receive God. Ἀγάπη is the love that is dedicated to the good of others, the dedication that goes toward self-sacrifice.

Eros means "the common love", while *Agape* is "the love that freely chooses its love". *The Eros* "seeks in the other the satisfaction of its thirst to live", often translated by "manifesting love".[39] In the broad lexical field of love of the Greek language, portrays the "disinterested affection", *agápē* has, since the first Christian centuries, new connotations, which ensure to it a true career. By designating God's love for people and the love that people owe to God as also to their fellowship, with *agápē* we find ourselves in front of the last and the highest form of love, that penetrates the depths of life. It is only now that we are about to understand the deity in its simplicity and essentiality, beyond the limits of our thinking. *Agápē* is the depth dimension of love, the one through which love is in direct relation to the fundamental notion of existence. In *agápē,* we are revealed the ultimate reality, and life and love are transfigured. "*Agape* is a love that invades into love, just as revelation is reason that invades into reason, and the Word of God is the Word that invades into all words".[40] For the soul to know God does not mean anything other than to love Him because this is how you know love. The union is expressed in terms of knowledge and vision.[41] It is the privilege and honor of those who live a good life to enter deeply into the mystery of God's commandments.

Conclusions

Staint Gregory the Great elaborated, starting from the living doctrine received from his predecessors, an original work that aroused the fervor and admiration of his time. The legacy of the past comes back in his writings integrated with his own thinking, enriched with his personal experience and revalued through a language that fructifies and renews its importance. Saint Gregory presents us in his work, his rich human, Christian and guiding experience. His word, abundantly fed by the divine Word, comes to translate with simplicity and without artifice what in the beginning was in himself a fiery search of God, of life with grace and ministering the Church.

Commentaries on *the Song of Songs* show the attention he gives to the emotional impulses of the heart, his reflection developing in this work, truly as a true tribute to the greatness of the heart of God, which opens without reservation before the poverty of the human heart, in an insistent invitation to celebrate the engagement of the Groom and the Bride, the relationship between the Groom and the Bride signifying the union of Jesus Christ with the church or with the human soul.

The interpretation of Saint Gregory is allegorical par excellence, having a special theological and literary value.

The parallels between the ideas expressed in *the Song of Songs* and *the Commentaries* related to it of Saint Gregory the Great are: love/mercy toward the history of the chosen people/kindness/awakening of souls/the human effort/the messianic salvation/justice/salvation.

After all, *the Song of Songs* is essentially the image of the purifications and successive ascensions of the repentant Israel under the action of the divine demands, which only evade to cause a deeper transformation and then to continue to live completely.

The interpretation of Saint Gregory the Great of the sacred poem is that of the preacher who knew how to carefully read the prophetic literature. Love is a unique reality, but with different dimensions, and the biblical faith does not build a world that is opposed to the original human phenomenon that is love, but accepts the whole man, opening new dimensions to him.

Saint Gregory the Great tries to bring into the souls the theological virtues of faith, a faith that is never more alive than when they obey the Word of God.

The Song of Songs, says Saint Gregory the Great, sings the faith that, despite all obstacles, does not cease to rely on the word of God.

Saint Gregory the Great remains one of the greatest Doctors of the Church. His influence was undoubtedly that of a moralist, approaching, from this point of view to the style of Saint Ambrose. His style is unpretentious, and this simplicity assures the phrase, with the gravity characteristic of the bishops, a vivid clarity, his thought comes off through this penetrating force which is one of Gregory's main gifts.

Even if Saint Gregory is not the creator of the mentality of his time, he belongs to his time, whose weaknesses he knows, and which he strives to combat. His spiritual and pastoral doctrine mirrors the fact that he was a guide for souls on the path of enlightenment and purification.

Notes

1 *Dictionnaire de Spiritualité, ascétique et mystique doctrine et histoire*, fondé M. Viller, F. Cavallera, J. de Guibert, Tome VI, Fascicules XLII–XLIII, Beauchesne, Paris 1967, 905.

2 *Dictionnaire de Spiritualité, ascétique et mystique doctrine et histoire*, 905.

3 Justinian Cârstoiu, "Interpretarea alegorică a Cântării Cântărilor în tradiţia iudaică şi în tradiţia creştină", https://www.crestinortodox.ro/religie/interpretarea-alegorica-cantarii-cantarilor-traditia-iudaica-in-traditia-crestina-69436.html.

4 Constantin Voicu, *Patrologie*, Vol. III, (Bucureşti: Institutul Biblic si de Msiune al Bisericii Ortodoxe Române Publishing House), 143.

5 Pierre Batiffol, *Saint Grégoire le Grand*, Paris, Librairie Lecoffre, J. Gabalda et Fils, Éditeurs, 1931, 10.

6 Grégoire le Grand, *Commentaire sur le Cantique des Cantiques*, Sources Chrétiennes, introduction, traduction, notes et index par Rodrigue Bélanger, Les Éditions du Cerf, Paris, 1984, 68.

7 *Dictionnaire de Spiritualité, ascétique et mystique doctrine et histoire*, 896.

8 P. Migne, *P.L.*, vol.75, 509.
9 Grégoire le Grand, *Commentaire sur le Cantique des Cantiques*, 70.
10 Grégoire le Grand, *Commentaire sur le Cantique des Cantiques*, 78.
11 Grégoire le Grand, Commentaire sur le Cantique des Cantiques, 30.
12 Fulbert, Cayré, *Patrologie et Histoire de la Théologie*, Sociéte de S. Jean L'Évangéliste, Paris, 1933, 240.
13 Grégoire le Grand, *Commentaire sur le Cantique des Cantiques*, Sources Chrétiennes, introduction, traduction, notes et index par Rodrigue Bélanger, Les Éditions du Cerf, Paris, 1984, 35.
14 Grégoire le Grand, Commentaire sur le Cantique des Cantiques, 41.
15 Grégoire le Grand, Commentaire sur le Cantique des Cantiques, 41.
16 Grégoire le Grand, *Commentaire sur le Cantique des Cantiques*, 44.
17 Grégoire le Grand, *Commentaire sur le Cantique des Cantiques*, 72.
18 *Dictionnaire de Spiritualité, ascétique et mystique doctrine et histoire*, 872.
19 Grégoire le Grand, *Commentaire sur le Cantique des Cantiques*, 80.
20 Grégoire le Grand, *Commentaire sur le Cantique des Cantiques*, 78.
21 Grégoire le Grand, *Commentaire sur le Cantique des Cantiques*, 83.
22 Grégoire le Grand, *Commentaire sur le Cantique des Cantiques*, 82.
23 Grégoire le Grand, *Commentaire sur le Cantique des Cantiques*, 89–90.
24 Grégoire le Grand, *Commentaire sur le Cantique des Cantiques*, 84.
25 Grégoire le Grand, *Commentaire sur le Cantique des Cantiques*, 143.
26 Grégoire le Grand, *Commentaire sur le Cantique des Cantiques*, 92.
27 For the term *sponsa*, Saint Gregory the Great indicates a double meaning, soul or group of souls, cf. pf. 9, 15, 39.
28 Grégoire le Grand, *Commentaire sur le Cantique des Cantiques*, 10.
29 Grégoire le Grand, *Commentaire sur le Cantique des Cantiques*, 68.
30 *Poezia Vechiului Testament*, version revised after *the Septuagint*, written and commented on by Bartolomeu Valeriu Anania, (București: Institutul Biblic si de Misiune al Bisericii Ortodoxe Române Publishing House), 490.
31 Grégoire le Grand, *Commentaire sur le Cantique des Cantiques*, 491.
32 Grégoire le Grand, *Commentaire sur le Cantique des Cantiques*, 100.
33 Grégoire le Grand, *Commentaire sur le Cantique des Cantiques*, 90.
34 Grégoire le Grand, *Commentaire sur le Cantique des Cantiques*, 90.
35 Grégoire le Grand, *Commentaire sur le Cantique des Cantiques*, 102.
36 Grégoire le Grand, *Commentaire sur le Cantique des Cantiques*, 110.
37 Gerhard Kittel, Otto Bauernfeind, *Theologisches Wörterbuchzum Neuen Testament*, Stuttgart, 1933, 37–38.
38 Isidor Todoran, "Eros and Agape", *Studii Teologice*, VIII 1956, no.3–4, 143.
39 Isidor Todoran, "Eros and Agape", 85.
40 Paul Tillich, "O ontologie a iubirii" *Viața Românească LXXXV (1990), no.11*, 91.
41 *Dictionnaire de Spiritualité, ascétique et mystique doctrine et histoire*, 899.

Bibliography

Anania, Valeriu, *Poezia Vechiului Testament,* Institutul Biblic si de Msiune al Bisericii Ortodoxe Române Publishing House, București, 2000.

Batiffol, Pierre, *Saint Grégoire le Grand*, Librairie Lecoffre, J. Gabalda et Fils, Éditeurs, Paris, 1931. Cayré, F., *Patrologie et Histoire de la Théologie*, Sociéte de S. Jean L'Évangéliste, Paris, 1933.

Cayré, Fulbert, *Patrologie et Histoire de la Théologie*, Sociéte de S. Jean L'Évangéliste, Paris, 1933.

Grégoire le Grand, *Commentaire sur le Cantique des Cantiques*, Sources Chrétiennes, Les Éditions du Cerf, Paris, 1984.
Kittel, Gerhard, Otto Bauernfeind, *Theologisches Wörterbuchzum Neuen Testament*, Stuttgart, 1933.
Migne, Jaques-Paul, *Patrologiae Cursus completes*, Series Latinae, Paris, 1844.
Nygren, Anders, *Eros și Agape. Prefaceri ale iubirii creștine*, Humanitas Publishing House, București, 2018.
Tillich, Paul, "O ontologie a iubirii" *Viața Românească* 11, 1990.
Todoran, Isidor, "Eros și Agape", *Studii Teologice* 3–4, 1956.
Viller, M., F. Cavallera, J. de Guibert, *Dictionnaire de Spiritualité, ascétique et mystique doctrine et histoire*, Beauchesne, Paris, 1967.
Voicu, Constantin, *Patrologie*, Vol. III, Institutul Biblic si de Msiune al Bisericii Ortodoxe Române Publishing House, București, 2009.

13 The Configuration of *Ethos* in Gregory Nazianzus's *First Theological Oration*

Anca Tomoioagă

Introduction

Gregory of Nazianzus has been known as being not only an extraordinary theologian of the Holy Trinity but also a critic who consecrated the canon for religious and theological discourse. Actually, he succeeds in delimitating the religious discourse *i.e.* preaching in the context of the fourth century very prodigious rhetorical market, from the common public discourse. Not only that he draws a line between the common public discourse and religious discourse but by regulating the preaching, he establishes a basic pattern for the act of speech of preaching and for the structural relationships developed between the addresser, the addressee and a topic/a message that is to be communicated. He was also much aware of the fact that such structural relationships are much influenced by the context (be it cultural or social) and even by the code.

All over his 44 orations, but especially in *Oration 20* and *Oration 27* (*First Theological Oration*), Gregory of Nazianzus discusses the status of the bishops/legitimate religious orators and the status of the religious discourse. In this respect, the issues that he ruminates in his works reflect our theologian's strive to define his own status as a preacher and himself as an authoritative voice inside the new religious discourse he frames.

The present study attempts to analyse this process of ethos configuration steadily developed by Gregory of Nazianzus through his orations with the main focus on *The First Theological Oration*. Also, it tables some questions for discussion: how come such a shy and emotive, introvert and reclusive personality as Gregory's succeeds in imposing such a powerful ethos not only in his epoch but also throughout ages till today? or What new light the contemporary pragmatic, sociologist and neo-rhetoric studies cast on ethos as configured by Gregory in his discourses?

Preliminaries

Religious discourse in Christianity evolved gradually and embraced, through the Church Fathers, the rhetorical, philosophical and cultural Greek legacy.

DOI: 10.4324/9781003273592-13

When referring to Christianity and culture, the Byzantine focus on education and on the public rhetoric as the second nature of the Byzantine population, created a very fertile social soil for the Christian scholar. Christian belief expanded also because of the increasing "emphasis on the verbal formulation of the faith",[1] a discursive attempt that reached its peak in the fourth century when "preaching became the mass medium *par excellence* that helped to shape public opinion".[2] Therefore, rhetoric started to serve as a very useful means of touching people's hearts and minds. For that matter, researchers identified in the époque a Christian sophistry, close to what the Second Sophistic meant. The sophist, the teacher of rhetoric, was supposed to use speeches as lessons "to expound views on political, moral, or aesthetic subjects"[3] and not as gratuitous exercises on different imaginary subjects. Libanius in Antioch, Themistitius in Constantinople, Saint Basil, Gregory of Nyssa and Gregory of Nazianzus[4] were associated with the Second Sophistic.

Apart from the early sophists, in the wake of Plato, the Christian orators rejected discourses as stylistic parades and despised "meretricious adornment" and "empty verbosity".[5] On numerous occasions, Gregory expressed his personal view upon the importance of the exhortations as guidance for the believer and not as verbal entertainment. Kinzig is right to assert that:

> for most believers the sermon as the most prominent form of Christian oratory was important as a source of information about their faith. It served a didactic and educational purpose. At the same time the sermon was a means of establishing Orthodoxy and combating deviant theological views.[6]

Therefore, when comes to the oration typology, sophistry could offer to Christians different oratorical genres such as deliberative (speaking or writing aimed at persuading an audience for or against a proposed course of action[7]), judicial or demonstrative orations, the *Demonstrativum genus* as "a type of speaking that aims to demonstrate either the good or the bad features of the subject under consideration".[8]

In his famous *Rhetoric*,[9] Aristotle referred to all the elements that constructed a discourse and made possible such an enterprise, including the speaker/the rhetor, the addressee, the message, the process of argumentation and the rhetorical devices. *Ethos*, *logos* and *pathos* were Aristotle's key terms to nominate the three technical, artistic (*entechnoi*) and internal means/proofs (*pisteis*) of persuasion that correspond to the three elements that configure the speech act *i.e.* addresser, addressee and message/speech.[10] What exists outside the oration, free of the rhetor's will, is considered to be non-technical, non-artistic such as the occasion, the social context and should be used by the orator in the discourse.

The three modes of persuasion are created and invented by the rhetor inside the oration and are dependent on the art of the discourse itself. *Ethos* represents the personal character of the speaker as projected in the speech[11] and only through the speech. *Pathos* is based on the emotion of the audience[12] and refers to how an audience may be emotionally moved by the discourse and how its reactions could vary according to the listeners' state of mind, from anger to agreement. *Logos* could be defined as the organisation and power of arguments and is "based upon reasoning, analysis, argument, as contained in the language of the speaker".[13]

When describing *ethos*,[14] Aristotle referred exclusively to the rhetoric ego as configured inside the discourse by the rhetors themselves through the voicing, gesticulation and presence, simultaneously working at their credibility. A rhetor becomes credible in front of his audience by displaying throughout the oration some qualities (much appreciated by the sophists[15]) such as practical intelligence (*phronêsis*), a virtuous character and good will.[16] In other words,

> speaker develops *ethos* artistically by showing good sense, the virtue by which one makes right judgments about practical affairs, and good moral character, the other virtues such as justice and courage, and also good will, which Aristotle takes as the equivalent of arguing that one is in an emotional state of friendliness toward the auditors.[17]

Therefore, the speaker's credibility is being constructed within the discourse by the speaker's efforts to show qualities that make him/her worthy of thrust. As long as the speaker's person is trustful (a strong *ethos* has been built), consequently, the message is also offered credence. Conclusively, the mechanism of *ethos* functions in a system that correlates it with both *logos* and *pathos*.

It is well known that Aristotle had discussed the *ethos* as both a direct and immediate product and a means of the discourse itself. Thus *ethos* is being created intrinsically throughout the speech as a way of influencing the auditory.

Recent studies in the field of neo-rhetoric deal with many categories that belong to classical rhetoric through an upgrade by means of pragmatics and sociology. In a study dedicated to *ethos* as a construct in modern discourses, researcher Ruth Amossy calls it "a spectacular comeback under various guises in contemporary theories".[18] Pragmatics analyses not only the tripartite verbal relation *speaker–message–receiver* but also refers to the context of this communicative act, the intentions of the speaker and the meaning of the speech act related to its context. Pragmatics tries to focus mainly on the contextualisation of the linguistic sentences in search of a holistic interpretation of the act of speech.

Levinson defines pragmatics as the study of any reference of a speaker to a context.[19] The main pragmatics preoccupation represents the effect of speaking in a specific context, but also the speaker's attitude and intentions when delivering the speech, the influence of the context on the act of speech, the connections between language and context.

J. L. Austin's famous theory of the acts of speech[20] describes three types of speech act: the locutionary act of speech that involves simple uttering of a sentence; the illocutionary act that involves not only uttering, but also performing a sentence (which includes the so-called performatives – verbs that clearly define the nature of the speech act performed such as: promise, order, apologise, invitation and vow); the perlocutionary act that focuses mainly on the reaction of the audience and the speech effects on the interlocutor. Coming back to the illocutionary act, this speech act focuses mainly on the speaker as it reflects the speaker's intention during the communicative act. This intention is also called illocutionary force and it is manifested towards the listener as means of persuasion.[21] Sociologists such as Bourdieu brought into discussion the social context and the speaker's social status that might have a major influence as an extralinguistic unit in the act of speech. Such aspects like social context or social status were considered by Aristotle *atechnoi* and consequently they were left aside by the philosopher.

Modern rhetoric has taken into account not only the *ethos* as an intrinsic mode of the discourse but also exterior aspects that belong to the *ethos* from before the discourse: public fame, institutional authority and legitimacy that could seriously contribute to the persuasive efficiency of a discourse. A distinction has been made between the prediscursive/prior *ethos* which expresses what the auditory already knows about the orator and the discursive *ethos* that could confirm its prediscursive image or could deconstruct it through the discourse.[22]

Ruth Amossy's study *Ethos at the Crossroads of Disciplines: Rhetoric, Pragmatics, Sociology* demonstrates a more integrative perspective upon the *ethos*, excluding unilateral approaches. Analysing two types of discursive *ethos*, within the theoretical framework based on several reseachers' studies (such as Bourdieu, Oswald Ducrot, Perelman, Dominique Maingueneau), professor Ruth Amossy reaches several conclusions that have also represented a starting point for the present topic.

One of the premises Amossy starts with is represented by a pre-Aristotelian "tradition founded by Isocrates and mainly followed by the Romans" which "defines *ethos* as the previous reputation and social status of the speaker".[23] Aristotle redefined *ethos* as being constructed only within the discourse. New research confirmed that *ethos* does not exclusively belong to the verbal exchange among the speaker and the audience, being only an internal dimension of the discourse, but it is also constructed by the prior image/fame of the speaker the audience has in mind, the institutional authority the speaker is endowed with or the preconceptions of the audience regarding the speaker. In Amossy's words, the final conclusion is comprehensive: "The discursive construction, the social imaginary, and the institutional authority contribute, then, to construct a suitable *ethos*".[24] Therefore, the sociological perspective on the *ethos*, the pragmatic and (neo)rhetoric views on *ethos* do not exclude/contradict each other but are complementary.[25] Furthermore, the power of the discourse might increase exactly because of the counterbalance between the prior *ethos* and the discursive *ethos*. This kind of *pitching* functions as a binding agent and creates a coherent, hence trustworthy image of the speaker: "Yet the construction of the image of self within the discourse has, in turn, the capacity to modify the prior representations and to confer credibility and authority upon the speaker".[26]

Thus, the present study focuses not only on *ethos* in the Aristotelian understanding of the word, but also on what seems to be exterior to the discursive *ethos*, namely, authority, legitimacy and fame as elements that may define the prior *ethos* and collaborate with the features the discursive *ethos* infers within a speech. In regard to Gregory of Nazianzus, how does the discursive *ethos* reconfigures itself pursuant to the out of the discourse features such as legitimacy, authority and social context? How do the social imaginary and the institutional authority contribute to the configuration of the discursive *ethos* in Gregory's preaching? Prior to develop a response for the two questions just mentioned, some notions and terms should be mentioned here as they are very useful for our enterprise.

The sociologist Pierre Bourdieu analyses *ethos* from the perspective of the authority it gains not only through the discourse itself, but also because of the exterior authority of the speaker, because of the social context the speech takes place. The authority of language does not reside

> in the set of prosodic and articulatory variations which define distinguished pronunciation, or in the complexity of the syntax or the richness of the vocabulary, in other words in the intrinsic properties of discourse itself, but rather in the social conditions of production and reproduction of the distribution between the classes of the knowledge and recognition of the legitimate language.[27]

Therefore, authority is created not only through the discourse itself, but also because of the social context and auditory which contribute to the setup of the speaker's authority. As Bourdieu puts it: "the language of authority never governs without the collaboration of those it governs".[28] Furthermore, Bourdieu states that "authority comes to language from outside". The spokesperson is given the *skeptron i.e.* delegated to represent, through words as symbols of authority, an institution, for instance. Power does not come from words *per se*, but also from the perspective of the social context the discourse is held in.[29] The French sociologist explains that the illocutionary force does not stay in performatives, but it

> is nothing other than the *delegated power* of the spokesperson, and his speech - that is, the substance of his discourse and, inseparably, his way of speaking- is no more than a testimony, and one among others, of the *guarantee of delegation* which is vested in him.[30]

In discourse analysis, linguists should look for answers not only referring to linguistic code, but also to social relations, the social context the discourse is delivered in, the typology of the audience participating to the discourse, the institutional and authoritative status of the speaker. In order to objectively decode the discourse meaning, one should take into account the relation between the linguistic product and the market. The term *market/field* is used by Bourdieu with reference to social contexts and settings where persons act. Such fields might be social, literary and linguistic and imply a circulation of capitals – linguistic capital (linguistic and various competences), cultural capital (knowledge and culture), symbolic capital (honour, prestige and recognised power).[31] These capitals are defining the individuals and synchronically contour their profile of potentialities.

Also, according to Bourdieu, each person is endowed with the so-called *habitus*, a concept that defines the individual diachronically. Habitus represents a sum of skills and predispositions, reactions and attitudes achieved throughout the life experiences from childhood to adulthood, which influences individuals in their vision upon life and defines their behaviour in society. Such dispositions are so deeply sowed in the individual that is even visible at a physical level in what has been defined as *bodily hexis*: "political mythology realized, *em-bodied,* turned into a permanent disposition, a durable way of standing, speaking, walking, and thereby of feeling and thinking".[32]

There is also a linguistic habitus Bourdieu writes about. This type of habitus implies a

> certain propensity to speak and to say determinate things (the expressive interest) and a certain capacity to speak, which involves both the linguistic capacity to generate an infinite number of grammatically correct discourses, and the social capacity to use this competence adequately in a determinate situation. This habitus manifests in a linguistic market whose structures impose themselves as a system of specific sanctions and censorships.[33]

A successful act of speech where *ethos* may communicate itself persuasively depends on the correlation between the speakers' (linguistic) potential and the hearers' potential (linguistic) profile within a social context that influences the power of discourse.

When linguistic habitus and linguistic market interact, the linguistic utterances are being produced throughout the dialogues that are established. Bourdieu explains the act of speech *via* economics terminology too. The act of speech is an "economic exchange established within a particular symbolic relation of power between a producer, endowed with a certain linguistic capital, and a consumer (or a market), and which is capable of procuring a certain material or symbolic profit. In other words, utterances are not only (save in exceptional circumstances) signs to be understood and deciphered; they are also *signs of wealth,* intended to be evaluated and appreciated, and *signs of authority,* intended to be believed and obeyed."[34] Hence, the discourse represents an expression of authority (consequently, of persuasiveness) manifested not only through the elements that construct the *ethos* inside the discourse itself, through verbal means, but also through the external elements that describe the relationship between the speaker and the listener as a relation of forces. In the same train of ideas, the authority also derives from the legitimacy of the speaker as the orator is frequently legitimated institutionally.

To summarise, in Bourdieu's vision, the act of speech represents the very moment of interaction between *habitus* and *market*. This interaction is produced synergically at various levels of such a relationship activating the latencies of each part, which attempt to correlate to each other. The success of such correlation, hence the success of each act of speech/discourse, depends in a great measure on the similarities between *habitus* and *market*, on the common potentialities they share and the incongruities they manage. *Ethos* cannot be seen only inside the discourse. When analysing the efficacy of a discourse, one should take account of the public fame, the social context, the social statuses, the institutional delegacy, the *habitus* and the *market*, and the various types of capital involved in the verbal exchange. Such factors, external to the discourse, are interactive and contribute to the success of a discourse as external means of persuasion. They also influence the building process of the discursive *ethos*.

Modern rhetoric adds audience as the main factor that has a major contribution in the configuration of the discursive *ethos*. Considering that the audience is made of those whom the spokesman intends to persuade,[35] Perelman and Olbrechts – Tyteca state that the audience determines the quality of the arguments and the orator's behaviour. The audience might be very heterogeneous, belonging to different social groups, but the speaker could perceive it differently and could situate it in personal social groups. When speakers recognise their audience, they also know how to condition it through the discourse itself which the orator continuously adapts to the audience. For the speaker, it is not important what he believes as true, but what the audience believes as true. Doing so, the orator takes into account the listeners, adapts to them and searches for the right arguments audience would react at.[36]

Therefore, for Perelman and Olbrechts – Tyteca, the audience is a representation/construct of the speaker. The orator's representation of the audience should identify with the real persons involved in the verbal exchange, and their expectations. The efficacy of the discourse is built on such correct identification of the image of the audience close to real, empirical audience.

Moreover, the speaker should also identify the image the audience holds of himself. The public image of the orator always affects *ethos*. Amossy writes that "when speakers take the floor, they evaluate the impact of the prior *ethos* on the current subject matter and operate to confirm their images, to rework and transform them".[37] The prior *ethos*, as named by Amossy in her study, might refer to institutional delegacy, public fame, social position, a sum of preconceptions and stereotypes that precede the discursive *ethos*. Stereotypes, common beliefs, familiar notions and shared values are being taken into consideration when creating a discourse and really influence the construction of *ethos*. Ruth Amossy insists on the role of stereotyping within the configuration of the *ethos* in discourse. As "Stereotyping consists of perceiving and understanding the real through a pre-existent cultural representation, a fixed collective schema",[38] both audience and speakers will use these patterns to associate the other to a pre-existent category (social, political, ethnic and cultural). The orator modifies the discourse and reformulates the discursive *ethos* according to what he/she thinks of the audience's pre-existent cultural schemas and expectations and according to what he/she thinks of the audience's opinion about the speaker. Amossy explains that

> the discursive construction of the *ethos* is realized through a series of mirror reflections. The orator builds his or her own image as a function of the image he or she forms of the audience, that is to say, of the representations of what a trustworthy and competent orator is in the eyes of the public as the orator imagines it. He or she has to guess how the audience conceives of a trustworthy politician, a reliable administrator, a genuine artist, or an intellectual. An orator also has to choose a presentation of self as fulfilling the expectations of the audience.[39]

Sometimes, the image of the prior *ethos* the audience holds should be assimilated in the discourse, sometimes it should be improved through the discursive *ethos*, sometimes it should be even replaced or "repaired" by the *ethos* constructed within the discourse. Therefore, there are two important premises we may start from, in our analysis of the discursive *ethos* constructing strategies within Gregory of Naziansus's oration:

When studying the discursive *ethos*, one could take into consideration the prior *ethos* and the fine *pitching* established within the discourse between the *ethos* and its prediscursive variant;

The modular relationship between the audience and the speaker contributes to the speaker's decisions when building his *ethos* through discourse.

To understand better the importance of prior *ethos* and audience in the configuration of the discursive *ethos*, we proceed to emphasising several aspects of Gregory's biography, relevant for understanding Gregory's rhetoric attitude.

Gregory of Nazianzus – A Diachronic Portrait

Gregory's family was part of the local aristocracy in Nazianzus, Cappadocia; his father was involved in public administration and politics, owned multiple properties and his household included slaves.[40] Later on, the father converted to Christianity and he was ordained bishop of Nazianzus. It was a common practice for Christians to ordain local aristocrats – the authoritative figures of the city – as there was a clerical staff crisis and the number of Christian believers was increasing. Some of these bishops and priests unfortunately were unskilled when it came to sermons and preaching and were mainly on the make.[41] This explains Gregory's breaking out in invectives against bishops from different works such as Oration 2 or the famous poems dedicated to bishops. His belonging to aristocracy and the expectations regarding such a destiny influenced his life and also his discourse.

Regarding his education, Gregory and his brother Cesario were sent to school in Caesarea, Cappadocia where Gregory met his best friend, Basil the Great. Their friendship was consecrated by the five years (350–355/356) they had been studying together at Athens the great philosophers and poets of Antiquity.[42] Actually, it was common for the aristocrats' offspring to be sent to study philosophy, rhetoric and literature.[43] Bernardi asserts[44] that Gregory knew the importance of being an educated Christian, a good Christian rhetor to whom the cultural, literary and philosophical legacy of Greece are nothing but helpful instruments in committing to the truth and sharing its light to the others. To be persuasive, he was aware that he had to be experienced in the common rhetorical techniques. He loved the Greek culture, but his evangelising purposes were never undermined by his passion for Greek culture, this is why he left Athens though he had been asked to become a professor. Consequently, after the study period spent in Athens, Gregory turned back home to help his 80-year-old father and to start studying the Scriptures, dedicating himself to continuing Athanasius's work.[45]

Regarding the circulation of theological ideas, the fourth century was much influenced by the Arians whilst the Orthodox, albeit encouraged by bishop Athanasius of Alexandria, were persecuted by emperor Constantius and subsequently tolerated by Constans.[46] Turning back home, Gregory felt the necessity to contribute to the spreading of the Orthodox Christian teachings and to serve the Truth. Simultaneously he understood that ascesis could define his way of being in the world. Nevertheless, these two natural inclinations were not totally compatible with the household and parish responsibilities waiting for him at home, in Nazianzus.

Ordained a priest, mostly because of his father's pressures,[47] Gregory retired for a while in Pontus, to free himself from the pressures he felt at the beginnings of his priesthood,[48] openly confessing his predisposition for recluseness and his inappentence for liturgy, for leading and counselling believers, for Church pragmatic affairs. Similarly, at his brother's death,

Gregory faced a lot of problems and conflicts regarding Cesario's fortune and employees; in such situations, he always felt unskilled and saddled.[49]

In fact, Gregory's biographers explained that he was always hold back by his inner struggle between his propensity towards ascesis and his sacerdotal duty, his responsibility to fight for truth: "Hesychia was charming him. Theology was a sacred duty". Papadopoulos wrote that Gregory spent his entire life endangering his *hesychia* and theologically struggling in the world.[50] His repeated self-exiles and withdrawals suggest a special delicacy, shyness and need for reclusiveness as a means of reestablishment of the ego in the world. His run to Pontus was followed by other such ascetic escapes.

Basil asked for Gregory's help against Emperor Valens[51] and he ordained his friend bishop of Sasima, a small town in Cappadocia Secunda whose metropolitan was Anthimos. As Basil, metropolitan of Cappadocia Prima, was in conflict with Anthimos and wanted to extend his influence in Cappadocia, he chose Gregory to plane the way. In the middle of such a conflict and in such a desolated town like Sasima was, Gregory, who was 43, stayed for several hours and fled to isolate himself in a wasteland close to Arianzum. Later on, at his father's death, he was again invoked to become Nazianzus's bishop but, consequently, he flew back to the monastic centre of Saint Thecla, from Seleucia where he retired for some years, till the Emperor Valens's death in August, 379.

As the new Emperor Theodosius who had Orthodox beliefs, was to enter Constantinople only at the end of January, 379, the Orthodox bishops from Asia Minor together with Basil the Great, Meletius of Antioch and Eusebius of Samosata (with some Constantinople political leaders' permission, as McGuckin adds[52]) agreed to send to Seleucia a delegation of Orthodox believers from Constantinople to ask Gregory to accept becoming their Orthodox representative in the Byzantine capital with an Arian majority led by bishop Demophilus.[53]

In other words, Gregory had been invited to "lead a preaching campaign" in Constantinople so that the important figures of the Constantinople, political leaders and aristocracy be informed upon the new religious (Nicene) vision the new emperor was coming with.[54] This invitation legitimated him as "the 'official' Nicene spokesman".[55]

At that time, Constantinople was inhabited by 250,000–300,000 people of whom only 250 were Orthodox Christians.[56] Constantinople clergy received him with indifference but soon after he started to preach, they expressed their "inbuilt racist xenophobia of the era" and their prejudices regarding Cappadocians, refusing him any access to the local churches.[57] Gregory was almost 49 years old when he came to Constantinople in 378 (Theodosius had not reached yet the capital) where people, incited by Demophilus, received him with stones.[58] Nobleman Avlavius and his cousin Theodosia protected him and offered him residence. In his cousin's house, he would soon preach and serve.

Till Theodosious's arrival to Constantinople, Gregory had to familiarise the population of the capital with the Orthodox theological views, paving the way for the new emperor. Gregory's enterprise might be seen as political. In fact, it has been observed that there was "a natural and powerful impulse toward demonstrating Christianity's compatibility with the political system of the empire. A realignment of Christian discourse toward the new political situation was essential".[59] Nevertheless, for the shy and introspective Gregory, not used to world affairs, this mission was not easy at all.

Apart from the traumatising welcome some of the inhabitants of Constantinople had prepared him, Gregory had to face other similar attacks. One of them happened on the Great Friday, year 379, when people had furiously come to Church Anastasia, armed with stones, for stopping bishop of Nazianzus. Demophilus was still the official bishop of Constantinople. Emperor Theodosius, baptised as Orthodox Christian, had not come yet to the capital and Gregory of Nazianzus, encouraged by Meletians, was serving in Anastasia. People from Constantinople knew him as a representative of the Nicene party. They were Semi-Arians as almost all the bishops in Constantinople. As there was a common practice the catechumens to be baptised by the local bishop before Easter and as Gregory was prepared to baptise them (a gesture that would have officialised his position as a bishop in Constantinople), Demofil sent his men to sabotage him.

When Theodosius finally came to Constantinople he recognised Gregory as the official archbishop of the capital, but everyone knew that Gregory of Nazianzus had not been nominated as a bishop according to the Church canon law[60] that presupposed the decision stated by a council of bishops and the members of the Church. Theodosius did not know this, but Gregory did. Papadopoulos insists on the fact[61] that Gregory could not fully consider himself a bishop because of his innate good sense and because he recoiled in the past from episcopal duties.

Later on, at one of the meetings of the Second Council of Nicaea whose president Gregory was after Meletius's death, some bishops' animadversions regarding the canonicity of his status as archbishop of Constantinople made him live the meeting and give up to his function as president.[62] Bernardi (176–177)[63] asserted that the main reason of Gregory's resignation was the omission of the word *homoousious* in describing the Holy Spirit, inside the new adopted Creed. The fact that his institutional authority was called into question for several times affected his discourses and contributed to the way he built his discursive *ethos*.

He retired in his last years of life (381–390) to Arianzum and this is the time when he corrected and rewrote some of his orations and poems.

Gregory's Prior-*ethos*

Such biographical data contribute to a more adequate configuration of the possible *prior-ethos* Gregory related to during his discourses. His biographical ups and downs partly reflect his character and partly his social status. He was introvert, reclusive, ascetical, perfectionist and a fighter for the Truth; he treasured culture, literature and philosophy and utilised them as catalysts for the spread of the Word. His inner struggle between sacerdotal responsibility and ascetical propensity defined his attitude and his way of being in the world. Such a personality would perceive any public situation or discourse as a step outside the comfort zone.

Moreover, when facing the Constantinople public, he confronted with a lot of the prejudices regarding his person and the Nicene party he was representing. Most of the Constantinople inhabitants were Neo-Arians and they were reactive to what the Orthodox had to say. In other words, Gregory was sent among adversaries. Nevertheless, he was sent to speak to an educated public made of aristocrats and political leaders, both Orthodox and Arian; some of them might also have been foreigners/newcomers.[64] It is important to add the fact that church Anastasia was placed in the most select neighbour and this made possible the aristocrats' gatherings in the church: "The whole area was a center of intellectuals and senatorial aristocrats, and one of the most expensive pieces of real estate in fourth-century Constantinople".[65]

Certainly, Gregory was aware of what his audience in Constantinople was like and what expectations they had. The inhabitants' appeal for rhetoric, eloquence and polemics was famous. McGuckin argues that Gregory was quite unpopular in the capital because of his statements regarding the simple's people restricted accessibility to theological speculation, but this is, McGuckin continues, a part of the Gregory's strategy to address himself to the educated and influential people of the city who, therefore, by adhering to his new perspective, should not fear of losing their intellectual credibility or their reputation.[66]

Bernardi describes them as being an exuberant and rebelling population, dominated by arrivestes and adventurers, militaries and jurists, scriveners and court bishops, eunuchs and senators.[67] Constantinople was flourishing, it was the New Rome. Most of the inhabitants enjoyed disputes on theological issues no matter the context *i.e.* the inner circle of the family or the market square. Theology was everywhere and suscitated controversies and ambitions, even parodies and mockery.[68] However people from Constantinople lack spiritual guidance and real catechesis,[69] this is how they begun to group and regroup around a momentary religious conviction or another and to accuse each other of heresy and cacodoxy. This antagonist atmosphere in the Church determined Gregory to preach about theology and the profile of the theologian so that to reduce the conflicts among the believers. For him, seeing people's arguing on serious theological issues was as if he would have seen the bull in the china shop.[70] Therefore, in front of such an audience as the Constantinople's inhabitants were, Gregory was aware of his listeners, their habits, their convictions and expectations; in Bourdieu's terms, he knew the field/ the market where the verbal exchange would take place. Also he was aware of their social status, linguistic capital and habitus. For sure, he constructed and modulated his discourses adapting to what he knew about his audience, about their prejudices and expectations regarding preaching and religious leading. In Perelman's words, Gregory created a pre-discursive personal construct that would have represented his audience in the Byzantine capital: political leaders and aristocrats, educated and select people, reactive, inquisitive and interactional public, used to cultivate their minds towards polemics, enjoying rhetoric and speculation as a gratuitous means of entertainment.

From a different point of view, the audience itself had also in mind a pre-discursive image of their speaker to be, a set of prejudices that definitely influenced the public's attitude towards Gregory. This prior *ethos* could have been correlated to public fame, social preconceptions, religious convictions affiliation, the legitimacy and the institutional delegation. Gregory was famous among Constantinople inhabitants who knew him as a very educated person, an extraordinary rhetor and an exemplary theologian, but simultaneously seemed a lost provincial.[71] Gregory's public fame was contradicting the inhabitants' common prejudices regarding newcomers.

Apart from the fact that, in Constantinople, Gregory was seen as a representative of the Nicene party which was not popular in the capital, he was also associated with the preconceptions regarding his origins. He was seen as a simple, provincial man, a peasant who came from a region behind times[72] (as Cappadocia was considered[73]) and who wanted to educate the people from the capital, addressing especially to aristocrats. Cappadocian accent was annoying because the inhabitants from Constantinople had a finer orthoepy this is why they criticised him for confusing long vocals for short vocals[74] and also funny, this is why he had repeatedly been the victim of their mockery.[75] McGuckin stated that Gregory was aware of the prejudices circulated among the Constantinople inhabitants regarding Cappadocians, seeing "a 'Cappadocian' rhetor as a contradiction in terms", as a flying turtle (a metaphor deduced from Ps. Lucian's *Epigram 43*).[76] Moreover, even his *bodily hexis* vexed them: an aristocrat as Gregory was expected to enforce respect not only through discourse but also through vestments, attitude, gestures and mimicry. They saw the contradiction between his rich, aristocratic origins and his humble, ascetic life[77] and despised him because of his humbleness and apparent lack of stateliness.[78]These prejudices, the people of Constantinople welcomed Gregory with, were an immense wall that stood still between the bishop and his parishioners. But Gregory made his auditory to face a new type of preacher that could have overturned their stereotypes. Indeed, by preaching and lecturing, Gregory tried to legitimate such contradictions he embodied, by deconstructing the prior *ethos* his audience preconceived, by offering them a model in flesh and blood, but also by managing discourse strategies for the purpose of a persuasive discursive *ethos*. The stakes were high. Gregory came to Constantinople to frame a new vision upon the new theologian: educated, select, profound, authentic, honest and humble, introverted, ascetically exercised, responsible and rational, blessed by revelation. Such a credible theologian could have transmitted a credible theological message *i.e.* Orthodoxy. Let's see how Gregory manages to deal with *the prior ethos* he was aware of and to replace it with the model of theologian he trusts the most and wished his audience to credit too as to make his teaching valuable and life changing.

Ethos in *The First Theological Oration*

The five Theological Orations were intended to form a treatise on the Holy Trinity; initially, they were five independent works comprising also some excerpts from different orations. Jean Bernardi asserted that the five theological orations were meant to form a treat about the Holy Trinity. He is not sure whether they were ever uttered, but, for sure, after his retirement, Gregory had enough time to reunite and modify them as he wished.[79] John McGuckin asserted that the five orations were successfully presented in the summer of 380, from July to August, not under the form of preaching, but as lectures in the Anastasia Church.[80]

The First Theological Oration, namely, *Oration 27*, is quite short and, probably later on, had been entitled by Gregory "A preliminary Discourse Against the Eunomians" – Arians who extremely denied consubstantialism inside the Holy Trinity.

From the very beginning, Gregory denounced, *ex abrupto*, with no *captatio benevolentiae* at all (as every speech driven by illocutionary force will normally do) the members of the audience that he was going to speak against:

> I am to speak against persons who pride themselves on their eloquence; so, to begin with text of Scripture, 'Behold, I am against thee, O thou proud one,' not only in thy system of teaching, but also in thy hearing, and in thy tone of mind. For there are certain persons who have not only their ears and their tongues, but even, as I now perceive, their hands too, itching for our words.[81]

No protective attitude is being displayed, except maybe for the usage of third person for personal pronouns such as them/they/themselves, so that a part of the addressees could exclude themselves. Still, he went on and made open references to older conflicts (such as his receiving to Constantinople, for instance) without sparing anyone's feelings. Arians (some of them Eunomius's adepts) used to send to church Anastasia their spies, always well-educated nobles, to write down what Gregory was preaching.[82] It is obvious that he knew whom he was speaking at and against. In the first part of the oration, he describes the typology of the rhetor he was delimitating himself from. In the eyes of the audience, he had to deconstruct this type of speaker whom he believes the audience used to appreciate those days. His enterprise was meant to discredit such orators in theological matters *i.e.* Eunomius. These rhetors who made of their discourses "profane babblings" and gratuitous verbal performances, "words, which tend to no profit" did not intend to theologically educate the public, but to arrogantly distinguish themselves through their rhetoric talent. Actually, what Gregory suggested was that these false rhetors did not conceive themselves as delegates, spokesmen of the Truth. Rodica Zafiu explains that, in the case of the religious discourses, the speakers, institutionally delegated and authorised by the Church, create within the discourse a discreet, implicit and restrained *ethos*[83] and subjectivity. Soon after mentioning such discursive weaknesses, Gregory legitimises his statements by invoking Apostle Paul whose example and authority could not be contested by the Constantinople parishioners. To the rhetor of the long gratuitous and stylistically embellished talks, Gregory opposed the incontestable rhetor of the "word cut short", the simple and direct discourses accessible to everyone. Probably, Gregory was aware of the fact that "Christian discourse could only be effective in all these respects if it was intelligible and comprehensible to the general public",[84] nevertheless he succeeded in integrating the classical rhetoric with the simplicity Christians claimed, a fact observed by Averil Cameron[85] but also obvious in the argumentative part of his orations. But brevity and simplicity are not enough as long as the discourse has no performative force. Words are actions. The rhetor's authenticity should stay in actions and message, not in stylistics. McGuckin[86] asserts that Gregory often confessed that rhetoric is but superficiality and ornament and in order to persuade his audience and to justify his rejection of exaggerated rhetoric, he tried to infer the idea that, in a discourse, the rhetoric intensity is in inverse ratio to the intensity of the message and the quality of arguments. In other words, Gregory educated his audience, guiding its reason towards the force of ideas that are to become acts and not towards the "stylistic brilliance" that frequently obliterated the audience's expectations to find a truth or deflect it from revelations.

Notwithstanding, Gregory did not renounce to the stylistic brilliance (evident in all orations) but he submitted it to transmitting the Christian Orthodox message he had been endowed with. His educational background and classical formation (achieved in Athens) helped him in mastering the secular art of rhetoric in the service of God but also in relating to an aristocratic audience, similarly educated, which mostly appreciated such talent. This "art of taking account of the relative positions of the sender and the receiver in the hierarchy of different kinds of capital, and also of sex and age, and of the limits inscribed in this relation" is called by Bourdieu tact or adroitness[87] and contributes to the configuration of the *ethos* as credible and reliable voice.

Furthermore, Gregory took advantage of his public fame as an exquisite rhetor and his aristocratic origins (being aware of this prior *ethos* as a construct in the imaginary of the auditory), legitimated himself through the association with the Apostle and revealed the purposelessness of some rhetoricians the Neo-Arian school used to promote. In such cases, Gregory's irony emphasises his delimitation from such orators calling them "acrobats of words", easing the tension and accomplishing the audience through laughter: "If I may use a ridiculous expression about a ridiculous subject".[88] Then he continued to speak about public orators' silly talk and market place buzz comparing them to wrestling matches in public. These comparisons with social activities that belong to simple people might be a strategy of convincing his aristocratic audience that permanent chit-chat belongs to low social classes Gregory spoke against Eunomius, the best representative of the Neo-Arian School. In this respect, McGuckin states that as this school had important imperial protection, Gregory Nazianzus, Gregory of Nyssa and his brother, Basil, considered it a servile school that practiced rhetoric based on syllogistic argumentative methods. Such a method was suitable for lower social classes ("like those persons who in theatres perform wrestling matches in public"[89]) as Gregory exemplifies, making references to Eunomius's humble origins as a slave. As Eunomius used to legitimate his discourse by invoking Aristotle's logic method, Gregory mentions Aristotle's opinion regarding who was habilitated to practice the great virtue of philosophy *i.e.* the free social classes, not the slaves.[90]

Anyhow, Gregory warns of the greatest risk of deriding the Truth itself through such verbal spectacles: "since, I say this is so, the evil is intolerable and not to be borne, and our Great Mystery is in danger of being made a thing of little moment".[91] Here, the speaker openly and without a doubt declared his position regarding the matter of discussion and diagnosed the excessive appetite for superfluous rhetoric as a threat to real Christian responsibilities. Gregory continued his diatribe making direct references to the potential spies whose presence at his discourses he was aware of: "let them bear with us so far as not to give a savage reception to our discourse upon this subject; and let them, if indeed they can, restrain their tongues for a short while and lend us their ears".[92] He obviously alluded to the Arian party spies, but also to their previous reactions, typical for the period, probably even more aggressive because of the dogmatic disagreements (as the stone attack before Easter).

It is well-known that the old audiences were not passive at all in the act of speech and conceived the discourse as bidirectional. As George Alexander asserts, in Greece and Rome, public discourses were seen as means of entertainment because the declamatory speeches, in sophistic school, were exercises, not real attempts at persuasion, in which they were often judged more for the cleverness or novelty of what they said or the ornamentation of their style than for the cogency of their argument.[93] Most of such discourses were held in the public market, thus an open space that offered a setting freed from restrictions. This also permitted listeners to react as they were standing in the right and legitimated place to express their opinions as a large public. Orators searched their audiences and came towards their public *i.e.* orators were conditioned by their audiences and not vice versa. This aspect mainly justified the reactive audience. Kinzig describes such audiences as being also present in front of a Christian preacher: "Generally speaking, the audiences virtually never appear to have listened in passive silence. When the sermon did not live up to their expectations, perhaps it was too long or the preacher was not well prepared or plainly boring, they began to murmur and create other disturbances. An additional nuisance was the habit of entering or leaving the church before, during and after the sermon, which distracted the preacher".[94] Gregory made reference to such audiences for at least two reasons we could identify. First, he wanted to draw his listeners' attention to the fact that he was aware of such *prior* audience and its risky manifestations. Second, this was also a method of self-securing, but by referring to *the spies* as being responsible for such aggressions, he also made his audience feel as a party to discourse and to anything that could happen.

Moreover, Gregory used first-person plural (we, our, ours), kept utilising third person plural (them, their) for referring to the "spies" and included direct addressing to the audience through second person plural (you, yourselves). By means of such pronouns he clearly dissociated between the orator, auditory and improper auditory. Moreover, for referring to himself, he used plural, not singular (as he would later on do) not necessary for the purpose of emphasising the authoritarian voice of the speaker, but more for its inclusive meaning (you and I, both audience and orator). This kind of verbal partisanship and declared alliance could have meant Gregory's attempt to transmit to his improper auditory that it is minority. Consequently, he openly declared his tolerance: "let them bear with us" because for them his words would bear fruit either in a positive way or in a destructive way as they could only fuel their carping. This verbal game of opposites is one of the common rhetorical figures in Gregory's orations. Averil Cameron observed that among the Christian rhetors, Gregory "draws heavily on the classical rhetorical technique of antithesis".[95] Indeed, the Cappadocian Father built his discourses on counter-examples and examples trying to replace, *via* discursive strategies, the first with the latter within the collective mentality. For instance, the same procedure is operated on the contrast between auditory and improper auditory. By contrasting the two and declaring open tolerance towards the latter, Gregory intended to form and educate a proper auditory, not dismissing however the improper, for the religious discourse, simultaneously working on the authoritarian status of the preacher in the Church.

He actually confronts us with three contrasts whose first parts should be replaced by new ones he describes: the public market and the solemn space of church, the public *per se* and the faithful as a proper audience, the public speaker/the secular rhetor and the religious spokesman. Gregory referred to the common opinions of his audience regarding rhetoric, rhetors, audience and setting of the discourse. He did not dismiss them but tried to redefine them, working on such stereotypes and pre-existent schemas that he identified in the collective mentality. In fact, in Averil Cameron's words, the Christian discourse "made its way in the wider world less by revolutionary novelty than by the procedure of working through the familiar, by appealing from the known to the unknown".[96] This is also a persuasive technique of the discourse. The speaker takes into consideration prediscursive convictions of the audience in order to gain credibility as an informed and perfectly aware orator of the profile of his audience. This common background represents a good starting point for a discourse. Averil Cameron adds that "in the spreading of ideas there is a tension between the need to show compatibility with an existing framework and the attraction of a complete change".[97] This is why Gregory described the profile of the secular rhetors and their much-admired spectacular verbosity because he knew the listeners' appreciation for such speakers and their expectations towards himself. He reflected through his discourse their expectations regarding a credible and worthy *ethos* and such mirror reflections (Amossy identified) built steadily the discursive *ethos*.

Nevertheless, Gregory did not stop to this faithful reflection. He indeed used "spectacular verbosity" too, but as he knew that he had already been recognised as a very talented orator, a public fame/ prior *ethos* he was aware of, he did not want to be associated with such acrobats of words. He did not speak for the sake of aesthetics or for emphasising or exercising his talent. He spoke for the Truth and this was how he configured an authoritarian voice inside the oration. Also, neither the audience should let itself deceived of such artistic performances, but it should look at the very true core of the speech.

This was the way Gregory invited all to adjust their endeavour to a new type of discourse, the religious discourse in which the public voice and its entertaining verbal devices lost their centrality in favour of the Truth. In the fourth century, Gregory tried to cultivate the theocentricism within the religious discourse that was at its beginnings and started to be delimitated from the public discourse. In contrast to common rhetoric, theocentricism defined the religious discourse in the sense that the setting of the discourse (church – a sacred space, impregnated by the presence of God) imposed a certain respectful and solemn behaviour, the audience had a common belief and trust in God as its absolute benchmark, the preacher was not presenting himself or his personal vision on life and Truth but he was the legitimate delegate of God whom all serve. Gregory educated his listeners on how to behave in the church, how to relate to the Christian rhetor and to the religious discourses. In fact, regarding the setting of the discourse, Kinzig stated that the Christian discourses happened within a liturgical setting that "shaped the Christian discourse".[98] In fact, by educating his public, Gregory's purposes were meant to have both a local impact and a long term impact.

Regarding the local impact, the Constantinople inhabitants had to understand the new theological vision the Cappadocian was coming with, but first he had to create a proper context, a proper audience and to overthrow the patterns that defined the prior image of the preacher in the collective mentality. Once these changes would have made, our theologian had gained legitimacy, authority and credibility when teaching dogmatic theological serious issues.

When referring to long-term impact, in his times, Gregory of Nazianzus set the standards for the right context, the right figure of the preacher/theologian, the right audience and right theological message, all within the specificity of religious discourse. Working with Aristotelian categories, he succeeds to submit *ethos*, *pathos* and *logos* to the authority of the Word of God. From these beginnings, the religious discourse evolved to its contemporary description as mass communication within a formal context, influenced by the speaker's social and privileged status that the audience recognises as such. The numerous and heterogeneous listeners are placed on an inferior and passive position in relation to the speaker whose qualities and competences are recognised by the audience as signs of authority and legitimacy.[99]

Coming back to *Oration 27*, Gregory of Nazianzus continued his discourse by insisting on the novelty he was (re)presenting in front of the audience, after delimitating himself, his discourse and his audience from the common secular rhetors (which he associated the Neo-Arian rhetors with), from the public market demonstrations and the noisy audiences. He adds a warning addressed to his listeners, a warning meant to prepare his audience for the new vision he was going to describe to them:

> And you must not be astonished if I speak a language which is strange to you and contrary to your custom, who profess to know everything and to teach everything in a too impetuous and generous manner…not to pain you by saying ignorant and rash.

This statement that introduced the auditory to the problematic and built a type of *captatio* actually ends the introductive part of the oration that presented the counter-example he as an orator was delimitating from. Once he deconstructed the typology of the public rhetor, trying simultaneously to change the expectations of the audience regarding himself as such a rhetor he had denied being, he had to put something else in place. Before that, he first assured the auditory that he was empathetic and understood how different his perspective was for his listeners. He also divulged the discrepancies he saw between his listeners' custom to impetuously pretend to know and teach everything and his humbleness and modesty in approaching important theological topics such as the consubstantialism of the Holy Trinity.

The preacher should be humble (as he was only the delegate of the Truth), not arrogant – this is a new step in the process of the configuration of the discursive *ethos*. People perceived him as too humble for such status he had among them. They expected to see this authoritarian position of a speaker in Gregory. He himself was, in this case too, very different from what they were used to see in an orator. He countered their impetuosity as listeners with a natural humility they did not expect. This shocked the audience and made it confused as it could not relate to anything it knew before. His physical appearance, in Bourdieu's terms, his *hexis* brought forth a new model. To understand it, the auditory appealed to their social preconceptions regarding, for instance, Cappadocians. For them, Gregory was a new type of aristocrat they could not understand: humble, simple, not searching for public fame, not nurturing his own vanity. Again, Gregory knew these expectations but he preached humility because a God's spokesman gains his authoritarian voice and credibility not by means of appearance (such as vestments, figures of speech), but by the power of words that tell the truth. The force of Gregory's discourse derives from his trust in the righteousness of what he had to say, legitimated by his experience as a theologian, but also by his continuous ascetic efforts as purification stages. For such an introvert and loner, the public discourses in front of the audience Constantinople offered were a break out of the comfort zone. Still, he understood his campaign as a missionary and this made him resistant and confident. Papadopoulos wrote that although physically tender, Gregory stood in front of his opponents with fervour, in Constantinople and did not seek for hesychia like in the past.[100]

In the next part of the oration, he started describing the new language he was coming with among his listeners. This new "language" had a holistic meaning as Gregory referred not only to its linguistic dimension, but to a way of being in the world as Christian and to a way of relating to God within an existential act of speech where all its components should be adjusted: message, emitter, receiver, code and context: "Christians built themselves a new world… partly through practice, partly through a discourse that was itself constantly brought under control and disciplined".[101] Nevertheless, a connection with the linguistic field should also be made. Historians noticed that Christian speakers had to look for verbal solutions to express the new vision upon the world and the sacred they were presenting. That is why Christians

> were linguistically stunningly innovative. The institutions, rites and doctrines of the new religion necessitated a new terminology and language. The semantic fields of traditional terms were extended to cover the new realities, partly under the influence of the Septuagint and the New Testament.[102]

Moreover, we should take into consideration also the personal Cappadocian accent Gregory had. This could have also been a barrier of prejudices between him and his listeners – incongruence between the linguistic capital of the audience and that of the speaker. But this time too, Gregory drew attention towards essence and not towards form. Accent represents an apparent aspect that could feature *ethos* (as preconception), but he replaced it with a new and deeper signification he gave to the word "language". In fact, as Bourdieu put it, his approach to language and his rich linguistic capital (including theological and secular, philosophical dimensions) was an advantage:

> differences in terms of accent, grammar and vocabulary - the very differences overlooked by formal linguistics- are indices of the social positions of speakers and reflections of the quantities of linguistic capital (and other capital) which they possess. The more linguistic capital the speakers possess, the more they are able to exploit the system of differences to their advantage and thereby secure a profit of distinction.[103]

As in the first parts of the oration, Gregory started deconstructing the counter-examples and he steadily rebuilt afterwards the image of appropriate audience, message and preacher. After speaking about the Constantinople inhabitants' pleasure to use rhetoric, eloquence everywhere and whenever they wanted, he addresses: "my friends". The discursive voice is somehow changed. This vocative changed the register of the discourse. Once the enemies/the spies/the counter-examples had been identified, Gregory's friendly addressability is meant to create complacency. The tone is fatherly. Several advices were to be given. Also, as Christian, religious discourses were generally begun with standardised formulas such as "my brethren", Gregory begun this part of his oration as such and not the oration as a whole. Such stereotyped formulas are part of the discursive strategies that express institutional delegacy. Bourdieu asserted that "the stylistic features which characterize the language of priests, teachers and, more generally, all institutions, like routinization, stereotyping and neutralization, all stem from the position occupied in a competitive field by these persons entrusted with delegated authority".[104] Nevertheless, Gregory does not resort to the typical institutional form of address but deliberately to a more temperate expression. He himself confessed why: "Surely not, my friends and brethren (for I will still call you Brethren, though you do not behave like brothers)".[105] Gregory was aware that a part of his listeners (the spies) did not recognise his institutional authority and legitimacy (as they were Demophilus's delegates) but still kept *a state of friendliness* for the sake of the efficacy of the discourse. Simultaneously, he proved that he knew well his audience and modulated his discourse according to how he represented the audience for himself and to what audience believed about him. He did not pretend that his authority was recognised by everybody, nor that he intended to flatter his opponents. This is why he avoided using openly such formulas (my brethren). His frankness did not spare anybody and had had a reverse effect. Instead of casting out the listeners, his direct remarks and refusal to hypocrisy might have had a positive impact on the configuration of *ethos* and increased reliability. Gregory did not want to lie or pretend that there was harmony between him and his auditory, nor he wanted to create a gratuitous emotional *captatio*. He starts his oration *ex abrupto*. This discursive sincerity showed the speaker's qualities such as honesty, morality and courage, the courage of putting things straight, of identifying them as spies and ignorant, of openly criticising them, discussing about their prejudices and accusing the power of taking them to the task.

Actually, the impetuosity of such direct and frank audiences (Constantinople had) was countered by Gregory's courage to call things by their name. Perelman and Olbrechts –Tyteca were right to state that the audience determines the quality of the arguments and the orator's behaviour. Most of the *First Theological Oration*, apart from its sophistic, educative purposes, is constructed by Gregory according to his representation of the audience. This strong voice of the *ethos* in his discourses was meant to respond to a strong and reactive audience with the same force. By means of words, Gregory was committed to impose himself as a reliable leader, stronger than such audiences difficult to "tame". The illocutionary force of this oration, in particular, is very impressive. No one, least of all his contesters, would have expected such force from such a humble, introvert and solitary personality.

Receiver and emitter, in this case, were highly contrastive but Gregory succeeded in identifying the fine *pitching* he should create (to use Bourdieu's terminology) as a balance between his *habitus* (highly educated in secular philosophy, deeply involved and formed in the Christian culture and legacy, with sacerdotal responsibilities, ascetically exercised, permanently oriented towards Truth and the right words to faithfully express It, his fame as a good rhetor *i.e.* cultural, linguistic, symbolic capitals) and a market (where inhabitants of Constantinople with definite capitals had a different cultural and linguistic potential). By comparing the two (producer and consumer) some incongruities emerge: Gregory's structural humbleness and his listeners' arrogance, his option regarding language as a vehicle of the truth and his listeners' appetite for verbal embellishments, his solemn attitude towards great subjects of talk and their chit-chat on heavy topics, his well-defined vision upon the religious discourses inside a liturgical setting and their mistaking the sermon for a public discourse, his attitude towards cultural heritage and philosophy and their convictions regarding it "as a bogey word". Referring to this latter aspect, McGuckin stated that

> trying to argue, throughout his life, that Christianity had a pressing obligation to address and refine its cultural impact, a duty to form and beautify the aesthetic character of the human race as much as the moral, Gregory sometimes felt like a voice in the wilderness.[106]

Certainly, for Gregory, such discrepancies did not smooth his way but he did not run from them either. Not this time. The theological stake was too important.

Still, Gregory was not confronted only with these inadvertences, but also with institutional delegacy issues that affected his preaching in Constantinople. If we follow Bourdieu, inside an act of speech, seen as an economic exchange between a producer and a market, utterances are signs of wealth and signs of authority which should be believed and obeyed. Once the speaker appears as sincere, direct and courageous *via* discourse, he himself becomes trustful in the eyes of the public, therefore, his message and arguments gain steadily credence and authority. Gregory's main focus was on the power of the discourse and the authoritative *ethos* that the discursive enterprise mirrored. Nevertheless, Bourdieu's statement that the power of words derives also from the institutional status of the speaker brings up other problems. The sociologist asserted that the power of words resides in the fact that an institutionally legitimated person pronounces them. The institutional authority derives from the discourse "because his speech concentrates within it the accumulated symbolic capital of the group which has delegated him and of which he is the *authorized representative*".[107] A priest is a legitimated person to speak in the Church and he receives authority from the authority of the Church because he, among all, "had access to the legitimate instruments of expression, and therefore the participation in the authority of the institution, which makes *all* the difference".[108] In the first centuries of Christianity, religious discourses were as important as secular rhetoric. Kinzig asserted that "As secular rhetoric in general was both a technique and a means of institutional power, the same could be argued for its ecclesiastical counterpart".[109] When Gregory of Nazianzus came to Constantinople, he was aware of the fact that he was not officially and fully recognised as the bishop of Constantinople, but believers had heard about Nazianzus's talent and faith, and also about the credit given to him by the emperor Theodosius and the Antiochians. Institutionally, Demophilus was still the official delegate of the Church and Gregory came to Constantinople as the representative of the Nicene party with very few adherents in the capital. From the very beginning, Gregory was not in a convenient situation, although even the new imperial policy was dogmatically Christian Orthodox. Theodosius authorised Gregory to preach and named him official bishop, but he knew that he had not been nominated as a bishop according to the Church canon law. What testify that this institutional delegation mattered for Gregory is his departure from the synod and his resignation from his function as president. Therefore, as long as Gregory did not feel enough legitimated to speak on behalf of the institution whose members were still contesting his authority, he was left with a single modality of constructing his legitimacy: discourse itself. The discursive *ethos* should have been enough powerful so that to convince auditory of his reliability as a spokesperson of the Truth itself and not of an institution still grinded by bishops' fight for power. In fact, the spokesperson of the Truth is the theologian himself. Gregory mainly identified as theologian.

In the *First Theological Oration,* he delimitates the theologian's field of competence. His endeavour is based on a series of rhetorical questions that set certain limits regarding how, when, who and what people should speak about God and his Trinitarian nature. Theology should not be "pleasant gossip, amusement when regarding to subject"; he refers to topics "within our reach" – to speak about God is good, but with moderation. Still, some of the subjects are not accessible to everyone, such as the subject of the Holy Trinity – a subject of the chosen one.

Also, he speaks about the type of the audience ready for such discussions. For sure, we should avoid fault finders: "we will not cast to ears profane that which may not uttered" and "Let even our disputing then be kept within bounds". Such people should not be allowed to speak about the nature of God. The theologian proposes a new type of speaker who has the authority to express thoroughly these ideas:

> But when we have put away those who are strangers to it and sent the great legion on its way to the abyss into the herd of swine, the next thing is to look to ourselves and polish our theological self to beauty like a statue.

The theologian should be visionary, following the model of Moses, "purified in soul and body", really concerned of the subject of discussion, moderate, uttering "holy things in a holy manner", very cult, aware of Greek high culture, the theologian that restrains oneself closes the windows of senses, fasts, censor excessive thought. Certainly, he worked on his prior *ethos* in that moment of the discourse, subtly justifying his retractile life dynamic as spiritual preparation for the encounter with the knowledge of God. In fact, "the convenient season" for speaking about God, Gregory was referring to, was not an exterior time, but a spiritual time – the right moment when the theologian is ready, prepared, spiritually mature for truly speaking about the Truth of God. This is what could give to the theologian credibility and authority in front of the others – his beforehand walk with God. These ample experiences into the knowledge of God also empowered Gregory and made him stay still in front of all the adversities he faced in Constantinople. Furthermore, theologians should not confuse theology with everyday discussions and should know themselves and their limits as well: "but let us philosophize within our proper bounds".[110]

Analysing Gregory's words, McGuckin wrote in this respect: "The exposition of theological dogma is, like a sacrament, something that should be reserved for the church, and a mystery that is part of the *proprium* of the ordained bishop, his peculiar priestly 'office'".[111] Theological discourse should give up to speculations and should become more sober and simple. Simultaneously, the theologian should embody both the educated philosopher and the profound believer. A theologian has to have both qualifications, according to "the principle of the essentially necessary union of intellectual training and personal religious ecstasy" – this balance between "logic and spiritual insight", prioritising the latter, is one of Gregory's most distinctive marks, McGuckin writes.[112] Therefore, these desiderata regarding an authoritarian and reliable, but also legitimate theologian contoured, in fact, Gregory's own portrait. Most of these represented himself. By deconstructing the image of the improper theologian/speaker he reconstructs his own *ethos* through discursive strategies. He picked his authoritative force from this image he created gradually in the discourse and he was credible because he was deeply authentic. He was what he uttered; he was not just words, but flesh and blood, convincing reality of what he pleaded for. This coherence in his behaviour, discourse and his way of being in the world brought forth consistency and reliability.

In the last part of the oration, he turned towards the Dialectician with a tirade of questions, demonstrating *via* dialectics that there is one virtue, the simple way of teaching others, considering arguments and speculations – frivolities and quackeries. The last part of the oration was Gregory's open demonstration that he could defeat dialecticians through their own weapons.

He referred to Anomoeans who had accused Gregory of too simple approach. Gregory never mentioned Eunomius in the oration but certainly his contemporaries detected the subtext and the allusions. Eunomius was well known for his saloon theology among aristocrats. By accusing theological talks in any environment, Gregory tries to suggest that theological issues such as the Holy Trinity need a proper context of discussion "holy things in a holy manner" and a proper listener who had a special ear for such solemn, delicate and sacred matters. Theology was not entertaining philosophy and theological issues were not for everyone, especially not for the "the hostile listeners" to whom every word could be used against the speaker. Once again, Gregory frankness impresses us. The power of his discourse comes out from the powerful *ethos* that emerges for the text itself. Gregory's multiple questions and direct references did not spare anybody. Moreover, he sincerely approached every "unpleasant" aspect he disagreed with and gave to the Theology of the Word an aura of exclusivity preserved for the prepared ones, the vested ones by the Grace of God. This investment is a gift, the sceptre of the Christian spokesman. Such sceptre was not given to everyone no matter their spiritual maturity, but to the chosen one who experienced purity and strove for the Revelation. This could not be otherwise as long as the theologian did not speak for himself, he had to be a reliable representative of God on Earth.

Also, not without irony, he suggests subjects of discussion instead of those regarding the Trinitarian nature – the silence of Pythagoras, for example, or "Void or full" or even philosophical topics, worthy of discussion such as the world matter, the soul, the good or the bad. Thus he excludes the delicate and problematic issue of the Holy Trinity and its nature. Such subject is preserved for those who prepared for it, who meditated, being ordained and had an ascetical life. By deconstructing, he adds step by step the contours of his *ethos* that authorise him to continue the next four orations.

Conclusions

Certainly, Gregory himself had to embody such a model in order to convince his auditory of its legitimacy. This model first had to face the prejudices forming the prior *ethos* (and that strongly related to Gregory as real individual) in the public's imaginary and to deconstruct these prediscursive schemas. Second, it had to replace the already deconstructed prior *ethos* with a possible alternative it included. This happened *via* discourses Gregory created, configuring a discursive *ethos*. This discursive *ethos* had to be a means of persuasion and had to contribute to the efficacy of the discourse. It increases the value of the discourse in proportion as it becomes more and more credible and reliable. Now, the discourse, such as *Oration 27*, theorised and proposed a new type of theologian speaker that is to say a new type of *ethos* (in religious discourses) that to be credible and reliable, a very different preacher's voice from the classical rhetor's, commonly recognised by the Byzantine. Confronted with the stereotyped image of the rhetor, seriously rooted in the public imaginary, Gregory had to start reconfiguring and redefining the rhetor as a typology already rooted in people's conceptions in order to infer a correct and authentic image of the Orthodox Christian rhetor. This image should afterwards fix the standards for a trustworthy and legitimated Christian rhetor in the long run and modify the expectations of the audience when regarding a trustworthy preacher. In other words, Gregory seemed to intend to change even the prior *ethos* of the Christian orator in the public eye *i.e.* to redirect the expectations of the audience towards the new model he showed up. A Christian faithful should expect an educated, select, profound, authentic, honest and humble, introverted, ascetically exercised, responsible and rational, blessed by revelation Christian orator. Also, this should be the only credible and trustworthy theological voice. Any speaker that accomplishes such expectations should be credible to the audience and should seriously increase the efficacy and the persuasiveness of the discourse itself. In other words, the message of the discourse becomes credible, real and trustworthy because of the orator's credibility. When the message refers to Truth and Orthodoxy, the messenger' reliability (discursive *ethos*) is crucial.

Gregory wanted to teach people about the Truth and the Word, but for his enterprise to be successful, he had to build a strong *ethos* which to be worthy of such a message. While configuring such an *ethos*, he tried to convince his audience that this model is the only one credible when coming to theology. Once the audience understood as legitimated such a model, it would always credit only such orators in the theological field. Though Gregory set the standards very high, the model of theologian he proposed then was of outmost credibility because he himself embodied it. Therefore, by determining the audience to expect a model of theologian as the only one to credit, Gregory of Nazianzus, the embodiment of the model he presented, worked at his credibility as preacher and paved the way for the teachings he had brought to Constantinople. The authoritarian force of the discursive *ethos* in Gregory's sermons mainly comes from this symphony between what he preached and what he was like as a person and theologian in the world.

Throughout the centuries, Gregory's model of the legitimated theologian influenced the nature of the religious discourse and the relation between the protagonists of this type of speech act.

Notes

1 Averil Cameron *Christianity and the Rhetoric of Empire: The Development of Christian Discourse Sather Classical Lectures*; V. 55 (Berkeley, Los Angeles, London: University of California Press, 1991), 19.
2 Wolfram Kinzig "The Greek Christian Writers" in Stainley E. Porter (ed.) *Handbook of Classical Rhetoric in the Hellenistic Period 330 B.C.- 440 A.D.*, (Leiden, New York, Koln: Brill, 1997), 655.
3 George A. Kennedy, *Classical Rhetoric and its Christian and Secular Tradition from Ancient to Modern Times*, (Chapel Hill and London: The University of North Carolina Press, 1999), 47.
4 Wolfram Kinzig "The Greek Christian Writers", 645–646.
5 George A. Kennedy, *Classical Rhetoric and its Christian and Secular Tradition from Ancient to Modern Times*, 50.
6 Wolfram Kinzig, "The Greek Christian Writers", 653.
7 Thomas Habinek, *Ancient Rhetoric and Oratory* (Oxford: Blackwell Publishing, 2005), 102.
8 Thomas Habinek, *Ancient Rhetoric and Oratory*, 102.
9 Aristotel, "Retorica", II, translated by. M.-C. Andrieş, (Bucureşti: IRI, 2004), 1: 1377b-1378 a.
10 George A. Kennedy, *Classical Rhetoric and its Christian and Secular Tradition from Ancient to Modern Times*, 80–82.
11 George A. Kennedy, *Classical Rhetoric and its Christian and Secular Tradition from Ancient to Modern Times*, 102.
12 Thomas Habinek, *Ancient Rhetoric and Oratory*, 102.
13 Thomas Habinek, *Ancient Rhetoric and Oratory*, 102.
14 Aristotel "Retorica", 1: 1377b-1378.
15 George A. Kennedy, *Classical Rhetoric and its Christian and Secular Tradition from Ancient to Modern Times*, 45.
16 Christof Rapp, "Aristotle's Rhetoric", in Edward N. Zalta (ed.) *The Stanford Encyclopedia of Philosophy* (Spring, 2010), https://plato.stanford.edu/archives/spr2010/entries/aristotle-rhetoric/.
17 Forbes I. Hill, "Aristotle's Rhetorical Theory. With a Synopsis of 59 Aristotle's Rhetoric" in James J. Murphy and Richard A. Katula with Forbes I. Hill, Donovan J. Ochs, (eds.) *A Synoptic History of Classical Rhetoric* (Mahwah, NJ, London: Lawrence Erlbaum Associates, 2003), 95.

18 Ruth Amossy, "Ethos at the *Crossroad* of Disciplines: Rhetoric, Pragmatics, Sociology", in *Poetics Today*, vol. 22, no 1 (Durham, NC: Duke University Press, 2001), 1.
19 S. C. Levinson, *Pragmatics* (Cambridge: Cambridge University Press, 1984), 5.
20 J. L. Austin, *How to do Things with Words* (Cambridge, MA: Harvard University Press, 1977).
21 Malcolm Coulthard, *An Introduction to Discourse Analysis*, New Edition (UK: Longman Group, 1985), 18–24.
22 Rodica Zafiu, "Ethos, pathos, logos în textul predicii" in *Text şi discurs religios*, II (Iaşi: Editura Universităţii "Alexandru Ioan Cuza", 2010), 27.
23 Ruth Amossy,"Ethos at the *Crossroad* of Disciplines: Rhetoric, Pragmatics, Sociology", 2.
24 Ruth Amossy, "Ethos at the *Crossroad* of Disciplines: Rhetoric, Pragmatics, Sociology", 25.
25 Ruth Amossy, "Ethos at the *Crossroad* of Disciplines: Rhetoric, Pragmatics, Sociology", 4–5.
26 Ruth Amossy, "Ethos at the *Crossroad* of Disciplines: Rhetoric, Pragmatics, Sociology", 21.
27 Pierre Bourdieu, *Language and Symbolic Power*, ed. and introd. by John B. Thompson, transl. by Gino Raymond and Matthew Adamson, (Cambridge: Polity Press, 1991), 113.
28 Pierre Bourdieu, *Language and Symbolic Power*, 113.
29 Pierre Bourdieu, *Language and Symbolic Power*, 109.
30 Pierre Bourdieu, *Language and Symbolic Power*, 107.
31 Pierre Bourdieu, *Language and Symbolic Power*, 72.
32 Pierre Bourdieu, *Language and Symbolic Power*, 20.
33 Pierre Bourdieu, *Language and Symbolic Power*, 7–38.
34 Pierre Bourdieu, *Language and Symbolic Power*, 66.
35 Chai"m Perelman şi Lucie Olbrechts-Tyteca "Tratat de argumentare Noua Retorică", translated by Aurelia Stoica, preface by Michel Meyer (Iași: Editura Universității „Alexandru Ioan Cuza", 2012), 32.
36 Chai"m Perelman şi Lucie Olbrechts-Tyteca "Tratat de argumentare Noua Retorică, 35–38.
37 Ruth Amossy, "Ethos at the *Crossroad* of Disciplines: Rhetoric, Pragmatics, Sociology", 7.
38 Ruth Amossy, "Ethos at the *Crossroad* of Disciplines: Rhetoric, Pragmatics, Sociology", 7.
39 Ruth Amossy, "Ethos at the *Crossroad* of Disciplines: Rhetoric, Pragmatics, Sociology", 6.
40 Stelianos *Papadopoulos*, "*Vulturul Rănit*. Viața Sfântului Grigorie Teologul", transl. by Constantin Coman, Cornel Coman (București: *Editura* Bizantină, 2002), 10.
41 Jean Bernardi, *Grigorie din Nazianz, Teologul și epoca sa*, transl. by Cristian Pop (Sibiu: Editura Deisis, 2002), 52–53.
42 Stelianos *Papadopoulos*, "*Vulturul Rănit*. Viața Sfântului Grigorie Teologul", 29.
43 Jean Bernardi, "*Grigorie din Nazianz, Teologul și epoca sa*", 23.
44 Jean Bernardi, "*Grigorie din Nazianz, Teologul și epoca sa*", 88.
45 Stelianos *Papadopoulos*, „*Vulturul Rănit*. Viața Sfântului Grigorie Teologul", 47.
46 Stelianos *Papadopoulos*, "*Vulturul Rănit*. Viața Sfântului Grigorie Teologul", 26.

47 Jean Bernardi, "*Grigorie din Nazianz, Teologul și epoca sa*", 94–95; McGuckin referred to the Roman notion of *patria-potestas* that defined the father-son relationship as "fundamentally one of power and service, and the benefits of inheritance were offered as incentives to those who served well and conformed" in John Anthony McGuckin, *St. Gregory of Nazianzus: An Intellectual Biography* (Crestwood, NY: St Vladimir's Seminary Press, 2001), 16.
48 Stelianos *Papadopoulos*, "*Vulturul Rănit.* Viața Sfântului Grigorie Teologul", 54.
49 Stelianos *Papadopoulos*, "*Vulturul Rănit.* Viața Sfântului Grigorie Teologul", 68–69.
50 Stelianos *Papadopoulos*, "*Vulturul Rănit.* Viața Sfântului Grigorie Teologul", 48–49.
51 Stelianos *Papadopoulos*, "*Vulturul Rănit.* Viața Sfântului Grigorie Teologul", 99.
52 John Anthony McGuckin, *St. Gregory of Nazianzus: An Intellectual Biography*, 236.
53 Stelianos *Papadopoulos*, "*Vulturul Rănit.* Viața Sfântului Grigorie Teologul", 108.
54 John Anthony McGuckin, *St. Gregory of Nazianzus: An Intellectual Biography*, 237.
55 John Anthony McGuckin, *St. Gregory of Nazianzus: An Intellectual Biography*, 243.
56 Stelianos *Papadopoulos*, "*Vulturul Rănit.* Viața Sfântului Grigorie Teologul", 114.
57 John Anthony McGuckin, *St. Gregory of Nazianzus: An Intellectual Biography*, 241.
58 Stelianos *Papadopoulos*, "*Vulturul Rănit.* Viața Sfântului Grigorie Teologul", 116.
59 Averil Cameron, *Christianity and the Rhetoric of Empire: The Development of Christian Discourse Sather Classical Lectures*, 130.
60 Stelianos *Papadopoulos*, "*Vulturul Rănit.* Viața Sfântului Grigorie Teologul", 188; Bernardi 159.
61 Stelianos *Papadopoulos*, "*Vulturul Rănit.* Viața Sfântului Grigorie Teologul", 188.
62 Stelianos *Papadopoulos*, "*Vulturul Rănit.* Viața Sfântului Grigorie Teologul", 188.
63 Jean Bernardi, "*Grigorie din Nazianz, Teologul și epoca sa*", 176–177.
64 Stelianos *Papadopoulos*, "*Vulturul Rănit.* Viața Sfântului Grigorie Teologul", 122.
65 John Anthony McGuckin, *St. Gregory of Nazianzus: An Intellectual Biography*, 243.
66 John Anthony McGuckin, *St. Gregory of Nazianzus: An Intellectual Biography*, 241.
67 Jean Bernardi, "*Grigorie din Nazianz, Teologul și epoca sa*", 124.
68 Jean Bernardi, "*Grigorie din Nazianz, Teologul și epoca sa*", 135–146.
69 Stelianos *Papadopoulos*, "*Vulturul Rănit.* Viața Sfântului Grigorie Teologul", 125.
70 Stelianos *Papadopoulos*, "*Vulturul Rănit.* Viața Sfântului Grigorie Teologul", 165.
71 Stelianos *Papadopoulos*, "*Vulturul Rănit.* Viața Sfântului Grigorie Teologul", 115.
72 Stelianos *Papadopoulos*, "*Vulturul Rănit.* Viața Sfântului Grigorie Teologul", 149.

73 Jean Bernardi, "*Grigorie din Nazianz, Teologul şi epoca sa*", 63.
74 Stelianos *Papadopoulos*, "*Vulturul Rănit.* Viaţa Sfântului Grigorie Teologul", 150.
75 John Anthony McGuckin, *St. Gregory of Nazianzus: An Intellectual Biography*, 240.
76 see John Anthony McGuckin, *St. Gregory of Nazianzus: An Intellectual Biography*, footnote 31, 43.
77 Stelianos *Papadopoulos*, "*Vulturul Rănit.* Viaţa Sfântului Grigorie Teologul", 130.
78 Stelianos *Papadopoulos*, "*Vulturul Rănit.* Viaţa Sfântului Grigorie Teologul", 121.
79 Jean Bernardi, "*Grigorie din Nazianz, Teologul şi epoca sa*", 210.
80 John Anthony McGuckin, *St. Gregory of Nazianzus: An Intellectual Biography*, 310.
81 St. Gregory of Nazianzus, "First Theological Oration (Oration XXVII)," in Schaff Philip, trans. Charles Gordon Browne and James Edward Swallow (eds.) *The Nicene and Post-Nicene Fathers of the Christian Church*, 2nd series, vol. 7 (New York: Christian Literature, 1893), 285.
82 Stelianos *Papadopoulos*, "*Vulturul Rănit.* Viaţa Sfântului Grigorie Teologul", 121.
83 Rodica Zafiu, "Ethos, pathos, logos în textul predicii", 30.
84 Wolfram Kinzig, "The Greek Christian Writers", 654.
85 Averil Cameron, *Christianity and the Rhetoric of Empire: The Development of Christian Discourse Sather Classical Lectures*, 144.
86 John Anthony McGuckin, *St. Gregory of Nazianzus: An Intellectual Biography*, 42.
87 Pierre Bourdieu, *Language and Symbolic Power*, 80.
88 St. Gregory of Nazianzus, "First Theological Oration (Oration XXVII)", 285.
89 St. Gregory of Nazianzus, "First Theological Oration (Oration XXVII)", 285.
90 John Anthony McGuckin, *St. Gregory of Nazianzus: An Intellectual Biography*, 279.
91 St. Gregory of Nazianzus, "First Theological Oration (Oration XXVII)", 285.
92 St. Gregory of Nazianzus, "First Theological Oration (Oration XXVII)", 285.
93 George A. Kennedy, *Classical Rhetoric and its Christian and Secular Tradition from Ancient to Modern Times*, 46.
94 Wolfram Kinzig, "The Greek Christian Writers", 652.
95 Averil Cameron, *Christianity and the Rhetoric of Empire: The Development of Christian Discourse Sather Classical Lectures*, 17.
96 Averil Cameron, *Christianity and the Rhetoric of Empire: The Development of Christian Discourse Sather Classical Lectures*, 35.
97 Averil Cameron, *Christianity and the Rhetoric of Empire: The Development of Christian Discourse Sather Classical Lectures*, 130.
98 Wolfram Kinzig, "The Greek Christian Writers", 648.
99 Daniela Obreja Răducănescu, "*Discursul religios - discurs specializat*" in "*Text şi discurs religios*", III, Section *Retorica discursului religios* (Iaşi: Editura Universităţii "Alexandru Ioan Cuza", 2011), 339.
100 Stelianos *Papadopoulos*, "*Vulturul Rănit.* Viaţa Sfântului Grigorie Teologul", 124.
101 Averil Cameron, *Christianity and the Rhetoric of Empire: The Development of Christian Discourse Sather Classical Lectures*, 21.
102 Wolfram Kinzig, "The Greek Christian Writers", 650.
103 Pierre Bourdieu, *Language and Symbolic Power*, 56.

104 Pierre Bourdieu, *Language and Symbolic Power*, 108.
105 St. Gregory of Nazianzus, "First Theological Oration (Oration XXVII)", 286.
106 John Anthony McGuckin, *St. Gregory of Nazianzus: An Intellectual Biography*, xxviii.
107 Pierre Bourdieu, *Language and Symbolic Power*, 109–111.
108 Pierre Bourdieu, *Language and Symbolic Power*, 109.
109 Wolfram Kinzig, "The Greek Christian Writers", 653.
110 Pierre Bourdieu, *Language and Symbolic Power*, 286.
111 John Anthony McGuckin, *St. Gregory of Nazianzus: An Intellectual Biography*, 244.
112 John Anthony McGuckin, *St. Gregory of Nazianzus: An Intellectual Biography*, 74.

Bibliography

Amossy, Ruth. "Ethos at the *Crossroad* of Disciplines: Rhetoric, Pragmatics, Sociology", in "Poetics Today", vol. 22, no. 1 (Durham, NC: Duke University Press, 2001).

Aristotel. "Retorica", II, translated by. M.-C. Andrieş (Bucureşti: IRI, 2004).

Austin, J. L. *How to do Things with Words* (Cambridge, MA: Harvard University Press, 1977).

Bernardi, Jean. "Grigorie din Nazianz, Teologul şi epoca sa", transl. by Cristian Pop (Sibiu: Editura Deisis, 2002).

Bourdieu, Pierre. "Language and Symbolic Power", ed. and introd. by John B. Thompson, transl. by Gino Raymond and Matthew Adamson (Cambridge: Polity Press, 1991).

Cameron, Averil. *Christianity and the Rhetoric of Empire: The Development of Christian Discourse Sather Classical Lectures*; V. 55, (Berkeley, Los Angeles, London: University of California Press, 1991).

Coulthard, Malcolm. *An Introduction to Discourse Analysis*, New Edition (London: Longman Group, 1985).

Forbes, I. Hill. "Aristotle's Rhetorical Theory. With a Synopsis of 59 Aristotle's Rhetoric" in James J. Murphy and Richard A. Katula with Forbes I. Hill, Donovan J. Ochs, "A Synoptic History of Classical Rhetoric" (Mahwah, NJ, London: Lawrence Erlbaum Associates, 2003).

Habinek, Thomas. *Ancient Rhetoric and Oratory* (Oxford: Blackwell Publishing, 2005).

Kennedy, George A. *Classical Rhetoric and its Christian and Secular Tradition from Ancient to Modern Times* (Chapel Hill and London: The University of North Carolina Press, 1999).

Kinzig, Wolfram. "The Greek Christian Writers" in Stainley E. Porter (ed.) *Handbook of Classical Rhetoric in the Hellenistic Period 330 B.C.- 440 A.D.* (Leiden, New York, Koln: Brill, 1997).

Levinson, S. C. *Pragmatics* (Cambridge: Cambridge University Press, 1984).

McGuckin, John Anthony. *St. Gregory of Nazianzus: An Intellectual Biography* (Crestwood, NY: St Vladimir's Seminary Press, 2001).

Papadopoulos, Stelianos. "*Vulturul Rănit.* Viaţa Sfântului Grigorie Teologul, transl. by Constantin Coman, Cornel Coman (Bucureşti: *Editura* Bizantină, 2002).

Perelman, Chaim and Olbrechts-Tyteca, Lucie. "Tratat de argumentare Noua Retorică", translated by Aurelia Stoica, preface by Michel Meyer (Iaşi: Editura Universităţii "Alexandru Ioan Cuza", 2012).
Răducănescu, Daniela Obreja. "Discursul religios - discurs specializat" in "Text şi discurs religios", III, Section Retorica discursului religios (Iaşi: Editura Universităţii "Alexandru Ioan Cuza", 2011).
Rapp, Christof. "Aristotle's Rhetoric", in Edward N. Zalta (ed.) "*The Stanford Encyclopedia of Philosophy*" (Spring, 2010), https://plato.stanford.edu/archives/spr2010/entries/aristotle-rhetoric/.
Zafiu, Rodica. "Ethos, pathos, logos în textul predicii" in Alexandru Gafton, Sorin Guia, Ioan Milică (ed.), "Text şi discurs religios", II (Iaşi: Editura Universităţii "Alexandru Ioan Cuza", 2010).

14 The Contribution of St. John Chrysostom to the Understanding of Pauline Hamartiology

Ştefan Florea

Introduction

Sin is a notion specific to the Judeo-Christian theological ambiance, which refers to the reality of fallen man, that means to the new existential state of man after the disobedience of our forefathers. The notion of sin takes in consideration both a dogmatic component and a moral and social one, being actually a reality that includes the fallen state of man. In the Gospels, we often find references to the notion of sin, but the one who theorized, developed, and grounded this reality, from a theological standpoint, was St Apostle Paul. In fact, he was the pioneer of Christian theology; therefore, the notion of sin could not have escaped his missionary and theological concerns, once that is midmost to Christianity.

The present study regards the development of the notion of sin at Saint Paul through the means of the theological vision of Saint John Chrysostom, the greatest homilist of all times. The notion of sin has many connotations, from the violation of the divine law to the alienation from the meaning of life or to moral decay or ontological deformation, depending on the theological or philosophical approach of the concept. The contemporary world, as can be easily seen lately, has moved away from the Christian roots of our civilization, preferring either an aggressive adogmatism or importing oriental meanings or even retaining, slightly distorted, the old meanings of the concept of sin.[1]

History of the Concept of "Hamartiology" and Pauline Terminology

The notion of sin is essential to the understanding of history, as well as of the presence of humanity, to know what we are, where we come from and where are going at. Some would prefer to give up the notion of sin and, unfortunately, we notice a worrying trend even among some Christians, or theologians or those who think of themselves as practitioners, who prefer not to talk about sin, in the spirit of the unfortunate neo-Marxist theory of political correctness.

Regardless of this, the concept of sin synthesizes a true existential and ontological historical reality, without which we cannot understand

DOI: 10.4324/9781003273592-14

either Christology or anthropology, and nowise soteriology or Christian eschatology.[2]

A great pioneer in the field of theology, the one who unparalleled synthesized Christian doctrine was St. Paul the Apostle, the heroic and ingenious Jewish rabbi converted to Christianity, who suddenly gave universal scope to Christianity and carried out the command of the Divine Saviour during his generation.

During Antiquity, the notion of sin referred mainly to the violation of a norm of social coexistence, of a rule of the polis (Gr. stronghold), of a social convention, so it had an external, social meaning. In the Old Testament, the notion also had a predominantly external character, referring to the violation of the divine law (I Kings 12, 19; Is. 1, 28), of a religious or moral prescription[3] or the intentional realization of evil, or it is an iniquity (Lev. 4, 2; I Sam. 26, 21), willingly or unwillingly (Is. 24, 1; I Kings 8, 50), or it is either a matter of rebellion against God, due to the world order instituted by Him, or it refers to the commission of evil intentionally or through negligence.[4]

For the St Apostle Paul, evil is not a phantasmagoria or a linguistic trick like the ones close to us, the lack of good or a reality without ontological support or other such bland and unnecessary definitions. Evil does exist! It is a terrible reality, engaged by the forces of darkness, to which the poor human being can only face with the help of God. Of course, Christianity as it was in Pauline times saw evil as an aggressive, dark, antihuman, concrete reality that tormented and afflicted the human being, as we see with great clarity in the Gospels, where the Saviour often frees people from the tyrannical power of the devil.

Evil is, therefore, connected with the devil, and this is an obvious reality from which there is no exception. And we, humans, our souls, are real battlefields for good and evil. Of course, evil is never equal to good and cannot rule over good, but runs away from it. From many gospel passages, we realize that evil is scared of good, that good can heal those affected by evil, and here good is meant as a Person; that evil never triumphs over good, but man can be sickened or affected by evil. That is why the Eastern Christianity prefers the thaumaturgical vision and often speaks, following the Pauline and evangelical model, of healing the man from evil.

Sin itself is seen as a disease that affects human life, but not irreparably, as the repentance of the thief on the Cross shows us. The New Testament uses a number of consecrated terms for the notion of sin, and the most common of these is "αμαρτία",[5] which means "betraying a purpose", "failing a goal[6]", "disregarding the divine will" or "breaking the law of God" (Rom 5:12).[7]

A commonly used Pauline term is παραπτόμα,[8] meaning unintentional mistake, error, or simple violation of the law (Eph. 2:1). And, with a similar meaning, the term παραβάσις (Rom 4:15) is often used, which has as specific the meaning of deviation from a clearly established norm, therefore an external, social meaning. On the strictly religious realm, in order to designate a lack of piety or impiety, the term ασεβία is used (Rom 1:18). Also, for violation of a social norm, the term ανομία (2 Cor 6:14) is preferred, which has especially the meaning of lawlessness, iniquity. Two other terms, κακία and πονερεία, used by St Paul refer to the major moral and spiritual decline (Rom 1:29). The apostle also uses the term αδικία, with the meaning of immediate harm done to the neighbor or, in other words, repeating or overlapping with some of the terms mentioned above, "injustice" (Rom. 9:14), "iniquity" (Rom. 2, 8) or "trespass" (2 Tim. 2:19).

All these terms that St. Paul uses refer to different aspects of sin, to its dynamic, current part, to what it produces into man and society, to different but complementary aspects of the notion of evil.

Of course, the Apostle Paul is a tributary of the Jewish conception, but also of the ancient one of his time. It couldn't be otherwise. He lived but in a concrete milieu, was a Jewish scholar and had known very well the theological and philosophical subtleties of his time.[9]

Paul was aware that sin is a disease that affects the human soul and often the body, that it has many social and community implications and that it must be fought against as the one that hinders the human being from achieving his purpose.[10]

The terms used by the Apostle are complementary, each depicting or highlighting another reality of evil that affects man and the human community, constituting itself on as many occasions to impel us to leave this decadent and inhuman captivity.[11]

St. John Chrysostom: "Exegete" of St. Paul the Apostle

In Pauline theology, sin is summed up to disobedience (Rom. 5:19) to God, which leads to an alienation from one's own purpose in life, from one's neighbor, and from the Creator Himself. It is about a loss of meaning, about getting sick by the soul that no longer allows clear vision and the pursuit of one's own meaning of life.

Saint John Chrysostom also deepens this perspective, insisting especially on the immediate moral, pastoral connotations. In fact, this is the general vision of St. John, by giving moral, immediate connotations to the doctrinal perspective of St. Paul the Apostle. And this is not bad at all, because he could not have resumed that doctrinal perspective and deepened it, taking into account the pastoral-missionary specifics of his time, the general ambience of the time and the fact that the social side of sin was the one which had obviously troubled.

Poverty and a lack of concern for one's neighbor's needs were the most upsetting in Christian communities, the place love was talked about, but not put it into practice. Under these conditions, St. John chose to give a moral application to the Pauline doctrinal concepts of sin.[12]

He sees sin as a disease, as a new existential reality that affects man and is the cause of death:

> As the most skillful doctors treat diseases from the beginning, and start with the very root of evil, so does the blessed Paul. Indeed, after pointing

> out that we are justified, and after indicating those about the patriarch, about the Holy Spirit, and about the death of Christ – Who would not have died if He was not going to straighten us up – he finally proves from another part of what has already been proved, and draws attention by the opposite to the subject in question, that is, to the death and sin. How and in which way? That is, he seeks to find out how death entered the world, and how after that took possession of it. So how did it come in and how did it take over? «Through one's sin», he says. But what does it mean «that all have sinned in him»? «When having fallen», he says, «then even those who did not eat from that tree became all mortal.[13]

In fact, it is important to see that the chrysostomic perspective always emphasizes the moral side of the dimension of sin for obvious reasons of missionary correction of it, in all its aspects.

The connection between sin and death, spoken of by St Apostle Paul in the fifth chapter of his Epistle to the Romans and the parallel between Adam and Christ, pedagogically and wisely presented by "the apostle of heathens" in order to show the reality of redemption and the importance of the work of salvation, is well-argued homiletically, from a moral perspective by St. John Chrysostom, in simple words and to the understanding of all categories of believers.

Using the rhetorical method of the age, he thus evokes the soteriological question

> If death has its root in sin, and since the law was not given and sin was not counted, then how come death was ruling? Hence it is conspicuous that not the sin followed by the breaking of the law, but that which results from the breaking of the commandment by Adam is the sin that has ruined everything.[14]

For this reason, pride and selfishness are two of the main signs of the major disease of sin that do not allow the man to manifest in a natural fashion. Missing his goal, man is no longer able to be free and keep himself in this state offered by the Creator, thus entering the most terrible existential slavery possible, i.e. that of the sin.[15]

Sin as a Limitation of Human Freedom

Sin robs man of his freedom. And here it is about an exceptional Pauline intuition that gives us the "correct lens" for interpreting human history. You are free, not when you are not physically closed or oppressed, but only when you are free from sin. Here, in fact, is the mistake of all political systems and human revolutions that claim the liberation of man and promise freedom without knowing what it really means.[16]

To be free means fundamentally to be freed from the bondage of sin and death, and the Single, the unique Liberator is only the Son of God

Incarnate, the One who broke the chains of sin and gives us until His second Coming, freedom through His grace, poured out through the Holy Sacraments and the other religious services.

For St. Paul, sin is: "disobedience against the will of God, willful transgression of His law, and the fall of man from the gracious communion with God".[17] The importance of disproving the sin and practicing virtue is very great in Pauline ethics, as evidenced by the numerous lists of sins (Cor. 5:10; 6: 9; Cor. 12:20; Gal. 5: 19–21; Rom. 1:29–31; Col. 3, 5–8; Ephesians 3, 5; 1 Tim. 1, 9; Titus 3, 3; 2 Tim. 3, 2–5) which the apostle listed in his letters. It shows that sin is a major obstacle in man's way to perfection, it is incompatible with the Kingdom of God, for it opposes salvation (1 Cor. 6: 9; Gal. 5:21).

To this perspective, St. John adds the idea that evil and sin are the fruit of the corruption of man's free will and cannot be imputed exclusively to evil,

> nor Eve's deception can be completely prescribed to Satan either, but woman was simply deceived by her own lust. This is what the Holy Scripture itself shows with the words, "When the woman saw that the fruit of the tree was good for food and pleasing to the eye, and also desirable for gaining wisdom, she took some and ate it".
>
> (Gen 3: 6)[18]

St. John Chrysostom comes here with a moral deepening and says that the will of man must be subject to freedom and not to necessity, that is, not to the immediate, but to the transcendent, of course, expressed with simple and beautiful words

> Human affairs are not subject to necessity, but, as I said, everything here is enlightened by the dignity that free will gives... So, to will good and will not evil, was planted in man from the beginning, and the Law coming, it became a greater accuser of evil deeds, as well as he became ...a greater praise and encourager of the good ones.[19]

St. Paul had the intuition that sin presupposes slavery to the powers of darkness, distance from the meaning of life and the Creator, but also a failure from a wrongly founded project of life, which leads to isolation, alienation, suffering and death (Eph. 2, 1–3).

Sin - Herald of Death

For St Apostle Paul, sin appears as a power of evil, so it is personified, because he intuited that behind evil there is not merely a lack of good, but the concrete, fallen spiritual forces, and the devil himself. That is, exactly what theology adapted to what contemporary man wants to hear, hesitates to state clearly. And as I affirmed at the beginning of my paper, today we increasingly want to blur the existence of evil and sin, as well as emphasize the guilt of sin for psychological reasons, false and superficial.

This Pauline vision is completed by St. John, who highlights the clear connection between sin-evil and death, but also offers the pastoral remedy of this morally decadent state, namely justification.

> Only one sin had the power to usher death and punishment into the world, while grace not only abolished that single sin, but also those introduced after that... But where there is justification, there is necessarily life, and after that thousands of goods must follow; as well as where their sin, necessarily is also death.[20]

Saint Paul presents sin as a power of evil, personified,[21] as a concrete reality that affects the good of the human being and his soul, body, and community integrity,[22] as that lever through which the devil acts on man, as the one who presents himself like "the master of this age" (2 Cor. 4: 4).

St. John Chrysostom went further, realizing that the evil that acts through sin leads man to despair and therefore says

> When we know that we are sinners, we must neither despair nor be light-minded and lazy, for both of these would lead us to destruction... This, therefore, robs us of the good we possess, and that, i.e. the despair, does not allow us to free ourselves from the evils under which we sigh.[23]

The connection between sin and despair is an interesting and necessary deepening in the context of the chrysostomic epoch, but valid at any time, which shows the spiritual skill of St. John, starting from the Pauline doctrinal considerations: "Therefore, do not despair, but have strong hope in God, let us think of the immeasurable stack of His grace and love of men, let us get rid of the evil conscience.[24]"

Justification in Christ, Healing of Sin, and Restoration of Human Nature

St. Paul knew that the reality of sin is terribly concrete and never illusory, because:

> sin is an implicitly aggressive trait, a cruelty, a damage, a separation from God and other people, a partial removal or an act of rebellion. ... a deliberate, defiant and disloyal act, through which someone is defied, or offended, or harmed.[25]

It is well-known the beautiful and famous antithesis between the New Adam, Christ and the Old Adam, with the help of which Saint Paul conceives a humanity in solidarity, ready to become either *massa damnata* or that *Corpus Christi*, dominated by grace (Rom. 5.14).

St. John uses in a pedagogical-pastoral way this type of Pauline antithesis: Christ–Adam, showing that the Old Law had only highlighted sin, without having the power to correct it because

> it showed that the world was condemned from Adam on, but saved and redeemed by Christ; therefore, in due time, he also speaks of the Law, again thwarting the faith that the Jews had in it... He showed that the law was temporary, and likewise its necessity, and not principled or from the beginning, as he says in the Epistle to the Galatians.[26]

The man of sin is in the Pauline conception the old, material or unspiritual man, who has Adam as a model and who is dominated by the spirit of this world, walking according to the will of the body in which the evil one works (cf. Eph. 2:12), becoming "Son of disobedience" (1 Thess. 5: 5). He is much dominated by passions, vices, and lusts, the image of God getting dimed and depersonalized in him day by day, and becoming a mere instrument of evil with too little will of his own, for he gradually gives way to his own sovereignty over evil; in other words, "being intimately connected with physical, intellectual, and moral weakness — he is inclined to sin and evil — therefore through the flesh (ἐν τῇ σαρκί, Eph. 2: 11–12), the apostle Paul repeatedly shows the condition of sin.[27]"

The power of reason, the determination of faith, and the example of the saints are meant to help us in the battle against sin. St. John recommends that "let everyone destroy the sin that upset him... to get rid of the passion. God has given us sufficiently good mind, capable if we want to open our eyes and make us victorious over the passions that are rising in us.[28]"

He considers that love, as the queen of all virtues, is the best remedy against sin, especially when he comments on the First Epistle to the Corinthians of St. Paul. So St. John advises us:

> do not behave as if we are isolated and do not say: this is not my friend, nor my relative, nor my neighbor and I have nothing in common with him... And if he participates in the same faith with you, lo! he is a member, because is part as you are of the same body of Christ....[29]

In fact, the rhetoric of the love of neighbor is very important to St. John, being the key to his soteriology and the perfect remedy for the healing of sin.[30] Here is the rule of Christian perfection, its most precise definition, its highest peak: "to seek the common interest... nothing, indeed, can make you so imitative of Christ as to take care of your neighbor.[31]"

A practical spirit and careful observer of the realities of his time, St. John Chrysostom transposed the Pauline doctrine, including that of sin, in the context of his time. He viewed the sin especially as that evil that undermines the foundations of its society, which puts a barrier to solidarity and communion, which exacerbates individualism and selfishness, which makes the Christian indifferent to the needs of his neighbor. Therefore, he acted for the fundamental change of the decadent, aged and sinful mentality, pleading for the transformation of this pagan society into a truly Christian one, according to the *homo novus* (new man) in Christ.

He acted for the transformation of the old, sinful man, who walks on the way of darkness, and for the edification of the new man, full of light, guided by the Holy Spirit on the shining paths of perfection. This reality is obvious and is accurately recorded by history: "what characterizes worthy architects is first that they destroy the edifice of lying and lay the foundation of truth, as the prophet says (cf. Jer. 1:10).[32]" In other words, first you demolish the old building, and then you build a new one, from the ground up, keeping nothing of the old one, so that the new creation has nothing to do with the disease of corruption.[33]

It should be noted, however, that the body, likewise the soul, is only a gateway to evil, but the body never identifies, as does the matter with evil, as in the Platonic conception (Gal. 5:17).

Aspects of Pauline Hamartiology in Chrysostomic Thoroughgoing Study

With the volitional availability of faith, man can be healed of sin, giving primacy in his life to the spirit and thus succeeding in transforming himself from a carnal (σαρκός), natural (σώμα) or external (ό έξω) man into a new man (κάινος άνθρώπος), beneficially ruled by the Spirit.[34] St. John sees the correction or healing of sin only through repentance. "Let us not, however, do such a thing, but come first to the knowledge of ourselves. Let us learn how to know our wounds, and then we will find the right cure".[35]

St. Paul believes that sin is "also a denial of the glory of God, and an arrogant attempt of man to be his own master ... it is life in the flesh deprived of the Holy Spirit (Rom. 1: 18–32).[36] This perspective is highlighted by St. John Chrysostom through the example given by the sinner, through his alienation from freedom and eschatological reality, because most often, the dissipation of thoughts about evil, sin, and hell gives way to sin. "Therefore, let us not doubt hell, but speak much of it, so that we may sin much the less.[37]"

The body of man is the temple of the Holy Spirit (1 Cor 3:16), and sin desecrates it, depriving its freedom, and St. Paul sees it as a: "all-encompassing situation in which men exist" (Rom 6: 1), or as a demonic force that dominates and holds people captive (Rom 3: 9; 5:12; 6: 16–23; 7: 8)".[38]

St. John emphasizes this perspective, but in the style of moral oratory, to urge his contemporaries to value the body as the seat of the Spirit, not as a ruin of sin:

> we confess that the body is smaller than the spirit, and inferior to it, but not contrary to and in battle with it, or malicious against the spirit, but as the harp in relation to the one who plays to it, or as the ship in relation to its helmsman, so also the body is in relation to the spirit.[39]

In a very plastic way, St. John shows the role of the evil one in tempting the believer, as a kidnapper and destroyer of human freedom. "Beware, therefore, and strengthen yourself with spiritual weapons on all sides, so that you cannot be conquered, but easily to crush it".[40]

In a direction that will be much appreciated and deepened by St. John Chrysostom, St. Paul sees the social, communitarian component of sin, especially if we consider the image of the Church as the **Mystical Body of Jesus Christ** (1 Cor. 12, 26); like the principle of communicating vessels, the sin of a member affects the whole body: "it hinders the transmission of the life of grace, it diminishes the irradiation of goodness and holiness".[41] The social repercussion of sin is also viewed in the fact that the sin which affects an individual will gradually spread throughout the social body (cf. Rom. 5:21; 6: 12–14).

Although St. John Chrysostom is known as the greatest homilist and moralist of the Church throughout the centuries, he is still blamed for the lack of a deeply dogmatic vision, or a systemic mystical-moral construction. But we must also take into account the context of his life, the fact that after the age of great persecution and doctrinal and apologetic insights, he lived in a time when the determination of the will of contemporaries to attune their lives to the principles of Christ gospel was essential, much more since that context was dominated by the pagan, materialistic view of life.

The Chrysostomic Interpretation Topicality of Pauline Hamartiology

At the end of my paper, I will try to bring this discussion into the contemporary space, where temptations are permanent and the means of spiritual survival more and more discreet. Therefore, there is a need for a re-evaluation of Pauline hamartiology in the vision of St. John, taking into account, of course, the image and moral structure of today's society. We have seen what are the main determinants of Pauline hamartiology in the deepening of St. John Chrysostom, but what relevance do they have today?

St. apostle Paul stressed out the terrible reality of sin as a form of manifestation of evil in our lives, and St. John Chrysostom dealt with the moral deepening and updating, in the context of his time, of this reality. Today, more than ever, we need, first of all, a deepening of the consciousness of sin. It has almost disappeared from many of our contemporaries, under the assault of secular ideologies and a nearly apocatastasis conception, very common in almost all denominational circles.

There are a lot of those who preach an exclusive God of love, who forgives absolutely anything, even if man does nothing in this regard and who militates for leaving the classical vision of sin. They conceive that God never condemns anyone, neither can a man condemn himself, nor can anyone else do so, regardless of the sins committed and the lack of proper repentance, which is only a deception and a huge one. In turn, we also believe in an

Almighty God who forgives everything, provided we are aware of sin and of repentance, otherwise there would be no point in forgiveness because redemption is a work of awareness of the traces of evil through sin in our lives and of its healing.

It is not about a vengeful God, but about the fact that in the Eastern conception sin is a disease that must be healed, and this is done through the collaboration between man and God. As in real life, without the help of the patient, the doctor cannot do everything that depends on him, just as in the spiritual life, without the help of man, God cannot do anything that violates his free will, not that he cannot, but that he does not want (paraphrasing St. John of Damascus), because He is good, but He is also just.

It is not the story of a vengeful God, but about the fact that in the Eastern theological conception sin is a disease that must be healed, and this is done through the collaboration between man and God. As in real life, without the help of the patient, the doctor cannot do everything that depends on him, just as in the spiritual life, without the help of man, God cannot do anything that violates his free will, and not because He cannot do, but He doesn't want to (paraphrasing St. John of Damascus), because He is good, not only just.

The return to the Pauline doctrinal and chrysostomic moral perspective is a major, pressing, and current necessity because without the consciousness of sin, man cannot rise from the bondage of it and cannot be healed. The homilies of St. John Chrysostom are more relevant than ever. In fact, almost overwhelmingly, everything he says can be actual and applied in all times and places, especially today. Our task, as theologians, is to bring back the true vision of life, starting from the Church Fathers, reinterpreting the reality of our age through their lens and instruments, because the ages are changing and the theological lens only need to be cleansed. Under the pretext of renewal (*aggiornamento)* or modernization, fundamental transformations of meaning in theology cannot take place and new contents cannot be given to theological concepts either, in such a way that they were totally opposed to the old ones.

First, because we must not violate the admirable rule of Vincent of Lérins and absolutize theologoumena or passing theological ideas; secondly, because we cannot overturn the two-millennial theological perspective under the pressure of neo-Marxist perfunctory that have made their way even in theology. More actual than ever, St. John Chrysostom, with his hamartiology of Pauline origin, is necessary, current, and saving, because it proposes the traditional response, always new and inspired of the Church, to the problems facing today's society.

Conclusion

Regarding the Pauline conception of sin, the great merit of St. John Chrysostom is that he gave it a significant moral interpretation, updating it to the level of understanding of his time and giving it practical utility in his homiletic discourse. In other words, St. John updated the meanings of sin in Pauline times for the possibilities of reception, understanding, and application of his contemporary Christians. This pastoral missionary, exegetic and homiletical contribution brought many benefits to the Church of the Chrysostom era, the faithful optimally having received the message of the Archbishop of Constantinople.

Broadly speaking, this is the Pauline conception of sin. Of course, many reproaches can be brought into this vision, perhaps the too accentuated a dogmatism or neglecting the role of human will in choosing evil, but we must not forget that St Apostle Paul was the real pioneer in the field of Christian theology, giving the measure, meaning, and only after that the latter was to develop in different directions.[42]

He gave it a concrete, practical application through his sermons, homilies, and catechesis, through which he wanted to change the mentality of contemporaries. Therefore, his style is a paternalistic, moralistic one and even if the lack of a dogmatic depth gives it an apparent superficiality, we must think about the purpose of the pastoral-missionary activity of Chrysostom. He did not seek to deepen the doctrine and to establish a doctrinal pattern of interpretation, but the rapid transformation of the mentality of contemporaries.[43]

Even though St. John Chrysostom is not a creator of theology, being rather a moralist, a kind of new prophet of his time, yet his originality, necessity, and missionary success cannot be denied.

The lack of a substantial contribution of St. John in the field of doctrine is explained by way of his fundamental disinterest in theological and philosophical speculation and of the inclination to the concrete social problems, social evil, and its correction, of the exorcising of sin in the community, through education, faith and will[44]; then, by dint of the fact that during his time there were no major theological debates and conflicts, and his contemporaries were more concerned with concrete social issues.[45] However, we must not forget that he is quoted by two ecumenical synods in the dogmatic matters (the Fourth Ecumenical Council of Chalcedon on the mode of hypostatic union, and the Seventh Ecumenical Council of Nicaea on *iconodulism*).

Commenting on the Pauline corpus, especially where sin is spoken about, St. John adapts and interprets it through a social angle and sees it as a concubinage of the Christian with his time, a kind of secularization *avant la lettre*, as a hardening in the project, as a deviation from the primary purpose. For him, sin presupposes a superficial faith, a refusal of renewal by grace, an attraction to the material and a surrender to it.[46]

It has been said of him that

> there are few who follow man with so much attention and warmth in all situations, at all stages and in all moments of life... there is no human being who does not show a special interest... No one can be excluded from the field of life's honor, endeavor and joy.[47]

To all Pauline expressions of sin and by and large to the consequent hamartiology, St. John brings the logic of love of neighbor and solidarity, somehow diverting everything in the social sphere, in the concrete side of philanthropic activism, because he finds the sin especially in indifference, and believes that evil affects the power of love, as well as human solidarity.

What St. Paul emphasized and developed doctrinally, St. John deepens socially and morally, philanthropically and communitarian, that is, he applies perfectly and practically, what the apostle had intuited and had seen dogmatically. We could say that St Paul beholds evil, identifies it, whereas Saint John finds the remedy; one is apparently more theoretical, the other more practical, but, ultimately, both views are undoubtedly complementary.

Notes

1 Paul Evdokimov, *The Ages of the Spiritual Life* (Bucureşti: Christiana, 1993), 133.
2 Carlo Maria Martini, *Mărturisirile Sfântului Paul. Meditaţii* (*The confessions of St. Paul. Meditations*), (Bucureşti: Editura Arhiepiscopiei Romano-Catolice de Bucureşti), 2003, 46.
3 John D. Douglas, *Dicţionar Biblic* (Oradea: Editura Cartea Creştină, 1995), 988.
4 Adolf Gustav Deissmann, *Paul, A Study in Social and Religious History* (Londra: Hodder & Stoughton, 1926), 116.
5 Jean Claude Ingelaere, Pierre Maraval, Paul Prigent, *Dictionnaire Grec-Français du Nouveau Testament* (Coreea: Alliance Biblique Universelle, 1998), 118.
6 John Stott, *Crucea lui Cristos* (Cross of Christ) (Wheaton, IL: SMR, 1992), 87.
7 Maurice Carrez, Georges Metzger, Laurent Galy, *Nouveau Testament Interlineaire Grec/Francais* (Paris: Cerf, 1988), 698.
8 Jean Claude Ingelaere, Pierre Maraval, Paul Prigent, *Dictionnaire Grec-Français du Nouveau Testament*, 113.
9 Douglas Moo, *Romans 1-8* (Chicago, IL: Moody, 1991), 372.
10 Sf. Ioan Gură de Aur, *Cele şapte cuvântări encomiastice în cinstea apostolului Pavel* (*Seven laudatory speeches in honor of the apostle Paul*), (Iaşi: Editura Doxologia, 2016), 137.
11 Leon Xavier Dufour, *Vocabular de Teologie Biblică (Vocabulary of Biblical Theology)* (Bucureşti: Editura Arhiepiscopiei Romano-Catolice de Bucureşti, 2001), 517.
12 Jean Chrysostome, *Panegyriques de Saint Paul* (Paris: Cerf, 1982), 201.
13 Jean Chrysostome, *Omilii la epistolele Pauline. Omilii la epistola către Romani (Homilies on the Pauline Epistles. Homilies on the Epistle to the Romans)* (Bucureşti: Christiana, 2005), 321.
14 Alexander J. M. Wedderburn, *Baptism and Resurrection: Studies in Pauline Theology Against Its Graeco-Roman Background* (Tubingen: Mohr, 1987), 345.
15 Karl Menninger, *Whatever Became of Sin?* (New York: Hawthorn Books, 1973), 19.
16 John Stott, *Noua Societate a lui Dumnezeu. Mesajul Epistolei către Efeseni, (The New Society of God. The Message of the Epistle to the Ephesians)* (Oradea: Cartea Creştină).

17 Valeriu Pietreanu, "*Virtute şi păcat în concepţia Sfântului Apostol Pavel*" (Virtue and sin in the conception of St. Paul) *Studii Teologice* 9-10 (1957), 673.
18 Sf. Ioan Gură de Aur, *Omilii la epistolele Pauline. Omilii la epistola către Romani (Homilies on the Pauline Epistles. Homilies on the Epistle to the Romans)* (Bucureşti: Editura Christiana, 2005), 389.
19 Sf. Ioan Gură de Aur, *Homilies on the Pauline Epistles. Homilies on the Epistle to the Romans*, 389.
20 Sf. Ioan Gură de Aur, *Homilies on the Pauline Epistles. Homilies on the Epistle to the Romans*, 392.
21 Arialdo Beni, Giambattista Biffi, *La grazia di Cristo*, Marietti, Torino, 1974, 20–21.
22 Leon Xavier Dufour, *Vocabular de Teologie Biblică (Vocabulary of Biblical Theology)* (Bucureşti: Editura Arhiepiscopiei Romano-Catolice de Bucureşti, 2001), 519.
23 Sf. Ioan Gură de Aur, *Epistulam I ad Corinthios argumentum et homiliae 25,3*, PG 61, col.160.
24 Sf. Ioan Gură de Aur, *Homilies on the Pauline Epistles. Homilies on the Epistle to the Romans*, 398.
25 Karl Menninger, *Whatever Became of Sin?*, 19.
26 Sf. Ioan Gură de Aur, *Despre îndurare* (On mercy), P.G. 51, col. 261–272.
27 Valeriu Pietreanu, "*Virtute şi păcat în concepţia Sfântului Apostol* Pavel" (Virtue and sin in the conception of St. Paul), 678.
28 Sf. Ioan Gură de Aur, *Omilii la Geneză* (*Homilies on Genesis*), P.G. 53, col. 71.
29 Sf. Ioan Gură de Aur, *Homilies on Genesis*, P.G. 53, col. 71.
30 Marin Stamate, *Educaţia Creştină în Opera Sfântului Ioan Gură de Aur* (Christian Education in the work of Saint John Chrysostom), (Galaţi: Episcopia Dunării de Jos, 2003), 69.
31 Sf. Ioan Gură de Aur, *In epistulam I ad Corinhios argumentum et homiliae 25,3*, PG 61, col.160.
32 Paladiu, *Dialog istoric cu Teodor, diacon al Bisericii Romane, despre viaţa şi activitatea fericitului Ioan Gură de Aur, episcop al Constantinopolului*, 5, P.G. 47, col. 20.
33 Sf. Ioan Gură de Aur, *Omilii la epistolele Pauline. Omilii la epistola către Romani (Homilies on the Pauline Epistles. Homilies on the Epistle to the Romans)* (Bucureşti: Christiana, 2005), 403.
34 Ioan Paul al II-lea, *Planul lui Dumnezeu. Decalog pentru mileniul III* (God's plan. Decalogue for the third millennium) (Bucureşti: Enciclopedică, 1999), 27.
35 Sf. Ioan Gură de Aur *Omilie la 1 Cor.* 18, 3, P.G. 61 col.654.
36 Karl Heintz Peschke, *Etica Creştină* (Christian Ethics) (Lugoj: Editura Dacia Nova, 2003), 249.
37 Sf. Ioan Gură de Aur, *Omilii la Postul Mare* (*Homilies at Lent*) (Bucureşti : Anastasia, 1997), 18.
38 Karl Heintz Peschke, *Christian Ethics*, 250.
39 Sf. Ioan Gură de Aur, *Omilii la epistolele Pauline. Omilii la epistola către Romani* (Homilies on the Pauline Epistles. Homilies on the Epistle to the Romans) (Bucureşti: Christiana, 2005), 417.
40 Sf. Ioan Gură de Aur, *Homilies on the Pauline Epistles. Homilies on the Epistle to the Romans*, 417.
41 Sf. Ioan Gură de Aur, *Homilies on the Pauline Epistles. Homilies on the Epistle to the Romans*, 417.
42 Orest Bucevschi, "*Sfântul Ioan Gură de Aur: Omiliile despre Pocăinţă*" (Saint John Chrysostom: Homilies on Repentance") *Sudii Teologice* 9-10 (1957), 626.
43 Ioan G. Coman, "Personalitatea Sfântului Ioan Gură de Aur (The personality of Saint John Chrysostom)" *Studii Teologice* 9-10 (1957), 603.

44 Carlo Moreschini, Enrico Norelli, *Istoria literaturii creştine vechi, greceşti şi latine (The history of ancient Christian, Greek and Latin literature)*, II/1 (Iaşi: Editura Polirom, 2004), 167.
45 Ferdinand Cavallera, Jean Danielou, *Jean Chrysostome sur l'incomprehensibilite de Dieu* (Paris,1951), 17.
46 Sf. Ioan Gură de Aur, *Sermonesin Genesim*, IX, 3, PG 54, col. 630.
47 Ioan G. Coman, "Personalitatea Sfântului Ioan Gură de Aur", 603.

Bibliography

Beni, Arialdo. Biffi, Giambattista. *La grazia di Cristo*, Torino: Marietti, 1974.

Borel, Brooke. *The Chicago Guide to Fact-Checking*, Chicago, IL: University of Chicago Press, 2016. ProQuest Ebrary.

Bucevschi, Orest. "Sfântul Ioan Gură de Aur: Omiliile despre Pocăinţă (Saint John Chrysostom: Homilies on Repentance)" *Studii Teologice* 9–10 (1957)

Carrez, Maurice. Metzger, Georges. Galy, Laurent. *Nouveau Testament Interlineaire Grec/Français*, Paris: Cerf, 1988.

Cavallera, Ferdinand; Danielou, Jean. *Jean Chrysostome sur l'incomprehensibilite de Dieu*, Paris: Cerf, 1951.

Chrysostome, Jean. *Panegyriques de Saint Paul*, Paris: Cerf, 1982.

Coman, Ioan G. "Personalitatea Sfântului Ioan Gură de Aur (The personality of Saint John Chrysostom)" *Studii Teologice* 9–10 (1957)

Deissmann, Adolf Gustav. *Paul, a Study in Social and Religious History*. Londra: Hodder & Stoughton, 1926.

Douglas, John D., *Biblical Dictionary*, Oradea: Editura Cartea Creştină, 1995.

Dufour, Leon Xavier. *Vocabular de Teologie Biblică (Vocabulary of Biblical Theology)*, Bucureşti: Editura Arhiepiscopiei Romano-Catolice de Bucureşti, 2001.

Evdokimov, Paul. *Vârstele vieţii spirituale (The ages of the spiritual life)*, Bucureşti: Christiana, 1993.

Ingelaere, Jean Claude. Maraval, Pierre Prigent, Paul. *Dictionnaire Grec-Français du Nouveau Testament*, Coreea: Alliance Biblique Universelle, 1998.

Ioan, Gură de Aur. *Cele şapte cuvântări encomiastice in cinstea apostolului Pavel (Seven laudatory speeches in honor of the apostle Paul)*, Iaşi: Doxologia, 2016.

———. *Epistulam I ad Corinhios argumentum et homiliae*. 1–44. PG 61, 9–382.

———. *In epistulam I ad Corinhios argumentum et homiliae 25, 3*. PG 61, col.160.

———. *Omilii la Postul Mare (Homilies at Lent)*, Bucureşti: Anastasia, 1997.

———. *Omilii la epistolele pauline. Omilii la Epistola către Romani* (Homilies on the Pauline Epistles. Homilies on the Epistle to the Romans), Christiana, 2005.

———. *In Epistulam ad Galatas commentarius*. Fiblb. IV 1–103, P. G. col. 661–682.

Ioan Paul, al II-lea, *Planul lui Dumnezeu. Decalog pentru mileniul III*. (God's plan. Decalogue for the third millennium), Bucureşti: Enciclopedică, 1999.

Kurland, Philip B., and Ralph Lerner, eds. *The Founders' Constitution*. Chicago, IL: University of Chicago Press, 1987. http://press-pubs.uchicago.edu/founders/.

Martini, Carlo Maria. *Mărturisirile Sfântului Paul. Meditaţii (The confessions of St. Paul. Meditations)*, Bucureşti: Edit. Arhiepiscopiei Romano-Catolice de Bucureşti, 2003.

Melville, Herman. *Moby-Dick; or, The Whale*, New York: Harper & Brothers, 1851. http://mel.hofstra.edu/moby-dick-the-whale-proofs.html.

Menninger, Karl. *Whatever Became of Sin?* New York: Hawthorn Books, 1973.

Moo, Douglas. *Romans 1–8*, Chicago, IL: Moody, 1991.
Moreschini, Carlo; Norelli, Enrico. *Istoria literaturii creştine vechi, greceşti şi latine* (*The history of ancient Christian, Greek and Latin literature*), II/1, Iaşi: Polirom, 2004.
Peschke, Karl Heintz. *Etica Creştină* (Christian Ethics), Lugoj: Editura Dacia Nova, 2003.
Pietreanu, Valeriu. "*Virtute şi păcat in concepţia Sfântului Apostol Pavel*" (Virtue and sin in the conception of St. Apostle Paul) *Studii Teologice* 9–10, Bucureşti: EIBMBOR, 1957.
Stamate, Marin, *Educaţia Creştină in opera Sfântului Ioan Gură de Aur* (Christian Education in the work of Saint John Chrysostom), Galaţi: Episcopia Dunării de Jos, 2003.
Stott, John. *Crucea lui Cristos* (*Cross of Christ*), Wheaton, IL: SMR, 1992.
———, *Noua Societate a lui Dumnezeu. Mesajul Epistolei către Efeseni* (The New Society of God. The Message of the Epistle to the Ephesians), Oradea: Editura Cartea Creştină, 1994.
Wedderburn, Alexander J. M., *Baptism and Resurrection: Studies in Pauline Theology Against Its Graeco-Roman Background*, Tubingen: Mohr, 1987.

15 Between Sacrament and Vocation

Augustine's Biblical Teaching on Marriage and its Influence on Luther's Theology

Piotr Kopiec

Introduction

There is a common conviction the thought of Augustine influenced Martin Luther's thinking. The cornerstone of the Lutheran theology, the teaching on the justification by faith alone, and many other main fields of the Reformer's teaching as Christology, anthropology, hamartiology, and social doctrine, to mention only the most important, reflected a theological genetic relation between both authors, a heritage of Augustine tradition which has shaped Luther's interpretation of religious questions. After all, for more than ten years, he was an Augustinian monk.

This observation is not merely a simple intellectual remark, significant only due to purely theological reasons. It is also crucial for countering false beliefs that the Protestant theology would have rejected the tradition of the Fathers when adopting the hermeneutical principle of *Sola Scriptura*. Obviously, it is a vast misinterpretation, stemming from both the interconfessional polemics and the identity formation processes. Enough to mention the main book of the Lutheran Reformation, the Augsburg Confession, where Melanchthon referred mainly to the teaching of Augustine but also to John Chrysostom, Gregory I, Ambrose and Cyprian, and stressed the unity with the early Church and Fathers, as in the conclusion of part I of the book: "This is a summary of our teaching, in which, as you can see, there is nothing that differs from the Scriptures, from the Catholic Church or the Church of Rome as known from its early writers", or in the article 24 about the mass: "Thus we celebrate the mass according to the example of the church, taken from the Scriptures and the Church Fathers".[1] Also, an unambiguous confirmation of the seven ecumenical councils of the early Church by the Lutheran symbolical books shows an allegiance to the tradition of the Fathers.

Thus Augustine's impact on Luther's and Lutheran theology is indisputable, especially when considering the soteriological thoughts of both theologians. Nevertheless, the scope and particular fields of interrelations raise the question about similarities and differences in the teaching on marriage. It seems to be interesting insofar as both authors vastly contributed to the

DOI: 10.4324/9781003273592-15

doctrinal history of marriage and family in the Christian civilization; in other words, to all the issues like the nature and value of marriage, its functions, its sacramentality, and relationships of spouses that constitutes the Christian model of marriage and family.

The purpose of the chapter is to present Augustine's doctrine of marriage and ask about the scope it influenced the marital teaching of Luther. The chapter aims to show an ambiguous interrelation between both theologians in their marital doctrine. It could also be essential for the interconfessional and ecumenical conversations on the resemblances and differences concerning the teaching on marriage and family.

Marriage in Early Christianity

The theology of marriage has been developed in a long process. Today's teaching of Churches, regardless of confession, results from the centuries of theological reflection and canonical statements. For the early Christians, marriage was holy and gifted by the grace of God, yet such conviction has not been grounded in the systematic theological reflection and terminology. Instead, it reflected both reception of the words of the Gospel (including Paul's letter to Ephesian and the account about the wedding in Cana in Galilee) and the cultural prevalence of the institution of marriage. Moreover, the early Church adopted the legal form of marriage according to Roman law and did not impose its own ceremonies of the wedding. Also, unlike Roman law, she acknowledged the right to marry among slaves and in couples where one of the spouses was a slave. It was ultimately confirmed by the decree of Pope St Julius I issued in 352.[2]

The widespread conviction marriage is a unique union, different from all others, to which God offers unique gifts, echoed in the writings of early theologians. It is worthwhile to refer to the thought of Tertullian, who wrote more than three treatizes on the meaning of Christian marriage, and who countered its gnostic demotion. In likely the most famous treatise, entitled *Ad uxorem* ("To his wife"), he warmly, emotionally, and personally expressed the significance of marriage: "How beautiful, then, the marriage of two Christians, two who are one in hope, one in desire, one in the way of life they follow, one in the religion they practice. They are as brother and sister, both servants of the same Master. Nothing divides them, either in the flesh or in spirit. They are, in very truth, two in one flesh, and where there is but one flesh, there is also but one spirit. They pray together, they worship together, they fast together; instructing one another, encouraging one another, strengthening one another. Side by side, they visit God's church and partake of God's banquet; side by side, they face difficulties and persecution, share their consolations. They have no secrets from one another; they never shun each other's company; they never bring sorrow to each other's hearts... Psalms and hymns they sing to one another, striving to see which one of them will chant more beautifully the praises of their Lord.

Hearing and seeing this, Christ rejoices. To such as these He gives His peace. Where there are two together, there also He is present, and where He is there evil is not".[3]

Thus Tertullian's words illustrate the beliefs of the early Christians about standing assistance of Jesus Christ himself to marriage. On the other hand, they help to discern the oncoming teachings of its sacramentality. Tertullian was not the only one who wrote about marriage; for instance, John Chrysostom, Origen, and Ambrose undertook this topic. Yet, the very systematic reflection had been developed by Augustine, who might be considered the first theologian of marriage.[4]

St. Augustine as the First Theologian of Marriage

The principal author of the ancient Christian West left a relatively coherent reflection on marriage and paved the way to further developing the theology of sacramental marriage. His relevant thought was expanding while the polemics with Donatism, Manichaeism, and Pelagianism, moreover, it was coined by the reflection on the marriages of Jews and Gentiles and was influenced by the teaching of Apostle Paul, especially by the 1 Corinthians and Ephesians.[5] Finally, this thought reflects the core motif of St. Augustine entire teaching, namely, the dialectic schema of the fight between good and evil, comprehensively explained in his *opus magnum* "De civitatae Dei" ("The City of God"). It is also worthwhile to mention the influence of the personal experience of Augustine, who has had two concubines and who has lived a celibate life after his conversion.

Marriage is essentially involved in this dialectic. It belongs to the "City of God" ("In the City of God, where marriage is sealed by the first act of intercourse between the two persons"[6]); it is an integral part of the *Civitas Christiana*, of the social and political values grounded in the Christian virtues, and it is called to act for their proliferation in the worldly order. Consequently, its significance is considered in the anthropological, hamartiological, Christological, soteriological, and sociological dimensions of the works of the theologian from Hippo. Furthermore, Augustine, in his writings, referred notion of marriage to the three relationships: first, to that between Christ and Church, second, between man and woman and third, between flash and spirit.[7]

The topic of marriage appears in his many writings. Apart from "De civitatae Dei", significant for the marital doctrine are the following works: "De bono coniugali", "De bono viduitatis", "Contra Julianum", "Contra duas epistulas Pelagianorum", "De gratia Christi et de peccato originali", "De nuptiis et concupiscentia", and "De sancta virginitate". Obviously, some elements of the teaching on marriage might also be found in his other books.

The starting point of Augustine's theology of marriage is the remark that it is good for the sake of itself; in other words, its value stands on its own.

Such judgment is especially striking when compared to the Manichean demotion of corporeality. The Bishop of Hippo expressed this conviction in a very indirectly way, as, for instance, when stating: "We can say now that in that condition of being born and dying with which we are acquainted, and in which we were created, the union of man and woman is something of value".[8] Marriage is also intended in God's plan of creation:

> to increase and multiply and replenish the earth in virtue of the blessing of God, is a gift of marriage as God instituted it from the beginning before man sinned when He created them male and female – in other words, two sexes manifestly distinct.[9]

This creational dimension of Augustine's teaching is upheld by his soteriological as well as hamartiological belief marriage is good and precious also after the original sin:

> But that blessing upon marriage, which encouraged them to increase and multiply and replenish the earth, though it continued even after they had sinned, was yet given before they sinned, in order that the procreation of children might be recognized as part of the glory of marriage, and not of the punishment of sin.[10]

Last but not least, the value of marriage touches the most intrinsic anthropological truth. Namely, human nature, perverted after the fall, prompts sexual intercourse, of which purpose is different than having children. Thus man, affected by the original sin, weak and susceptible to unordered behaviours, also in his sexuality, is given marriage, as a perfect union between man and woman.

> So, even if a perverted morality motivates them to have intercourse like that, marriage still saves them from adultery or fornication. It is not that conduct of that kind is accepted because of marriage, but it is forgiven because of marriage.[11]

This claiming of the Bishop of Hippo reveals an extraordinary dignity of marriage.

This dignity must not hide the supreme value of virginity. For Augustine, even though the marital knot is good as intended by God, sexual abstinence is of high importance. This opinion was staunchly espoused by the Bishop of Hippo while the polemics with Jovinian, for whom marriage and celibacy were equal. Stemming from the anthropological teaching and Paul's letters (especially 1 Cor.), Augustine saw chastity as a more appropriate condition for Christian. He confirmed this opinion by the arguments derived either from human nature or the thoughts about the Christian mission towards society.

In summary, marriage is good, because it is a union of people of the different complementary sex wanted by God, it is a natural relation of friendship between spouses, it founds the most rudimentary unit of society ("the first natural bond of human society, therefore, is that of husband and wife")[12] and, finally, it was affirmed by Jesus Christ while his participation in the Wedding in Cana ("concerning the good of marriage, which the Lord also confirmed in the Gospel, not only in that He forbade to put away a wife, save because of fornication, but also in that He came by invitation to a marriage").[13] In Augustine's teaching, marriage is to be defined as

> the good, and not as a sin, also because it creates a community of woman and man, which is indissoluble and faithful, which follow the same ideas, and which has social value because it founds a primary cell of society.[14]

The Values-Goals of Marriage in Augustine's Theology

Moreover, this affirmation of marriage is derived from its three values-goals: the begetting and upbringing of offspring (*proles*), mutual fidelity of spouses (*fides*) and sacrament.[15] All these points simultaneously depict the functions of marriage and highlight its good; also, all have to be regarded as complementary. This thought was clearly expounded in the above-mentioned treatise on marriage "On the Good of Marriage" ("De bono coniugali"), perhaps the most relevant book on this topic:

> The value of marriage, therefore, for all races and all people, lies in the objective of procreation and the faithful observance of chastity. For the people of God, however, it lies also in the sanctity of sacrament, and this has the consequence that it is forbidden for a woman to marry anyone else while her husband is still living, even if she has been divorced by him, and even if it is only for the purpose of having children.[16]

This conviction about the three complementary values-goals of marriage was also repeated in other writings, as, for instance, in the "On Genesis" ("Genesi Ad Litteram"):

> I mean, just because immoderate sexuality is an evil, it does not follow that marriage, even between over-sexed persons, is not a good. Quite the contrary; not only does that evil not make this good blameworthy, this good makes that evil pardonable, since what is good in marriage can never be a sin. This good, in fact is threefold: fidelity, offspring, sacrament. What fidelity means that neither partner should sleep with another person outside the marriage bond; offspring means that children should be welcomed with love, brought up with kindness, given a

> religious education; sacrament means that the union should not be broken up, and that if either husband or wife is sent away, neither should marry another even for the sake of having children. This is, so to say, the set-square of marriage, good either for embellishing the fertility of nature, or putting straight the crookedness of lust.[17]

Two values-goals, fidelity and offspring, are understandable enough and do not need a more detailed explanation. The sacramentality of marriage is more enigmatic provided that the sacramental doctrine was *in statu nascendi* at that time; in other words, integral sacramentology has not existed yet,[18] and the Bishop of Hippo employed the word of the sacrament in different meanings. Nevertheless, marriage was officially listed as a sacrament during the local Synod of Verona in 1138 as a response to its condemnation by Cathars. Moreover, the Catholic sacramentology was finally shaped on the Second Council of Lyon (1272–1274), where the Church confirmed the number of seven sacraments and on the Council of Florence (1438–1445), which formulated the teaching about the three sacraments: Baptism, Confirmation and Eucharist as the "seal" of the Holy Spirit. Thus the teaching about marriage as a sacrament in early Christianity reflected rather an intuition of theologians.

Consequently, the research on Augustine's theology distinguished three traditions of how his teaching of the sacramentality of marriage should be understood. First, many historians of theology imposed a contemporary understanding of sacrament on Augustine's meaning of marriage; in other words, his teaching on baptism and Eucharist is being referred to as marriage. It is, therefore, the sacramentality of marriage *implicit*. The second group of researchers insisted that the notion of a sacrament in the strict theological definition, as the outward and visible form of invisible grace, and the sign instituted by Christ himself, must not be linked to Augustine's understanding of marriage, since it is a lack of scriptural confirmation of both sacramental elements and a lack of explicit acknowledgement of marriage as a sacrament. And finally, the last research position stated that for Augustine, not marriage but rather its attributes: fidelity, unity and indissolubility should be regarded as a sacrament.[19]

Regardless of the polemics, as mentioned earlier, one must admit that Augustine's understanding of sacramental marriage was often different from the contemporary definition of sacrament. Yet following the discussions of the scholars, it seems to be justified to say that Bishop of Hippo addressed to marriage these attributes that are today included in the definition of a sacrament: the visible sign of the sanctifying reality, God's institution and grace.[20] When teaching about marriage, he predominantly referred it to the mystical relationship between Christ and Church as described in Paul's Letter to Ephesians:

> For this reason, a man will leave his father and mother and be united to his wife, and the two will become one flesh. This is a profound

> mystery - but I am talking about Christ and the Church. However, each one of you also must love his wife as he loves himself, and the wife must respect her husband.
>
> (Ephesians 5:31–33)

Thus marriage as a sacrament should not be understood and confined to a contract or a rite only, but it is a holy mystery reflecting the paradigm of union between Christ and the Church. As Antoni Swoboda stated, Augustine discerned the holiness and mystery of marriage; consequently, in his interpretation, marriage is not only a sign but an ontological reality.[21] In other words, marriage belongs to the ontological rather than to the moral order.

The teaching on the marriage of the Bishop of Hippo has decisively determined the marital doctrine of the Christian Churches of the West. It remains, until today, an essential source of reflection and inspiration for marital life. Especially several points of his thoughts seem to be crucial: first of all, Augustine has taught marriage is something of value; it is good for itself and not only good in comparison to evil. It is a primary social particle as a natural union between man and woman, and it is an instrument of the Church for the proliferation of Christian moral patterns; it is a source of grace and the way to sanctity for spouses, and, finally, it is a mysterious participation in the holy union of the Christ and Church, marriage is an ontological reality.

Luther's Teaching on Marriage

As mentioned above, Augustine's theology profoundly influenced the Fathers of the Protestant Reformation. The theology of grace and salvation, the doctrine on original sin, the teaching on Church and sacraments predominantly impacted Reformers' theological outlook. Calvin's *opus magnum*, "Institutio Christianae Religionis", is full of references to Augustine's works and of personal confessions of reverence to Bishop of Hippo.[22] Luther repeatedly admitted and considered his theology as a heritage of Augustine's thinking.[23] This genetic relation between both theologians is something evident for historians of the Reformation.[24] Yet the Doctor from Wittenberg was not an unconditional follower of the Bishop of Hippo's theology what reflects in the Reformer's approach to marriage.

Many interpreters of Luther's theology considered the question of whether Reformer had demoted or, reversely, affirmed marriage. The first position pointed out Luther denied the sacramentality of marriage, whereas the latter discerned Reformer's reverence to marriage as a vocation and the primary social entity.[25] The polemics between both approaches were obviously often confessionally grounded and thus hindering a relevant interpretation. Yet, they also reached the core of Luther's view on soteriological and anthropological issues.

The theologian from Wittenberg had much written about marriage, but his teaching is dispersed, less systematized, and therefore less internally coherent than Augustine's. It was unfolding *ad hoc*, while the polemics with the Roman Church and the criticism of Catholicism had marked this thought from the very beginning. Also, Luther's treatise lacks that would comprehensively present his teaching on marriage.[26] In Luther's marital doctrine, one may distinguish three crucial push factors: the criticism of the monasticism and the late Middle Ages' approach to human sexuality,[27] the Lutheran main theological principles, especially the doctrine of the universal priesthood, and, last but not least; the personal experiences of Luther himself. They open the way to a more detailed presentation of the marital doctrine. It was shaping somehow between Luther's teaching on vocation and the conviction that "marriage is a pure worldly thing". Both create the space for further doctrinal elucidations.

Marriage in the Perspective of the Teaching on Vocation

The first idea is closely related to the understanding of the Christian vocation. Yet it is also touching the most central anthropological truth about a Christian person who is justified by Jesus Christ, who is living in the hope of salvation given by Jesus and, at the same time, in the worldly reality corrupted by sin. It is a theological background for the entire system of social teaching. All Christians, when participating in Christ's dignity, are substantially equal. They must not be differentiated depending on the office they take. Thereby every vocation and, using more sociological terms, every social role they play must be regarded as essential and complementary. Thus Luther seems to deny any theological stratification.[28]

The teaching on vocation vastly influenced the social reflection of the Reformer. Even though his thinking about politics was shaped by the teaching of two Kingdoms and two Regiments, the notion of vocation given to every member of Church and society might be regarded as a crossroad of concepts of Luther's soteriology anthropology and sociology. Complementary interrelated Church and state, vocations and offices establish a system leading Christians to God's Kingdom.

Marriage plays a crucial role in this system. A number of writings and sermons confirm Luther's concern about marriage. He even occasionally introduced in his dichotomic scheme of the two Regiments (state and Church), household as the third Regiment (*Hausregiment*). In his opinion, the marital state is the primary of all vocations and offices, mainly because of its functions. Marriage is good because of its role in fighting good and evil and in God's salvific plan. This is why Luther insisted that marriage is both "particularly blessed" and "particularly necessary". His reverence to the marital state and its functions he blatantly expressed in the "Large Catechism", the crucial source of the Lutheran tradition:

> Let us carefully note, first, how highly God honours and glorifies the married life, sanctioning and protecting it by his commandment. He

> sanctioned it above in the fourth commandment, «You shall honor father and mother»; but here, as I said, he has secured it and protected it. Therefore he also wishes us to honor, maintain, and cherish it as a divine and blessed estate. Significantly he established it as the first of all institutions, and he created man and woman differently (as is evident) not for lewdness but to be true to each other, be fruitful, beget children, and support and bring them up to the glory of God.[29]

This quotation seems to be the best commentary for Luther's thinking about marriage. It is the crucial, the most blessed and the most necessary state and vocation due to its function, of which the most important are upbringing of children, a friendship between spouses and ordering of human sexuality. And insofar as the first and the second of these functions are already well described, the third appears as particularly interesting.

Despite the patriarchal outlook, Luther steadily affirmed an ideal of marriage which should have been a relation of love, fidelity and trust. A conviction about the supreme value of a marital relationship links with the next function of marriage, namely, the ordering of human sexuality. The question of sexual intercourses refers obviously to the doctrine on original sin, which he took over, at least to a certain extent, from Augustine. Luther claimed that the sexual drive is an extremely strong force. Though there are people that are gifted to live in chastity, yet in the case of the "ordinary" Christian, sexual drive, like eating, drinking and sleep, becomes a need that has to be fulfilled. He insisted that as human flesh and blood remain flesh and blood, like the sexual drive cannot be suppressed. The vows of chastity are as difficult as a struggle to destroy the Turkish Empire or to live to the age of Matusalem.[30]

Consequently, Reformer has discerned a special place of human sexuality in the struggle of good and evil and insisted that sexual intercourse outside marriage provides an exceptional opportunity for the devil (*Knechtschaft des Teufels*)[31] which corrupted and disordered its proper functions and purposes designated by God. On the contrary, sexual intercourse in marriage is not a sin since marriage protects against fornication, adultery and unchastity. Marriage sanctifies human sexual life, following the sanctification of the marital relation itself, the most precious treasure of human beings (*magnus thesaurus*).[32]

Marriage as the "Pure Worldly Thing"

Luther's utterance "marriage is a pure worldly thing" is at times regarded as a slogan illustrating his entire doctrine on marriage. Such an illustration seems to be exaggerated; furthermore, only thorough elucidations allow us to comprehend its proper meaning. It contains two main points: first, the issue of lack of sacramentality of marriage and second, the ascribing of marriage to the worldly order.

The fact Luther denied the sacramentality of marriage stemmed from a different theological perspective adopted by Luther in its teaching on the sacrament. While following the methodological principle of *Sola Scriptura*, he rejected all these theological contents that the Scripture has not confirmed. Consequently, he also acknowledged merely these sacraments that had been instituted by Jesus Christ himself (*ab ipso Christus institutis*). Nevertheless, the Gospel was not merely a criterion; it also founded the content of sacraments.

The formula of *ab ipso Christus institutis* was the first dimension of Luther's sacramentology. The next was an image of the structure of the sacrament. Reformer from Wittenberg has followed Augustine's definition about its binary composition: "When the Word is added to the element or the natural substance, it becomes a sacrament" (*Accedat verbum ad sacramentum et fit elementum*). The sacrament is constituted by both the internal element – the content of Christ's institution and the external element – the ritual sign. Yet its significance consists not in its substantial attributes but in its dynamic aspect of the invisible grace Christ gives in the visible sign. The only way to receive this grace is faith. This structural definition leads to the last important dimension of the sacramental doctrine concerning the number of sacraments. Luther admitted there are only two sacraments: Baptism and Eucharist (though he occasionally wrote about repentance as the third), that meet the theological conditions.

Considering the above-presented summary of Luther's teaching on the sacrament, it is comprehensible why he didn't accept the sacramentality of marriage. Though in the sermon on the marital state (*Ein Sermon von ehelichen Stand*) from 1519, he still regarded marriage as a sacrament, yet already on a year later, in the treatise "On the Babylonian Captivity of the Church", he radically denied its sacramentality. In his opinion, marriage is not a particularly important issue from the theological perspective, yet, it must not be regarded as a sacrament – it would be a triumph of the human thought on God's Word. This theological denial of the sacramentality of marriage is often supported by a historical argumentation. Luther, namely, often noticed that marriage is not a specific Christian reality. As it is from the beginning and also exists in unchristian societies, there is no serious reason to regard it as a sacrament. The denial of sacramentality links to the second dimension. According to Luther, unlike baptism and Eucharist belonging to the spiritual order, marriage is ascribed to the worldly one. This classification reflects Luther's political theory, which comprises the above-mentioned dualistic schemes of two Kingdoms and two Regiments. The first one echoed Augustinian thinking about relations of power and social institutions from the *Civitas Dei*. The Bishop of Hippo formulated a vision of history as a steady fight between the *civitas terrena* and *Civitas Dei*, the Kingdom of World and the Kingdom of God. The second refers to the teaching of two Regiments used by God in this continued struggle: the spiritual (*geistliches Regiment Gottes*) and the worldly one (*weltliches Regiment Gottes*). The instruments of the former are faith, freedom and conscience. The spiritual Regiment enables man/woman to love his/her neighbour, and it gives them hope for approaching the Kingdom of God and the rule of peace and justice. It is represented by the Church, which wields the Gospel and sacraments. The worldly Regiment has to protect against the evil in the carnal perspective. Its particular tasks are as follows: external freedom, political and social peace and natural health and life and its instruments are law, reason and coercion. It is represented by the state.[33] Marriage, with all its functions, belongs to this Regiment.

Conclusion: Augustine and Luther on Marriage – Ambiguous Interrelation

The short outlines of the teaching on the marriage of both Augustine and Luther confirm, to a certain degree, a deep genetic interrelation between both theologians. However, the question of Augustine's impact on Luther's doctrine of marriage is more ambiguous. It is obvious that Reformer from Wittenberg developed his theology of marriage in the Augustinian theological tradition. The question of original sin, the political teaching of two Kingdoms, the understanding of grace, the structural definition of the sacrament – all these parts of the Bishop of Hippo's theology have deeply influenced Luther's theological thinking and all have set the context for his teaching of marriage. Thus one could claim, in terms of its contextualization, Luther's marital doctrine is undoubtedly Augustinian. When considering the direct utterances on a marriage of both theologians, there is also much in common, especially when listing the purposes of marriage: the upbringing of children and the mutual relation of love and trust of spouses.

Yet also one may bring out the differences between them. First, it is a different attitude towards the vows of chastity and celibacy. Whereas Augustine is eager to confirm a supreme value of virginity, Luther is far from this affirmation, particularly when considering his criticism of monasticism. Second, and this is the crucial point of divergences, Augustine, even though the sacramentology was in its very beginning at that time, has written about the sacramentality of marriage. Many scholars insist that the Bishop of Hippo understood the sacramental character of marriage as in the present Catholic definition of the sacrament. On the contrary, Luther staunchly denied the sacramentality of marriage, following his teaching on sacraments as instituted by Jesus Christ himself.

This juxtaposition of divergences and similarities might be completed by a remark made from the wider perspective. Augustine's teaching on marriage is more substantial; in other words, he considered marriage more as an autotelic value and purpose in itself. For Luther, marriage is defined predominantly through its functions in the broader context of the salvific plan of Gog. Thus the Reformer's teaching is more functional. Yet, even considering the above-mentioned differences, either for Augustine or for Luther, marriage is theological of the supreme value. It is the "highest good".

Notes

1 *The Unaltered Augsburg Confession*, trans. Glen L. Thompson (Milwaukee: Northwestern Publishing House, 2005), 13.18.
2 Augusto Sarmiento, Javier Escrivá-Ivars, *Enchiridion Familiae. Textos del Magisterio Pontificio y Conciliar sobre el Matrimonio y la Familia* (Madrid: Ediciones Rialp, 1992), 11f.
3 Tertullian, *Ad Uxorem* II, 8, 7–8, *Corpus Christianorum, Series Latina*. English translation: Tertullian, *Ad Uxorem*, in: Johannes Quasten, *Patrology*, vol. 1 (*The Beginnings of Patristic Literature. From the Apostle's Creed to Irenaeus*) (Allen: Christian Classics, 1951), 303f.
4 Cormac Burke, *The Theology of Marriage. Personalism, Doctrine, and Canon Law* (Washington: Catholic University of America Press, 2015), 125.
5 Antoni Swoboda, "Bonum sacramenti w nauce św. Augustyna o małżeństwie," *Poznańskie Studia Teologiczne*, 22(2008): 68.
6 Augustine, *The Excellence of Marriage*, trans. Ray Kearney, in: David G. Hunter, ed., *Marriage and Virginity* (New York: New City Press, 1999), 15.
7 Swoboda, *Bonum sacramenti*, ibid., 73.
8 Augustine, *The Excellence of Marriage*, ibid., 3.
9 Augustine, *The City of God*, trans. Marcus Dodd (New York: Random House, 2010), 469 (book xiv).
10 Ibid., 470 (book xiv).
11 Augustine, *The Excellence of Marriage*, ibid., 6.
12 Ibid., 1.
13 Ibid. 3.
14 Swoboda, *Bonum sacramenti*, ibid., 76.
15 Ibid., 79.
16 Augustine, *The Excellence of Marriage*, ibid., 24.
17 Augustine, *On Genesis. A Refutation of the Manichees* (New York: New York City Press, 2002), 382.
18 Wincenty Granat, *Dogmatyka katolicka*, t. 2 *Sakramenty święte* (Lublin: Towarzystwo Naukowe KUL, 1966), 9.
19 Swoboda, *Bonum sacramenti*, 75.
20 Ibid., 76.
21 Ibid.
22 John Calvin, *The Institutes of the Christian Religion*, trans. Henry Beveridge (Grand Rapids: Christian Classics Ethereal Library, 2002), 53.
23 Alistair McGrath, *Christianity's Dangerous Idea. The Protestant Reformation. A History from the Sixteenth Century to the Twenty-First* (London: SPCK, 2007), 43.
24 Heiko Obermann, *Luther: Man between God and the Devil* (New Haven-London: Yale University Press, 2006), 159.
25 Michael Parsons, *Reformation Marriage: The Husband and Wife Relationship in the Theology of Luther and Calvin* (Eugene: Wipf and Stock, 2005), 148.
26 Jan Motyka, *Luter o rodzinie i w rodzinie* (Bielsko-Biała: Augustana, 1997), 88.
27 Derrick Bailey, *The Man-Woman Relation in Christian Thought* (London: Longmans, Green, 1959), 103.

28 Martin Luther, *Open Letter to the Christian Nobility of the German Nation Concerning the Reform of the Christian Estate.* trans. Jacobs C. M. (Philadelphia: A. J. Holman Company, 1915), 2.
29 Martin Luther, *The Large Catechism*, in: Theodore Gerhardt Tappert, ed., *The Book of Concord: The Confessions of the Evangelical Lutheran Church* (Philadelphia: Fortress Press, 1959b), 393.
30 Olavi Lähteenmäki, *Sexus und Ehe bei Luther* (Turku: Luther-Agricola-Gesellschaft, 1955), 32.
31 Björn Björnsson, *The Lutheran Doctrine of Marriage in Modern Icelandic Society* (Oslo: Univeristetsforlaget, 1971).
32 Lähteenmäki, *Sexus...*, ibid., 65.
33 Eberhard Röhm, Jörg Thierfelder, *Kirche-Staat-Politik. Zum Öffentlichkeitsauftrag der Kirche* (Stuttgart: Calwer Verlag, 1979), 12.

References

Augustine. The Excellence of Marriage. Trans. Ray Kearney. In: Hunter, David G. (Ed.). *Marriage and Virginity* (pp. 33–61). New York: New City Press, 1999.

Augustine. *On Genesis. A Refutation of the Manichees.* New York: New York City Press, 2002.

Augustine. *The City of God.* Dodd M. (Trans.). New York: Random House, 2010.

Bailey D. *The Man-Woman Relation in Christian Thought.* London: Longmans, Green, 1959.

Björnsson B. *The Lutheran Doctrine of Marriage in Modern Icelandic Society.* Oslo: Univeristetsforlaget, 1971.

Burke C. *The Theology of Marriage. Personalism, Doctrine, and Canon Law.* Washington: Catholic University of America Press, 2015.

Calvin J. *The Institutes of the Christian Religion.* Beveridge H. (Trans.). Grand Rapids: Christian Classics Ethereal Library, 2002.

Granat W. *Dogmatyka katolicka, t. 2. Sakramenty święte.* Lublin: Towarzystwo Naukowe KUL, 1966.

Lähteenmäki O. *Sexus und Ehe bei Luther.* Turku: Luther-Agricola-Gesellschaft, 1955.

Luther M. *Open Letter to the Christian Nobility of the German Nation Concerning the Reform of the Christian Estate.* Jacobs C. M. (Trans.). Philadelphia: A. J. Holman Company, 1915.

Luther M. *The Babylonian Captivity of the Church.* Steinhäuser A. T. W. (Trans.) Ahrens F. C., Ross W.A. (Rev.). In: Lehman H. (Ed.) Luther's Work, Vol. 36. Ross W. A. (Ed.) Word and Sacrament II (pp. 3–126). Philadelphia: Fortress Press, 1959a.

Luther M. The Large Catechism. In: Tappert T. G. (Ed.). *The Book of Concord: The Confessions of the Evangelical Lutheran Church.* Philadelphia: Fortress Press, 1959b.

McGrath A. *Christianity's Dangerous Idea. The Protestant Reformation. A History from the Sixteenth Century to the Twenty-First.* London: SPCK, 2007.

Motyka J. *Luter o rodzinie i w rodzinie.* Bielsko-Biała: Augustana, 1997.

Obermann H. *Luther: Man between God and the Devil.* New Haven-London: Yale University Press, 2006.

Parsons M. *Reformation Marriage: The Husband and Wife Relationship in the Theology of Luther and Calvin*. Eugene: Wipf and Stock, 2005.

Röhm E., Thierfelder J. *Kirche-Staat-Politik. Zum Öffentlichkeitsauftrag der Kirche*. Stuttgart: Calwer Verlag, 1979.

Sarmiento A., Escrivá-Ivars J. *Enchiridion Familiae. Textos del Magisterio Pontificio y Conciliar sobre el Matrimonio y la Familia*. Madrid: Ediciones Rialp, 1992.

Swoboda A. Bonum sacramenti w nauce św. Augustyna o małżeństwie. "*Poznańskie Studia Teologiczne*" 22 (2008): 67–89.

Tertullian. *Ad Uxorem. In: Quasten J. Patrology, vol. 1 (The Beginnings of Patristic Literature. From the Apostle's Creed to Irenaeus)*. Allen: Christian Classics, 1951.

The Unaltered Augsburg Confession . Glen L. Thompson G.L. (Trans.). Milwaukee: Northwestern Publishing House, 2005.

Index

Note: Page numbers followed by "n" denote endnotes.